"Almost all state-based criminal justice professionals in recent years have instinctively feared and disliked the "privatisation" that they were persistently being threatened with, and fought as best they could to keep their services public. Sometimes, the wider public themselves were indifferent to their struggles (as with probation), and others, more supportive (as with legal aid). What all the struggling agencies had in common was a shallow understanding of what they were up against, and a naive belief that merely empirical and ethical arguments could resist it. Hamerton and Hobbs' fine book, the first comprehensive British treatment of the subject for more than a decade, offers a new way of conceptualising privatisation, maps the dramatic changes that have already occurred and indicates what may be to come. Not all privatisations go smoothly—recent attempts to upgrade electronic monitoring have been a foreseeable fiasco—but without a book like this to guide us, all attempts to salvage and sustain best practice in the new penal landscape will be futile."

Emeritus Professor Mike Nellis, *University of Strathclyde*

"Hamerton and Hobbs' *Privatising Criminal Justice* is an authoritative and timely discussion of the most disturbing commercialized intrusion into the criminal justice arena since Thatcher and Reagan introduced the idea in the 1980s. It is essential reading for anyone—politicians, the public, students and practitioners—interested in the role global business plays in the delivery of commercialized justice."

Emeritus Professor Bob Lilly, *Northern Kentucky University*

"At one point in time, not so very long ago, the idea of 'private prisons' or 'private police' was either something 'that happened in the USA' or in dystopian visions of 'the future'. But today, that 'future' is here, the private justice sector is as familiar in the UK as in the USA, and the long history of commercial engagement in the criminal justice system needs re-visiting and explaining. This needs expert guides. Hamerton and Hobbs provide an exemplary account of comparative and contemporary influences and events that have shaped a complex story of operational crises, public finance austerity, privatisation and profiteering, and failure to sustain principles of democratic welfarism. Highly recommended for anyone wishing to get to grips with these issues and debates."

Emeritus Professor Nigel South, *University of Essex*

PRIVATISING CRIMINAL JUSTICE

Privatising Criminal Justice explores the social, cultural and political context of privatisation in the criminal justice sector. In recent years, the criminal justice sector has made various strategic partnerships with the private sector, exemplified by initiatives within the police, the prison system and offender services. This has seen unprecedented growth in the past 30 years and a veritable explosion under the tenure of the coalition government in the UK.

This book highlights key areas of domestic and global concern and illustrates, with detailed case studies of important developments. It connects the study of criminology and criminal justice to the wider study of public policy, government institutions and political decision making. In doing so, *Privatising Criminal Justice* provides a theoretical and practical framework for evaluating collaborative public- and private-sector response to social problems at the beginning of the twenty first century.

An accessible and compelling read, this book will appeal to students and scholars of criminology, criminal justice, sociology and politics and all those interested in how privatisation has shaped the contemporary criminal justice system.

Christopher Hamerton is currently Deputy Director of the Institute of Criminal Justice Research in the School of Economic, Social and Political Sciences at the University of Southampton, UK.

Sue Hobbs is an Adjunct Fellow with the School of Social Sciences and Psychology at the University of Western Sydney, Australia. She has wide practice experience in social and criminal justice.

PRIVATISING CRIMINAL JUSTICE

History, Neoliberal Penality and the Commodification of Crime

Christopher Hamerton and Sue Hobbs

LONDON AND NEW YORK

Cover image: monsitj

First published 2023
by Routledge
4 Park Square, Milton Park, Abingdon, Oxon OX14 4RN

and by Routledge
605 Third Avenue, New York, NY 10158

Routledge is an imprint of the Taylor & Francis Group, an informa business

© 2023 Christopher Hamerton and Sue Hobbs

The right of Christopher Hamerton and Sue Hobbs to be identified as authors of this work has been asserted in accordance with sections 77 and 78 of the Copyright, Designs and Patents Act 1988.

All rights reserved. No part of this book may be reprinted or reproduced or utilised in any form or by any electronic, mechanical, or other means, now known or hereafter invented, including photocopying and recording, or in any information storage or retrieval system, without permission in writing from the publishers.

Trademark notice: Product or corporate names may be trademarks or registered trademarks, and are used only for identification and explanation without intent to infringe.

British Library Cataloguing-in-Publication Data
A catalogue record for this book is available from the British Library

Library of Congress Cataloging-in-Publication Data
Names: Hamerton, Christopher, author. | Hobbs, Sue, author.
Title: Privatising criminal justice : history, neoliberal penality and the
  commodification of crime / Christopher Hamerton and Sue Hobbs.
Description: Milton Park, Abingdon, Oxon ; New York, NY : Routledge,
  2022. | Includes bibliographical references and index.
Identifiers: LCCN 2022003469 | ISBN 9781138891166 (hardback) |
  ISBN 9781138891173 (paperback) | ISBN 9781315709819 (ebook)
Subjects: LCSH: Criminal justice, Administration of . | Privatization. |
  Police, Private. | Private prisons.
Classification: LCC HV7419 .H358 2022 | DDC 364—dc23/
  eng/20220128
LC record available at https://lccn.loc.gov/2022003469

ISBN: 978-1-138-89116-6 (hbk)
ISBN: 978-1-138-89117-3 (pbk)
ISBN: 978-1-315-70981-9 (ebk)

DOI: 10.4324/9781315709819

Typeset in Bembo
by Apex CoVantage, LLC

In memory of Roger Matthews (1948–2020).

This book is dedicated to our partners in crime, Gaby and Dick; our children, Laura, Henry, and Lizi, and Patrick and Nik; and our grandchildren, Archie and Alfie.

CONTENTS

About the authors   xi
Acknowledgements   xii
List of abbreviations   xiii

1 Introduction   1

2 From nationalisation to privatisation, or bringing capitalism to the people   15

3 The free market panacea and putting the State up for sale   39

4 Transatlantic crossing, or the appeal of American know-how in the age of risk, responsibilisation and rising crime   64

5 Public sector outsourcing, the contract culture and the myth of the regulatory State   86

6 The private and public police, or there and back   107

7 The public and private police, or back to the future   138

8 Prison privatisation and the foundation of public privilege   167

9 Prison privatisation and normalisation in the neoliberal State: between dispersal of decency and diffusion of duty   195

10 The ascendency of the business ideal and the marketisation of offender services   228

11 Interrogating the failed probation experiment, or it wasn't broken, so why did they try to fix it?   256

Index   *286*

ABOUT THE AUTHORS

Christopher Hamerton is currently Deputy Director of the Institute of Criminal Justice Research in the School of Economic, Social and Political Sciences at the University of Southampton, UK.

Educated at the Universities of Oxford and Southampton, he is a Barrister of the Honourable Society of the Middle Temple (NP) and an elected fellow of both the Royal Anthropological Institute (FRAI) and the Linnean Society (FLS). He is co-author, with Sue Hobbs, of *The Making of Criminal Justice Policy*, also published by Routledge. His research interests in the field of criminal justice encompass law, crime and history.

Sue Hobbs is an Adjunct Fellow with the School of Social Sciences and Psychology at the University of Western Sydney. She has wide practice experience in social and criminal justice.

Having started her working life as a social worker in east London in the 80s, she transferred to the Probation Service in the 90s. On leaving the service in the mid-90s she taught on the probation qualifying degree programme at both Northumbria and Portsmouth University and later joined Kingston University as a Senior Lecturer in Criminology.

She has acted as an academic consultant to HM Inspectorate of Probation, and worked for the independent panel on the Daniel Morgan murder case.

ACKNOWLEDGEMENTS

The authors are indebted to the late Roger Matthews (1948–2020) who offered to write the foreword for our book and was an enthusiastic supporter of the project. They would like to thank him for his friendship, helpful feedback and encouragement during the early writing process. Roger felt that a detailed treatment of the role of privatisation within the sphere of contemporary criminal justice was long overdue. His pioneering *Privatizing Criminal Justice,* published in 1989, was the inspirational foundation for our project.

The authors are saddened that Roger was unable to see this book come to fruition and trust that they have made a half decent attempt at producing a book that he would have been willing to put his name to.

The authors would like to express special thanks to Bob Lilly, Mike Nellis and Nigel South, who have kindly endorsed the book, and Tom Sutton and his team at Routledge, whose patience and fortitude have been tested on more than one occasion.

ABBREVIATIONS

ACBA	Advisory Committee on Business Appointments
ACPO	Association of Chief Police Officers
AGM	Annual General Meeting
ASI	Adam Smith Institute
CCA	Corrections Corporation of America
CCT	Compulsory Competitive Tendering
CCTV	Closed Circuit Television
CPO	Chief Probation Officer
CPS	Centre for Policy Studies
CRC	Community Rehabilitation Company
DETR	Department of the Environment, Transport and the Regions
DWP	Department of Work and Pensions
DPA	Deferred Prosecution Agreement
EFI	Effective Practice Initiative
EM	Electronic Monitoring
FMI	Financial Management Initiative
GNP	Gross National Product
HAC	Home Affairs Committee
HCJC	House of Commons Justice Committee
HDC	Home Detention Curfew
HM	Her Majesty's
HMCIP	Her Majesty's Chief Inspector of Prisons
HMI	Her Majesty's Inspectorate(s)
HMP	Her Majesty's Prison
HMPS	Her Majesty's Prison Service
HOC	House of Commons
ICA	Institute of Economic Affairs

KPI	Key Performance Indicators
MOJ	Ministry of Justice
MP	Member of Parliament
NAO	National Audit Office
NAPO	National Association of Probation Officers
NATS	National Air Traffic Service
NCVO	National Council of Voluntary Organisations
NHS	National Health Service
NOMS	National Offender Management Service
NPM	New Public Management
NPS	National Probation Service
NS	National Standards
Ofsted	Office for Standards in Education
OTA	Offender Tagging Association
PAC	Public Accounts Committee
PACAC	Public Administration and Constitutional Affairs Committee
PbR	Payment by Results
PFI	Private Finance Initiative
POA	Prison Officers' Association
PPPs	Public Private Partnerships
PPS	Premier Prison Services
PwC	PricewaterhouseCoopers
SNOP	Statement of National Objectives and Priorities
STC	Special Training Centre
TR	Transforming Rehabilitation
UK	United Kingdom
UKDS	UK Detention Services,
US(A)	United States (of America)
WCC	Wackenhut Corrections Corporation
WW	What Works

1
INTRODUCTION

In 1989, Roger Matthews' controversial edited collection, *Privatizing Criminal Justice*, was published. A Left Realist, he sought to dispel the comforting myth that privatisation was something happening over there that 'couldn't happen' over here by highlighting 'two basic realizations' (1989: 1), namely that there had been a major shift in thinking about the State's role in the provision of criminal justice services and that privatisation had already made considerable inroads into the criminal justice system. Provoking hostility from academics, reformers, practitioners, trade unionists and radicals alike, he took issue with the prevailing view that crime control and punishment represent unique aspects of social life that should be the sole preserve of the State and contested the orthodoxy that the dispersal of coercive power to private agencies would undermine the State's legitimacy. To prove his point, he cited the incorporation and expansion of non-statutory service providers, in the main, voluntary sector agencies, into the criminal justice system and posited the contentious view that 'it is becoming apparent that many services can be readily provided by a range of State providers without impairing the legitimacy of the State' (1989: 2). Signposting what was to evolve as the regulatory State perspective (Braithwaite, 2000), he argued that, rather than being diminished, as long as the State retained administrative control of privately delivered services, the range and depth of its authority would be extended.

In his collection, Matthews considered the issues of non-State provision in relation to policing, prisons, the juvenile justice system and electronic monitoring (EM). Although many of his observations tended towards speculation extrapolated from the US experience, his empirically driven realism provided concrete examples of non-State incursions in the criminal justice system, such as the use of private contractors in the prison system, private security in industrial and commercial premises, the use of private security firms in the immigration and detention services, the piloting of EM in the UK, civilianisation of the police force and the increasing involvement of the not-for-profit sector in juvenile justice, to support what has proved incontestable: privatisation was not operating at the margins in the background but rather was moving into the mainstream.

Highlighting the polarisation of the debate into public versus private, which pitted the Left Idealists against the 'New Right and disenchanted liberals' (1989: 3), he argued that the reality of privatisation presented the Left with 'a window of opportunity for those wishing to exert influence' (Taylor and Pease, 1989: 181) that should not be shirked. Embracing a pluralist approach, most of the contributors (South being the exception) cautiously welcomed the mixed economy of criminal justice and the multiplicity of relationships between sectors as a means of improving the quality of services and thereby serving the public interest. For example, whilst hindsight has proved this not to be the case, he argued that competition had the potential to drive down the cost of legal services and improve accessibility.

Stating that privatisation was a real phenomenon with real consequences for the criminal justice system and its users, Matthews rehearsed the dilemmas, issues and challenges faced by contemporary critical authors that have framed this book. Inspired by his original text and bolstered by the many positive accolades we received from Matthews during the writing of this book, we have sought to explore the central administrator/provision distinction posed in his original thesis and, with the benefit of the insights provided by three decades of criminal justice privatisation, critically examine the economics, politics and culture that shape the contemporary privatisation landscape. Additionally, in an attempt to revisit the central tenets of his thesis, we return to the original questions posed by the contributors in his collection, namely how far can the privatisation process go? Will it achieve a cheaper, more flexible, effective service? What problems of accountability and safeguards does it raise? How far does privatisation test the limits of legitimacy? Does the State abrogate its authority when it abrogates its responsibility to deliver public services to the private sector? What regulatory control is the State able to exert over private providers? What is the relationship between private provision and public good? Will privatisation and competition improve the quality of service users' provision?

1989, the watershed year

In hindsight, 1989, the year when *Privatizing Criminal Justice* was published, has proven to be a watershed moment: the tipping point in the privatisation trajectory. Prime Minister Thatcher, who is credited with promoting a neoliberal free market and privatisation, was in her third term, and radical free market reforms of contracting out and privatisation of public services loomed large; the penal system was in crisis, buckling under overcrowding, riots and strikes; the pro-privatisation of the prisons lobby was at its peak; and the Home Affairs Committee, under the chairmanship of Garner and his successor Wheeler, who had been favourably impressed by both the facilities and conditions observed in privately run prisons during visits to the US (Jones and Newburn, 2007: 52–55), had published the 1988 green paper

Private Sector Involvement in the Penal State (HAC, 1988). Envisaged as the most cost effective solution to the crisis, and in line with the government's determination to promote private enterprise and extend the free market into public services, the Parliamentary Home Affairs Select Committee concluded that the contracting out of prison building and management to the private sector offered the advantages that: it relieved the taxpayer of the initial capital cost; it offered the possibility of an accelerated building process; and, faced with a squalid and decaying infrastructure, greatly enhanced architectural efficiency and excellence (Prison Reform Trust, 2005: n.p.). In 1992 under the premiership of Major following a tendering process from which the public sector was excluded, Group 4 was awarded the contract to manage HMP Wolds. The following year it was announced that all new prisons would be built under the Private Finance Initiative and privately operated. In the decades since, the private prison, which was the exception, has become the norm. As of 30 October 2020, there were 13 private prisons in England and Wales, housing 14,603 (18% of the prisoner population) at an annual cost of £563.9m in 2019–20 (PRT, 2021).

Whilst there was a recognised reluctance within government in 1989 to pursue privatisation beyond the prison estate (Mawby, 1989), the three decades since have seen privatisation tentacles extending into increasingly sensitive areas of core police, prison and offender management services, frequently in defiance of the evidence, reaching its zenith with what would have been unimaginable in 1989, the privatisation of the Probation Service. What is more, with outsourcing and tendering favouring big business, the not-for-profit and voluntary sector, which quite rightly featured as a positive force for supplementing mainstream service provision in *Privatizing Criminal Justice*, has almost exclusively been superseded by an exclusive club of 'too big to fail' private providers that dominate the market. These providers have effectively driven off all other competitors and essentially operate as a cartel that exerts considerable influence over the government departments and their ministers who depend on them to ensure they fulfil their public duty and responsibilities.

Defining privatisation

As Matthews (1989) observed, privatisation is multi-modal. It represents a 'catch-all' term applied 'to a disparate set of processes', whilst it is most frequently associated with activities 'ranging from the sale of public companies to contracting out, as well as various forms of deregulation' 1989: 1). As there is no one privatisation, it may be helpful to talk of privatisations, of different interlinking dimensions as delineated by Vickers and Wright (1989):

- abolishing or severely curtailing public services on the assumption that private provision will fill the gap (e.g. cutting local authority provision of nurseries and care homes, creating a gap to be filled by private providers);
- squeezing the financial resources of publicly funded bodies in the hope of inducing them to seek compensating private funding (e.g. local authorities

relying on private developers of large housing projects such as the South West London Nine Elms Project to build schools and colleges as part of planning agreements);
- increasing the financial contribution of consumers for public goods and services (e.g. the reduction in publicly funded legal aid, whereby fewer are eligible for legal aid in the first place, and the contribution is raised for those who are. With publicly funded representation cuts, a two-tiered system has been created whereby those who can afford to pay for representation do so, and those who cannot are either forced to plead guilty or to become litigants-in-person);
- transferring public policy responsibilities to the private sector (e.g. the transfer of responsibility for the protection of property to the individual or business and the rise of commercialised security);
- encouraging private finance to build and operate public works (e.g. the introduction of the Private Finance Initiative in the design, construction and management of prisons);
- introducing private sector personnel and notions of efficiency and management techniques into the public sector in the hope of imparting a greater 'commercial orientation' into its ethos and functioning (e.g. the introduction of New Public Management to impose business principles of economy, effectiveness and efficiency);
- contracting out public services to private agents (e.g. the outsourcing of offender services to private businesses and not-for-profit organisations as part of the Rehabilitation Revolution in the delivery of the Probation Service);
- selling land and publicly owned housing stock and other tangible assets (e.g. the selling off of the sites of 'outdated' prisons and buildings, many on prime real estate, to housing developers).

In its purest form privatisation implies the total transfer of public assets to the private sector as manifested in the selling off of State-owned businesses, industries and utilities. Whilst this model was successfully adopted in the early decades of privatisation, as privatisation gained momentum, moving from the industrial to the public sector, it became more limited in its scope, requiring greater innovation and adaptability. Selling off of criminal justice assets has been primarily restricted to the sale of land or property (e.g. police stations, prison and court buildings). Due in no small part to austerity cuts and budgetary demands, criminal justice sell offs include: 100 police stations across London alone, the headquarters of the Metropolitan Police Scotland Yard (sold for £1billion to private developers) (Charity, 2018), and 164 of the 320 magistrates courts that existed in 2010 (sold to developers for a total of £223m and turned into hotels and apartments) (Campbell, 2021). The dominant model for criminal justice privatisation has been outsourcing: the process by which the State continued to fund services but contracted out discrete segments of provision/delivery to private enterprise. Its most bold manifestation was the bifurcation of the Probation Service, with the largest of the two parts contracted out to private providers.

History

Since the 1970s, the central State has been restructured and is now much more restricted in its scope. Whilst the post-war State settlement, predicated on social democratic principles of common good and collectivism, favoured State provision and was accompanied by the expansion of the public sector, the gradual incursion of neoliberalism into social, political and economic life over the last four decades is associated with the shrinking of the public domain, the rolling back of the State and the expansion of the private domain. In the new hollowed-out State, the private sector has become pivotal to the day-to-day function of the body politic, and a new 'Shadow State' of powerful corporate interests has evolved (White, 2016). Locked into a reciprocal relationship with an increasingly powerful oligopoly of big private firms whose tentacles reach into the deepest crevices of government, the State has become residualised, reduced to the provider of last resort waiting in the wings to step back onto the main stage when the private actors' incompetence can no longer be covered up.

Although at its inception an experimental, marginal policy initiative, confined to the Conservative party, privatisation as a movement has gained in momentum over the last 40 years, crossing party political boundaries and entering the mainstream thinking of all major political parties. Adapted to comply with party political priorities, privatisation is now a central plank of contemporary public policy orthodoxy. Initially pursued as a limited revenue raising experiment confined to the selling off of profitable publicly owned industries, privatisation has expanded exponentially. As neoliberalism gained a hold on political and economic thinking, the privatisation remit expanded first to include the delivery of local authority services such as refuse collection and later to a growing number of 'soft services . . . performed on or for people' (Nelson, 1980: 431), including criminal justice, where outsourcing of the provision/delivery to private enterprise has become the norm.

As privatisation has become embedded in public policy, the market for private contracted-out services has both expanded and accelerated: the private provision of public services has become a highly lucrative business. With provision dominated by a small group of contractors, an oligopoly of ever diversifying private providers has emerged which, heavily reliant on the fulfilment of government contracts for their revenue, engage in activities that are neither niche nor departmentally specific. Profit driven, with expansion built into their *modus operandi*, too big-to-fail companies, aided and abetted by State departments, who depend on them to fulfil their State responsibilities, operate as mutating predators, encroaching into increasingly sensitive areas of social life. Whether it is high-profile provision of non-fire resistant cladding for social housing, 'track and trace' in the COVID crisis, food parcels for asylum seekers or the more benign provision of light bulbs to bail hostels, nothing is deemed out of bounds; nothing is sacrosanct.

With the State abrogating its traditional responsibilities, the post-war social contract has been rewritten: new social relationships and responsibilities have emerged.

Neoliberal penality

As O'Malley (2015) reminds us neoliberal penality is a contested concept: the 'debate over the impact of neoliberalism on penal policy and practice is by now familiar to criminologists' (2015: 1). With neoliberalism associated with economic deregulation, promotion of competitive markets and the rolling back of the Welfare State, discussions about neoliberal penality have tended to coalesce around the key ideas of the rise of New Right penology and the new punitiveness (Pratt et al., 2005), the ascendancy of a culture of control and the decline of penal welfarism (Garland, 2000) and the emergence of risk-based strategies and practices (O'Malley, 1992), as well as the creation of a market for penal products and services.

Whilst the degree to which penal policies have been shaped by neoliberalism remains open to debate, what is generally accepted is that neoliberal precepts underpin the marketisation and privatisation of the criminal justice system. Although the criminal justice system initially eluded privatisation (it was one of the last of the public sectors to be privatised), the speed, breadth and depth of the incursion of privatisation, once complementary, into the mainstream, has been unparalleled. That said, with the criminal justice system made up of distinct and separate agencies with their own organisational structures and operational requirements, as well as penal philosophies and statutory responsibilities, which straddle two ministries, the degree to which privatisation has reconfigured individual agencies is varied. Indeed, pre-existing institutional forms, organisational cultures and histories, as well as political imperatives and public sensibilities, have all shaped the degree to which criminal justice professionals, their representatives and their supporters have been able to successfully resist the prevailing trend. It is these nuances, continuities and discontinuities that are the focus of this book.

The commodification of crime

Central to the neoliberal penality thesis is the concept that crime, its products and its objects can be transformed into commodities to be sold on the open market. Reliance on the private sector to satisfy the need for new products and services to control crime means that crime is the gift that keeps giving. Crime pays; it 'means money. Big money' (Christie, 2003: 117). The crime control industry has a voracious appetite and, thanks to neoliberal crime control policies, an ever expanding customer base.

The privatisation of criminal justice is without doubt highly controversial, posing unique dilemmas. Whilst the privatisation of any aspect of public service raises fundamental questions about the role and function of the State, the privatisation of law enforcement and crime control is 'qualitatively different on ethical and moral grounds, from other public services' (Shichor, 1995: 46). As Matthews (1989) acknowledged, for many critical writers, 'the power to lock people up, depriving them of their liberty and separating them from their families, is a responsibility that should be the preserve of the State' (*The Guardian*, 2019). Privatisation of the

State's prerogative to detain and punish tests the limits of the State's legitimacy and authority, compromising long-established principles, rights and liberties which are the bedrock of criminal justice. The establishment of the State as the sole provider of criminal justice, the sole body vested with the power to punish, is central to the civilisation process (Pratt and Clark, 2005: 263); the abrogation of the State's coercive power—the deprivation of a 'person's liberty . . . at the behest of government' (Robbins, 1989: 558–559) to business interests for commercial gain—is indicative of decivilisation (Pratt and Clark, 2005).

Relationships that were previously untainted by commerce have been recalibrated. The injection of the profit motive into sensitive decision-making processes has created perverse incentives which, among others, compromise the impartial administration of justice, threaten fundamental liberties and freedoms and pose a risk to public security and safety. With private corporations ultimately established for their owners and shareholders, not the public good (Shichor, 1995), the traditional public service ethos, its principles, values and professionalism have been tainted.

Notwithstanding this, as ex-practitioners in contact with former colleagues, the authors, whilst adopting a critical perspective towards privatisation, neither seek to act as apologists for the State system nor to valorise the public system. Indeed, mindful of contemporary examples of systemic failings of the criminal justice system exposed by the Black Lives Matter movement, we recognise that the State system is flawed; beset by scandals, wrongdoings and cover ups, institutional bias and prejudice; and capable of egregious abuses of power. With this in mind, whilst a rounded critique of the State system falls outside our remit in this instance, we remain indebted to the work of our fellow scholars (including, Nils Christie, David Garland, Penny Green, Alison Liebling, Bob Lilly, John Pratt, Jeffrey Reiman, Joe Sim, Steve Tombs and Tony Ward) and the campaigners, investigative journalists and penal reformers (e.g. the Howard League for Penal Reform, Inquest, The Prison Reform Trust) whose collective body of work meticulously catalogues public criminal justice failings and the wider abuses of State power.

The structure of the book

Whilst taking a minor liberty with Matthews' original formulation (given its central role in the roll-out of privatisation, we have substituted the Probation Service for Juvenile Justice), we have, in the main, replicated the focus on the main institutions featured in *Privatizing Criminal Justice*—police, prisons, electronic monitoring services—and have incorporated the voluntary sector in the chapter on the Probation Service. Additionally, mindful that the agencies under discussion operate in different political and social spheres, have occupational cultures and structural frameworks shaped by their unique historical precedents, developments and contingencies, we have incorporated a historiographical perspective that owes much to Matthews' (1999) later text *Doing Time*. In exploring how the past shapes the present, we seek to explore the degree to which the roll-out of privatisation of criminal justice has had to adapt and evolve to encompass historically determined differences of administrative and institutional structures, professional priorities and penal philosophy differences. In so doing, we provide a context for understanding the divergences, similarities, continuities, contradictions and discontinuities, as well as acceptance, reluctant capitulation, compromise, resignation, resistance and reversal that constitute *Privatizing Criminal Justice*.

The book can be summarised as follows:

Chapters 2 and 3, which should be read together, provide the theoretical building blocks of privatisation and trace its development across four decades Adopting a broad-brush approach, the privatisation of the criminal justice system is located within a wider political and historical context, which recognises the strategic policy coherence across the diverse and (on the face of it) seemingly unconnected offices of the State. The intention is to avoid the 'silo effect' whereby criminal justice is divorced from wider developments in other government departments such as business, innovation and skills; energy and climate change; communities and local government; transport; education; health; and work and pensions.

Whilst the authors recognise at the outset that the process of transfer of services between the public and the private sector has not been exclusively in one direction, in these two chapters, significant events that exemplify the incremental erosion of the State monopoly on provision of public services in the UK are discussed. Chapter 2 starts by exploring the contested term 'privatisation' and proposes the adoption of a multi-modal framework for analysis that encapsulates the wide range of sector specific variants. The chapter continues by identifying the ideological roots of privatisation and explores the role of transatlantic think tanks in developing and disseminating ideas. In tracing the trajectory of privatisation, the authors argue that the model of privatisation of the industrial sector, which predated the privatisation of welfare provision and delivery, was typified by fiscally driven wholesale industry sell offs, differs from that of the Welfare State where sell offs have been more limited in scope.

Although creation of internal markets and outsourcing has been a predominant mode of privatisation for the welfare sector, the technical, legislative, administrative, political and ideological precedents established by industrial sector privatisation provided the platform for the later more innovative and creative incursions of the private sector into public service provision. In this chapter, the enabling environment the interconnecting social, economic and political factors that served as the launch pad for the seismic shift in public policy thinking and action (a shift that transformed the State from one founded on social democratic principles into a hollowed out one shaped by neoliberalism) are analysed.

With the foundations established, the bulk of Chapters 2 and 3 is given over to the discussion of the economic and political influences that have shaped different stages of privatisation. Starting with denationalisation, Chapter 2 explores the incremental ratcheting up of privatisation, the changing scope and range, that characterised the four terms of Tory rule. With local authority services early targets, the chapter focusses on how the policy of putting public service provision out to tender, facilitated the creation of an internal market in the reconfigured the Welfare State.

With privatisation embedded into public policy by the time that New Labour emerged from the political doldrums in 1979, Chapter 3 starts by discussing how, despite claims to the contrary whilst in opposition, privatisation emerged as an accepted aspect of the party's political agenda. In this chapter, the authors explain how key ideas and practices, tried and tested by the Tories, were incorporated into the New Labour public policy agenda. They describe how, under the auspices of the Third Way and modernisation, the outsourcing of public services, albeit 'repackaged and justified on a new set of objectives' (Whitfield, 2000: 82), carried on apace. With New Labour keen to promote new infrastructure projects, initiatives such as private financing, introduced in a limited form by Major, became the norm.

The chapter proceeds with a discussion of privatisation under the Con/Dem coalition, in particular the austerity agenda and public sector cost-cutting policies, characterised by the opening up of all public services to a new market of providers, the introduction of new funding arrangements with Payment by Results and the extension of privatisation to increasingly sensitive areas of public provision. The chapter concludes with the return of the Tory Party under May and then Johnson. Highlighting the degree to which Brexit dominated policy making under May, the chapter concludes by exploring the COVID crisis under Johnson's administration and the role of private companies in providing the bulk of new services demanded to respond to the pandemic.

In Chapter 4, the key themes of: globalisation, neoliberalism, risk, responsibilisation and securitisation; the development of the US as the penal workshop of the world; and the transfer of penal policy ideas and products to the UK are discussed. The chapter starts by acknowledging that the study of contemporary criminal justice policy is increasingly a global endeavour, encompassing both the economic opportunity and social risk brought about by globalisation. In this chapter, the authors argue that a feature of neoliberalism and State contraction has been the redrawing of the social contract between the State and the individual, with the transfer of responsibility for risk prevention and management from the State to the individual or organisation: a development which created a market for the provision of private security goods and services.

The chapter continues by exploring the forging of the special relationship between Reagan and Thatcher in the 1980s and the willingness of successive UK governments to gain inspiration from America crime control and punishment policy solutions. The authors argue that the emergence of New Right penal policy in the 1970s and the subsequent penal crisis created a market in penal goods and services in the United States, which provided the impetus for the nascent private security industry to diversify into commercial corrections industry. In this chapter, the authors focus on how, faced with its own penal crisis a decade later, the UK (influenced in part by lobbying from the US), lacking its own off-the-shelf solutions, looked to the US to supply the know-how, technologies, services and personnel: a development which allowed the US security and corrections industry to expand its global footprint.

In Chapter 5, the authors explore how, despite the fact that privatisation has been accompanied by a plethora of regulatory bodies, systemic flaws in the regulatory apparatus, in part a consequence of the symbiotic relationship between the State and commercial interests, have contributed to multiple incidents of malfeasance, disasters and scandal. The chapter exposes how the privatisation and market imperatives have become associated with the loss of transparency and good governance, poor performance, corner-cutting, lax contract scrutiny and oversight, malpractice, negligence and on occasion culpable criminality.

Taking issue with the regulatory State literature, the authors argue that as privatisation has grown in scope and size, the boundaries between the public and the private sector have become increasingly permeable, and the regulatory State has incrementally conceded its authority to the commercial interests. Light-touch regulation has given rise to practices and procedures that have undermined the due diligence that should be exercised by officials in the procurement and oversight of private contracts. The emergence of a powerful new public sector oligopoly of multi-national 'too big to fail' companies has created an operational environment in which private companies have been able to exploit systemic fault lines, putting the public, service users and employees at risk.

In Chapter 6, the authors offer the first of two inter-related consecutive chapters on policing which examine and evaluate the development of both public and private policing perspectives, primarily in the context of England and Wales but also drawing on relevant comparative theoretical and practice models when appropriate. Given the breadth of the field of policing in terms of perspectives of privatisation, the principal aim, therefore, is to provide a critical historical foundation to the subject area, highlighting social conflict, continuity and change. The chapter explores the customary system which preceded considerations of public policing, which is offered as a precursor to the development of the public sphere and burgeoning centralised governance.

The creation of the 'new police' and moreover public policing and the increasingly complementary blending of private security are then examined as counterpoints through the social, disciplinary and technological changes of the nineteenth and twentieth centuries up until the post-World War Two apex for the public service role in policing, which has been frequently termed the 'Golden Age'. The challenges of recession and discord which followed the post-war boom are then explored, with the perceived need for the modernisation of public policing prior to the emergence of the New Right politics of the late 1970s, highlighting the impact on policing practice and its administration enacted by consecutive Conservative administrations led by Margaret Thatcher during the 1980s and the progress of the private security industry as amalgam and supplement and reflecting that this era provided the catalyst for the profound relational changes between the public, the police and private enterprise that have influenced and informed the policy of all governments that have followed, regardless of personality or ideological tinge.

Chapter 7 builds on the preceding chapter to explore public and private policing developments in England and Wales and the UK since the early 1990s, beginning at the end of the Thatcher administration. These last four decades have witnessed a period of precipitous social and technological change, with public policing increasingly forced to play catch up and second fiddle to the private security industry. In this chapter the authors examine the continuing privatisation ethos of the Major government, which saw policing increasingly placed under the political microscope, at turns viewed as saviour, service industry and Aunt Sally. Such close scrutiny continued with the rise of New Labour under Blair, with its particular brand of driven neoliberalism, placing emphasis on tough-smart tech-smart crime policy, and an attempt at public police responsibilisation through pluralism, civilianisation and legislation.

The strategic shrinking of the State during the 1990s and 2000s ensured that the arrival of the global credit crunch and ensuing austerity effecting Western countries from 2010 could be utilised to initiate further attacks by consecutive coalition and Conservative administrations on the public sector, including the cutting of public policing services to the bone. Within the volatile political environment of the last decade a wider more operational role for the private security industry has been conceived and trialled, alongside increasing numbers of private watch and patrol services and a belief that dataveillance, technology and analytics can provide a panacea in policing precarity which drives traditional social control methodologies towards redundancy.

Chapter 8 adopts the historiographic approach used in Chapter 6 in seeking to provide socio-historical underpinning to an extensive and long established subject area. Here, focus is on the early modern history of punishment and imprisonment to inform the present—with explicit linkage to the chapter that immediately follows, which critically considers the contemporary penal landscape. Its emphasis is primarily on the UK, though continental and American historical models are utilised where relevant. The chapter commences with an examination of symbolic punitive custom in the early modern period to demonstrate the dramatic impact of social change and the move from corporal punishment towards formalised incapacitation. Growing public awareness and fear of crime, the resultant demand for discipline and the development of corrective technologies are explored, alongside the inherent profit imperatives and structures of early organised penality.

As the central State became involved with plans for prison design, construction and reform and aware of the associated costs—fiscal, political and social—a modern concept of the prison emerges. It is argued that a turning point is reached in the early nineteenth century with an evolving desire towards bureaucratic formalism, coherent rationale and centralised control. The chapter then develops to reveal the construction of what might be termed a 'public edifice' through various regimes and representations during the Victorian era, to emerge as a model of purpose for modern public penality up until the middle of the twentieth century. Conceptions of idealistic decay and administrative idealism, essentially the deterioration and degradation of the public edifice, are discussed, with the move towards the muted surrender of public sovereignty and control at the commencement of the final decade of the twentieth century

Chapter 9 follows and builds on the content of Chapter 8 in mapping the development of privatisation within the contemporary prison system of the UK. It does this by chronologically exploring four overlapping intensive phases of criminal justice policy, covering the last 40 years in critical overview. The first considers aspects of the ideological justification for the use of competition as a tool of penal reform in the late 1980s and early 1990s, the ensuing clamour for its adoption and its formal realisation as government policy under the Conservatives. The second explores the rapid manufacture and public acceptance of a private prison complex under the Major administrations at the start of the 1990s—a move which conceptually owed much to the American model but was supplied with a distinctly British flavour. The third phase evaluates the response of a succession of Blairite Labour governments between 1997 and 2010, firmly against penal privatisation in opposition but shown to be exacting neoliberalists in governance. Finally, the last decade is scrutinised, a period framed by austerity and intense social change, where normalised penal privatisation went beyond rationalisation towards a culture of denigration and drift.

Chapters 10 and 11 are interlinked chapters that address the privatisation of offender management services. In these two chapters, two parallel but inter-related developments are explored. These are the rise of electronic monitoring as the first exclusively private provision of offenders' services and the slow demise of the Probation Service, culminating in the largest privatisation venture in the criminal justice system. With private companies predators rather than partners, the two chapters explore how the Probation Service was particularly vulnerable to the vagaries of successive governments' forays into privatisation and in a series of incremental changes, including increasing outsourcing of peripheral services, softened up for selling off to the private sector.

In the first of these two chapters the different stages of the 'privatisation by stealth' (Burgess and MacDonald, 1999: 8) (e.g. the introduction of the business ethos into the service, the emergence of command and control style management by targets and the creation of an internal market), which laid the groundwork for privatisation of 70% of the Probation Services, and the awarding of the electronic monitoring of offenders to private contractors—a pivotal moment that signalled the eve of destruction—are debated.

The second of the two chapters focuses exclusively on the balkanisation of probation, with the majority of the community sentences and rehabilitation packaged off and outsourced to the private sector through Transforming Rehabilitation. With the reconfigured National Probation Service marginalised (reduced to initial risk assessment, advising courts on sentencing options and the direct management of convicted lawbreakers deemed high risk), the various steps involved in turning the policy vision of a privatiser zealot, Grayling, the then Minister of Justice, into a programme of action from consultation, to green papers, to bills and enacted legislation are traced, alongside the campaign of resistance by penal reformers, trade unionists and parliamentary allies.

In Chapter 11, the authors turn their attention to the risks of privatising the delivery of mainstream probation services identified by opponents during the consultation stage and discuss how these came to fruition once the policy was operationalised. Through the analysis of the series of excoriating reports compiled by watchdogs since its implementation, including the incendiary 2018 House of Commons Justice Committee report (HOC, Justice Committee, 2018), the authors describe how the new arrangements were ultimately condemned as 'not fit for purpose'. Mindful of the catalogue of private company failures that were the hallmark of the privatisation of the Probation Service experiment, the authors expose the costly consequences for offenders, practitioners and the public of political hubris. Having charted the many twists and turns in the flawed probation privatisation experiment, the chapter finishes by urging a cautious welcome to the unexpected U-turn with the renationalisation of the service in 2020 under the smokescreen of the COVID-19 crisis.

References

Braithwaite, J. (2000) 'The New Regulatory State and the Transformation of Criminology' *British Journal of Criminology* 40 (2): 222–238

Burgess, J., and MacDonald, D. (1999) 'Outsourcing, Employment and Industrial Relations in the Public Sector' *The Economic and Labour Relations Review* 10 (1): 36–55

Campbell, D. (2021, November 2) 'Britain's Prisons Are Becoming More Like the Failed US System' *The Guardian*

Charity, N. (2018, September 3) 'Revealed: £1bn of Properties Sold by Scotland Yard' *Evening Standard*

Christie, N. (2003) *Crime Control as Industry* (3rd edition), London: Routledge

Garland, D. (2000) *Culture of Control*, Oxford: Oxford University Press

The Guardian (2019, May 13) 'The Guardian View on Private Jails: Flaws in the System' *The Guardian*

Home Affairs Committee (1988) *Private Sector Involvement in the Penal State*, London: HAC

House of Commons (HOC) Justice Committee (2018) *Transforming Rehabilitation*, London: HOC Justice Committee

Jones, T., and Newburn, T. (2007) *Policy Transfer and Criminal Justice*, Milton Keynes: Open University Press

Matthews, R. (1989) 'Privatization in Perspective' in R. Matthews (ed) *Privatizing Criminal Justice*, London: Sage

Matthews, R. (1999) *Doing Time: A Sociological Introduction*, London: Palgrave Macmillan

Mawby, R.I. (1989) 'The Voluntary Sector's Role in a Mixed Economy of Criminal Justice' in R. Matthews (ed) *Privatizing Criminal Justice*, London: Sage

Nelson, B.J. (1980) 'Purchase and Service' in G.J. Washnis (ed) *Productivity Improvement Handbook for State and Local Government*, New York: Wiley

O'Malley, P. (1992) 'Risk, Power and Crime Prevention' *Economy and Society* 21: 252–275

O'Malley, P. (2015) *Rethinking Neoliberal Penality*. Legal Studies Research Paper no. 15/67, Sydney: University of Sydney Law School

Pratt, J., and Clark, M. (2005) 'Penal Populism in New Zealand' *Punishment and Society* 7 (3): 303–322

Pratt, J., Pratt, D., Brown, D., Hallsworth, S., and Morrison, W. (2005) *The New Punitiveness: Trends, Theories, Perspectives,* London: Sage

Prison Reform Trust (2005) *Private Punishment: Who Profits?* London: PRT

Prison Reform Trust (2021) *Bromley Briefings Prison Factfile, Winter 2021,* London: PRT

Robbins, I.P. (1989) 'The Legal Dimension of Private Incarceration' *American University Law Review* 50: 24–30

Shichor, D. (1995) *Punishment for Profit,* London: Sage

Taylor, M., and Pease, K. (1989) 'Private Prisons and Penal Purpose' in R. Matthews (ed) *Privatizing Criminal Justice,* London: Sage

Vickers, J., and Wright, V. (1989) 'The Politics of Industrial Privatisation in Western Europe' in J. Vickers and V. Wright (eds) *The Politics of Privatization in Western Europe,* London: Frank Cass

White, A. (2016) *Shadow State: Inside the Secret Companies that Run Britain,* London: Oneworld

Whitfield, D. (2000) 'The Third Way for Education: Privatisation and Marketisation' *Forum* 42 (2): 82–85

2
FROM NATIONALISATION TO PRIVATISATION, OR BRINGING CAPITALISM TO THE PEOPLE

> As a Conservative minister once stated, 'privatisation is an ugly word for a beautiful concept'.
>
> (Heald, 1984: 36)

Introduction

The study of contemporary penal policy making all too often creates a 'silo effect' with the study of criminal justice and thereby the actions of Home Office ministers and officials, divorced from wider developments in other government departments such as business, innovation and skills; energy and climate change; communities and local government; transport; education; health; and work and pensions. The lack of recognition of strategic policy coherence across the diverse and (on the face of it) seemingly unconnected offices of the State means that too often there is a failure to acknowledge the degree to which the current attack on the basic provisions of key aspects of criminal justice is merely the latest manifestation of the over 40 years of successive governments' actions to hollow out the State. This short history, which provides a snapshot of key developments (see the two volumes by Parker, 2009, 2012 for a comprehensive account), is intended as a corrective to this.

Distinguishing between the industrial and the welfare sectors under public ownership at the beginning of the 1980s, and the different modes of privatisation imposed upon them, the trajectory of government policy making during the 13 years of Tory administration is traced: a trajectory which, motivated by the primary objectives of raising revenue, widening share ownership (giving investors a stake in the reconfigured, hollowed-out State) and reducing the power of the unions began with the early tentative, experimental steps of denationalisation of profit-making public enterprises and grew more ambitious in scope and range, expanding beyond the industrial sphere into core public services of the Welfare State. Indeed, with the creation of the internal markets and the outsourcing to private companies of key functions of the Welfare State, in the expectation that the smoke and mirrors of consumer choice, improved quality of service delivery and reduced cost to the public purse would have popular appeal, a blueprint for the privatisation of public services was created: a blueprint which, emulated and augmented by later governments of different party political outlooks, moved privatisation from the margins to the centre of policy making embraced by all political parties.

Although 'the organisation of economic activity and the ownership of the means of production and trade have moved throughout history from the State sector to the private sector and back at many times in many different ways', and the transfer is not one directional, it is nonetheless the case that one of the defining features of public policy over the last four decades has been the hollowing out of the State and the transfer of State industries and public services to the private sector. With this in mind, the starting point for discussions of privatisation are major events of the thirties and forties which provided the impetus for a programme of nationalisation (Megginson and Netter, 2003: 26–27): namely the Great Depression of the thirties, which gave credence to the view that unbridled capitalism was a failed venture, incapable of delivering 'economic growth and a decent life' (Yergin and Stanislaw, 1998: 22), and the Second World War, which proved to the public that the national interest of providing essential war resources could best be served by large-scale government intervention in industrial production.

Elected in a landslide victory in July 1945, the Labour government under the premiership of Clement Attlee 'came into power totally committed to nationalization and determined to conquer the "commanding heights" of the economy' (Yergin and Stanislaw, 1998: 25). Under invested and poorly managed industries such as coal, iron and steel, railways, utilities and international telecommunications were transferred from the private sector to the public. Simultaneously, the Welfare State, outlined in the Beveridge report was implemented, creating a national health service in 1948 which provided universal free medical care and a system of 'cradle to grave' welfare benefits (Megginson and Netter, 2003: 27). Public sector expansion became a key feature of the post-war political consensus, and by the late 1970s 'the UK possessed one on the largest public enterprise sectors in Europe' (Heald, 1989: 33). In common with other developed countries at the time, the State became both a major employer and provider of goods and services (Bishop and Thompson, 1993: 2). By 1979 (the year that Margaret Thatcher was elected Prime Minister) the nationalised industries alone accounted for 10% of the gross domestic product (GDP), employing nearly 10% of the total workforce. State-owned monopolies dominated transport, communications and the energy sector. Local authority services such as refuse collection, as well as welfare sector services provided by local and central government, 'accounted for a further (extensive) slice of economic activity' (Bishop and Thompson, 1993: 2).

Despite this, during the four terms of Tory administration (1979–1997) the political, economic and social landscape had shifted. By the time that Thatcher, whose premiership some claim was defined by privatisation, left office in 1990, to be replaced by Major, more than 40 State-owned businesses, employing 600,000 workers, had been privatised (Groom and Pfeifer, 2011). Additionally, central government and local authorities had been transformed by a series of measures: namely, the introduction of internal markets, 'competitive tendering and contracting out of work' (Parker, 2012: 504). The culmination of these initiatives was the reduction of the contribution of publicly owned industries to about 3% of GDP, with employment in the public sector a mere 1.5% by the late 1990s (Parker, 2012: 504).

As these two linked chapters demonstrate, privatisation, which started at the margins of public policy, over a period of four decades became mainstream, forming part of the public policy agenda of all major political parties. Consequently:

> Where we once had public services which were democratically accountable, funded through a fair taxation system and available to all, we now have a 'shadow state', run by private management only accountable to their wealthy shareholders, who cream off profits while the taxpayer taxes the risks.
> *(The Trade Union Co-Ordinating Group, 2013: 3)*

The pursuit of 'a predominantly free enterprise economy' (Thatcher, 1995: 574) ensured that most of the previously State-owned industries were returned to private ownership, and those that remained were considerably reduced in size through the 'policy of fragmentation' (The Conservative Research Department, 1979: 16): a process by which publicly owned businesses and services are broken up into smaller delivery units in order to reduce public service trade union power, and to prepare them for being sold off piece by piece (in the case of the post office, this divided up into giro bank, parcels, post and counter services as a precursor to privatisation [Johnson, 2014: 292). In addition, the transformation of local authority and central government reduced the role of a range of public services, most notably the Health Service, from being the primary 'providers of services to suppliers of services produced by others' (Bishop and Thompson, 1993: 2).

Although there have been some reversals (a case in point being the return of network rail to the public sector), over the last four decades the scope and range of privatisation have expanded and accelerated, encroaching into all areas of public service delivery. In this process, the State has been increasingly marginalised, relegated to the provider of last resort. Privatisation and the underpinning belief that public services are best managed by markets has become the political orthodoxy across all political parties. Complex and sensitive areas of public service are increasingly outsourced to private providers. In 2014, the Public Accounts Committee reported that £90 billion, which amounts to half of all the public sector expenditure on goods and service, goes to private companies (Evans, 2016).

What is privatisation?

Privatisation, as a word of 'every-day vocabulary' (replacing the more cumbersome term denationalisation), was 'launched' in July 1979 by *The Financial Times* following a telephone interview with Nigel Lawson, who had just become financial secretary at the Treasury (Elliott, 2013). An imprecise and highly contested term, the meaning of privatisation is 'at best uncertain and tenacious' (Dennison,1984: 107): a 'fuzzy concept that evokes sharp political reactions' (Starr, 1988: 6). The term, which has spawned a variety of definitions, is best understood as an 'umbrella term for many different policies loosely linked by the way in which they are taken to mean a strengthening of the market at the expense of the state' (Heald, 1983: 398). As discussed earlier, privatisation is a

> catch-all term referring to any process where the State is no longer the provider of particular goods and services . . . [It] has . . . come to be used to refer to a disparate set of processes ranging from the sale of public companies to contracting out, as well as various forms of deregulation.
> *(Matthews, 1989: 1)*

The variety of disparate manifestations, which are outlined in detail in the introduction, can be summed up as: redrawing the public/private boundary in favour of the private sector; the shrinking of the State's role as the provider (but not necessarily purchaser) of goods and services; and reducing the scope, limiting the functions and generally weakening the influence of the public sector and its representatives (Vickers and Wright, 1989: 2). With its roots in 'the countermovement against the growth of government in the West', it signifies a 'new chapter in the conflict over the public-private balance' (Starr, 1988: 6).

Multi-modal privatisation has proved highly adaptable, changing and mutating to meet sector specific contingencies. It encompasses a range of activities, including deregulation, liberalisation, the dispensing of vouchers to individuals to purchase private goods or services, 'charging for public services previously provided at zero price', as well as the 'transfer of assets (sales) from the state to the private sector' (Hartley, 1990: 180). Although at first glance this range of activities may appear disparate and separate, what provides 'strategic policy coherence' (Rose, 2000) are shared underlying ideological imperatives and beliefs. Indeed, whilst privatisation initiatives differ both in form and scope, involve 'different actors and policy communities, . . . [are] motivated by different ambitions and . . . [are shaped] by different constraints' (Vickers and Wright, 1989: 3), what provides the 'high level of continuity' (Whitfield, 2002: 235) are the 'family resemblances amongst the various ways of thinking and acting' (Rose, 2000: 323). Seemingly discrete activities across different policy realms involving different offices of State share a common ideological core: one that is summed up in the 'private good, public bad' dogma.

Whilst the privatisation of nationalised industries and the Welfare State differ in both scope and form, the privatisation of public services was dependent on the successful transfer of a 'whole range of industries and services back to the private sector' (Ryan and Ward, 1989: 1) which preceded it. With earlier policy successes providing the impetus, by the time government attention turned to the social welfare sector, 'many of the concerns which had to be addressed from the technical to the political had already been rehearsed' (Drakeford, 2000: 20). The post-war settlement had been breached, and in the process public sensibilities and priorities had realigned. In the wake of mediated industrial disputes and unrest that accompanied the economic and political changes, a less communitarian, more individualistic public emerged: a public receptive to the pro-privatisation arguments. Additionally, perhaps mostly importantly, as a consequence of Thatcher's industrial policy of curtailing the union's power, once omnipotent industrial trade unions that failed to hold back the tide of change were no longer perceived by politicians and Whitehall mandarins as a major threat or obstacle.

Total and partial privatisation: two parts of the State

As outlined in the previous chapter, privatisation is multi-modal. It takes a variety of forms, and can adapt to sector specific contingencies, cultures and history. One way of understanding the different faces of privatisation is to divide State-owned assets and services into two distinct parts—the nationalised industrial sector and the public service/welfare sector—and to recognise that different logistical, technical, institutional and political challenges, including public sensibilities, created sector specific obstacles that militated against the adoption of a 'one size fits all', uniform approach. As Heald (1989) points out:

> [There is] a distinction between the public market sector [public enterprises] and the public non market sector [broadly, the welfare state] . . . [which] reflects institutional features and past political choices about financing as well as the characteristics of the goods and services supplied.
>
> *(1989: 30)*

With 'the extent to which . . . ownership, finance and accountability [could be moved] out of the public sector' (1989: 24), the range of State actions can be broadly depicted as encompassing total privatisation (the preferred model for the industrial sector), whereby the State transfers the complete ownership of public assets to private individuals or enterprises to partial privatisation (the preferred model for the welfare sector) to partial ownership, whereby the State retains the ownership but contracts out the management to a private company (as in the case of the private management of custody suites) or retains the financial role but divests itself of the operating role of services (through the contracting out service provision or issuing vouchers to individuals to buy private goods or services such as nursery places). What is more, the wide range of forms of privatisation means that there are different levels of post-privatisation government involvement: in some cases, the

State's direct involvement in effect ceases, and at other times, partnerships between government and private service providers are created whereby government retains an active presence and/or seeks to be the dominant partner (Starr, 1988).

Whilst industrial sector privatisation has been primarily characterised by total privatisation, privatisation in the public service/welfare sector, with a few notable exceptions, is best characterised as partial, more limited in its scope and consequently requiring greater innovation and experimentation. With the selling off of welfare assets restricted to the sale of land or property (e.g. to the sale of prison and court buildings), the dominant forms of welfare sector privatisation have involved: the hiving off or contracting out of discrete segments of provision/delivery to private enterprise (outsourcing); inviting the private sector to become partners in the finance, construction and management of new institutions; and looking to the private sector to plug the gaps in public services created by State withdrawal.

Differences between the two sectors reflect cultural context (Heald, 1989). Each stage of privatisation has been shaped by sector specific logistical obstacles and political challenges: challenges which are not only indicative of differences in institutional features (themselves the result of previous political decisions about the financing and organisation of goods and services delivered), but also arise from 'huge differences in public perception about the two parts of the UK public sector'. Indeed, although contemporary polls suggest that the public from the mid-1970s was increasingly receptive to the view that 'nationalised industries are less efficient than private enterprises' and are a drain on the public purse, by contrast, parts of the Welfare State services, in particular the National Health Service then (and now) commanded a level of public support which provided protection from wholesale sell off (Heald, 1989: 30).

The rise of privatisation: motives and objectives

Where nationalisation was a response to the perceived failures of capitalism in the 30s and 40s, the rise of privatisation had its roots in the perceived failures of State ownership and control in the 1970s. Although the stated motives, priorities and objectives of pro-privatisation lobbyists, politicians and policy makers have been multiple and have changed over time (e.g. cost cutting and economic efficiency have replaced reducing the power of the trade unions as the dominant narrative), and policy decisions have been framed by historically and sector specific circumstances, contingencies and characteristics, shared ideological, economic, political and fiscal considerations provide linkage between seemingly unconnected State actions.

In terms of ideological motives, Vickers and Wright (1989) differentiate between the broader and the more specific. In their analysis privatisation is not a series of isolated acts, but rather a set of specific policy activities that form part of a much broader and more far-reaching onslaught against the 'social democratic, semi-collectivist consensus of the post-war era' (1989: 5): policy activities which sought to push back of the frontiers of the State; to promote the virtues of self-help, self-responsibility and self-reliance; to abolish inhibitors to the market; and to promote private investment, as well as creating a proper environment for individual actors through the provision of tax incentives (1989: 5).

Theories of ownership and privatisation: ideological roots

As Starr points out:

> The normative theories justifying privatization as a direction for public policy draw their inspiration from several different visions of a good society . . . grounded in laissez-faire individualism and freemarket economics that promises greater efficiency, a smaller government and more individual choice.
> *(1989: 26)*

Privatisation is predicated on three core beliefs, namely that public industries function as monopolies and place restrictions on consumers' individual choice; public ownership deprives individuals of economic freedom as the public are in effect shareholders, whether they choose to be or not, in public sector enterprises; and finally privatisation creates a 'property-owning democracy' and nurtures 'popular capitalism' through the selling off of shares to the public, including employees.

Parker (2009), in his comprehensive *Official History of Privatisation*, describes five inter-related economic arguments which, converging in the 1970s, offered a 'powerful critique of State ownership'. The theories that provided the 'intellectual underpinnings of privatisation' (Parker, 2009: 25) were Austrian economics, public choice theory, agency theory, regulation theory and monetarism.

Austrian school of economics

The importance of competition is central to the ideas of the Austrian school of economics, of which Hayek was a key exponent, that underwent a renaissance in the 1970s. According to the economists of the Austrian school, private ownership and competition hold the key to innovation, efficiency and personal freedom. Whilst private industries are lauded for their capacity to seek out new methods of production and new markets, State-owned industries, by comparison, devoid of the profit motive and private property rights, lack the incentive, and their managers lack the know-how to respond innovatively to the market forces of supply and demand.

Even when politicians and civil servants are 'minded to try and mimic the market', the 'absence of competitive marketing signals' limits their ability to make the right decisions. Parker, 2009: 19). Protected from the

> bracing winds of market forces, and . . . cushioned by the statutory obligation by the state to pick up the bill for any losses made, public sector managers,

> exempt from the risk of bankruptcy and are not answerable to shareholders, lack the incentive to achieve greater efficiency and to maximise profit.
>
> *(Vickers and Wright, 1989: 6)*

Exempt from the financial disciplines of the private sector, the public sector, not dependent on commercial rates of borrowing to cover its losses, and able to anticipate being bailed out by the Treasury, exerts considerable competitive advantage over the private sector (Conservative Research Department, 1977).

Public choice theory

Public choice theory draws upon neoclassical ideas. Based on the notion of 'individual utility maximization', its central tenet is the belief that individuals are motivated by self-interest rather than public interest. Consequently, government employees are self-serving when making 'economic policy and taking political decisions' (Parker, 2009: 20). From this perspective, politicians, despite claims to the contrary, engage in behaviour (e.g. courting pressure groups and financers) and make decisions that promote the utility of particular interests 'both inside and outside of' parliament. Vulnerable to lobbyists that seek to promote their own interests, the key determinant in economic policy and public programme resource allocation is political expediency. State ownership is synonymous with 'empire building, gold plating of public investments, union restrictive practices and waste' (Parker, 2009: 20).

Agency theory

In the 1970s there was a growing attraction to the ideas associated with agency theory, specifically the role contractual arrangements play in the control of agents' behaviour. Ownership *per se* is not the issue; rather what matters is the completeness of the contracts entered into. A complete contract is one that covers all 'possible contingencies during the contractual period' and ensures compliant agent behaviour (Parker, 2009: 21). Incomplete contracts fail to ensure behavioural compliance and are dependent on the establishment of different strategies of governance. In the private sector carrot and stick incentives exert disciplinary leverage. The carrot includes 'profit-related pay, stock options and the like', whereas the stick is the threat of takeover by new management that will eradicate waste and increase profits (Parker, 2009: 21). The State sector, however, lacks these incentives as salaries are fixed, stock options are not available and there is no risk of takeover. In contrast with the private sector, poor performance in the public sector is rarely subject to sanctions:

> Like Austrian economics and public choice theory, agency theory leads to the conclusion that state enterprises will be managed less efficiently than private enterprises and will be less responsive to changes in consumer demands and input cost.
>
> *(Parker, 2009: 21)*

Although open to challenges at both an ideological and empirical level, the three key theories provided a compelling case for changes in ownership for politicians (particularly within the right wing of the Conservative Party) and lobbyists who, disillusioned with the post-war compromise, were in search of new ways of thinking and acting. They share a common belief that differences between the two sectors in terms of incentives, objectives and managerial constraints account for the public sector 'over manning and wasteful investment' (Parker, 2009: 21), where as private management, characterised by profit and efficiency, is more likely to confront the unions and tackle inefficient work practices (Vickers and Wright, 1989: 5).

Informed by the central tenets of these ideas, in 1977, the Conservative Party's Nationalised Industry Group, chaired by freemarket advocate Nicholas Ridley, published its infamous report on the future of nationalised industries. Judged by critics at the time to be a two-pronged blueprint, the author had in his sight the punishment of the trade unions for the defeat of the Heath government and denationalisation 'by stealth', rather than direct 'frontal attack', of the wasteful monopolistic industrial sector 'run for the benefit of the boys that work in them', not the customer. The report recommended the breaking up of State monopolies, fragmenting them into smaller units (in order to reduce the power of public sector unions) and edging them back into the private sector. Reproducing the arguments of the economists from whom he drew inspiration, Ridley stated:

> There are fundamental differences between the private and the public sector. In the private sector there is the risk of bankruptcy and redundancy—'the stick', there is also the hope of reward in the form of higher dividends, salaries or wages as the result of success—'the carrot' . . . There is a need to provide sticks, and carrots in the public sector. They are bound to be infinitely less effective than those in the private sector—by the very nature of the public sector and its immunity from bankruptcy . . . The public sector is very seldom found in successful direct competition with the private sector . . . [Where] competition [does exist it] nearly always results in heavy public sector losses, rather than in an attempt being made in the public enterprise to improve its performance. The usual reaction is to seek ways of disguising the loss, and/or of disadvantaging the private sector competitor or better still obliterating it . . . [rather than increasing] efficiency to meet the competition.
>
> (*The Conservative Research Department, 1977: 1*)

The new economics of regulation

A further idea that came to prominence in the 1970s related to the economics of regulation and extolled the virtues of de-regulation and market liberalisation. Concern with the potential of State regulators to introduce measures that distort the market, creating less favourable performance such as 'over-investment in industries where the rate of return was regulated', it underpinned a growing interest in 'how best to structure regulation to avoid monopoly abuse, while maintaining efficiency incentives' (Parker, 2009: 23). With the emergence of research on 'contestable markets', focussing on monopolies, competition and pricing, privatisers were handed the empirical evidence to support their ideological beliefs in the imperative of removing barriers to competition and erasing monopolistic State-owned industries. It provided the impetus for opening up the market to competition from new providers (an early example was telecommunications), the introduction of competitive tendering and the contracting out of the provision of public services (an early example was refuse collection) (Parker, 2009: 23–24).

Monetarism

Finally, the 1970s witnessed a retreat from Keynesianism: the 'dominant force in macroeconomics' in the post-war period. Writing in 1936, during a period of mass unemployment across the major developed economies, Keynes proposed that general unemployment could be reversed through government intervention to stimulate 'demand using tax and spending powers' (Parker, 2009: 24). Adopted by both the Conservative and the Labour Party, successive governments sought to increase demand at times of recession and to reduce demand at times when the economy was overheating in order to manage the boom/slump cycle, creating in its place 'stop/go' cycles (Parker, 2009: 24). Where Keynesians advocated a State-managed economy, monetarist economists favoured leaving 'economic adjustments to the freemarket' (Parker, 2009: 24). While Keynesians were driven by the imperative to reverse recession, monetarists had in their sight the reversal of inflation. Pivotal to the monetarist perspective are the twin beliefs that inflation is the result of 'monetary expansion' (printing too much money) and that the creation of real jobs is dependent on bringing inflation under control.

Although privatisation was not a central tenet of monetarist economics, one of its key proponents, Milton Friedman, was a freemarket advocate who promoted tax reduction as the means of creating an environment that would increase entrepreneurial activity and improve investment. His ideas were taken up in the 1970s by Bacon and Ellis in Britain, who argued that public spending and borrowing was 'crowding out' the private sector and placing restrictions on private sector jobs and investments. Encapsulated in the image of the State as a jackboot stamping on prosperity and wealth creation, the concept of 'crowding out' gained considerable favourable media coverage. Embraced by Thatcher, the Conservative government's post 1979 policy of tax cuts, public spending restraint and monetary control proved an 'important stimulus for a privatisation programme' (Parker, 2009: 25).

The importance of think tanks

Although there is little evidence to suggest that key political figures in the Conservative Party of the 70s and 80s read the original economic texts, there is little doubt that developments in economic thinking disseminated through right wing think tanks that came to prominence in the period provided the momentum, intellectual rationale and legitimacy for Thatcher's privatisation programme (Ryan and Ward, 1989; Parker, 2009). Between the 1940s and the 1970s, a transatlantic network of businessmen, academics, journalists and politicians was established to populise the freemarket ideas of the Austrian economist Hayek and the monetarist ideas of Milton Friedman. This network was formalised through the creation of a series of interlinked think tanks, which serve as 'second hand dealers in ideas' (Stedman Jones, 2012: 153). In 1955, the Institute of Economic Affairs (ICA), whose events Margaret Thatcher[1] attended both prior to and during her premiership, was formed to promote the ideas of Hayek, who was pivotal to its foundation (Parker, 2009: 20). Along with the Centre for Policy Studies (CPS), which became a *de facto* 'policy arm of the Conservative Party', and the Adam Smith Institute (ASI), the ICA played a significant role in the formulation of Conservative Party policy. Under the stewardship of Sherman, the CPS, drawing on the ideas of the two political philosophers, was 'tasked explicitly with the drawing up a new economic agenda that would provide a solution to the twin evils of trade unionism and inflation' (Steadman Jones, 2012: 161).

Informed by the values and beliefs of Hayek (Parker, 2009: 20), in particular the promotion of individualism and personal freedom in tandem with the monetarist principles of budgetary restraint, public spending reduction, low taxation and deregulation (Parker, 2009: 24), Conservative Party policies of the 1980s and 1990s, reversing the post-war political compromise between capital and labour which had given rise to the social market economy, transformed society into one that was more individualistic, competitive and self-governing, with consumption, choice, competition and self-sufficiency the driving forces (Ryan, 2005).

How did neoliberal and monetarists ideas translate into policy? The importance of the enabling environment

Whilst neoliberal and monetarist ideas were gaining an ideological foothold in the 1970s, there is never a seamless transition from theory to policy. Ideas may provide a vision, an end to reach, but do not provide a 'road map'. Politics is both a pragmatic and an ideological business; 'ideas count for little without the practical measures to realise them or the opportunities to provide them' (Heffernan, 2005: 267). For one set of ideas and related policy initiatives to replace another, new ideas must not only fit with dominant political and economic interests (such as those represented in the pro-business, right wing think tanks) but also require enabling societal, social, economic and political contexts. In short, whilst ideas can provide the catalyst for change, in the messy world where politics remains the 'art of the possible', it is the wider socio-economic, political and institutional conditions that either facilitate or frustrate their translation into policy measures.

In the event, translating ideas into policy was the culmination of interrelated factors: the emergence of an 'ideationally informed policy paradigm' in which neoliberal ideas could provide both a causal explanation for the problems and a solution to them; political actors willing to take advantage of the opportunity afforded by the crisis of the social democratic State and its perceived policy failure, institutional willingness and capacity to pursue the policy agenda; as well as key interest groups willing to promote the initiative to a willing electorate (Heffernan, 2005: 268).

Although it was generally accepted by the Conservative Party grandees that turning ideas into practical policies would be hard to achieve (The Conservative Research Department, 1977: 15), and that, in particular, the economic embeddedness of nationalised industries and powerful lobbyists militated against a 'frontal attack', '[a]fter 1973 . . . the emergence of a new set of macroeconomic conditions' provided the impetus for 'the rise of neoliberal ideas. This new set of microeconomic conditions provided the enabling environment (both materially and ideologically) which facilitated the repositioning of privatisation, once at the margins of party policy, closer to centre stage (Heffernan, 2005: 265).

The 1970s were an economically, socially and politically volatile period that precipitated a crisis for the post-war social democratic State and its guiding principles. The oil embargo of 1973 (occasioned by Arab/Israeli conflict and the US government's decision to back the Israelis); the ensuing economic recession, competition from emerging nations, stagflation (inflation coupled with low productivity); rising unemployment (it reached nearly 1.4 million); and successive government attempts to exert control over first the nationalised industrial unions (under Heath) and later the wider public sector (under Callaghan) ushered in considerable economic instability and industrial unrest (Evans, 2013: 14; Garland, 2001: 81). The 1970s witnessed both the three day week in 1974 and the Winter of Discontent in 1978.

In the winter of 1973–1974, in a policy aimed at clamping down on price/wage inflation, the Conservative Prime Minister, Edward Heath, locked horns with the traditional elite of the trade union movement, the National Union of Miners, introducing the three day week, cutting electricity supplies to three consecutive days per week, to conserve coal in the face of a threatened strike by the mineworkers. A snap election in 1974 sealed Heath's fate, with the Labour Party forming a minority government (Taylor, 1996). Four years later in the midst of the winter of 1978/9, Jim Callaghan, the Labour Prime Minister, was embroiled in snowballing strike action (there were more than 2,000 strikes) across Britain as union after union rejected the then Labour government's attempts to impose a wage restraint policy. The 'Winter of Discontent', which become synonymous with the mediated image of 'greedy' local authority worker, piles of uncollected waste (when the refuse collectors came out on strike) and unburied bodies (when the grave diggers joined them) irreversibly changed the social, economic and political landscape (Martin-López and Rowbotham, 2014). Despite the fact that the industrial rest was not confined to the public sector, the backlash against State employees and their trade union representatives (Evans, 2013: 16), orchestrated by the right wing press, made it easier for the electorate to countenance a range of measures which, favouring business interests, challenged the post-war consensus of Keynesian economics, collective corporatism and public ownership.

By the end of the 1970s privatisation was gaining ground as the solution to the 'problems' of the decade, namely trade union militancy, low productivity, and industrial loss making and inefficiency. A drain on the public purse, publicly owned industries and publicly provided services became the focus of criticism from not just an increasingly broad spectrum of the Conservative Party members, but also, perhaps more importantly, the senior civil servant mandarins: a powerful elite at the heart of the government machinery, who, under the direction of ministers, ultimately transform ideas into pragmatic policy (Heffernan, 2005; Hobbs and Hamerton, 2014).

Total privatisation: the nationalised industrial sector

The first phase of privatisation exemplifies Starr's definition of total privatisation: the selling off of publicly owned industrial assets and the creation of new private enterprises. Fiscally driven by the need to raise revenue in the wake of the financial crisis of the 1970s and ideologically driven by neoliberal politics, the multiple aims of privatisation can be summed up as: increasing efficiency by transferring enterprises from public to private ownership and increasing the exposure of organisations to competitive market forces; enhancing freedom by reducing State ownership; deregulation by cutting back the web of State regulation; establishing people's capitalism by building into denationalisation plans special provisions for extending equity ownership by individuals and employees; relieving budgetary pressure on the government by means of denationalisation which generates cash from asset sales, removes the financing of investment by profitable public enterprises from budgetary entanglement and may stem the drain of finance into persistent loss-makers; and finally weakening trade unions by avoiding the obligation placed upon public bodies to be 'good employers, by facilitating anti-union tactics and employment practices which statutory provisions and political pressures make unacceptable within the public sector and by disengaging government from the intractable questions surrounding public sector pay' (Heald and Steel, 1982 as cited in Heald, 1989: 29).

1979–1997: the Tory years

Although most accounts of privatisation take as their starting point 1979 when the grocer's daughter from Grantham, Margaret Thatcher, became Prime Minister in a 'decisive, but not overwhelming' (Evans, 2013: 17) electoral victory, the transfer of ownership of a State-owned industry to the private sector was not new. Indeed, its precedents were Churchill's denationalisation of the British steel industry in the 1950s (Megginson and Netter, 2003: 31), and Callaghan's selling off of State assets in the form of British Petroleum (Vickers and Wright, 1989: 4) in contravention of its own constitutional commitment under Clause 4 to achieve the 'common ownership of the means of production' (Singleton, 1995: 14).

Notwithstanding this, what distinguishes the four terms of Tory rule was the incremental ratcheting up of the scope and scale of the process, the transformation of the prevailing economic orthodoxy and the realisation of the vision of a new social order (Heffernan, 2005: 264). Prior to the 1980s 'privatisation was sporadic and limited, with no ideological roots, no political implications and belonging to no overall industrial strategy. It was not until the 1980s that privatisation was to assume its wide-ranging and politically significant form' (Vickers and Wright, 1989: 2). In spite of the fact that the Conservative Party manifesto of 1979 made no mention of 'privatisation' *per se* (Hastings, 1983: 16), the section on nationalisation included proposals that *de facto* encompassed the politics and practice of privatisation. These included proposals in the first term to: return to private ownership the recently nationalised aerospace and shipbuilding industries with the lure of offering the purchase of shares to employees, raise revenue by selling shares in the National Freight Company to the public; to encourage the emergence of new private bus contractors by amending the system of licensing; to interfere less with the management of the remaining nationalised industries; and set them a clearer financial discipline in which to work and to reduce the powers of National Enterprise Board to ensure that its assets were sold off. Furthermore, the manifesto included the party's populist plans to create a 'property-owning democracy' by selling off council housing to tenants at a below-market price (Hastings, 1983: 16–17; The Conservative Party General Election Manifesto (1979: n.p.).

Selling off State-owned assets: industrial privatisation

Until 1979, the UK 'possessed one of the largest public enterprise sectors in Europe' (Keyser and Windle, 1978 as cited in Heald, 1989: 33). Whilst injecting competition and breaking the economic stranglehold of monopolistic industry were central planks of Tory thinking, arguments that only privatisation could achieve this goal remain highly contested. Although the claim that privatisation was driven by publicly owned enterprises which functioned either as monopolies or were dominated by internal cartels (Heald, 1989: 40) became the dominant political orthodoxy, this was not universally accepted. Indeed, there were (and remain) those who dispute this, arguing that State monopolies such as telecommunications, gas, electricity, water, rail, transport and postal services co-existed with enterprises that either operated competitively or had the potential so to do. The latter included: steel, oil, coal and vehicles (Vickers and Yarrow, 1991: 121).

The first phase of 'denationalisation was relatively modest and exploratory' (Heald, 1989: 34). The 1979 manifesto was limited in its scope and did not commit the policy to engage in 'wide spread' denationalisation (Parker, 2009). Indeed, as stated previously, the Ridley Report cautioned against a frontal attack on State industries and urged a policy of 'preparation' for return to private ownership 'more or less by stealth' (Conservative Research Department, 1977: 15). The main focus of the first administration was the State of the economy and the need to reduce public spending and the public spending borrowing requirement. Under political pressure from the Treasury to balance the books, the pursuit of pragmatic fiscally driven solutions, as much as ideological predilections, provided the impetus for selling off assets quickly: the effect of this was privatisation assuming a higher policy priority than had originally been envisaged (Parker, 2009: 53–54).

Progress at the outset was slow. Although the governing party had a comfortable majority in parliament, there were hurdles to overcome at each stage in the process: preparing the legislative instruments, securing parliamentary assent and then organising the flotation process was time consuming (Heald, 1989: 43). Difficulties arose from the fact that, as a government official of the time observed, 'to all extents and purposes it had never been done before . . . there was no departmental dossier to dust down' (Yergin and Stanislaw, 1998: 117; Megginson and Netter, 2003: 31). The early years were characterised by trial and error: experimenting with methods of denationalisation, finding out what would work and 'testing the market'. As this was uncharted territory, there was no certainty either that the equity market could cope with a large share flotation or that 'businesses tarred with the brush of being nationalised industries' would appeal to private investors (Heald, 1989: 34). Uncertainty about how the market would respond once the statutory measures were in place meant there was 'considerable experimentation with different methods of flotation' (Heffernan, 2005: 266). While some industries were transferred directly by private sale, others were subject to in-house buyouts by employees or managers (Bishop and Thompson, 1993: 5).

In 1980, six Acts were passed that provided the enabling provisions allowing privatisation to take place on a sector by sector basis. Based on the premise that the industry/sector in question was 'unsuitable' for nationalisation, the acts included: *the Industry Act,* which, among other measures, altered the 'status and financing' of the National Enterprise Board; the *Housing Act,* which enshrined in legislation the 'Right to Buy' local authority houses and flats by their tenants; the *Local Government Planning and Land Act,* which introduced the model of local authorities putting out to private companies the provision of services through competitive tender; the *British Aerospace Act,* which was intended to 'rest all property, rights etc. of British Aerospace in a company nominated by the Secretary of State'; the *Civil Aviation Act,* which set in motion the dissolution of the British Airways Board and establishment of a public company; and the *Transport Act,* which foreshadowed the conversion of the National Freight Corporation into a public liability company (Hastings, 1983: 19).

With the outright sale of State-owned industries confined to Thatcher's first term of office, primarily to profitable entities, a range of different flotation models were experimented with:

> Britoil (1982), British Petroleum (1983), Enterprise Oil (1983) and Cable and Wireless (1983) were tender offers; British Aerospace (1981), Amersham International (1982) and Associated British Ports (1983) were offered for sale at a fixed striking price; British Sugar was a private placing; and National

Freight was an employee buyout. Later flotations (were), however, dominated by the offer for sale method.

(Heffernan, 2005: 266)

While Thatcher's early forays were marked by experimentation and caution, her subsequent terms were characterised by a rolling programme of privatisation. The catalyst for this was '(t)he successful sale of Telecom in November 1984 (which) was the key to the entire privatisation programme that followed' (Heffernan, 2005: 256). Spurred on by electoral successes, including Thatcher's much heralded 'third term', privatisation became increasingly 'radical'. Successful implementation and populist appeal meant that the question of whether to privatise had been replaced by 'why not?' (Heffernan, 2005: 267).

With the floodgates open after the sale of British Telecom in November1984, privatisation was extended to include British Gas (1986), British Airways, Rolls Royce, the British Airports Authority (1987) and British Steel (1988), as well as the utilities of war and electricity between 1989 and 1991. What is more, under Thatcher's successor, John Major, further asset sales, including British Coal (1984), which had previously been the site of fierce opposition by one of the strongest trade unions (National Union of Miners) to government's earlier attempts to introduce market principles in 1984–5 by closing down unprofitable pits, was transacted 'as the fact that the policy could be undertaken proved its viability' (Heffernan, 2005: 266).

Popular capitalism

Although Thatcher's policy of selling off State assets was not accepted by all sections of her party, with Macmillan (a former Conservative prime minister) famously criticising her for 'selling off the family silver' (*The Telegraph*, 2008), Thatcher's plans to both sell off the public housing stock and to embark upon a public share flotations formed part of a wider political agenda (announced in her address to the 1986 Conservative Party Conference) which was driven by a heady mix of ideology and populism: popular capitalism. She stated:

> We Conservatives believe in popular capitalism—believe in a property-owning democracy. And it works! Popular capitalism is nothing less than a crusade to enfranchise the many in the economic life of the nation. We Conservatives are returning power to the people. That is the way to one nation, one people.
>
> *(Thatcher, 1986: n.p.)*

The most enduring feature of popular capitalism was the discounted selling off of council housing to tenants. Appealing to the aspirant working class, Right to Buy, which appeared in the 1979 Conservative Party Manifesto, captured the public mood, which was turning against State provided housing (a central plank of the post-war Beveridge settlement). With mortgages for council tenants made easy to come by and initial discounts ranging from 33% after 3 years, rising with length of tenancy to a maximum of 50% after 20 years (further inducements were later introduced when the scheme stalled), electorally and financially the policy was an unprecedented success. The revenue raised from 'housing receipts represented 43% of all privatisation proceeds and was both the largest and the most sustained source of capital receipts' (Forrest and Murrie, 1993: 255).

What is more, although public share flotation was not initially a key feature of privatisation, the decision to offer market shares in a limited number of newly created private companies to the general public had a populist appeal that not only provided legitimacy but also (more importantly) gave the public a tangible stake in the process. As Heald (1989) points out:

> (W)ider share ownership through privatisation issues [was] a device of symbolic brilliance . . . Rarely can two, four or six million people have taken active steps in response to an impending government policy decision: privatisation issues have become a yuppie version of the football pools.
>
> *(1989:49)*

Accompanied by a series of highly successful publicity campaigns, the policy of encouraging the general public to become shareholders formed part of a larger vision in which trade unionists ('bad symbols of restrictive practice') would be outnumbered by shareholders ('good symbols of freedom') (Evans, 2013: 36). The 1986 British Gas sell off, epitomised by the famous, "If you see Sid . . . Tell him"' publicity campaign (Insley, 2011), saw share ownership, previously the preserve of an elite minority, opened up to the man in the street only too eager to pass on the word about the benefits of share ownership (Evans, 2013: 36).

Not simply concerned to maximise sale proceeds, Thatcher, never averse to 'rigging the rules of share selling', artificially set the share figure low to ensure an initial quick take-up (an accusation that has resonance with the recent debacle surrounding the Royal Mail flotation, [Neate, 2013]). Indeed, a feature of the various flotations was that

> [e]ach asset was sold fast and cheap. This led to many under valuations which cost the taxpayer dear. At the end of the decade the National Audit Office calculated that the manner of privatisation cost the taxpayer £2.4 billion in expenses and asset values forgone, half of it on electricity and water.
>
> *(Heffernan, 2005: 269)*

In the event, the appeal to the public of maintaining a long-term stake in the running of the newly privatised companies was short lived. For many small shareholders the lure was less about having a say in how the new private business operated but more about the prospect of making a quick profit. Although the numbers purchasing shares increased dramatically during the successive periods of Thatcher's administration, the preference for selling on of shares by private individuals meant that share ownership was not democratised, as Thatcher envisaged, but rather was concentrated in the hands of traditional shareholding elites such as pension managers (Evans, 2013: 37).

Partial privatisation: public services and the Welfare State

Although selling off of nationalised services and utilities, once the enabling legislation and administrative processes had been established, was relatively straightforward, the wholesale selling off of the Welfare State was a step too far. A complex process, requiring greater innovation and creativity, the preferred model for privatisation for Welfare State services from the late 1980s onwards was the creation of a mixed economy of provision. The new arrangements, predicated on new modes of procurement that signalled the end of the State provision monopoly, encouraged non-traditional State providers of goods and services to compete for State funds: funds dispersed either by the intermediaries of newly created budget holding organisations or directly by local or central government departments (Drakeford, 2007: 64–65). By these means, a 'Shadow State' was created in which private companies gained an increasingly large share of the delivery of services that had previously been provided by the State (White, 2016)

Compulsory Competitive Tendering

Although the NHS is seen by many as the public sector privatisation exemplar, providing the model that was emulated or copied by other key departments, the marketisation of the public sector had its origins with the introduction of Compulsory Competitive Tendering (CCT) in 1980's *Local Government and Planning Act* and the *1988 Local Government Act*. Motivated primarily by their cost-cutting potential, these Acts placed local authorities under a statutory duty to subject publicly delivered services to competitive tender.

Under the new arrangements, in-house organisations employing a direct labour force were increasingly required to compete with new private providers. Although initially limited in its scope to new construction work and some estate maintenance, the 1988 Act widened the remit, placing a statutory duty on local authorities to put out to competitive tender five 'designated activities': refuse collection, public building and street cleaning, vehicle maintenance, maintenance of playing fields and parks and catering. Additionally, signposting the government's intention to expand the scheme still further, the Act included a facilitating proviso which not only permitted the Secretary of State to increase the range of designated activities as it deemed necessary, but also to set out the conditions that had to be applied in the bidding process: conditions which ensured the primacy of commercial considerations and exempted criteria such as trade union recognition (Cope, 1999: 175–176; Parker, 2009: 182–183).

Despite the fact that CCT was at the outset restricted to a comparatively narrow range of local authority blue collar workers (leading some critics at the time to argue that this was a punitive response to the Winter of Discontent), the scheme quickly expanded to include a wider range of non-manual and managerial functions. From 1996 onwards, the scheme was extended to include both central and local government white collar functions. Although in the event nearly three quarters of local authority contracts awarded under CCT were in-house and included previous employees, the significance of CCT was that it established the principles, practices and organisational structures that could be emulated in later phases of privatisation, as well as and providing the financial and institutional impetus for the creation of new private contractors ready and willing to ply their trade in the emerging market. During the six year period from 1991–1997 the value of services subject to CCT more than doubled from £1.6 billion to £3.5 billion, and over 100 private firms were set up to deliver contracted-out services (Whitfield, 2002: 239).

The internal market and the National Health Service

In terms of the privatisation of the Welfare State, the most far-reaching and bold development was the creation of the National Health Service (NHS) purchaser/provider split that was to provide the blueprint for later privatisation initiatives such as the Probation Service. The introduction of the internal market into the NHS was preceded by a softening up period of centrally imposed New Public Managerialism (NPM) that broke with tradition of managers being recruited from within the health professions and health provision. Under NPM, managers were employed on the basis of their 'managerial skills and expertise', not disciplinary background (Butler and Calnan, 1999: 324). The intention was to introduce into the State sector 'private sector personnel and notions of efficiency and of management techniques . . . in the hope of imparting a greater "commercial orientation" into its ethos and functioning' (Vickers and Wright, 1989: 3).

The incursion of NPM into the NHS set the stage for the next phase of privatisation: the creation of the internal market (Butler and Calnan, 1999: 324–325). Heavily influenced by the ideas of the American Enthoven, writing in 1985, the introduction of 'market like incentives' (Mays et al., 2011: 2) into the NHS, creating an 'internal market within the NHS in which providers would compete for funds' (Drakeford, 2000: 128), was predicated on the belief that inefficiencies, lack of patient choice and poor performance could be corrected by competition. While the new 'public service market' idea shared the political ideology that underpinned the privatisation of former public sector industries and functions, it was distinct from these and far more experimental. Where the initial phase of privatisation was characterised by the wholesale transfer of public assets and service functions from the public to the private sector, the 'distinction between public and private sector economic activity in the 'internal market' was blurred. Under the new policy the 'NHS would remain a public sector service: its assets would remain publicly owned; expenditure would remain taxpayer funded; and its effective delivery would remain the democratic responsibility of elected politicians'. However, discipline and practices imported from the private sector would improve quality and choice (Evans, 2016).

Although the NHS had experimented with privatisation in the 1980s by contracting out ancillary services (such as hospital domestic services) to the private sector, it was the publication of the landmark 1989 white paper *Working for Patients*, spearheaded by Kenneth Clarke, the Health Minister, which signalled the audacious, 'staggering ambition' to break with the structures set in place by Bevan and Beveridge by restructuring the NHS in a way that would open it up to market forces (Butler and Calnan, 1999: 324). Conveniently side-stepping the longstanding issue of underfunding which had plagued the NHS, new structural and financial arrangements, predicated on the belief that competition would improve the quality service provision, consumer choice and efficiency savings (Hunter, 1997: 48), would be imposed. The intention of these was to establish

> a funding system in which successful hospitals can flourish . . . [that] . . . will encourage greater competition. All this in turn will ensure a better deal for the public, improving choice and quality of services offered and the efficiency with which these services are delivered.
> (DOH, 1989: 22 as cited in Drakeford, 2000: 128)

In its 'explicit preference for market over planning' (Drakeford, 2000: 129), the white paper signalled a radical, game-changing departure from the structures for welfare service delivery that were established in the post-war settlement.

Despite professional resistance and opposition from 'almost every interest group in the NHS', the *1990 National Health Service and Community Care Act* became law in 1999, imposing a new structure for the NHS: a structure which separated the roles of purchaser (demand for services) and provider (supply for services) (Butler and Calnan, 1999: 325). On the demand side, new budget holder arrangements were created through the devolution of budgets to general practitioners and district health authorities. On the supply side, services would be provided by those hospitals which remained under the direct management of the NHS or by self-governing trusts, which had opted out, supplemented by private and voluntary providers (Drakeford, 2000). With the emphasis on the market rather than planning, the newly enfranchised budget holders, free to purchase services not only from their 'own hospitals' but also from neighbouring and/or private hospitals, could determine the 'quantity and quality of (local patient) care' (Butler and Calnan, 1999: 325).

Although there are many excellent accounts (e.g. Ranade, 1997) of how the internal market developed within the NHS, for our purposes, what is significant is that 'new' funding and structural delivery arrangements provided policy decision makers with a model, a blueprint, a dossier that could be applied, albeit with institutionally specific adaptations, to other sections of the Welfare State. With the creation of a market for private services, the successful separation of funding (provided by the State) and delivery (provided by a range of suppliers, including the private sector under the auspices of the mixed economy) provided the impetus for the outsourcing of an ever widening range of central government services. As privatisation gained a foothold across all offices of State, it was only a matter of time before the opportunity would arise for the model adopted by the whale of the welfare sector to be imposed upon the minnows of the criminal justice system, specifically the Probation Service. These developments are discussed in the following chapters.

Conclusion

Driven at the outset by a heady mix of neoliberal ideology, fiscal pragmatism and a visceral hatred of trade unions, the early years of privatisation (Thatcher's first administration), which formed part of the Conservative Party's industrial strategy, were initially characterised by cautious experimentation: limited to the selling off of profitable State controlled industries (total privatisation) and the contracting out of a narrow range of public services such as refuse collection and hospital cleaning (partial privatisation). However, buoyed up by the success of quick wins, the range and scope became more ambitious. The programme quickly accelerated into a rolling programme of privatisation that extended to the utilities as well as the less profitable State industries, most notably the *bête noire* of the Conservative Party, the coal industry.

Although initially intended to apply exclusively to the industrial realm, within the space of a decade, ministers, reversing the post-war social reconstruction, had turned their sights from the privatisation of the industrial sector to the privatisation of the welfare sector. Where the selling off of nationalised industries, once the enabling legislation and administrative processes had been established, was relatively straightforward, the wholesale selling off of the Welfare State was more complicated, partly due to the fear that it would be unlikely to receive public approval. Consequently, a series of creative and innovative measures, starting with the compulsory tendering of a limited range of local authority services, which created a market for private outsourcing companies, were tested out. As these proved successful, the scope and range of services put out to tender accelerated. With the opening up of discrete areas of public service provision to market conditions and the consequent fragmentation of service delivery established in the 1980s, and the more ambitious creation of an internal market within the NHS in 1990, splitting of the service into a purchaser and provider, the way was paved for the radical transformation of the Welfare State and the delivery of public services. As Whitfield and Hall, writing at the time, opined:

> Privatisation and restructuring of public services is a clear strategy to concentrate wealth in the hands of the wealthy. It covers all services—from cradle to the grave—including those we all use regularly a well as those traditionally seen as part of the welfare state'.
>
> *(1983: 180)*

By the time New Labour emerged from the political doldrums in 1997, privatisation had become political orthodoxy, and putting public service provision out to tender was embedded in public policy.

Note

1 Metcalfe (2017) claims that 'to anyone who would listen, Thatcher lionised Hayek, promising to bring together his free market philosophy with a revival of Victorian values: family, commitment and hard work'

References

Bishop, M., and Thompson, D. (1993) 'Privatisation in the UK: Deregulatory Reform and Public Enterprise Performance' in V.V. Ramanadham (ed) *Privatisation: A Global Perspective*, London: Routledge

Butler, J.R., and Calnan, S. (1999) 'Health and Health Policy' in J.C. Baldock, N. Manning, S. Miller and S. Vickers (eds) *Social Policy*, Oxford: Oxford University Press

The Conservative Party (1979) 'The Conservative Party Manifesto' www.conservative-party.net/manifestos/1979/1979-conservative-manifesto.shtml. Retrieved 14 October 2014

The Conservative Research Department (1977) 'The Final Report of the Policy Group on Nationalised Industries' www.margaretthatcher.org/document/110795. Retrieved 20 November 2014

Cope, S. (1999) 'Contracting and Globalisation: Implications for Governance, Policy Learning and Strategic Management' in A. Kouzmin and A. Hayne (eds) *Essays in Economic Globalization, Transnational Policies and Vulnerability*, Oxford: IOS

Dennison, D. (1984) 'The Progressive Potential of Privatisation' in J. Le Grande and R. Robinson (eds) *Privatisation and the Welfare State*, London: Allen and Unwin

Drakeford, M. (2000) *Privatisation and Social Policy*, Harlow: Pearson

Drakeford, M. (2007) 'Private Welfare' in M. Powell (ed) *Understanding the Mixed Economy of Welfare*, Bristol: Policy Press

Elliott, J. (2013, April 11) 'How We Launched Thatcher's "Privatisation" Word in the FT in 1979' *The Independent*

Evans, E. (2013) *Thatcher and Thatcherism*, London: Routledge

Evans, K. (2016) 'Public Service Markets Aren't Working for the Public Good . . . or as Markets' in C. Pell, R. Wilson and T. Lowe (eds) *Kittens are Evil: Little Heresies in Public Policy*, Devon: Triarchy Press

Forrest, R., and Murrie, A. (1993) *Selling the Welfare State: The Privatisation of Public Housing*, London: Routledge

Garland, D. (2001) *The Culture of Control: Crime and Social Order in Contemporary Society*, Oxford: Oxford University Press

Groom, B., and Pfeifer, S. (2011, December 7) 'Privatisation Defined the Thatcher era' *The Financial Times*

Hartley, K. (1990) 'Contracting out in Britain: achievements and problems' in J.J. Richardson (ed) *Privatization and Deregulation in Canada and Britain*. Dartmouth. IRPP

Hastings, S. (1983) 'Privatization 1979–1982' in S. Hastings and H. Levie (eds) *Privatisation?* Nottingham: Spokesman

Heald, D. (1983) *Public Expenditure: Its Defence and Reform*, Oxford: Robertson

Heald, D. (1984) 'Privatisation: Analysing Its Appeal and Limitations' *Fiscal Studies* 5(1): 36–46

Heald, D. (1989) 'The United Kingdom: Privatisation and Its Political Context' in J. Vickers and V. Wright (eds) *The Politics of Privatization in Western Europe*, London: Frank Cass

Heffernan, R. (2005) 'UK Privatisation Revisited: Ideas and Policy Change 1979–1992' *The Political Quarterly* 76 (2): 264–272

Hobbs, S., and Hamerton, C. (2014) *The Making of Criminal Justice Policy*, Oxford: Routledge

Hunter, D.J. (1997) *Desperately Seeking Solutions: Rationing Health Care*, London: Longman

Insley, J. (2011, November 12) 'Tell Sid That British Gas Shares Are Now Worth a Packet' *The Observer*

Johnson, A. (2014) *Please, Mister Postman*, London: Bantam

Martin López, T., and Rowbotham, S. (2014) *The Winter of Discontent—Myth, Memory and History*, Liverpool: Liverpool University Press

Mays, N., Dixon, A., and Jones, L. (2011) *Understanding New Labour's Market Reforms of the English NHS*, London: King's Fund

Matthews, R. (1989) 'Privatization in Perspective' in R. Matthews (ed) *Privatizing Criminal Justice*, London: Sage

Megginson, W., and Netter, J. (2003) 'History and Methods of Privatisation' in D. Parker and D. Saal (eds) *International Handbook of Privatisation*, Chelmsford: Edward Elgar

Metcalfe, S. (2017, August 18) 'Neo-liberalism: the idea that swallowed the world'. *The Guardian*

Neate (2013, November 27) 'Vince Cable Defends Royal Mail Float after Profits Double—as it Happened' *The Guardian*

Parker, D. (2009) *The Official History of Privatisation, Volume 1: The Formative Years 1970–1987*, London: Routledge

Parker, D. (2012) *The Official History of Privatisation, Volume 2: Popular Capitalism 1987–1997*, London: Routledge

Ranade, W. (1997) *A Future for the NHS? Health Care for the Millennium*, London: Longman

Rose, N. (2000) 'Government and Control' *British Journal of Criminology* 40 (2): 321–339

Ryan, M. (2005) 'Engaging with Punitive Attitudes Towards Crime and Punishment: Some Strategic Lessons from England and Wales' in J. Pratt, D. Brown, M. Brown, S. Wallsworth and W. Morrison (eds) *The New Puintiveness: Trends, Theories and Perspectives*, Cullompton: Willan

Ryan, M., and Ward, T. (1989) *Privatization and the Penal System: The American Experience and Debate in Britain*, Milton Keynes: Open University Press

Singleton, J. (1995) 'Labour, the Conservatives and Nationalisation' in R. Millward and J. Singleton (eds) *The Political Economy of Nationalisation in Britain, 1920–1950*, Cambridge: Cambridge University Press

Starr, P. (1988) 'The Meaning of Privatisation' *Yale Law and Policy Review* 6 (1): 6–41

Starr, P. (1989) 'The Meaning of Privatisation' (reprinted) in S. Kamerman and A. Kahn (eds) *Privatization and the Welfare State*, Princeton: Princeton University Press

Stedman Jones, D. (2012) *Masters of the Universe: Hayek, Friedman, and the Birth of Neoliberal Politics*, Princetown: Princetown University Press

Taylor, R. (1996) 'The Heath Government and Industrial Relations: Myth and Reality' in S. Ball and A. Seldon (eds) *The Heath Government 1970–1974: A Reappraisal*, Oxford: Routledge

The Telegraph (2008, August 24) 'It's Labour's Turn to Sell the Family Silver' *The Telegraph*

Thatcher, M. (1986) 'Speech to the Conservative Party Conference' Margaret Thatcher Foundation. Retrieved 3rd January 2015 from www.margaretthatcher.org/document/106498

Thatcher, M. (1995) *The Path to Power*, London: Harper Collins

The Trade Union Co-Ordinating Group (2013) *The Real Cost of Privatisation*, London: Centre for Legal and Social Studies

Vickers, J., and Wright, V. (1989) 'The Politics of Industrial Privatisation in Western Europe' in J. Vickers and V. Wright (eds) *The Politics of Privatization in Western Europe*, London: Frank Cass

Vickers, J., and Yarrow, G. (1991) 'Economic Perspectives on Privatization' *The Journal of Economic Perspectives* 5 (2): 111–132

White, A. (2016) *Shadow State: Inside the Secret Companies that Run Britain*, London: Oneworld

Whitfield, D. (2002) 'Impact of Privatisation and Commercialisation on Municipal Services in the UK' *Transfer: European Review of Labour and Research* 8 (2): 234–251

Whitfield, D., and Hall, D. (1983) 'Strategies to Fight Privatisation' in S. Hastings and L. Hugo (eds) *Privatisation?* Spokesman: Nottingham

Yergin, D., and Stanislaw, J. (1998) *The Commanding Heights; The Battle between Government and Market Place That Is Remaking the Modern World*, New York: Simon and Schuster

3
THE FREE MARKET PANACEA AND PUTTING THE STATE UP FOR SALE

> New Labour since 1997 swallowed the ideology, or rather the theology of global free market fundamentalism, whole.
>
> (Hobsbawm 2009)

Introduction

Since its introduction into public policy, privatisation (particularly in the form of outsourcing), at the outset a Tory-led initiative, has become common ground among the political parties. Repackaged and adapted to meet specific party political agendas, promoting the illusion of pluralism, over the last four decades, a cross party consensus has developed in which privatisation has become the mainstay of political thinking and action. Its remit has gained in scope and pace, encompassing an ever widening circle of State provided and delivered service. Currently it is estimated that one half of the UK's budget for public services is devoted to privately delivered but taxpayer-funded public services. In this process the recipients of services (patients, offenders, the public) have been reduced to commodities, all too often sold to the lowest bidder in what has become known as a 'race to the bottom'.

By the end of the 90s, despite claims to the contrary, key ideas and practices tried and tested by the Tories had become incorporated into the New Labour public policy agenda. Under Blair not only was the prevailing public policy of internal markets in welfare, competition and contracting out accepted (Johnson, 2001: 186), but also, under the auspices of the Third Way and modernisation, the outsourcing of public services, albeit 'repackaged and justified on a new set of objectives' (Whitfield, 2000: 82), expanded exponentially. Keen to redress the neglect of schools, hospitals and prisons that had characterised the Conservative term of office, New Labour embarked upon an ambitious programme of new infrastructure projects funded by private financing, introduced in a limited form by Major. Simultaneously, under the Best Value programme, price competitive tendering and outsourcing became central planks of public policy.

In 2010, in the aftermath of the banking crisis and global recession, the Conservative led coalition government was formed, and privatisation gained a new momentum. Under the new administration, deficit reduction became priority (Toynbee and Walker, 2015), and an austerity programme to reduce the budgetary deficit was introduced, characterised by a draconian package of cuts in public expenditure, public sector retrenchment 'greater than any retrenchment since the end of the Second World War', and public service 'restructuring of Beveridgean proportions' (Taylor-Gooby, 2012: 62). With privatisation and cost cutting aligned in Conservative party thinking, price-competitive tendering gained a new impetus. Under the policy of Open Public Services, all public services were opened to a new market of providers, and privatisation was extended to increasingly sensitive areas of public provision. In the case of the NHS, legislation was passed stipulating that all contracts worth more than £615,278 over their lifetime should be put out to tender (NHS England, 2019). Simultaneously, the Prime Minister, David Cameron, pressed ahead with his flagship programme of Payment by Results: deeply flawed new funding arrangements which contributed to significant underfunding of outsourced services by linking resource allocation to private providers to results.

In 2015 the Conservative Party came to power under the leadership of David Cameron. A year later Cameron resigned following the results of the Brexit referendum and was succeeded by Theresa May. With Brexit dominating the policy agenda, and the government's loss of its majority, following a snap election in 2017, the pursuit of new public policy initiatives stalled. In spite of this, outsourcing continued apace, with the farcical Grayling Brexit ferry contract fiasco (wasting £33 million of public money) epitomising the recklessness at the heart of ideologically driven privatisation (Hutton, 2019).

The 2018s and 2019s were marked by the exposure of the endemic financial risks at the heart of austerity-driven privatisation. With cash-strapped Whitehall departments (mandated to cut expenditure) left with little/no option but to pursue the most economically advantageous tenders and competing contractors, either partially or fully dependent on publicly funded contracts, a systemic 'race to the bottom' of underpricing or undercutting has become the norm, with contractors reliant on government bailouts when the quality of services diminishes and the real cost of delivery outstrips the original tender bid. In 2018/9, a series of financial watchdog reports drew attention to the poor service delivery and poor value for money—the NAO (2019) report into Capita's failure to fulfil its contract to provide human resources to the Ministry of Defence (MOD) is a case in point—simultaneously three large outsourcing companies with a wide range of contracts across government went into administration. What is more, in 2019, NHS England, in recognition of the damage to service delivery associated with unfettered outsourcing, called for the repeal of section 75 of the *2012 Health and Social Care Act* that compelled commissioners to put contracts out to tender. In the same year Grayling, a privatisation ideologue, in his role as the Minister of Transport was embroiled in yet another outsourcing debacle, attracting humiliating media derision, when he awarded a contract to provide ferry services to a firm that had no ferries.

Finally, in 2019, Boris Johnson replaced May as the leader of the Conservative Party and Prime Minister. With a collapsing majority, he called a snap election in December 2019 on a pro-Brexit ticket and was returned to power with a majority of 80. During his period in office, Johnson, a radical right, Machiavellian populist, signalled both his willingness to roll back unpopular, inefficient aspects of privatisation—the partial renationalisation of the railways was a case in point—and in response to the COVID-19 crisis to expand outsourcing by the awarding of contracts worth £1bn to private companies. With a determination to get Brexit done and to forge new trade agreements outside of the European Union, there was considerable speculation that his premiership would be marred by more rather than less privatisation.

New Labour 1997–2010

In 1997, after four terms in the doldrums, the reformed Labour Party, inspired by the success of Clinton's New Democrats, was elected. Despite the fact that Labour (the party traditionally associated with State ownership) in opposition, seeking to gain electoral advantage from the growing disillusionment with privatisation, was highly critical of the new measures and made promises to bring privatised services back in house, the reversal of public policy (Massey, 2001: 23), which many had eagerly anticipated, proved illusory, and a remarkable 'degree of continuity' prevailed (Whitfield, 2002). Whilst New Labour stopped short of a total sell off of assets (under the public private partnership there was a partial sale of the National Air Traffic Service), from the early 1990s onwards it became clear that the rebranded New Labour, under its leader Tony Blair, derided by Hobsbawm as 'Thatcher in trousers', was pro-marketisation not only in 'commerce and business, but also in welfare' (Johnson, 2001: 186).

An adopter of the 'enabling model of the State' with its concomitant withdrawal of the State from its the role of direct service provision(Whitfield, 2002: 234), Blair did not merely accept the prevailing public policy of internal markets in welfare, competition and contracting out (Johnson, 2001: 186) but also oversaw an unprecedented level of expansion of privatisation into public services and the Welfare State sector, in particular 'local government services, the defence sector and the criminal justice system' (Whitfield, 2002: 235). To the disbelief of many of Labour's key constituents, workers and trade unionists in the welfare services, who harboured high hopes that New Labour would turn back the privatisation tide, there was no reprieve from the Thatcherite policy of restructuring of public services into purchasers and competing private providers.

Although explanations for this development vary, key broad themes emerge from the literature, which are summed up by Harrison and McDonald (2008):

> The first suggests that New Labour's approach is simply a pragmatic piece of statecraft aimed at presenting a favourable impression of its policies. The second suggests that current policies derive substantially from the spread of contemporary ideas about 'new public management', whilst the third attributes the policies to a response to globalisation.
>
> (as cited in Hill, 2013: 140)

While it is clear that Blair never accepted markets and competition as 'the sole policy vehicle' (Johnson, 2001: 188), and in pursuit of communitarianism and social cohesion (Johnson, 2001: 188) implemented a range of publicly funded 'welfarist' measures (Downes and Hansen, 2006), it is nonetheless the case that under his Third Way, 'compromise between social democratisation and the market orientation of Conservative neo-liberalism' (White, 2016: 10), there was 'minimal reversal of Tory Legislation'. The Conservative's transformation of the public services continued apace, albeit 'repackaged and justified on a new set of objectives' (Whitfield, 2000: 82). With central and local government service provision and functions in its sights, the range of privatisation activities can be summarised as: the further development of a performance-competition State with inspection regimes and centrally imposed cash-linked performance targets; the continuation of the marketisation, privatisation and private management of public services; the promotion of the externalisation and transfer of local government services to the private and social enterprise sectors; the escalation of corporatisation and commercialisation of the State; the expansion of private funding of the public infrastructure through private-public partnerships; the adoption of deregulation; and the establishment of a flexible workforce (Whitfield, 2002: 235–236).

From Compulsory Competitive Tendering to Best Value

Under New Labour, CCT was abolished and replaced by the Best Value programme enshrined in the *1999 Local Government Act*. However, in spite of the nomenclature change, the Act established a statutory framework for the 'modernisation' of local government which shared many of its predecessor's features, including price competitiveness and outsourcing. Although New Labour was keen to establish its credentials, departing from what it perceived as a dogmatic and rigid preference for the private sector (expanding the range of suppliers to include the voluntary and public sector), the requirement to search for the 'best supplier', the retention of competition and price-competitive tendering favoured the private sector (Cabinet Office, 1999: 41).

As White (2016) points out, 'New Labour picked up the Conservatives' ball and ran with it. Public services were handed to the private sector on an ever increasing scale' (2016: 10–11). Indeed, such was the willingness of Blair and his successor,

Brown, to hand out public contracts to private providers that in 2009 the *Telegraph* announced that Serco, one of the key private providers of public services with a portfolio that extended across the different offices of the State, was 'effectively running the country'. The article stated:

> Most of the general public has never come across the name Serco, but the company inspects Britain's schools, trains the armed forces, helps to protect our borders, maintains our nuclear weapons, runs our trains and operates our prisons . . . Figures for the half year, released yesterday, showed Serco has secured a record number of contracts in 2009 so far, worth £4bn, as revenues climbed 31pc to £1.95bn. Pre-tax profits jumped 33pc to £83.4m. Alongside rivals Capita and Interserve, Serco has grown into the lives of Britons amid a growing culture of outsourcing public services, which began under Margaret Thatcher and has accelerated under Labour. Last December, Serco's rapid rise propelled it into the FTSE 100.
>
> *(Ruddick, 2009)*

Under the Best Value regime, all services remaining within the public realm were subjected to performance scrutiny. A 'five year cycle' of review was implemented in which services were judged in relation to five dimensions of performance (Whitfield, 2002: 239). These were strategic objectives questioning the efficacy of existing service provision (why the service exists and what it seeks to achieve); cost/efficiency (the financial resources committed to a service and the efficiency with which they are turned into outputs); service delivery outcomes (how well the service is being operated in order to achieve the strategic objectives); quality (the quality of the services delivered, explicitly reflecting users' experience of services); and fair access (ease and equality of access to services) (DETR, 1999: 12).

Pivotal to the Best Value initiative was the creation of a statutory performance management framework with a centrally driven set of national performance indicators and standards, which, as stated by the DETR (1999), were 'designed to provide for a rounded view of performance, reflecting as far as possible service users' experience of service delivery (outputs and outcomes) rather than the resources devoted to them (inputs)' (DETR, 1999: 11). These performance targets were cash linked: services that failed to meet the targets were subject to financial penalties (see later).

Partnerships

Seeking to distance itself from aspects of Tory policy, which by the end of the administration had fallen out of favour with voters, New Labour employed its spin doctors[1] to reshape the narrative (Dean, 2012), putting 'clear blue water' between itself and its predecessors. If privatisation was the watchword of two decades of Tory administration, reflecting the shift in justifications and rhetorical devices, partnership became the watchword for New Labour's repackaging of a range of public policy initiatives that transferred public service delivery to non-State providers. As laid out in the 1999 white paper, *Modernising Government*, Blair's Thatcher mark two vision for 'modernisation' of public services included bringing 'together partner organisations in the public, voluntary and private sector' (Cabinet Office, 1999: 29) and 'opening the way to new ideas, partnerships and opportunities for devising and delivering what the public wants' (Cabinet Office, 1999: 9).

With obscuration, rebranding and spinning the narrative key features of Blairite public policy initiatives, New Labour sought to muddy the waters by redefining the parameters of privatisation. In an attempt to create an artificial wedge between the selling off of assets and outsourcing, with the latter redefined as partnership.

> New Labour . . . attempted to redefine privatisation as being limited to the sale of assets. There have been attempts to brand PPPs[2] and outsourcing as partnerships. However, these projects involve the transfer of resources (staff, equipment and intellectual capital), private investment in public services and private management of a wide range of services. This is privatisation. Staff are frequently not categorised as assets but commodities . . . [that] can thus be transferred from one employer to another with impunity.
>
> *(Whitfield, 2002: 238)*

Despite this sleight of hand, with the private sector predators rather than partners, partnership working (outsourcing), which gained greater momentum as the New Labour term of office proceeded, provided further opportunities for multi-national businesses to increase their foothold.

Private Finance Initiatives

Of the various partnerships created under New Labour, Private Finance Initiatives (PFIs) are among the most controversial. An aspect of public policy that most clearly demonstrates New Labour's rejection of the '(p)arty's longstanding ideological preference for publicly provided welfare services' (Bochel et al., 2009: 152), PFIs constituted an unambiguous manifestation of the government's willingness to encourage private sector involvement in the financing, building, management and delivery of public services.

Introduced in 1992 by the Major government, PFI provided the means of attracting private finance into capital projects. Emerging from a deep recession and keen to use money flooding into the city to fund public services, Major embarked upon a scheme that involved 'shifting the risk of cost overruns and delays on building to the private sector in return for the guaranteed payments over the lifetime of the contract, which could run for 20 years' (Inman, 2018). As the NAO (2018a) explains:

> The fundamental difference between conventional public procurement and PFI procurement for capital investment relates to which party raises finance for the asset's construction. In conventional procurement the private sector

is still involved (private contractors build the asset) but the public sector provides the finance. When the public sector procures an asset using PFI, a private company (SPV) is formed and it raises finance from debt and equity investors to pay for construction. Once the asset is constructed and available for use the taxpayer makes 'unitary charge' payments to the SPV over the contract term, usually 25 to 30 years. This charge includes debt and interest repayments, shareholder dividends, asset maintenance, and in some cases other services like cleaning.

(2018a: 6)

Despite the fact that Labour in opposition was highly critical of the measure, PFI was to prove highly seductive politically. 'Haunted by the hoary accusation' of being a party that was 'congenitally profligate with public finances', and seeking to distance itself from its electorally damaging 'tax, borrow and spend' image, PFI provided the means by which much needed infrastructure construction projects could proceed whilst avoiding the public wrath that making a 'big dent in the public balanced sheet' would draw (Freedland, 2018).

The ticking time bomb of PFI exposed

With no upfront expenditure required by the Treasury, the prospect of rebuilding the crumbling infrastructure of schools, hospitals and controversially prisons (required as draconian sentencing became the norm after 1993) on the 'never-never' was to prove politically irresistible for New Labour. As North (2001) succinctly puts it, although PFI left the government with a debt to repay, 'delivering new . . . buildings for relatively little outlay [was] . . . every politician's dream' (131). However, although the New Labour administration enthusiastically pursued PFI as a means of injecting capital into much needed infrastructure projects, PFI, which expanded exponentially under its auspices, has proved a double-edged sword, a financial ticking time bomb, which in recent years exploded into public consciousness. Significantly more expensive than conventional government borrowing (HOC, Treasury Committee, 2014),[3] PFI schemes have been repeatedly excoriated by the National Audit Office, the Treasury Committee and the Public Accounts Committee for providing poor value for money, burdening individual institutions and thereby taxpayers with spiralling debt. Between 2016 and 2017 the annual charges for servicing the over 700 PFI deals amounted to £10.3 billion, and the projected costs of projects until 2040 was £199 billion (NAO, 2018a). The estimated cost of a privately financed hospital was 70% higher than if the project had been directly financed by the Treasury.

Further, with contracts awarded to a small group of multi-national companies that dominate the privatisation market (evidence from the NAO showed that in 33% of PFI projects examined between 2004–2006, there were only two viable bidders, mostly due to other bidders pulling out or to lack of interest), big businesses 'flipping' or selling on their projects shortly after completion have been able to amass enormous profits. With companies exploiting the deals to build and maintain schools, hospitals and prisons, figures obtained by the *Independent* in 2014 revealed that:

> Four contractors alone made profits of more than £300m. Of the companies studied—Balfour Beatty, Carillion, Interserve and Kier-Balfour Beatty—are by far the biggest beneficiary of the rising value of its Private Finance Initiative and Private Partnership deals. It alone has made profits of £188.9m.
> (Armitage and Holmes, 2014)

In 2017 Margaret Hodge, the chair of the PAC from 2010 to 2015, described the 'scandal' of the excessive profits made by PFI companies, many of whom are based in tax havens and avoid contributing towards UK tax. She stated:

> My time on the Public Accounts Committee convinced me that PFI . . . was a total scandal. Using PFI costs the tax payer more than if the public sector financed investment directly. Interests rates are over 2% higher . . . The extra cost was justified on the grounds that the private expenditure didn't count against expenditure rules . . . but . . . that justification no longer applies.
> (Hodge, 2017)

In January 2018 the NAO published a report into its investigation of PFI, which received unprecedented press coverage. Released mere days after the Carillion collapse when the public was confronted with the realities of the 'Shadow State' (White, 2016): abandoned, half finished construction projects, locked out workers, directors skimming off bonuses and paying dividends to shareholders when the company was failing, and the Treasury stepping in to pick up the pieces. The report, which would normally have been relegated to couple of columns in the inside pages of the red top papers, was headline news. Indeed, on the day of its release, the *Sun* stepped up to condemn private suppliers for shafting the public with 'shoddy Government deals' (Dathan, 2018). In common with previous government reports, the report shined the spotlight on the excessive costs of using PFI to finance major construction works, judging PFI 'a dereliction of public value for money' (Toynbee, 2018). Whilst acknowledging the benefits of PFI in terms of construction that would probably not otherwise have been completed, the report spelt out that while PFI has been politically attractive to governments seeking to obscure the level of government debt by avoiding upfront capital expenditure, the maintenance of the smoke and mirrors 'fiscal illusion' has been 'catastrophically costly' (Mance and Parker, 2018). Higher borrowing and insurance costs, and fees to external advisers and lenders incurred by private investors had seen the expenditure on servicing the debt escalate.[4]

As the costs of servicing the debt have eaten into the budgets of cash-strapped schools, hospitals and prisons, reducing the money available to provide frontline services, many institutions have either bought out their contract to save money or have considered the option. Whilst those that have done so claim to have been able to recoup short-term losses by applying innovation that the inflexible and rigid contracts (despite claims to the contrary) militated against (Toynbee, 2018), it is estimated that the price for breaking the 75 largest PFIs amounts to £2billion—25% more than the outstanding debt (Mance and Parker, 2018).

The lifting of the lid on the failure of PFI, which since its inception had been a central pillar of cross party policy-making, drew criticism pro-nationalisation leader of the opposition, Jeremy Corbyn, and trade unions, but also some Tory ministers. In a scathing response to the 2018 report, Meg Hillier, the chair of the PAC, concluded:

> after 25 years of PFI, there is still little evidence that it delivers enough to offset the additional costs of borrowing money privately . . . many local bodies are shackled to inflexible PFI contracts that are exorbitantly expensive to change.

Similarly, the national secretary of the GMB union denounced PFI as 'a catastrophic waste of the tax payer's money' (Syal, 2018). These sentiments echoed the succinct points made some seven years earlier by Lord Oakeshott, a Liberal Democrat Treasury spokesman, who pointedly observed:

> PFI contracts will be a millstone around taxpayers' necks for most of our lifetimes, at least the next quarter century. Dreamt up under John Major and rolled out by Gordon Brown, they are the disastrous result of Treasury short-termism under both governments. They didn't just sell the family silver, they paid the banks to take it away by handing them blank cheques in the form of guaranteed long term contracts we can't afford.
>
> *(Prince, 2011)*

Introduced under the Tories and vastly expanded under New Labour, PFI represents an area of 'public policy in which the imbalance of power and interest' has become unsustainable (Young, 2018). Politically expedient short-term savings that PFI can bring look to be overshadowed by a recognition of the long-term costs both financially to the taxpayer, as well as morally and socially to those who are the supposed beneficiaries: the sick, the offender, the school child. Indeed, in 2012 with strain within Whitehall over the 'toxic' scheme becoming increasingly transparent, George Osborne, the coalition chancellor, backed a review of the PFI: a move that was reversed in 2016, when Osborne's successor Philip Hammond relaunched PFI as PF2 (Inman, 2018). This signaled a change of name rather than a change of direction.

The National Air Traffic Service sell off

As well as PFI and contracting out publicly provided services to a range of non–public sector providers, Public Private Partnership, the term of choice adopted, provided a smokescreen for partial sell off of the National Air Traffic Service. Despite the fact that the divisive decision to take the Tory plans forward created one of 'the biggest backbench rebellions of the first Blair government', the sell off was completed in 2001, raising £750 million. The sale, which not only raised questions about New Labour's ideological preferences but also reignited debates about transport safety, was announced in 1998 as a Public Private Partnership (PPP), with the government retaining a 'golden share' of 49%. Under the sale agreement, 5% was made available to staff, and the rest was sold to Airline Group (a consortium of seven airlines). The selling off was justified on fiscal grounds that it

> would free NATS from public sector borrowing constraints, subject the company to private sector financial disciplines and raise money for investment from the sale, while retaining a substantial public sector interest, with the Government as a partner in the business.
>
> *(NATS, 2012)*

Management by targets: cash-linked KPIs and extension of New Public Management

During the Blair administration New Public Management (NPM), originally introduced with limited success under Thatcher, acquired greater impetus. As part of the far reaching modernisation project, a new, more invasive level of accountability and centralised control of performance and service delivery was introduced to all government departments. Promoted as the means of 'improving efficiency and effectiveness', the new system, emulating the lexicon and practice of business, transformed the management and delivery of public services (Hyndman and Eden, 2001: 579). As stated in *Modernising Government:*

> Ministers and their Departments will be held to delivery of the priorities set out in the PSAs. The Government will ensure that these priorities are cascaded through the targets and measures which will be set for all public bodies, in consultations with those who receive services. On both targets and inspections, we will focus on key outcomes and strike an appropriate balance between intervening where services are failing and giving successful organisations the freedom to manage.
>
> *(Cabinet Office, 1999: 36)*

Variously derided by critics as 'management by targets' or 'target world', a newly reinvigorated, highly bureaucratised public management regime was introduced that linked the funding of public services to performance. Under the new arrangements, in exchange for extra funding, all aspects of public services were subjected to an unprecedented regime of centralised control:

> Building on initiatives . . . by previous governments, the . . . government issued more than 300 headline performance targets applying to all

government departments. The targets were linked to agreed-upon budgetary allocations with Her Majesty's Treasury, Britain's all powerful central co-ordinating department, and applied to everything.

(Hood, 2006: 515)

To ensure compliance with the targets drawn up by civil servants, financial inducements and penalties were put in place which rewarded those who met targets and penalised those who fell short. In effect, managers were held to task with the sword of Damocles poised to fall on those who were either unwilling or unable to submit to micromanagement. In order to monitor target achievement, departments were required to audit the organisations that they were responsible for on a regular basis. Ultimately answerable to the newly established Prime Minister's Delivery Unit, departments operated under the watchful gaze of a prime minister who was determined that his political imperatives be implemented.

> Blair himself held "stocktakes" to assess progress on the key public service targets every two or three months . . . Every governmental department was subjected to an elaborate reporting cycle, and its higher echelons had to learn a new and daunting bureaucratic vocabulary of milestones, trajectories, monthly reports, and priority review.
>
> (Hood, 2006: 515)

Criticised for creating a wide range of inverse incentive anomalies, such as the de-prioritising of activities that were not included in the 'basket of targets', the target culture was responsible for the burgeoning of game playing, including forms of creative compliance practice whereby managers hit the target but missed the point. Documented examples include: hospitals responding to the target that patients be admitted to a hospital bed within 12 hours of emergency admission by transforming gurneys into beds by removing their wheels; ambulances failing to deliver patients to the doors of emergency rooms to meet Accident and Emergency waiting time targets of 4 hours; and general practitioners meeting a target that patients should be able to see a doctor within 48 hours by refusing to book an appointment more than 48 hours in advance (Hood, 2006: 517–518). Disliked by professionals, whose autonomy and discretion were threatened, the highly elaborate systems of monitoring, recording and reporting that evolved led many demoralised professionals to claim that new work practices, introduced by managers to both meet targets set and capture performance data, reduced work to a 'tick box culture'.

2010–2015: austerity and the Conservative-Liberal Democrat coalition

As Mitchell, writing in 1990, observed, one of the enduring attractions to successive governments of privatisation has been the potential it offers to governments to simultaneously expand the range and depth of control of political objectives whilst reducing the level of public expenditure that would have otherwise been necessary to achieve this outcome (Mitchell, 1990: 4). In 2010, in the wake of the banking crisis and global recession, the Conservative led coalition government was formed following an election in which the Conservative Party had the highest number of MPs returned to Parliament but did not command an overall majority in the House of Commons. With deficit reduction given priority over all other policy considerations (Toynbee and Walker, 2015), austerity became the focus of public spending with a renewed programme of hollowing out of the State, which would be mitigated by the pursuit of the PM's 'panacea for social ills' (Levitas, 2012: 320): the Big Society of voluntary and not-for-profit organisations.

With the balance of deficit reduction weighted towards public expenditure cuts, particularly in relation to increasingly unpopular welfare spending (with the binary of strivers pitted against skivers), rather than revenue raising through taxation, large year-on-year cuts to public expenditure were implemented which left local authorities, as well as other unprotected departments, struggling to meet their statutory obligations (in 2014 the National Audit Office [2014a] predicted that over half of councils were at risk of financial failure); penalised those of working age on benefits and living in social housing under the bedroom tax; and led to NHS executives complaining that the NHS was at 'crisis point'. Simultaneously, the rate of income tax for the wealthiest was cut and the personal tax allowance raised, reducing revenue collected by the treasury (Toynbee and Walker, 2015). With public spending 'projected to fall to 35.2% of GDP by 2019–20', some commentators predicted that public sector funding would be at its 'lowest level in 80 years' (Wintour and Elliott, 2014).

Open Public Services

Key to the achievement of budgetary cuts was the rebalancing of the public and private sector and marketisation, leaving critics in little doubt that, contrary to government's claims that they harboured no ideological preference for one sector, the private sector would play a major role in the new arrangements (Taylor-Gooby, 2012: 67). In July 2011, the white paper *Open Public Services* was published. Setting out the government's plan to create a new marketplace of providers, including charities, social enterprises, private companies and employee-led mutuals, the paper underlined the centrality of budgetary considerations:

> in this economic climate, when times are tight and budgets are being cut to stabilise the economy and reduce our debts, opening public services is more important than ever—if we want to deliver better services for less money, improve public service productivity and stimulate innovation to drive the wider growth of the UK economy.
>
> *(HM Government, 2011: 6)*

However, with price competitive tendering built-in to the procurement process, complex legal and accounting challenges limited the capacity of all but the big multi-national outsourcing giants like Serco to tender. With the usual oligopoly of providers positioned to reap yet more rewards, critics observed that the 'Big Society' language was deployed as a 'Trojan Horse used to overcome public opposition to straight-forward privatisation'.

(The Trade Union Co-Ordinating Group, 2013: 5)

In an attempt to resolve the tension between the two public policy objectives of ensuring financial efficiency and improving the quality of service delivery, the white paper outlined the government's plans to create a new variant of 'payment by performance' (Appleby et al., 2012): Payment by Results (PbR). Payments would be based 'primarily on the results they achieve, with challenging minimum performance levels and year-on-year price reductions to drive improved performance continuously' (HM Government, 2011: 33). Under PbR a series of financially driven checks and balances would be introduced to reward those who achieved contracted outcomes and penalise those who failed (Dominey, 2012: 345). The funding system provided contractors with a basic tariff to cover their costs, supplemented by additional payments for meeting contracted targets (Fox and Albertson, 2021). With the intention to ensure that providers met contractual obligations and performance targets, the stated aim of PbR was to 'build yet more accountability into the system, creating a direct financial incentive to focus on what works, but also encouraging providers to find better ways of delivering services' (HM Government, 2011: 34).

By its own account, public service delivery was transformed under the coalition. With privatisation viewed as the primary means by which reductions in public expenditure could be accomplished, the scale and scope of the unrestrained encroachment of privatisation into public services was exceptional. Adopting the neoliberal rationale of 'choice, decentralisation, diverse provision, fairness and accountability' (NAO, 2014a: 3), the floodgates to privatisation were opened, with nothing deemed out of bounds, nothing sacrosanct, leading some commentators to accuse the coalition government of 'selling off the State itself' (Toynbee and Walker, 2015).

In 2012, after a year in Parliament, where it received 'more scrutiny than any bill in living memory, and more than 1,000 amendments in the House of Commons and the House of Lords', (Jowitt, 2012) the most 'controversial piece of legislation in the NHS for two decades' the *Health and Social Care Act,* was passed. Part of the 'Lansley reforms', the Act, condemned as 'dysfunctional', ensured that the purchaser/provider split, built into previous reforms, was not merely a 'way of managing the service, but rather as *the* way'. Driven by twin requirements to balance the books and improve services, commissioners were expected to reconcile the conflicting duties of embracing competition through outsourcing to a wide range of providers (building fragmentation into the system) whilst at the same time providing integrated service delivery for patients (NHS England, 2019).

Under Section 75 of the Act and the subsequent *Public Contracts Regulations* issued in 2015 rigid procurement requirements to put all contracts worth £615,278 over their lifetime out to tender, regardless of whether there was a strong rationale for retaining them within the NHS, were initiated (NHS England, 2019). A consequence of this is that since April 2013, £16 billion worth of clinical contracts have been awarded to non-NHS providers, with the majority (£5.5 billion) awarded to private contractors both in the UK and outside. A case in point was the NHS sale of Plasma Resources UK, a company providing blood products, to a US private equity company, Bain and Company (Rankin, 2013).

Examples of the contracts awarded within the UK include those made to large multi-national private companies: Capita and Virgin Care. In 2015 Capita, one of the 'big four UK' oligopoly of outsourcing firms (NAO, 2013)[5] with an extensive range of contracts across the different Whitehall departments, took over a contract worth £1 billion to provide primary care in the expectation that it would achieve cost reductions of 40%. Despite a chequered track record of service provision (e.g. in September 2014 West London Mental Health NHS Trust cancelled its human resources contract after serious shortfalls in its recruitment of nurses), in 2015 Capita was rewarded with a further contract worth £80 million to provide IT, finance and estate management services to the biggest health services provider in London. In 2015, Virgin Care, which currently holds over 400 NHS contracts, was awarded a £280 million contract in East Staffordshire to co-ordinate service provision to elderly and frail patients.

At the same time that the NHS was being propelled into awarding more and more contracts to outside providers, contracts were having to be terminated early due to problems of poor performance and/or financial instability. One of the highest-profile cases was the handing back in 2016, after a mere eight months of operation, of the £800 million contracted awarded to UnitingCare on the grounds that the contract was insufficiently funded to cover the cost of services to be provided. A costly waste of public money, the protracted procurement process alone had cost the NHS £1.1 million, with a further £20 million cost incurred by local hospitals, GPs and community care providers (NHS Support Federation, 2016) following the collapse of the contract.

In 2016, Interserve, which was awarded one of the earliest post-2012 contracts, worth £300 million over seven years, was stripped of its contract to improve estates and facilities managements service across Leicester, Leicestershire and Rutland NHS trusts following reports that its efforts to save the NHS trust £100 million had resulted in poor standards of performance (NHS Support Federation, 2016) that included patients receiving meals three hours late, bloodstains in the corridors and bins not being emptied (*BBC News*, 2016). During the period that Interserve delivered the contract, in a textbook case of a 'race to the bottom' where reductions in working conditions, wages and staffing were endemic, staffing levels were reduced by one fifth (500 to 400), and staff wages were cut to half those paid to NHS staff.

In late 2018, further outsourcing problems were exposed when Healthcare Environment Services, which failed to deliver on its contract to dispose of NHS body parts and hazardous waste, including amputated limbs and waste from cancer treatment, leading to the illegal storing of excess waste products at its depots (this prompted the Environment Agency to launch a criminal investigation), was stripped of its contracts to 35 trusts and subsequently went into administration (Campbell and Partington, 2018).

Finally in 2019, with too many contracts being put out to tender driving expense and delay into the system and too many contracts awarded not fit for purpose, NHS England announced proposals to change the procurement requirements, replacing competitive tendering with Best Value. As many welcomed the announcement as a timely recognition that privatisation had gone too far, Paul Evans, who runs the NHS Support Federation, which tracks privatisation in the NHS, issued the following damning evaluation of the initiative:

> The Lansley reforms have been a damaging and wasteful experiment in forcing competition on the NHS and inviting in the private sector. The market-based experiment has led to the collapse of multiple contracts, to patients getting substandard care or the denial of it altogether, and to the huge waste of public resources.
>
> *(Campbell, 2019)*

Selling off of the post office

In addition to the outsourcing of public services, the coalition government forged ahead with Thatcherite flotations of publicly owned companies. One of the most controversial of the flotations was the privatisation of the postal services, which attracted accusations that the haste to push through the flotation, and the desire to curry electoral favour with individual shareholders, had resulted in underselling reminiscent of the 80s. In a damning report, the NAO concluded that the government's sell off was flawed, prioritising speed and political expediency over financial responsibility. The report identified that, in the face of potential industrial action and short-term market uncertainty, a cautiously low price was set to 'reflect the price indications of a small number of priority investors whose participation was seen as vital, as well the views of over 500 other potential investors' (NAO, 2014b). Indeed, the prioritising of a small group of priority investors (half of whom sold their shares in the immediate aftermath for a substantial profit) over the public led to accusations that run the gamut from financial incompetence to cronyism (Farrell, 2014), or what Thatcher famously called looking after 'one of us'.

The return of the nasty party 2015

In May 2015, the Conservative Party returned to power under the leadership of David Cameron. He was replaced a year later by Theresa May following his resignation in direct response to the Brexit referendum results. Although in July 2016, the new Prime Minister set out her vision of a 'one nation' government that would embrace social justice, the 'enormity of the Brexit task quickly overwhelmed the government', and potential policy initiatives stalled (Garside et al., 2018: 7). The problem of legislative and public policy inertia was compounded by the reckless 2017 snap election which left the Conservative Party without a majority entering into a confidence and supply agreement with the Democratic Unionist Party.

The race to the bottom in the public sector outsourcing market

One of the noteworthy features of recent years has been the lifting of the lid on the risks/costs that underpin the privatisation edifice: risk/costs that significantly outweigh the hyped benefits. Namely, risks to the recipients through inadequate or curtailed services, financial risks to providers in exchange for contracts and risks to the treasury and the tax paying public when private contracts fail. With 2018/9 destined to go down in history as the years in which the myth that private companies can deliver more for less and still make a profit was laid bare, the privatisation bastion was buffeted by a wave of financial shocks. These included: the collapse of outsourcing providers Carillion, Working Links, and Interserve (in the case of Interserve a pre-pack administration deal was put in place to avert it descending into a Carillion style collapse); the issuing of a profit warning by a fourth company, Capita (one of the big four providers deemed 'too big to fail'), as well as the renationalisation of the East Coast Mainline in May 2018; and the return in August 2018 of HMP Birmingham, run by G4S, to the public sector (Eaton, 2018).

Whilst it is the case that privatisation has had a history of failed contracts in terms of service delivery for end customers and financial and reputational losses for providers, contract default was exacerbated and accelerated by the post-2010 austerity agenda. As cost cutting became the number one policy priority, private contractors, reliant on public sector contracts, and Whitehall procurers, constrained by budgetary cuts, were caught up in a 'who blinks first' cycle of underfunding, undercutting and underpricing: a 'race to the bottom' in which providers, aware that a procurement process structured on a most economically advantageous tenders process rewards the cheapest bidder, gamed the procurement process to gain advantage over the competitors in the expectation that when delivery costs outstrip the bid, government departments, dependent on the private sector to deliver its services, would absorb the financial fall, taking the necessary action on a contract by contract basis. Indeed, actions to reduce the financial impact for contractors included letting the contractor hand the contract back, terminating the contract early or bailing the contractor out by paying it enough to fulfil its contractual obligations. (See the later chapter on Transforming Rehabilitation, where all three strategies were adopted to shore up the contracts awarded to private companies.)

Not withstanding this, despite the company's expectation that the Treasury would intervene to avert its collapse, in January 2018, Carillion, the outsourcing giant, went into administration. For the multi-national firm employing over

45,000 people in the UK, Canada and the Middle East (18,200 in the UK), the collapse, which the NAO (2018b) estimated cost the taxpayer £148 million, was the first sign of the financial risks that concentrating the provision of services in the hands of a small group of suppliers posed. A major supplier of public services, its work spanned road and hospital construction as well as the provision of MOD accommodation, prison services and school meals. At the time of its demise it held around 420 contracts with UK public services worth an estimated £100 million a year. One of a small number of contractors with extensive portfolios of government contracts, the company had recklessly expanded in the expectation that rather than risk the public opprobrium that a full scale scandal (discussed later) would unleash, the government would step in and bail it out: given that the government had a year prior to its collapse, despite a profit warning, continued to award it £1.6 billion worth of contracts, this was not a fanciful expectation (HOC Committee of Public Accounts, 2018)

In February 2019, the same month that NHS England announced plans to curtail the outsourcing of all contracts worth more than £600,000, Working Links, an outsourcer with £1 billion of public contractors, mostly in education, employment and support services, despite being awarded a contract by the MOJ worth £924 million in 2015 to provide probation services, went into administration. Similarly, in early March 2019, it came to light that Interserve was teetering on the brink of collapse and banks were making contingency plans to avoid a Carillion-style collapse. On 15th March 2019, it went into administration.

Interserve, a multi-national company with a global workforce of 80,000, was one of the biggest beneficiaries of Blair's privately financed construction initiative in the 1990s and 2000s (being awarded 43 PFI contracts). Beginning life as construction and dredging company, it expanded rapidly into new spheres of provision under privatisation, acquiring public contracts ranging from construction and engineering, to catering and school meals, to security and support for the MOD, to rehabilitation and health care. In 2014, it was awarded five contracts to deliver probation services. In 2016, the company held nine contracts for facilities management with NHS hospitals as a result of the company's investment in PFI contracts.

In spite of this, in September 2018, indications that Interserve was in financial difficulties came to light when the company defaulted on its contract to provide a plant to turn waste into gas: this failure saw the company accrue £200 million losses (Chapman, 2018), precipitating a Treasury bailout. With a further profit downturn in its construction business (after delays and cancellations of projects) and rising staffing costs, Interserve announced in March 2019 that it was taking measures to ensure an orderly administration that would not jeopardise its public service provision. It collapsed on 15th March 2019 (Davies, 2019)

In January 2018, Capita, one of the 'big four' providers, with a UK workforce of 50,000, which was awarded 154 government contracts in 2017 alone, issued a shock profit warning as shares fell to a 15 year low (Wearden and Fletcher, 2018). In March 2019 its financial problems were compounded when the Public Accounts Committee, casting doubt on its financial viability, published the findings of its inquiry into the company's failure to fulfil its contractual obligations to the MOD: contractual obligations to recruit sufficient Army regulars and reserves and to achieve planned savings of £267 million. In the report, the committee stated that the creation of the ten year partnership with the British Army in 2012 was a naïve and costly endeavour that risked undermining public confidence in MOD planning (HOC Committee of Public Accounts, 2019).

Grayling and the ferry debacle

In 2019, with 29th March the then planned Brexit departure date, Grayling, in his role as the Minister for Transport, embarked upon the 'rushed and risky procurement of additional ferry capacity', which, in the scathing words of Meg Hillier, the chair of the Public Accounts Committee, landed the taxpayer 'with a £85m bill with very little show'(HOC, Public Accounts Committee, 2019). In a shambolic, reckless venture to increase capacity, Grayling, who was mercilessly mocked by all sections of the press, awarded and rapidly withdrew contracts totalling £107.7m to Brittany Ferries (£42.3m), DFDS Seaways (£46.6m), and an 'on paper' only, start-up company, Seaborne Freight (£13.8) (Davies, 2018), that had no ferries and no secure financial backing and whose website terms and conditions appeared to be intended for a food delivery firm (Quinn, 2019). With a flawed tendering process that proceeded without the call for competition, the government was challenged in court by Eurotunnel and forced to make a £33 m out-of-court settlement. An additional sum of £51.4m was paid out for cancelling the original contracts (HOC, Public Accounts Committee, 2019).

2020: Boris Johnson, privatisation and the COVID-19 crisis

In December 2019, Boris Johnson, who replaced Theresa May as leader of the Conservative Party and Prime Minister in July of the same year, won a snap election with a House of Commons majority of 80 on a populist, regaining 'control of our borders', anti-freedom of movement, pro-Brexit mandate. Despite fear mongering during the election that a Labour victory would herald a new era of renationalisation, with returning the railways to public ownership, a popular cause among commuters inured to massive disruption due to strikes, poor service and rising prices, Johnson announced that he was ordering a review of the franchising system, which encouraged private firms to overbid in the expectation that they will be subsidised by the government if they run into financial difficulties. He further indicated that he was not ruling out the prospect of further renationalisation. Subsequently Northern Rail was stripped of its franchise and returned to the operator of last resort, the State, and plans to return the privatised Probation Service, which had been bailed out on numerous occasions by the Treasury, in its totality to the public sector were announced.

COVID-19 contracts, corruption, chumocracy and cronyism: public finance and private profit

Notwithstanding this, in the first quarter of 2020, with the arrival of the COVID-19 pandemic in the UK, the policy priority shifted to the emergent economic, social and health priorities. Faced with a fragmented NHS, compromised by decades of 'privatisation, commercialisation, outsourcing and off shoring' (Monbiot, 2020), depleted by a decade of austerity and catastrophically ill prepared to respond to a pandemic, Johnson's government initiated a new privatisation wave. This was a response to the need for: protective clothing for NHS and social care staff; testing to determine who had the virus and needed to quarantine; the construction of Nightingale hospitals to increase bed capacity; and the recruitment of nurses and doctors. In a system open to bias and conflict of interest, contracts were hastily awarded to preferred private providers, often with insider connections to the department of Health. Indeed, £10.5 billion worth of a total of £18 billion in contracts was handed out in contravention of normal procurement rules on competitive tendering and due diligence through the creation of a fast-track high-priority channel (NAO, 2020). Beneficiaries of the system included the usual oligopoly of providers—Sodexo, G4S, Serco and Capita; the 'big four' accountancy firms—Deloitte and KPMG, PricewaterhouseCoopers (PwC) and Ernst and Young; and Mitie, Glaxo, Smith and Klein and Boots.(Taylor, 2020). Writing in *The Guardian* in May 2020, Evans *et al.* (2020) pointed out:

> In what amounts to a Covid-19 bonanza for some firms, ministers have suspended the standard rules to: enable contracts to be issued "with extreme urgency". Laws designed to ensure transparency and value for money in the way public funds are spent usually require government and other state bodies to advertise any new contract over a certain value, and invite several bidders to compete. However, in March, ministers told Whitehall departments, the NHS, local councils and other agencies that if they needed to act fast because of the public health risks posed by the pandemic, they could lawfully sign deals with private firms 'without competing or advertising the requirement'.

Mired in controversy, the opaque procurement system established by the government faced mounting criticism from its own watchdog, the NAO, as well as campaigning groups (i.e. Transparency International UK and The Good Law Project) about the way that the high-priority or 'VIP' channel system advantaged 'those in the know', particularly politically well-connected recipients with privileged access to information. Applicants with special relationships with ministers and civil servants, including party donors and Tory party 'chums' directed to the high-priority or 'VIP' channel, were ten times more likely to be successful (NAO, 2020). Having secured lucrative jobs in private firms through the 'revolving door', former special advisers, ministers and senior civil servants, seeking to profit from personal contacts, bombarded civil servants with requests. So much so that civil servants complained that, with suppliers with political connections directed to the 'VIP' channel where they could jump the queue, other suppliers with better credentials were relegated to slower channels and pushed aside. Civil servants were 'drowning under VIP requests to supply goods and services', frequently by firms unable to meet the necessary standards (Monbiot, 2021). The effect of this procurement fiasco was that contracts awarded were frequently not fulfilled: goods and services were not delivered, were unduly expensive or were substandard.

Despite repeated attempts by the government to obstruct scrutiny, the Good Law Project, which is pursuing a judicial review of 'VIP' contracts, as well as identifying a contract awarded to an insolvent firm with no employees, and Pestfix, a company specialising in pest control, highlighted £160 million for PPE contracts awarded to Meller Designs, run by David Meller, a large Tory donor, and further contracts worth £252 million awarded to Ayanda, negotiated by Andrew Mills, a ministerial adviser (Good Law Project, 2021). Similarly, Transparency International UK, who claim that 73, or one in five, government contracts worth £3.7 billion awarded contain red flag indicators of corruption, identified 30 awarded to companies with well-known connections to the Conservative Party. These included: 24 PPE contracts worth £1.6 billion, 3 testing contracts worth £536 million and a further 3 worth £4.1 million. In summarising the findings of their research, Transparency International UK argued that with critical safeguards suspended as procurement was ramped up in speed and scale, the system was vulnerable to corrupt practices, including cronyism and chumocracy:

> Undoubtedly, one of the most contentious and concerning aspects of procurement during the pandemic has been the awarding of Government contracts to companies with political connections. Whether rightfully or not, terms like 'chumocracy' and 'cronyism' are now highly associated with securing materials and services for the public health response. The insinuation being it is not what you know or have to offer that matters, it is who you know.
> (*Transparency International 2021: 22*)

The future of privatisation

Whilst it is clear at the time of going to press 'that sheer irrationality, expense and the failure of so many private contracts' (Toynbee, 2018) raises questions about the future outsourcing, if the government's knee-jerk reaction to a public health emergency to mobilise the private sector is an indicator of future government policy, it would be safe to assume that, despite early indications that a case-by-case reversal was under consideration (in the event initial plans to renationalise the railway were watered down and franchising retained), the public sector remains the provider of last resort, called upon when necessary to bail out failing private companies, and that a *volte face* on privatisation is not on the current political radar. Indeed with the awarding of COVID-19 contracts replete with cronyism, it seems to be business as usual. Furthermore, with Johnson's Conservative Party elected to deliver Brexit at all costs, privatisation, in which 'the public ethos is swallowed up in boardrooms controlled by shareholders with no interest in the public good' (Toynbee, 2018: n.p.), is on the ascendency.

Conclusion

Over the last four decades, privatisation of 'State-run institutions has become a dominant political issue' (Ryan and Ward, 1989: vii): a key driver of public policy across all major political parties. Once the preserve of the right wing fringes of the Conservative party, the selling off of State assets and outsourcing, although differentially packaged for the public to maintain the illusion of political pluralism, has become mainstream, adopted and adapted by all political leaders. By the end of the 90s, despite claims to the contrary, privatisation was emerging as an accepted aspect of all political parties' agendas.

During the period of New Labour, key ideas and practices, tried and tested by the Tories, were incorporated into its public policy agenda. Under the auspices of the Third Way and modernisation, the inculcation of business ethos, characterised by NPM, into the public sector was introduced, and the outsourcing of public services, albeit 'repackaged and justified on a new set of objectives' (Whitfield, 2000: 82), carried on apace. What is more, with New Labour keen to promote new infrastructure projects, initiatives such as private financing, introduced in a limited form by Major, became the norm.

With the establishment of the Con/Dem coalition in 2010, privatisation was given a new boost. Driven by the post-financial crisis austerity agenda, the opening up of all public services to a new market of providers was embraced as a means of reducing costs. In an indecent haste to outsource public services, the volume of new contracts awarded to private companies grew exponentially, and privatisation encroached into increasingly sensitive areas of provision. With budget reduction outstripping all other the policy objectives, underfunding, underpricing and undercutting became the norm in the procurement process.

Despite the claims of privatisers that the private sector outperforms the public and business can deliver more for less and still make a return, the assumptions that have propelled privatisation over the last four decades have been demonstrated to be increasingly worthless. The inherent risks in the procurement process, which has prompted companies to overclaim what was possible in absurdly demanding contracts, has been laid bare. Additionally, incidences of contract default leading to bailouts, cancellations and buy backs have increased. In 2017, a study by the European Services Strategy Unit revealed that the public cost of buyouts, bailouts and terminations associated with PFIs alone amounted to £3,755m (Whitfield, 2017). Further, with the financial fallacy at the heart of privatisation orthodoxy exposed, three major outsourcing firms, Carillion, Working Links and Interserve, within a month, went into administration.

Finally, as the pursuit of cost efficiency has emerged as the primary objective of public policy, the values of public service have eroded. The guiding principles of the social contract between the State and its citizens, in particular the State's responsibility to ensure fairness, to promote justice and to act in the public's interest, have been subsumed by the profit motive. There has been a retreat from liberal democratic principles that government's actions are for the common good, 'as opposed to that of a part' (Starr, 1989: 16). Not only has the public sector been transformed, but also the core purposes of businesses, which half a century ago included serving employees, communities and society as well as making profits, have been whittled down, though 'ideological shifts and changes in laws and rules, to little more than a single-minded focus on maximising the wealth of shareholders' (Shaxson, 2018). As the wave of privatisation has swept over, and professionals scramble to retain a foothold on their values and beliefs, the public ethos has been confined to diminishing rock pools.

Notes

1 With 'spin' at the heart of Blair's management of his policy agenda, it was no coincidence that his s first appointment on becoming party leader was a press director, Alastair Campbell.
2 Public private partnerships (PPPs).
3 In 2014 the House of Commons Treasury Committee announced that, 'the cost of capital for a typical PFI project is currently over 8%—double the government long term gilt rate of 4%' (HOC, Treasury Committee, 2014: 3).
4 With costs of borrowing having dropped in recent years, new PFI contracts for schools and other facilities are between 2% and 4% more expensive than government borrowing
5 In 2013, the National Audit Office (NAO, 2013) published *Managing Government Suppliers*, a report into the role of the private contracts in the delivery of public services, which revealed that contracts for both frontline and back office services across government departments were disproportionately awarded to the 'big four' private contractors (Serco, G4S, Capita and Atos) who between them in accounting period 2012–2013 held government contracts worth £4 billion. With the government dependent on this oligopoly of providers, concerns were expressed about the risks to recipients and the taxpayer if these 'too big to fail' companies failed.

References

Appleby, J., Harrison, T; Hawkins, L., and Dixon, A. (2012) *Payment by Results; How Can Payment Systems Help to Deliver Better Care?* London: The Kings Fund
Armitage, J., and Holmes, R. (2014, June 4) 'Exclusive: How Private Firms Make a Quick Killing from PFI' *The Independent*
BBC News (2016, February 8) 'Interserve Cleaning Contract in Leicester Ends Early' *BBC News*
Bochel, H., Bochel, C., Page, R., and Sykes, R. (2009) *Social Policy; Themes, Issues and Debates* (2nd edition), Basingstoke: Pearson
Cabinet Office (1999) *Modernising Government*, London: HMSO
Campbell, D. (2019, February 28) 'Scrap Laws Driving Privatisation of Health Service, Say NHS Bosses' *The Guardian*
Campbell, D., and Partington, R. (2018, October 5) 'NHS in Outsourcing Talks with Mitie after Body Parts Fiasco' *The Guardian*

Chapman, B. (2018, December 18) 'What Is Interserve and What Would Happen if the Outsourcing Firm Collapsed?' *The Independent*

Dathan, M. (2018, January 18) 'PFI Cry Day: Taxpayers Are Shelling Out £10billion a Year on PFI Fees and Shafted by Shoddy Government Deals, Report Reveals' *The Sun*

Davies, R. (2018, December 31) 'No-Deal Brexit Ferries; Who Gets Funds and How Was Contract Awarded' *The Guardian*

Davies, R. (2019, March 16) 'Interserve Goes into Administration after Shareholder Rebellion Scuppers Rescue Plan' *The Guardian*

Dean, M. (2012) *Democracy under Attack: How the Media Distort Policy and Politics*, Bristol: Policy Press

Department of the Environment, Transport and the Regions (DETR) (1999) *Commission Performance Indicators for 2000/2001 Volume One: The Performance Indicators, including the Publication of Information Direction*, London: DETR

Dominey, J. (2012) 'A Mixed Market of Probation Services: Can Lessons from the Recent Past Shape the Near Future' *Probation Journal* 59 (4): 339–354

Downes, D., and Hansen, K. (2006) *Welfare and Punishment: The Relationship between Welfare Spending and Imprisonment,* London: Crime and Society Foundation

Eaton, G. (2018, August 20) '2018: The Year Failure the Failure of Privatisation and Austerity Become Undisguisable' *New Statesman*

Evans, R., Garside, J., Smith, J., and Duncan, P. (2020, May 15) 'Firms Given £1bn of State Contracts without Tender in Covid-19 Crisis' *The Guardian*

Farrell, S. (2014, July 11) 'Royal Mail Sale Under Priced by £1bn, Says Scathing Select Committee Report' *The Guardian*

Fox, C., and Albertson, K. (2021) 'Is Payment by Results the Most Effective Way to Address the Challenges Facing by the Criminal Justice Sector' *Probation Journal* 59 (4): 355–375

Freedland, J. (2018, January 20) 'After Carillion We Have a Chance to Build a Better Country' *The Guardian*

Garside, R., Grimshaw, R., and Ford, M. (2018) *UK Justice Policy Review: Vol, 7,* London: Centre for Crime and Justice Studies

The Good Law Project (2021) 'Exclusive: 4 More VIP-Lane Companies Revealed' https://goodlawproject.org/update/awarded-contracts-vip-lane/. Retrieved 27 May 2021

Hill, M. (2013) *The Public Policy Process* (6th edition), Harlow: Pearson

HM Government (2011) *Open Public Services: White Paper,* London: HMSO

Hobsbawm, E. (2009, April 10) 'Socialism Has Failed. Now Capitalism Is Bankrupt. So What Comes Next?' *The Guardian*

HOC Committee of Public Accounts (2018) *Collapse of Carillion Inquiry*, London: House of Commons

HOC Committee of Public Accounts (2019) *Capita's Contracts with Ministry of Defence*, London: House of Commons

HOC, Public Accounts Committee (2019) *Brexit and the UK Border Out of Court Settlement with Eurotunnel*, London: House of Commons

HOC, Treasury Committee (2014) *Private Finance Initiative: Seventeenth Report of Session 2010–12*, London: House of Commons

Hodge, M. (2017, September 27) 'McDonnell's Hall of Smoke and Mirrors' *The Guardian*

Hood, C. (2006) 'Gaming in the Target World: The Targets Approach to Managing British Public Services' *Public Administration Review* 66 (4): 515–521

Hutton, W. (2019, March 3) 'At Last We Are Turning Away from Our Mania for Hiving Off Public Services' *The Guardian*

Hyndman, N., and Eden, R. (2001) 'Rational Management, Performance Targets and Executive Agencies: Views from Agency Chief Executives in Northern Ireland' *Public Administration* 79 (3): 578–598

Inman, P. (2018, February 2) 'Carillion Has Collapsed and Capita Is in Trouble. Is PFI Itself Now on the Critical List?' *The Guardian*

Johnson, N. (2001) 'The Personal Social Services' in S. Savage and R. Atkinson (eds) *Public Policy under Blair*, Basingstoke: Palgrave Macmillan

Jowitt, J. (2012 March 20) 'NHS Reform: Health and Social Care Bill Passes its Final Hurdle' *The Guardian*

Levitas, R. (2012) 'The Just's Umbrella: Austerity and the Big Society in Coalition Policy and Beyond' *Critical Social Policy* 32 (3): 320–342

Mance, H., and Parker, G. (2018, January 18) 'UK Finance Watchdog Exposes Lost PFI Billions' *The Financial Times*

Massey, A. (2001) 'Policy, Management and Implementation' in S. Savage and R. Atkinson (eds) *Public Policy under Blair*, Basingstoke: Palgrave Macmillan

Mitchell, J. (1990) 'Britain: Privatisation as Myth' in J.J. Richardson (ed) *Privatisation and Deregulation in Canada and Britain*, Dartmouth: IRPP

Monbiot, G. (2020, May 27) 'Privatisation Is to Blame for Our Tragic Covid-19 Response' *The Guardian*

Monbiot, G. (2021, April 28) 'As the Crony Contracts Kept Coming, Where Were the Media?' *The Guardian*

National Audit Office (2013) *The Role of Major Contractors in the Delivery of Public Services*, London: NAO

National Audit Office (2014a) *Impact of Funding Reductions Cuts on Local Authorities*, London: NAO

National Audit Office (2014b) *The Privatisation of Royal Mail*, London: NAO

National Audit Office (2018a) *PFI and PF2*, London: NAO

NAO (2018b) *Investigation into the Government's Handling of the Collapse of Carillion*, London: NAO

National Audit Office (2019) *The Award of Contracts for Additional Freight Capacity on Ferry Services. Report*, London: NAO

National Audit Office (2020) *Investigation into Government Procurement During the COVID-19*, London: NAO

NATS (2012) 'National Air Traffic Services' www.politics.co.uk/reference/national-air-traffic-services. Retrieved 6 January 2015

NHS England (2019) *Implementing NHS Long Term Plan*, London: NHS England

NHS Support Federation (2016) *NHS for Sale?* Brighton: NHS Support Federation:

North, N. (2001) 'Health Policy in Implementation' in S. Savage and R. Atkinson (eds) *Public Policy under Blair*, Basingstoke: Palgrave Macmillan

Prince, R., (2011, April 28) 'Public Finance Initiative schemes will cost every household nearly £400 next year' *The Telegraph*

Quinn, B. (2019, January 3) 'Brexit Ferry Firm Appears All Geared up to Deliver Pizzas' *The Guardian*

Rankin, J. (2013, August 25) 'UK Blood Plasma Company Sale to Bain Capital "Endangers NHS Supplies"' *The Guardian*

Ruddick, G. (2009, August 26) 'Meet Serco, the Company Running the Country' *Telegraph*

Ryan, M., and Ward, T. (1989) *Privatization and the Penal System: The American Experience and Debate in Britain*, Milton Keynes. Open University Press

Shaxson, N. (2018, October 5) 'The Financial Curse; How Outsized Power of the City Makes Britain Poorer' *The Guardian*

Starr, P. (1989) 'The Meaning of Privatisation' (reprinted) in S. Kamerman and A. Kahn (eds) *Privatization and the Welfare State*, Princeton: Princeton University Press

Syal, R. (2018, January 18) 'Taxpayers to Foot £200bn Bill for PFI Contracts—Audit Office' *The Guardian*

Taylor, D. (2020, June 1) 'Serco Wins Covid-19 Test and Trace Contract Despite £1m Fine' *The Guardian*

Taylor-Gooby, P. (2012) 'Root and Branch Restructuring to Achieve Major Cuts: The Social Policy Programme of the 2010 UK Coalition Government' *Social Policy & Administration* 46 (1): 61–82

Toynbee, P. (2018, January 22) 'At Last, the Privatisation Myth Has Been Exposed' *The Guardian*

Toynbee, P., and Walker, D. (2015) *Cameron's Coup: How the Tories Took Britain to the Brink*, London: Guardian Faber Publishing

The Trade Union Co-Ordinating Group (2013) *The Real Cost of Privatisation*, London: Centre for Legal and Social Studies

Transparency International UK (2021) 'Track and Trace: Identifying Corruption Risks in UK Public Procurement for the Covid-19 Pandemic' www.transparency.org.uk/sites/default/files/pdf/publications/Track%20and%20Trace%20-%20Transparency%20International%20UK.pdf. Retrieved 28 June 2021

Wearden, G., and Fletcher, N. (2018, January 31) 'Capita Shares Hit 15 Year Low after Shock Profits Warning—As It Happened' *The Guardian*

White, A. (2016) *Shadow State: Inside the Secret Companies that Run Britain*, London: Oneworld

Whitfield, D. (2000) 'The Third Way for Education: Privatisation and Marketisation' *Forum* 42 (2): 82–85

Whitfield, D. (2002) 'Impact of Privatisation and Commercialisation on Municipal Services in the UK' *Transfer: European Review of Labour and Research* 8 (2): 234–251

Whitfield, D. (2017) *PFI/PPP Buyouts, Bailouts, Terminations and Major Problem Contracts ESSU Research Report No 9*, Ireland: ESSU

Wintour, P., and Elliott, L. (2014, December 4) 'Osborne Moves to Cut Spending to 1930' *The Guardian*

Young, G. (2018, January 19) 'Restless for Change. Britain Needs New Solutions Not Old Dogmas' *The Guardian*

4

TRANSATLANTIC CROSSING, OR THE APPEAL OF AMERICAN KNOW-HOW IN THE AGE OF RISK, RESPONSIBILISATION AND RISING CRIME

> The crime control industry is . . . an industry with particular advantages, providing weapons for what is often seen as a permanent war against crime . . . like rabbits in Australia or wild mink in Norway—there are so few natural enemies around.
>
> (Nils Christie, 2003)

Introduction

Contemporary criminal justice policy is increasingly a global endeavour, encompassing both the economic opportunity and social risk brought about by globalisation. As constraints of geography on economic, political, social and cultural arrangements recede, risk, anxieties and threats expand. This creates a powerful modernist quest for safety and secure order: developments which shape policy making at both a local and a global level (Beck, 1992; Bauman, 2006). A political accompaniment to the rapid economic and social change brought about by globalisation has been the rise of neoliberalism. With the establishment of a free market in capital, goods and labour, there has been a growing interconnectedness between nation states, who in a quest to attract the international capital required to compete in the global market from institutions, such as the International Monetary Fund, have adapted their political economies to accommodate neoliberal principles. Despite opposing voices seeking to uphold the principle that fundamental public services such as education, health care, defence, and criminal justice should remain in the hands of the State, 'what marks out the 1980s is the rise of neo-liberal, market driven policies on both sides of the Atlantic' (Sinden, 2003: 41): policies predicated on the principles of 'economic deregulation, promotion of competitive markets as an optimal mechanism for distribution of goods and services, the hollowing out of the welfare state' (O'Malley, 2015: 1) and the rebalancing of the public/private spheres in favour of the commercial sector.

The study of contemporary criminal justice policy is increasingly a global endeavour, encompassing both the economic opportunity and social risk brought about by globalisation. The political accompaniment of neoliberalism has been the redrawing of the social contract between the State and the individual, with a key feature being the transfer of responsibility for risk prevention and management from the State to the individual or organisation. In the void, risk-averse individuals and organisations looked to the private sector to fill the gap between needs/wants and their satisfaction. With individual consumption and choice at the heart of the neoliberal ideal, this process created a market for security provision: a market within which the nascent private security industry of personnel and goods could flourish. Furthermore, as the State sought simultaneously to divest itself of the responsibility for providing existing public services, the incremental privatisation of the criminal justice system as a whole afforded the emergent industry opportunities to expand and diversify.

Pivotal to the trajectory of UK privatisation was the forging of the 'special relationship' between the UK and the US, initially under Reagan and Thatcher in the 1980s, and the concomitant willingness of successive UK governments to gain inspiration from America's crime control and punishment policy solutions. In the 1970s the emergence of the New Right penal policy in the US precipitated a rapid rise in the prison population, creating a penal crisis of overcrowding. With Reagan embracing neoliberal tenets, unwilling to invest public funding in a prison building programme to increase capacity, a market in penal construction, goods and service developed. Additionally, as the State became increasingly reliant on the private sector to fill the gap in goods, services and know-how, the boundaries separating the two entities eroded, enmeshing the State and commercial sector in a symbiotic relationship: the corrections commercial complex. Made up of 'governmental, professional, and not-for-profit organisations' (Nellis, 2000: 117), who share policy goals, vision and objectives, the corrections commercial complex (Lilly and Knepper, 1992) has exerted increasing influence over the policy making process, ensuring that the allocation of resources (e.g. the awarding of contracts) meets their needs for profit and expansion.

Indeed, with profit making and expansion built into the nascent US private punishment industry, the UK penal crisis that followed the UK's own adoption of New Right law and order policies provided the opportunity for US commercial entities to expand their sphere of influence. Lacking its own 'off-the-shelf' solutions, the UK, partly in response to combined US and UK commercial and political lobbying, looked to its ideological soul mates across the pond to supply the know-how, technologies, services and personnel needed to meet its provision in penal goods and services deficit: a development which allowed the burgeoning US industry to expand its global footprint.

Globalisation and glocalisation: key themes and trends

According to Bauman (2006):

> Globalization is on everyone's lips; a fad word fast turning into a shibboleth, a magic incantation, a pass-key, meant to unlock the gates to present and future mysteries. For some, 'globalization' is what we are bound to do if we wish to be happy; for others 'globalization' is the cause of our unhappiness. For everybody, though, 'globalization' is the intractable fate of the world; it is a process which affects us all in the same measure and in the same way.
>
> *(2006:1)*

Although until comparatively recently barely unknown outside the world of academe, globalisation now occupies a central position in public discourse. 'Its existence, benefits, and costs (are) routinely tussled over by politicians, commentators, corporate executives and social movements' (Loader and Sparks, 2007: 88). As Giddens has argued, '(g)lobalization may not be a particularly attractive or elegant word. But absolutely no one who wants to understand our prospects at century's end can ignore it' (2000: 25). For Giddens, globalisation is best understood as 'the intensification of worldwide social relationships'. It links different regions of the globes, creating interconnectedness in which 'local happenings are shaped by events occurring many miles away and visa versa' (1990: 64). Similarly, Bauman (2001) describes a 'network of dependences' that 'absorb and embrace the furthest corners of the globe': nothing that happens elsewhere, the causes and effects, can be left out of the calculations (2001: 11).

Whilst globalisation's reach means that political, economic, social and technological events and developments resonate across national borders, the convergence of both global dynamics and local contexts means that the global impact is not homogeneous, but rather globalising international pressures are negotiated at the local level, shaped by local contingencies, resistance, pre-existing institutional forms and political imperatives. Globalising effects are neither uniform nor consistent but are always 'mediated by distinctive national and sub-national cultures and socio-economic cultural norms' (Muncie, 2005: 57). The global and the local are interdependent, existing in a constantly evolving reflexive relationship. What may at first glance appear to be a global phenomenon (such as the spread of neoliberalism, the free market and *laissez faire* individualism) needs to be contextualised within the specific local context. With 'glocalisation' the preferred explanatory framework for understanding local configurations, Hobbs (2013), paraphrasing Latour argues, activities are '(l)ocal at all points' offering a vehicle for transferring from one sphere to another along 'continuous paths that lead from the local to the global, from the circumstantial to the universal, from the contingent to the necessary' (Latour, 1993: 117). Or, as Robertson (1995) notes:

> [I]it makes no good sense to define the global as if the global excludes the local . . . defining the global in such a way suggests that the global lies beyond

all localities, as having systematic properties over and beyond the attributes of units within a global system.

(1995:34)

Globalisation and neoliberalism: the hollowed-out State

One of the key ideas within the globalisation literature is the notion that globalisation is synonymous with the 'the diffusion of ideologies like liberalism and . . . (which has been a key driver for) the spread of the capitalist mode of production' (Mann, 2013: 11). Neoliberalism (Findlay, 2008), an 'umbrella term' that encompasses a 'cluster of interrelated features' (O'Malley, 2015: 1), is associated with free market ideology and practices, in particular privatisation:

> [N]eoliberalism refers to an economic and political school of thought on the relations between the state on the one hand, and citizens and the world of trade and commerce on the other. Because it espouses minimal or no state interference in the market and promotes the lifting of barriers to trade and business transactions across regional and national borders, it certainly becomes a motor of globalisation.
>
> *(Passas, 2000: 21)*

In the UK whilst the post-war State settlement, predicated on social democratic principles of common good and collectivism, favoured State provision and was accompanied by the expansion of the public sector, the gradual incursion of neoliberalism into social, political and economic life over the last four decades has been accompanied by the shrinking of the public domain, the rolling back of the State and increasing expectation that the individual, not the State, is a responsible agent. The renegotiation of the social contract between the State and its citizens has brought in its wake the State's retreat from being the sole provider of public goods and services, as the State's obligations have become redefined as steering (ensuring that services are provided) rather than rowing (providing services themselves) (Osborne and Gaebler, 1992). In the reconfigured context of the 'de-centring of the State and "rule at a distance"' (Braithwaite, 2000: 50), multi-national company, the globalised market and the global brand (Aas, 2007: 3–4) have provided the infrastructure: the means by which the public/private can be rebalanced. As the State has relinquished its duty to provide public services, the UK has proved a lucrative market for global welfare products and services, including crime control and punishment.

Globalisation and risk

Once restricted to the technical domain, risk has become part of the 'idiom of our contemporary moral and political conversations' (Loader and Sparks, 2007: 86). Having been deployed since the 1970s as a driver for 'forward thinking' policymaking in crime and security, notions of risk, risk control and risk management have become embedded in criminal justice practice. Further, with privately financed and developed technological advances the possibility of making profit from managing risk has become a pervasive feature of contemporary life.

Although not writing about crime, Beck (1986, 1992, 1999) has been highly influential in developing the notion that we live in a 'risk society':

> The argument is that, while in classic industrial society the 'logic' of wealth production dominates the 'logic' of risk production, in the risk society this relationship is reversed . . . The gain in power from techno-economic 'progress' is being increasingly overshadowed by the production of risks.
>
> *(1992: 12)*

In 'risk society' analyses, the negatives of risk take primacy over the positives of benefits. The optimistic modernist discourse of security and prosperity, which science and rational government can deliver, has been replaced by a pessimistic discourse of threats and ills that they pose. Risks are omnipresent and incalculable; risk thinking has become not only 'pervasive, but also routinised' (Hudson, 1993: 43). The 'fruits of this work' have been that the conceptualisation of risk has expanded to embrace a wide range of social problems: 'risk has become embedded in the intellectual infrastructure of the social disciplines as well as the natural sciences' (Baker and Roberts, 2005: 129).

A significant product of risk society is the emergence of the conventional wisdom that fear of crime has gained a 'global dimension' (Walklate and Mythen, 2008). Risk awareness and aversion, manifested in concern for global social order and personal threats, has given rise to a search for lost certainty, control and security. In a climate of 'self-propelling fear' (Bauman, 2006: 119) and insecurity, attendant upon globalisation (Loader and Sparks, 2007), 'the concrete experience of uncontrollability . . . the loss of credibility and trust' on both 'a large and small scale, in everyday family life and in global politics' (Beck, 2009: 18) has produced a powerful modernist quest for safety and order. In a defence against anxiety and fear, individuals are attracted to 'discourses and practices which appear to offer the hope of control and order' (Holloway and Jefferson, 2005: 573). Discourses and practices, which are represented in the protection from threats to spiritual and material comfort, become commodified in the defended space and the safe home (Bauman, 2006).

Managing risk: new penology paradigm

In the field of criminal justice, risk society analyses of everyday life, in which risk is a central, generalised preoccupation, are held responsible for 'emergent risk-based practices': practices predicated on 'neo-liberal economistic preferences for prevention over cure, for improved cost effectiveness, and for protecting the public'

(O'Malley, 2015: 3). With social life increasingly organised around risk-oriented thinking, risk prediction and prevention (Beck, 1992) have become a central motif of governance. Everyday criminal justice practice has increasingly been defined by

> bringing possible future undesired events into calculations in the present, making their avoidance the central objective of decision-making processes, and administering individuals, institutions, expertise and resources in the service of that ambition.
>
> *(Rose, 2000: 332)*

What is more, with the coalescence of the 'conditions and consequences of late modernity, in particular, the mutation of political liberalism into contemporary neoliberalism, and the emergence of the late modern preoccupation with risk, a new penology paradigm has emerged' (Hudson, 2003: 42):

> Risk is something undesired which may happen, and criminal justice is charged with managing the risk of crime. Risk is central to law and order politics, and it is hardly surprising, then, that the risk society perspective developed in writings like Beck . . . has been drawn on by criminal justice writers to understand recent developments in penal and social control.
>
> *(Hudson, 2003: 43)*

A forward-looking penology that is less concerned with past wrongdoing and more concerned with preventing future harms (Jones, 2007: 851), the new penology informed by risk and its control has brought in its wake new sites of inquiry and intervention, displacing traditional socially orientated and explanatory models (O'Malley, 2001) associated with rehabilitation offender and welfarism (Garland, 1997). The new penology in which the offender is either the 'situational man' whose behaviour could be managed and controlled by pragmatic, adaptive strategies which reduce the opportunities by manipulating incentives and risks, or is the 'Other' who requires surveillance, incapacitation and control, has fuelled a demand for new modes of intervention, new strategies and new techniques, creating a market for commercially provided crime prevention goods and services (e.g. CCTV, burglar alarms, etc.), as well as customised technologies in the security and telecommunications field (e.g. electronic monitoring) (Garland, 1997; Jones, 2007).

Responsibilisation and the privatisation of consumption

Starr (1989), in his analysis, distinguishes between policy-driven and demand-driven privatisation. He argues that where the former requires significant institutional changes and is characterised by a substitution of private for public goods, the latter shifts attention to the consumption sphere and self-conscious choice. Although not all may be able to access the goods and services on the grounds of cost, and the individual may acquire certain privileges and advantages as a consequence of this, demand-driven privatisation *per se* does not impinge upon the public good:

> shifts from publicly to privately produced services may arise not only from a deliberate government action, such as the sale of assets, but also from choices of individuals and firms if a government is unwilling or unable to satisfy or control . . . This *is demand-driven privatization.*
>
> *(1989: 22–23)*

With changes in economic and political spheres brought about by globalisation, particularly deindustrialisation, the social structure has become more complex, and previous social networks which provided informal sources of control have become fractured and fragmented. In the face of real and mediated threats—'random violence that seems to erupt at all levels of society, and the apparent inability of governments to do anything about these problems' (Jewkes, 2004: 28)—in the hollowed-out State, individuals that can afford to do so increasingly rely on the purchase and consumption of goods and services of anonymous others (e.g. professionals, security experts) (Baker and Roberts, 2005: 129).

In the neoliberal State 'reliance on the state, even for protection against crime is not to be encouraged' (O'Malley, 1992). Neoliberalism is predicated on a social contract between the State and the citizen in which the State 'retreats' from the direct, centralised provision of social welfare that socialises risk. In its place new arrangements that individualise risk and risk management are created. These arrangements lay stress upon the self-activating capacities of the autonomous individual, alongside the enterprise of the market to provide the services and goods for those that can afford it. With purchasing power and self-reliance elevated, consumption, choice, competition and self-sufficiency became the driving forces (Ryan, 2005). As McMahon points out, 'at the level of the Welfare State there was a huge shift away from an ethos of universal social insurance and a collective guaranteed minimum towards personal and family obligation' (2007: 24).

Whilst the responsibility for being both the 'ultimate and the proximate guarantor of security' was assumed by the social democratic State, in the down-sized, hollowed-out neoliberal State, public sector provision is simply one node of security amongst others in the commercial, voluntary and statutory sectors (Johnston and Shearing, 2003). Under the 'ethos of individual autonomy characteristic of advanced forms of liberalism, the self-actuating individual is expected to secure himself against crime risks' (Rose, 2000: 327–328). Securitisation of the individual is reflected away from the State, reconfigured as a private commodity that should be purchased by individual consumers in the marketplace (Jones, 2007: 845). The individualistic, risk-averse consumer is offered the choice to regain a 'semblance of control over an unpredictable and troubling future' (Loader, 1999: 381) through the purchase and consumption of the private goods and services provided by the globalised security industry.

With crime normalised as a 'routine phenomenon, as something that happens in the course of events, rather than a disruption of normality that has to be specially explained' (Garland, 1997), risk overstated and all individuals cast as potential victims (Christie, 2003), managing and controlling this eventuality through the adoption of situational crime prevention strategies has gained precedence (Sullivan, 2001). Attractive on a number of levels, it not only provides the risk-averse consumer commonsense solutions with tangible results, but it also fits the prevailing neoliberal ethos, with its emphasis on a small State and entrepreneurial activity (Crawford, 2007: 879). The State's relinquishment of its monopoly of crime control and the responsibility for crime control and crime prevention is associated with the dispersal to new providers and non-criminal justice agencies (Garland, 2003: 124). Under these arrangements, which lay stress upon the self-activating capacities of the autonomous, actualised individual alongside the enterprise of the market to provide the services and goods, the State and its citizens have become 'partners in prudence' (Rose, 2000):

> Increasingly political discourse lay stress not merely upon the economic and technical limits of what could be provided by the state for its citizens, but also the paradoxical and undesirable effects of the promise of total social protection . . . the social democratic promise of the social state gave way to the metaphor of the facilitating state, the state as partner and animator rather than provider and manager. Individuals, families, firms, organisations, communities were urged to take upon themselves the responsibility for the security of their property and their persons, and for that of their own families. Protection against risk of crime through investment in measures of security became part of the responsibilities of each active individual, each responsible employer.
>
> *(Rose 2000: 327)*

On both sides of the Atlantic, concerns by business about employee theft and liabilities for crimes committed on their premises, as well as privatised fears about domestic security created a lucrative market in the supply of surveillance equipment and other security measures. In the six years between 1988 and 1992, private individuals in the US handed over $65 billion to the private security industry. Simultaneously, gated communities patrolled by private security guards grew in popularity as families, emulating their forebears who sought safety behind stockades, were seduced by marketing promises of a 'totally new way of life' in 'an old community setting' (Shelden and Brown, 2000).

Circuits of security and insecurity: the haves and have-nots

Alongside the dispersal of the responsibility for crime prevention, the costs have been redistributed. With the emergence of a model which favours the haves at the expense of the have-nots, provision of security has become increasingly uneven, patchwork and polarised: determined by the ability to pay and market forces, rather than need (Loader, 1999: 374). The employment of private security patrols in affluent Altringham, Manchester, are a recent case in point. Whilst the

> rich and powerful can readily afford personal and property insurance premiums, burglar and car alarms, homes in gated communities and even security guards . . . the poor and unprotected (become) even more vulnerable to those who are thus driven to prey on their meagre resources.
> (Zedner, 2000: 209)

They are left to fend for themselves in the dangerous public places, policed by an 'increasingly militarized public police force' (Davis, 1999 as cited in Jones, 2007: 852). In the haves and have-nots binary, the particular features of demand-driven privatisation associated with neoliberal responsibilisation increasingly impinge upon the public good.

In the neoliberal city, 'circuits of security' coexist with 'circuits of insecurity'. With the municipal public spaces 'abandoned, desolate and dangerous', new 'secured spaces—shopping malls, arts centres and gourmet restaurant strips' have emerged. Under the watchful eye of police paid for by the mall's proprietors as well as private security police and monitors of electronic surveillance, access is guarded, and those whose intentions are not deemed consumerist can be excluded: 'expelled to spaces outside the circuits of security and inclusion, spaces which are increasingly avoided and feared by those who used to walk, shop and visit there'. Private spaces where strategies of inclusion exist (such as the gated community and the crowdfunding of public police by residents of a wealthy London borough) compete with public spaces where draconian strategies exist to further exclude and segregate those deemed dangerous or anti-social (Rose, 2000: 330).

Neoliberalism, New Right punitiveness and the Penal State

Whilst there is little dispute that neoliberalism is associated with the free market and the rebalancing of the private/public in favour of the private sector, the scope and scale of privatisation of the penal system were not inevitable. Although, as discussed in the previous chapter, Thatcher's government had already transferred a whole range of industries to the private sector, and the precedent was established, it was fiscally driven pragmatism (arguably dictated by neoliberalism's master narrative) as much as ideologically driven pro-privatisation fervour that triggered the incursion into the penal system. With America and the UK following similar trajectories, on both sides of the Atlantic, privatisation of the penal system was the pragmatic solution to the problem of penal excess, associated with the emergence of the neoliberal Penal State and New Right penology.

In the last quarter of the twentieth century, the rise of the 'high crime society' and its associated anxieties and insecurities (Garland, 2000) provided the impetus for the emergence of a 'new' punitive law and order agenda, variously referred to as the 'new punitiveness' (Pratt, 2005), the 'penal turn' (Meyer and O'Malley, 2005) or the 'great leap backwards' (Wacquant, 2005). Features of the new punitiveness include the creation of the 'Penal State' (Loader and Sparks, 2007: 87) in which law and order is politicised, New Right 'law and order' politics take precedence and poverty is penalised (Wacquant, 2001); the promotion of penal provisions at the expense of social welfare provisions (Hudson, 1993), 'stripping back . . . "welfare" or "therapeutic"' interventions in favour of corrective sanctions that promote individual responsibility'; and the 'sanctification of the victim' and the focus on penality as the means to protect the citizen (Garland, 2001). New punitiveness is associated with

> mass incarceration . . . longer sentences [and] . . . penal laws that seem to abandon long-standing limits to punishment in modern societies . . . as well as the emergence of penal sanctions that had previously thought to be extinct and inappropriate in the civilized state.
>
> *(Pratt et al., 2005: xii)*

Whilst much is made of American exceptionalism, mass incarceration and racialised penal excess (in the southern states, one in ten young black men experience the carceral system), a similar New Right repertoire of tough sentencing in the UK precipitated an unprecedented rise in the prison population, creating home-grown problems of capacity and funding: problems that, for the hollowed-out State, could best be met by private sector initiatives.

The US experience

The burgeoning of the American corrections commercial sector which was to prove so pivotal to UK privatisation initiatives (providing a ready-made template to emulate) was rooted in America's penal crisis. Driven by New Right penal policies, the penal crisis was the product of policies which, conflating welfare dependency with immorality and socially undesirable behaviour, signalled an important shift in penological thinking towards crime control. Underscored by the war on drugs and war on crime rhetoric, the dominant (regressive) principle in penology became incapacitation. The new punitive penal strategy of locking up more offenders for longer became synonymous in the public and political imagination with deterrence and public protection.

In the space of ten years the US prison population rose from an incarceration rate of 139 per 100,000 at the beginning of 1980 to 292 per 100,000 by 1990 (Shichor, 1995: 10–11). Disproportionately affecting 'men and people of colour', the prison population explosion reached its peak in 2009 when the 'prison population exceeded 2.4 million, with more than 1% of the country's adult population behind bars' (Eisenberg, 2016: 80–81). In New York alone in the ten years between 1974 and 1984, the prison population rose from 14,000 to 32,926, and spending on prisons and prison services rose nearly threefold from $192.7 million to $523.5 million (Ryan and Ward, 1989: 8).

With lobbying by powerful interest groups that could benefit from the growth of prisons (including private providers and prison officer unions) a contributory factor, the new political trend that gained momentum under Reagan capitalised 'on the public's fear of crime and their resulting openness to draconian criminal laws' (Eisenberg, 2016: 82). Electorally popular, punitive sentencing and concomitant mass incarceration not only appealed to public sensibilities, but also provided a welcome source of employment in rust belt America. The rapid rise in the prison population created capacity problems for the public prison system, which was quickly overwhelmed. With the demand for prison places outstripping supply, and individual states demanding more federal resources to cope with overcrowding, embarking on a programme of penal expansion seemed to be the solution (Ryan and Ward, 1989).

Despite the populist appeal of 'locking up bad people', the incarceration boom coincided with a period of economic crisis, pressure on public expenditure and middle class resistance to taxation (Wood, 2003), which created a junction between the end and means. With pressure experienced at both the Federal and State level to 'reduce expenditure by investigating in new and more efficient ways of running public services', Reagan embarked on a series of reforms and policy initiatives that 'involved the private sector more directly in the delivery of hitherto public services' (Ryan and Ward, 1989: 1). With the corrections commercial industry in its infancy and defence industry in decline (a casualty of the geopolitical changes brought about by the end of the Cold War) Reagan, an early advocate of private prisons, handed the defence industry a lifeline, challenging it to use its technology and know-how to wage war on the enemy within: the poor, the law breaker and the drug user.

'Keen to maintain profit margins in the absence of a clearly defined threat against the Western world' (Paterson, 2007: 109), defence contractors joined forces with the fledgling 'homeland' security industry. In a country with a historical and cultural distrust of big government, which gained a resurgence under Reagan (Shichor, 1995; Sinden, 2003), it was comparatively easy to gain public approval for measures that promised to make the streets safe whilst simultaneously offering taxation advantages to the public and employment opportunities to communities where the impact of deindustrialisation was being most keenly felt. As a consequence of the awarding of prison contracts to private suppliers 'between 1990 and 2009, the American private prison industry grew by more than 1600% (with) the two largest private corporations: Corrections Corporation of America (CCA) and the GEO Group (GEO)' (Eisenberg, 2016: 83).

The UK experience

'Despite the differences in government structure . . . it is easy to see parallels between the British and the American experience' (Ryan and Ward, 1989: 8). Although it is generally agreed that the UK, whilst sharing common features of

US neoliberal penal policy, retained elements derived from seemingly oppositional political rationalities, it is nonetheless the case that in the late 1980s and 1990s a noticeable sea change in penal thinking and action signalled a retreat from traditional social welfarism. Coinciding with the decline in the influence of the traditional liberal policy making elite (the Platonic guardians made up of senior civil servants, academics and strategic practitioners), a 'highly-politicized, over-dramatized and "'hot" penal climate' (Loader, 2008: 9) evolved in which the 'civilization project' of decency, humanity and restraint that balanced the competing civil liberties of offenders and the public was replaced by a new politics responsive to 'public demands for vengeance'(Loader, 2006: 564; Pratt, 2006). This reached its zenith in 1993, when in the wake of a series of high-profile murders, the Home Secretary, Michael Howard, harnessing the mediated sentiments of a public seemingly fixated on retribution, pitched himself against the prevailing penal orthodoxy of restricting imprisonment on the grounds that 'prison makes bad people worse' by promoting the new populist 'prison works' philosophy.

Reversing the long-established principle that penal policy should reduce the prison population, Howard set the course for an era of intense criminal justice hyperactivity. Changes in the climate of political and public crime and punishment debate sounded the death knell for penal welfarism, transforming the legislative framework and guidance within which sentencers operated (Millie et al., 2003). In the face of a succession of ministers seeking to assert their tough on crime credentials, sentencers, fearing the bad publicity that diverging from the dominant discourse would attract, felt increasingly obligated to resort to custody and longer sentences (Loader, 2008), fuelling penal expansion. Consequently, between 1993 and 2011, the prison population nearly doubled, from 44,246 (PRT, 2014) to an all-time high of 88,179 (Howard League for Penal Reform, 2015). As 'more and more offenders' became 'mired deeper and deeper within the criminal justice system for doing less and less' (Morgan, 2003: 14), England and Wales gained the dubious status of having the highest imprisonment rate in Europe (IPCR, 2015).

As the penal pendulum swung in favour of punitivism, the rising prison population not only placed a strain on the prisons' capacity to accommodate the new population, leading to the need to expand capacity by building more prisons or finding new alternative modes of punishment that chimed with the public mood, but also placed drain on the public purse. Between 1997 and 2005 there was a 5% average annual real terms increase in spending on public order and safety. By 2008 the criminal justice system as a whole in England and Wales received £22.7 billion, over a third more than it received ten years previously. Faced with the crisis of penal excess, politicians of both main parties, cognisant of the electoral perils of either promoting policies of decarceration or increasing taxation too steeply, in a bid to cut costs, became increasingly reliant upon 'market competition, privatised institutions, and subcontracted, at a distance forms of social control' (Paterson, 2007: 3). Emulating the US, with free market neoliberalism and the hollowed-out State the dominant paradigm, the scene was set for privatisation.

The US as the penal workshop of the world

Globalisation and the transfer of penal ideas

One of the consequences of the globalisation is that new communications technologies and the widespread use of English mean that 'little goes on that cannot be learnt about elsewhere' (Tonry, 2001: 527). With 'an evolving awareness of the global wealth of penal ideas' (Baker and Roberts, 2005: 124), as Dolowitz and Marsh point out:

> If governments are searching for policy solutions to new or changing problems, they are increasingly likely to look for 'solutions' abroad. This is much easier than it was in the past because of the growth in all forms of communication; politicians and civil servants from different countries now meet more frequently, in bilateral as well as multi-lateral meetings.
>
> *(2000: 21)*

Not only does the globalised exchange of penal ideas provide the means by which individual governments can 'pick and mix' policy solutions from elsewhere, it also provides a platform for policy entrepreneurs, backed by powerful business interests, to 'sell' their expertise around the world. With the decline in the influence of traditional criminological experts (Aas, 2007; Garland, 2003), what passes for knowledge has become diffused and diluted (Currie, 2007), opening up a space in which big business, either directly through its own 'experts' or through intermediaries masquerading as independent, non-partisan research organisations (e.g. think tanks), can market penal ideas and solutions that further their commercial interests.

Whilst the direction of policy transfer is neither 'one dimensional (n)or one directional' (Muncie, 2005: 42), much of the literature on the direction of policy transfer focuses upon the United States as the 'penal workshop of the world' (Downes and Howard, 1976), with the US depicted as at the forefront of the exportation of penal ideas, (Wacquant, 2001) technologies and penal hardware: 'the place where new ideas, new practices in criminal justice are pioneered, and then exported to, forced upon, or borrowed by other countries' (Nellis, 2000: 99). 'Neoliberal penality', characterised by social welfare retrenchment and the growing use of the penal system as an instrument for managing social insecurity and containing the social disorders created at the bottom of the class structure by neoliberal economic policies of deregulation, elaborated in the United States, diffused throughout the world.

Although there is evidence of importation to the UK of penal policies that do not have their origins in the US (Muncie, 2005), Dolowitz (2000), in his analysis of the direction of penal policy transfer, argues that in the lender/borrower relationship, the United States features frequently as the lender, exporting its variants of crime control and punishment, whereas Britain is invariably (but not exclusively) the borrower (2000). Jones and Newburn (2002), summing up the view, argue:

> There is a view, not always framed explicitly, that the field of British social policy in general (including crime control policy) has become increasingly

'Americanized' in recent years. Such arguments often suggest a rather straightforward exertion of American influence, which manifests itself via deliberate policy transfers from the USA, and the conscious emulation of US policy innovation by UK policy-makers.

(2002: 177)

Causal explanations for the Americanisation of UK penal policy vary. Nellis (2000) credits shared language, similarities in the legal system and 'common ideological outlooks' for the willingness of successive British governments to embrace penal ideas and policy formulations that originate from the United States (2000: 5). Similarly, for Dolowitz (2000), the exportation of ideas, practices and policies from the United States to Britain has its origins in common political economies, the rise of the New Right in the United States in the 70s and the forging of the 'special relationship'(characterised by unusually warm personal, political, cultural and military ties) with the United States during the Thatcher/Reagan administrations: a relationship that further developed during the period of the Blair administration, with Clinton's New Democrats providing an electability template for New Labour (Savage and Atkinson, 2001).

For Newburn (2002) the key determinants of policy transfer from the US to UK are: ideological proximity—shared neoliberal agenda, shared language and terminology with which to define the problem and shared models of the offender; the historically close relationship between the two countries; the emergence of the penal industrial complex in the US and global influence of corporations that profit from the building and running of prisons and the provision of other associated services; the adoption of New Right penality and discourse on both sides of the Atlantic, specifically key terms and phrases that have 'mesmeric appeal', such as the 'war' metaphor; symbolic politics; the formulation of electorally popular law and order policies or postures that are intended to communicate concern about an issue, to distinguish between 'good and bad', but are not necessarily believed to be instrumentally effective or implemented or, if implemented, assumed to be met by adaptive, nullifying responses by practitioners such as judges; and the emergence of the neoliberal penal policy network of think tanks and advocacy coalitions with interchangeable personnel which operate across national borders and export ideas (Newburn, 2002).

The emergence of the American crime control industry and penal imperialism

As Christie (2003) states:

Compared to most other industries, the crime control industry is in a most privileged position. There is no end to raw material; crime seems to be in endless supply. Endless are the demands for the service, as well as the willingness to pay for what is seen as security. And the usual industrial questions of

> contamination do not appear. On the contrary, this is an industry seen to be cleaning up, removing unwanted elements from the social system.
>
> (2003: 13)

There can be little doubt that, as Quinney (1977) observed in the late 1970s, 'there is a profit to be made from crime' (Shelden and Brown, 2000: 40). Whether it is through the provision of clothing, IT, accounting, catering services and building maintenance services, the building and management of prisons, the supply of custodial escort services, the provision of new technologies (such as electronic monitoring, tasers, bio-metric recognition systems), the delivery of drug services and offender management and/or the supply of security services, crime and its control offer a seemingly endless range of profit-making opportunities (Shelden, 2010). As Shelden succinctly summed it up, 'crime pays for big business and the "crime control industry"' (1999: 1).

With expansion built into the industrial thinking (Christie, 2003), pioneering US companies such as Corrections Corporation of America (CCA) and Wackenhut Corrections Corporation (WCC) which, emerging in the 1980s, were at 'the cutting edge of the brand new (punishment) industry' (Ryan and Ward, 1989: 13), cognisant of profit-making opportunities beyond their own borders, embarked on 'penal imperialism' (Lilly and Deflem, 1996). During the1980s and 1990s, American corporations, promoted by US government officials, were able to 'transfer the more concrete aspects of policy, both through some initial lobbying for policy change, and subsequently through their involvement in commercial contracts in running prisons and EM schemes' (Jones and Newburn, 2007: 61–62).

Although it was not until the late 1980s and 1990s that Conservative members of the Home Affairs Committee, seeking to address the social and fiscal implications of the penal crisis (including a series of high-profile prison riots), settled upon the idea of privatising key aspects of the criminal justice system, the fact that America had a ready-made source of private penal goods and services, which it was keen to export, militated against the delays and setup costs associated with starting from scratch. Indeed, the vacuum created by the absence of British firms with the necessary knowledge and experience to 'exploit the burgeoning (UK) corrections market' (Nathan, 2003a: 190) was filled by multi-national American companies, CCA and WCC, who were to prove pivotal to the development of the UK privatised penal system. In 1987, CCA formed a British company, UK Detention Services, with two regular contributors to the Conservative Party, Sir Robert MacAlpine and John Mowlem (long-established British construction companies). Instrumental in lobbying for private prisons, its aim was to 'promote the private design, financing, construction and management by private contractors and remand facilities in the UK' (Nathan, 2003b: 164).

In 1996, CCA bought out the two British firms and eventually sold half of UK Detention Services (UKDS) to Sodexho, a Paris based multi-national corporation. In September 2000, Sodexho became the sole owner of UKDS after CCA sold out. Similarly, in 1992, WCC joined with Serco Ltd., a British facilities management firm, to form Premier Prison Services: the company that was to establish itself as the UK's largest private prison provider in the UK. In May 2002, WWC was acquired by Group 4 Falck. In July 2003 Serco acquired control of Premier Prison Services (PRT, 2005).

As the market for penal products and service expanded, new players emerged. Whilst some companies came into being just to sell penal products, others had 'backgrounds in the military, security, IT and business processing industries' and (seeing the opportunities to make profit) diversified into the private corrections sector (Nellis, 2018). What is more as Nellis (2018) argues, with an industry that has never been stable, mergers and take overs have been commonplace, and smaller companies have been vulnerable to be buyout by larger companies.

Despite this, whilst 'the sometimes convoluted, multi-layered nature of company ownership' (Nellis, 2018) created by sell offs, mergers, take overs and the entry into the market of new commercial contractors has complicated the issue, at times obscuring the footprint of American corporation on the UK privatised corrections and security market, there is little doubt that the American multi-national company's influence on the UK penal market has not diminished (Nathan, 2003b). Indeed, in the post-Brexit world where the UK government is actively seeking to secure free trade arrangements with the US, there is every reason to believe that the US existing sphere of interest will increase.

The corrections commercial complex

As Nellis (2018) recently pointed out, Lilly and his partners were instrumental in sharpening the early debate in the USA. They equated the expansion of private security and punishment, in terms of surveillance technologies from the defence to the securities, with a newly emergent 'Corrections Commercial Complex' of sub-governments' comprising State, business and professional interests which encouraged uptake of the new measures (cc. Lilly and Ball, 1993). As Wood points out:

> (The concept) arises from critical perspectives on the American state, which see corporate colonization of the decision-making structures as the key to an understanding of American policy making. By using their resources to serve the needs of state and local politicians and bureaucrats, business interests and/or wealthy individuals are able to exercise disproportionate influence over policy making and contribute to a corporate welfare state. The 'revolving door' between government service and the private sector, substantial bureaucratic autonomy and the domination of electoral politics by corporate money all contribute to relative immunity from democratic accountability and . . . the downsizing the state.
>
> *(2003: 16)*

With a global reach, participants in the corrections commercial complex (Lilly and Deflem, 1996), comprising private companies that profit from privatised punishment, likeminded lobbyist and politicians, form part of a self-serving alliance that exerts its influence 'behind the scenes' (Nellis, 2000: 11), maintaining a 'low profile', which allows it to operate 'without public scrutiny' (Lilly and Knepper, 1992).

As the American criminal justice system has been transformed by the rapid growth and the increasing importance of private interests in criminal justice policy, a symbiotic relationship between the State and big business has evolved that, blurring the boundaries that separate the State and business, threatens the integrity of the policy making process, and by allowing business to gain a foothold, the allocation of contracts to deliver public services. The corrections commercial complex, made up of those industries that profit from policies that create high prison numbers (either through the building and management of prisons or through the provision of ancillary services and products such as catering, health care, transportation and drug detection as well as the provision of uniforms, protective vests, restraints, furniture, locks etc.) and those that make penal policy, reflects the enmeshed relationship between the two. Emulating key features of the earlier military industrial complex—the 'iron triangle' of the Pentagon, made up of various members of influential Congressional committees (e.g. armed services committees and defence appropriations committees) and private providers of defence and military services—the US corrections commercial complex has evolved as a small, largely unaccountable, elite circle of 'private corporations . . . devoted to profiting from imprisonment', 'government agencies anxious to maintain their existence' and 'professional organisations that sew together an otherwise fragmented group into a powerful alliance' that exerts influence over policy making (Lilly and Knepper, 1993: 154).

With expansion built into the business ethos of private contractors, and each new policy initiative welcomed as a business opportunity (Christie, 2003; Lilly and Knepper, 1992, 1993), the highly efficient mechanisms for expansion that evolved in the US have raised serious questions about the influence that business exerts over the legislative and judicial processes (such as sentencing) (Shichor, 1995: 238) and has prompted questions about whose interest it serves. The unholy alliance between policy makers and industry which seemingly allows industry to exert undue 'influence over corrections policy', ensuring among others that the allocation of government resources (e.g. service delivery contracts) meets their expansionary business interests (Lilly and Knepper, 1992: 175), promoted one commentator writing in the 1990s to predict that:

> In coming years, as the private prison companies expand their operations, the prison-industrial complex's influence over criminal justice policy is likely to grow significantly. Criminal justice policy may someday be as influenced by the Corrections Corporation of America as defence policy has been influenced by Lockheed Martin and McDonnell Douglas.
>
> *(Lotke, 1996: 21)*

Conclusion

Contemporary criminal justice is increasingly shaped both by the social risk and economic opportunity brought about by globalisation. With the spread of neoliberalism, the political companion of globalisation, providing a competitive profit imperative in the global market, rebalancing the public/private spheres, the privatisation of public assets and services has gained momentum in the Western world. Predicated on a relationship between the State and the citizen in which the State retreats from the centralised provision of social welfare, in the context of the risk society, management of risk is transferred from the State to the individual, with a market created to provide the services and goods needed to provide individualised security. This marketisation of security provided the impetus for the development of the security industry: an industry that expanded and developed as new opportunities for private services emerged with the penal crisis of the 70s in US, and the 80s in UK and the normalisation of the outsourcing of penal services on both sides of the Atlantic.

With the penal crisis in the US in the 1970s, caused by New Right laws and order agenda which saw the prison population expand rapidly, outstripping the capacity of public prisons, the US government, in search of a fiscally efficient solution, looked to the private sector to provide new prisons and other associated innovative penal services (e.g. electronic tagging). Similarly, by the late 1980s, as overcrowding in the UK prisons reached its own crisis point, exemplified by prison unrest and riots, it was clear that something had to be done. With the planned expansion of the UK prison system seen as a costly exercise and the government keen to reduce the role of the State, the American experience provided a model for service provision to be emulated. Inviting the private sector to deliver punishment (a tried and tested delivery model in the US) represented a pragmatic, fiscally efficient means of delivering capacity more cheaply and more quickly. What is more, with American private penal providers already in place keen to expand their operations globally and the US and UK sharing ideological proximity and linked in a special relationship, importing American penal know-how, hardware and services alleviated the problems associated with building a home-grown service base from scratch.

Finally, with the establishment of the privatisation of penal services in UK in the late 1980s/90s, the privatisation dice was cast. The scene was set for further incursions into the criminal justice system. Indeed, as discussed in the following chapters, as privatisation moved from the margins of public policy to the centre, crossing traditional party political boundaries, one sector after another, aided and abetted by pro-privatisation politicians, fell under the private industry gaze. The criminal justice system was irrevocably transformed.

References

Aas, F. (2007) 'The Ad and the Form: Punitiveness and Cultural Change' in J. Pratt, D. Brown, M. Brown, S. Hallsworth and W. Morrison (eds) *The New Punitiveness: Trends, Theories, Perspectives*, Cullompton: Willan

Baker, E., and Roberts, J.V. (2005) 'Globalization and the New Punitiveness' in J. Pratt, D. Brown, M. Brown, S. Hallsworth and W. Morrison (eds) *The New Punitiveness: Trends, Theories, Perspectives*, Cullompton: Willan

Bauman, Z. (2001) 'Wars in the Global Era', *Journal of Social Policy* 4 (1): 11–28

Bauman, Z. (2006) *Globalization: The Human Consequences*, Cambridge: Polity Press

Beck, U. (1986) *Risikogesellschaft*, Frankfurt: Suhrkamp

Beck, U. (1992) *Risk Society: Towards a New Modernity*, London: Sage

Beck, U. (1999) *World Risk Society*, Cambridge: Polity Press

Beck, U. (2009) 'Critical Theory of World Risk Society: A Cosmopolitan Vision' *Constellations* 16 (1): 4–22

Braithwaite, J. (2000) 'The New Regulatory State and the Transformation of Criminology' *British Journal of Criminology* 40 (2): 222–238

Christie, N. (2003) *Crime Control as Industry: Towards GULAGs, Western Style?* (3rd edition) London: Routledge

Crawford, A. (2007) 'Crime Prevention and Community Safety' in M. Maguire, R. Morgan and R. Reiner (eds) *The Oxford Handbook of Criminology* (4th edition), Oxford: Oxford University Press

Currie, E. (2007) 'Against Marginality; Arguments for Public Criminology' *Theoretical Criminology* 11 (2): 175–190

Dolowitz, D.P. (2000) 'Policy Transfer: A Framework for Analysis' in D.P. Dolowitz, R. Hume, M. Nellis and F. O'Neil (eds) *Policy Transfer and British Social Policy*, Maidenhead: Open University Press

Dolowitz, D.P., and Marsh, D. (2000) 'Learning from Abroad: The Role of Policy Transfer in Contemporary Policy-Making' *Governance* 13 (1): 5–24

Downes, D., and Howard, M. (1976) 'Law and Order Futures' *Criminal Justice Matters* 26 (10): 3–5

Eisenberg, A. (2016) 'Incarceration Incentives in the Decarceration Era' *Vanderbilt Law Review* 69 (1): 71–136

Findlay, M. (2008) *Governing through Globalised Crime*, Cullompton: Willan

Garland, D. (1997) '"Governmentality" and the Problem of Crime: Foucault, Criminology, Sociology' *Theoretical Criminology* 1 (2): 173–214

Garland, D. (2000) 'The Culture of High Crime Societies' *British Journal of Criminology* 40 (3): 347–375

Garland, D. (2001) *The Culture of Control*, Oxford: Oxford University

Garland, D. (2003) *The Culture of Control (reprinted)*, Oxford: Oxford University Press

Giddens, A. (1990) *The Consequences of Modernity*, Stanford: Stanford University Press

Giddens, A. (2000) *Runaway World: How Globalization Is Reshaping Our World*, New York: Routledge

Hobbs, D. (2013) *Lush Life*, Oxford: Oxford University Press

Holloway, W., and Jefferson, T. (2005) 'The Risk Society in an Age of Anxiety: Situating the Fear of Crime' *British Journal of Sociology* 48 (2): 252–266. Reprinted in E. McLaughlin, J. Muncie and G. Hughes (eds) (1997) *Criminological Perspectives: Essential Readings* (2nd edition), Milton Keynes: Open University Press

Howard League for Penal Reform (2015) *Week by Week Prison Population Breakdown*, London: Howard League for Penal Reform www.howardleague.org/weekly-prison-watch/. Retrieved 5 November 2015

Hudson, B. (1993) *Penal and Social Justice*, London: Palgrave Macmillan

Hudson, B. (2003) *Justice in the Risk Society: Challenging and Reaffirming Justice in Late Modernity*, London: Sage

ICPR (2015) *World Prison Brief*, London: ICPR www.prisonstudies.org/country/united-kingdom-england-wales. Retrieved 5 November 2015

Jewkes, Y. (2004) *Media and Crime*, London: Sage
Johnston, L., and Shearing, C. (2003) *Governing Security*, London: Routledge
Jones, T. (2007) 'The Governance of Security: Pluralization, Privatization, and Polarization in Crime Control' in M. Maguire, R. Morgan and R. Reiner (eds) *The Oxford Handbook of Criminology* (4th edition), Oxford: Oxford University Press
Jones, T., and Newburn, T. (2002) 'Policy Convergence and Crime Control in the USA and UK' *Criminal Justice* 2 (2): 173–203
Jones, T., and Newburn, T. (2007) *Policy Transfer and Criminal Justice*, Maidenhead: Open University
Latour, B. (1993) *We Have Never Been Modern*, London: Harvester Wheatsheaf
Lilly, J.R., and Ball, R.A. (1993) 'Selling Justice: Will Electronic Monitoring Last?' *Northern Kentucky Law Review* 20 (2): 505–530
Lilly, J.R., and Deflem, M. (1996) 'Profit and Penality: An Analysis of the Corrections-Commercial Complex' *Crime and Delinquency* 42 (1): 3–20
Lilly, J.R., and Knepper, P. (1992) 'An International Perspective of Corrections' *Howard Journal* 31 (3): 174–191
Lilly, J.R., and Knepper, P. (1993) 'The Corrections-Commercial Complex' *Crime & Delinquency* 39 (2): 150–166
Loader, I. (1999) 'Consumer Culture and the Commodification of Policing and Security' *Sociology* 33 (2): 273–292
Loader, I. (2006) 'Fall of the "Platonic Guardians": Liberalism, Criminology and Political Responses to Crime in England and Wales' *British Journal of Criminology* 46 (4): 561–586
Loader, I. (2008) 'Why Penal Moderation', Discussion Paper from the Penal Moderation Working Group. Commission on English Prisons Today www.howardleague.org/fileadmin/howard_league/user/pdf/Commission/Why_penal_moderation.pdf. Retrieved 5 November 2015
Loader, I., and Sparks, R. (2007) 'Contemporary Landscapes of Crime, Order, and Control: Governance, Risk, and Globalization' in M. Maguire, R. Morgan and R. Reiner (eds) *The Oxford Handbook of Criminology* (4th edition), Oxford: Oxford University Press)
Lotke, E. (1996) 'The Prison-Industrial Complex' *Multinational Monitor*
Mann, M. (2013) *The Sources of Social Power: Volume 3, Global Empires and Revolution, 1890–1945*, New York: Cambridge
McMahon, W. (2007) 'New Labour—Social Transformation and Social Order' in R. Roberts and W. McMahon (eds) *Social Justice and Criminal Justice,* London: Centre for Criminal Justice Studies
Meyer, J., and O'Malley, P. (2005) 'Missing the Punitive Turn? Canadian Criminal Justice, "Balance", and Penal Modernism' in J. Pratt, D. Brown, M. Brown, S. Hallsworth and W. Morrison (eds) *The New Punitiveness: Trends, Theories, Perspectives*, Cullompton: Willan
Millie, A., Jacobson, J., and Hough, M. (2003) 'Understanding the Growth in the Prison Population in England and Wales' *Criminology and Criminal Justice* 3 (4): 369–387
Morgan, R. (2003) 'Thinking about the Demand for Probation Service' *Probation Journal* 50 (1): 7–19
Muncie, J. (2005) 'Globalisation of Crime Control: The Case of Youth and Juvenile Justice' *Theoretical Criminology* 9 (1): 35–64
Nathan, S. (2003a) 'Prison Privatization in the United Kingdom' in A. Coyle, A. Campbell and R. Neufeld (eds) *Capitalist Punishment: Privatization and Human Rights*, London: Zed Books
Nathan, S. (2003b) 'Private Prisons and Emerging Economies' in A. Coyle, A. Campbell and R. Neufeld (eds) *Capitalist Punishment: Privatization and Human Rights,* London: Zed Books

Nellis, M. (2000) 'Law and Order: The Electronic Monitoring of Offenders' in D. Dolowitz, R. Hume, M. Nellis and F. O'Neil (eds) *Policy Transfer and Social Justice*, Maidenhead: Open University Press

Nellis, M. (2018) 'Electronically Monitoring Offenders as "Coercive Connectivity": Commerce and Penality in Surveillance Capitalism' in T. Daems and B. Vander (eds) *Privatising Punishment in Europe*, London: Routledge

Newburn, T. (2002) 'Atlantic Crossings: Policy Transfer and Crime Control in USA and Britain' *Punishment and Society* 4 (2): 165–194

O'Malley, P. (1992) 'Risk, Power and Crime Prevention' *Economy and Society* 21 (3): 361–374

O'Malley, P. (2001) 'Risk, Crime and Prudentialism Revisited' in K. Stenson and R. R. Sullivan (eds) *Crime, Risk and Justice*, Willan: Cullompton

O' Malley, P. (2015) *Rethinking Neoliberal Penality*, Sydney Law School Research Paper No. 15/67, Sydney: University of Sydney

Osborne, D., and Gaebler, T. (1992) *Reinventing Government*, New York: Addison-Wesley

Passas, N. (2000) 'Global Anomie, Dysnomie and Economic Crime: Hidden Consequences of Globalisation in Russia and Around the World' *Social Justice* 27 (2): 16–43

Paterson, C. (2007) 'Commercial Crime Control and the Electronic Monitoring of Offenders in England and Wales' *Social Justice* 30 (3–4): 98–110

Pratt, J. (2005) 'Elias, Punishment and Decivilization' in J. Pratt, D. Brown, M. Brown, S. Hallsworth and W. Morrison (eds) *The New Punitiveness: Trends, Theories, Perspectives*, Cullompton: Willan

Pratt, J. (2006) *Penal Populism*, London: Routledge

Pratt, J., Brown, D., Brown, M., Hallsworth, S., and Morrison, W. (2005) 'Introduction' in J. Pratt, D. Brown, M. Brown, S. Hallsworth and W. Morrison (eds) *The New Punitiveness: Trends, Theories, Perspectives*, Cullompton: Willan

Prison Reform Trust (PRT) (2005) *Private Punishment: Who Profits*, London: PRT

Prison Reform Trust (PRT) (2014) 'Bromley Briefings Summer 2014' www.prisonreformtrust.org.uk/Portals/0/Documents/Prison%20the%20facts%20May%202014.pdf. Retrieved 5 November 2015

Quinney (1977) *Class, State and Crime*, New York: Longman

Robertson, R. (1995) 'Glocalisation: Time-Space and Homogeneity-Heterogeneity' in M. Featherstone, S. Lash and R. Robertson (eds) *Global Modernities*, London: Sage

Rose, N. (2000) 'Government and Control' in D. Garland and R. Sparks (eds) *Criminology and Social Theory*, Oxford: Oxford University Press

Ryan, M. (2005) 'Engaging with Punitive Attitudes Towards Crime and Punishment. Some Strategic Lessons from England and Wales' in J. Pratt, D. Brown, S. Hallsworth and W. Morrison (eds) *The New Punitiveness: Trends, Theories, Perspectives*, Cullompton: Willan

Ryan, M., and Ward, T. (1989) *Privatization and the Penal System: The American Experience and Debate in Britain*, New York: St Martin's Press

Savage, S., and Atkinson, R. (2001) 'Introduction: New Labour and Blairism' in S. Savage and R. Atkinson (eds) *Public Policy under Blair*, London: Palgrave Macmillan

Shelden, R. (1999) 'The Prison Industrial Complex and the New American Apartheid' *The Critical Criminologist* 10 (1): 1–10

Shelden, R. (2010) *The Prison Industry*, San Francisco: Centre on Juvenile and Criminal Justice

Shelden, R., and Brown, W. (2000) 'The Crime Control Industry and the Management of the Surplus Population' *Critical Criminology* 9 (1/2): 39–62

Shichor, D. (1995) *Punishment for Profit*, London: Sage

Sinden, J. (2003) 'The Problem of Prison Privatization: The US Experience' in A. Coyle, A. Campbell and R. Neufeld (eds) *Capitalist Punishment: Privatization and Human Rights*, London: Zed Books

Starr, P. (1989) 'The Meaning of Privatisation' (reprinted) in S. Kamerman and A. Kahn (eds) *Privatization and the Welfare State*, Princeton: Princeton University Press

Sullivan, R.R. (2001) 'The Schizophrenic State: Neo-Liberal Criminal Justice' in K. Stenson and R.R. Sullivan (eds) *Crime, Risk and Justice,* Willan: Cullompton

Tonry, M. (2001) 'Symbol, Substance and Severity in Western Penal Policies' *Punishment and Society* 3 (4): 517–536

Wacquant, L. (2001) 'The Penalisation of Poverty and the Rise of Neo-Liberalism' *European Journal of Criminal Policy and Research* 9 (4): 401–412

Wacquant, L. (2005) 'The Great Penal Leap Backward: Incarceration in America from Nixon and Clinton' in J. Pratt, D. Brown, M. Brown, S. Hallsworth and W. Morrison (eds) *The New Punitiveness: Trends, Theories, Perspectives*, Cullompton: Willan

Walklate, S., and Mythen, G. (2008) 'How Scared Are We?' *British Journal of Criminology* 48: 209–225

Wood, P. (2003) 'The Rise of the Private Prison Industrial Complex' in A. Coyle, A. Campbell and R. Neufeld (eds) *Capitalist Punishment: Privatization and Human Rights,* London: Zed Books

Zedner, L. (2000) 'The Pursuit of Security' in T. Hope and R. Sparks (eds) *Crime Risk and Insecurity*, Abingdon: Routledge

5
PUBLIC SECTOR OUTSOURCING, THE CONTRACT CULTURE AND THE MYTH OF THE REGULATORY STATE

> Without doubt, the state has its fair share of bureaucratic cruelty and incompetence. But the introduction of the profit motive and the lack of transparency about that never fails to add an element of scandal to these tragedies.
> (White, 2016)

Introduction

As privatisation has become the norm, the risks associated with the pursuit of the vision of marketisation that would 'liberate governments from the public sector monopoly, and enable them to provide lower cost, higher quality and better managed services' (Ludlow, 2017: 915) have become increasingly self-evident. One debacle after another has chipped away at the privatisation edifice, exposing what critics have known from the outset: that the risks/costs significantly outweigh the benefits. The privatisation illusion that the private sector can do more for less has been laid bare. With corner-cutting, poor performance, light-touch governance[1] (to encourage private sector investment), malpractice, negligence and on occasions culpable criminality all too familiar accompaniments of privatisation, democratic accountability and legitimacy are under threat (Padfield, 2016).

A case in point is the recent Grenfell Tower tragedy, condemned as 'social murder' by one commentator (Chakrabortty, 2017), which has demonstrates the horrific consequences that can arise from ideologically and fiscally driven political decisions to outsource social housing management and maintenance and privatise building inspection: policies that have created a 'race to the bottom' to reduce costs by downgrading building materials and curtailing the number of safety inspections carried out (Davies, 2017). With 'the cost and cosmetic façade of the tower block' outweighing safety and fire prevention considerations (O'Neil and Karim, 2017), and 'the refurbishment of Grenfell Tower contracted out to a private construction firm, Rydon, which in turn subcontracted some of the work', the disaster is illustrative of the lucrative 'rewards on offer to private firms from social housing' (Grierson and Siddique, 2017).

In relation to the criminal justice system, criminal negligence and mistreatment of offenders, mismanagement and fraudulent behaviour have all raised serious concerns about the operating practices of contractors, their public accountability and the level of public scrutiny to which they are subject. Although most instances of malfeasance escape the public gaze, even when there are high-profile scandals which attract international attention and force reputation-saving resignations by senior managers, the new public sector oligopoly of multi-national private contractors, taking advantage of government dependence upon them and systemic weaknesses within the contracting government departments, continues to flaunt both the spirit and the letter of their contracts, in the expectation that public censure will be short lived, and the political appetite for the expansion of private domain will remain unabated (G4S's litany of scandals is a case in point).[2] With the financial grip on non-protected departments (including the MOJ and The Home Office) tightened in the fulfilment of the austerity agenda, over claims by commercial sector, in particular the promise of cost cutting, ensured that the privatisation gravy train ran rampant.

The appeal of privatisation: cutting the costs and expanding control

With the 'rolling back of the state' an integral part of the neoliberal agenda, one of the early attractions of privatisation was the private sector's capacity for technological innovation. The prospect of reducing the fiscal burden of providing public services by outsourcing delivery to commercial providers willing to pursue cost cutting practices, in particular the adoption of new forms of technological surveillance and control, which could achieve 'economies of the present', reducing the size of the labour force and staffing expenditure, was politically and fiscally attractive. What is more, with surveillance and control labour intensive, technological forms of control that could enhance the State's ability to manage social groups deemed 'disorderly or at risk' at a fraction of the cost, offered a win-win for successive US and UK governments (Paterson, 2004: 8).

As early as 1967, the US president's Crime Control Commission promoted the role that private sector science and technology could play in combating crime. The commission stated:

> More than 200,000 scientists and engineers have applied themselves to solving military problems and hundreds of thousands more to innovation in other areas of modern life, but only a handful are working to control the crimes that injure or frighten millions of Americans each year. Science and

technology is a valuable source of knowledge and techniques for combating crime; the criminal justice system represents a vast area of challenging problems.

(as quoted in Shelden and Brown, 2000: 41)

In 1993, the Attorney General, Ford, advocating 'non lethal violence', called for a 'crucial crusade', which would galvanise the 'know how' of the defence industry, turning 'skills that had served us so well in the cold war to helping us with the war we're now fighting daily in the streets of our towns and cities across the nation' (Christie, 2003: 124). With crime control a labour-intensive enterprise, reliant on an individual police officer, prison guard or offender supervisor being in the right place at the right time, changes in technology (e.g. CCTV, electronic monitoring, remote bionic reporting booths, remotely opening prison doors) reduced the costs associated with having a 'body right there, in some specific location to establish the possibility of direct face-to-face contact' (Mitchell, 2000: 129).

With the private sector willing and able to fund and develop technological advances, governments on both sides of the pond, embracing the allure of technological solutions, looked to the private sector to provide the goods that could extend their control at a fraction of the cost: replacing social interaction with a less costly electronic equivalent. This preoccupation with the power of technology has ensured that at each stage of the criminal justice, from detection to imprisonment, electronically achieved cost effective decisions have been made about the 'degree of presence' needed to accomplish a particular task.

However, in the 'race to the bottom', in which companies compete to undercut each other to secure contracts, technological economies alone can only partially achieve service provision costs that will give the competitive edge. In order to outbid competitors, private companies are associated with paying lower salaries to their staff, providing less generous fringe benefits (such as pensions, holiday entitlement and sick leave), and reducing the numbers of professionally qualified staff, restricting training and increasing workloads. These measures, which impact staff morale and performance, have been increasingly identified in reports by government watchdogs as contributing to diminished service delivery. Sodexo, awarded contracts to provide probation supervision in six areas in 2015, exemplifies the service-delivery economies driven by price-competitive tendering. A multinational company with close American links,[3] Sodexo, shortly after being awarded its contract, in order to order to create a new streamlined work force operating under new conditions and terms of employment, circumvented the TUPE[4] employment regulations that preserve the terms and conditions of staff when a business is transferred to a new employer by issuing redundancy notices to nearly 40% of the staff transferred to it from the public service. This clear breach of employer responsibilities and undertakings left the staff still in employment struggling with disproportionately high workloads and inadequate IT systems, overwhelmed and stressed (NAPO, 2014).

The creation of a private owned, public sector oligopoly

Since its inception, the outsourcing of public services to private providers has both 'attracted and built giant corporations' (Froud et al., 2017: 79), creating 'privately owned monopolies, which largely, or in some cases wholly, rely on taxpayers' money for their income' (HOC, 2014: 3). As the pace and scope of privatisation have increased, the lucrative outsourcing market has provided the impetus for a small oligopoly of commercial providers to expand their business output, churning out a steady flow of contracts and diversifying their business operations into areas of provision of which they have little or no knowledge, understanding or acumen. A recent example of this is the disgraced Carillion corporation, which, starting life as a construction business, evolved into one of the biggest outsourcing conglomerates with a diverse range of contracts across different government departments, providing essential, sensitive services to hospitals, schools and prisons whilst simultaneously undertaking numerous high-profile public and private construction projects. such as HS2 and London Heathrow Terminal 5 (West, 2018: 42–43).

Whilst a central tenet of privatisation orthodoxy has been the benefits to the public and service users in terms of improved services and cost effectiveness afforded by creating market competition, one of the abiding features of expansion of the global market in privatised criminal justice has been the multitude of mergers and acquisitions that have reduced competition in the marketplace, pushing aside small, niche providers and consolidating the dominant position of a select few multinationals (Paterson, 2013): a development that has contributed to creation of what the National Audit Office has identified as a 'private owned, public sector monopoly' (NAO, 2013).

In 2013, the National Audit Office (NAO, 2013) published *Managing Government Suppliers*, a report into the role of the private contracts in the delivery of public services, which exposed the fallacy of competition, revealing that contracts for both frontline and back office services across government departments were disproportionately awarded to the 'big four' private contractors (Serco, G4S, Capita and Atos). A exclusive group of providers, who between them in accounting period 2012–2013 held government contracts worth £4 billion, with 'three quarters of the contract budget' concentrated in the hands of two companies(G4S and Serco) (White, 2016: 174). These four giant conglomerates, 'with the exception of Capita, a FTSE 100 company built virtually entirely from British outsourcing contracts, . . . have multinational portfolios' (Froud et al., 2017: 79.

With the financial, legal and contractual demands of mounting a successful bid prohibitive to smaller and medium-sized companies, and Whitehall departments favouring the usual suspect companies that they know, the market has contracted, dominated by an oligopoly of suppliers that attract contracts across the different departments, diversifying and expanding to garner the privatisation zeal of successive governments. Despite government claims to the contrary, the 2013 NAO report concluded that, rather than creating a diverse range of providers with the skills and knowledge to meet locally defined need, outsourcing had narrowed the range of successful competitors. With debt-fuelled mergers and buyouts by bigger companies a feature of the private providers' business model, on the rare occasions when smaller businesses, against the odds, do win contracts, the risk remains that they will be subsumed by a larger contractor, leading to a further consolidation of the market (NAO, 2013: 14).

In 2013, 23% of Ministry of Justice's (the mostly highly outsourced of all Whitehall departments) expenditure went to commercial providers. From an annual budget of £2,847 million, it awarded £303 million to G4S, £214 million to Serco, £107 million to Atos, and £23 million to Capita (NAO, 2013: 8). In 2014, Margaret Hodge, MP, chair of the House of Commons Public Accounts Committee, warned that in 'the absence of real competition . . . privately owned public monopolies which have become too big to fail' (HOC, 2014), effectively holding the government captive. With small suppliers possessing local knowledge providing bespoke service effectively squeezed out of the bidding process (HOC Justice Committee, 2011), the market, beset by secrecy and weak competition, all too frequently has the government over a barrel, exposed 'to huge delivery and financial risks should the supplier fail' (Garside, 2014). The lack of competition means that even when companies fail to fulfil their contractual obligations, the dearth of alternative suppliers results in their being awarded further contracts: 'failure is rewarded again and again because there are so few companies to choose from' (White, 2016).

Regulation, accountability and fraud

For proponents of the regulatory State perspective, one of the ironies of privatisation in the UK is that it has not led to withdrawal of State involvement; rather the regulatory mode of government has displaced the 'welfare state mode of government' (Loughlin and Scott, 1977: 2016), a shift that New Right purists argue is a 'temporary phenomenon, pending the achievement of truly free markets' (Drakeford, 2000: 27). They argue that despite the rhetoric, there has been a noteworthy reluctance to give private providers of public services the freedom to self-regulate and self-direct (Nellis, 2011). Even when an enterprise is sold to the private sector, this is not an 'end to questions about public control and accountability . . . "Privatisation" is not so much a retreat by the state, as a shift in modes of intervention from ownership (by the state) to regulation by the state' (Moran and Proser, 1994: 3). As Braithwaite (2000: 24) explains:

> Contrary to the Hayekian philosophy of Thatcherism, deregulation did not always go hand in hand with privatization. Rather we saw what a number of scholars have discussed as the 'rise of a new regulatory state'.

With 'privatization, outsourcing and the like actually requir[ing] more regulation not less' (Goodin et al., 2003: 17), State involvement has not been not eliminated; rather the reforms brought about by privatisation have been accompanied by considerable 'strengthening of central power' (Drakeford, 2000: 28) through the creation of a plethora of new regulatory bodies. In short, in the UK the free economy and the strong State have gone hand in hand. Either as the purchaser of services or the partner in financial arrangements, the State has sought to retain control and oversight through the imposition of contractual obligations and service-level agreements intended to ensure that private contractors adhere to the government of the day's political agenda. What is more, just as the contractual arrangements with purchasers tie providers to the prevailing policy agenda, changes in labour relations between private contractors and their workforces (with considerable weakening of workers' rights) reduce the risks of staff resistance to policy initiatives.

As Crawford (2006), employing the Osborne and Gaebler 'nautical analogy of the state', explains, the State, despite delegating the 'rowing' task of providing direct services to separate (private) organisations, has retained its regulatory role of 'governing by setting the course, monitoring the direction and correcting deviations from the course set' (2006: 453). Freed from direct provision, the State operates at 'a distance' overseeing, managing and 'steering' the activities of 'new' providers through the imposition of a range of performance management measures such as service-level agreements, contract, targets, audits and inspections that constitute 'regulating privatization' (Crawford, 2006; Crawford and Lewis, 2007). The attractions of separation are that the 'political agenda can be set at the centre', politicians, freed from the responsibility for service delivery and the tedium of everyday minutiae, can retain control by 'steering not rowing' (Deakin and Walsh, 1996: 5).

Nellis (2011) goes further, arguing that private providers as exemplified by electronic monitoring contractors are in effect 'co-opted as an arm of the state':

> The tightness of the contracts and the closeness of the scrutiny to which the commercial suppliers are subject does indicate that EM is ultimately controlled by government and that policy and practice is primarily shaped by the regulatory ethos of 'the managerial state' rather than by purely commercial imperatives. The contractors are well networked into wider global developments in security technology and telecommunications, can act as powerful advisers to government in terms of what is feasible and possible in EM, and can even stimulate innovation, but they are not running the show . . . EM contractors in Britain are not operating as independent competing businesses in a free market: they are, in effect, a duopoly functioning as part of the state.
> *(2011: 296)*

Whilst it is indubitably the case that contractors lack the commercial freedom afforded to traditional private enterprises and are in effect co-opted members of the State, commercial interests, exploiting the hold over governments afforded by their monopoly status, have become proficient at gaming both the procurement and delivery process. Consequently, Whitehall, in its rush to create a business friendly environment, found it increasingly difficult to maintain its authority: its grip has been loosened. Indeed, as governmental dependence on for-profit enterprises has become the norm, exacerbated by the sheer volume of contracts and service-level agreements, State officials' capacity to exert the level of regulatory control and managerial oversight envisaged in the managerial State model has been eroded. As the incidences of malfeasance (discussed later) demonstrate, businesses have become adept at bypassing the processes and procedures intended to keep them in check

The UK Corrections Commercial Complex: the blurring of boundaries between the State and commercial interests

The ever increasing incursion of business interests into the State has incrementally compromised the traditional separation of business interests and policy making: the boundaries between the two have become blurred, and cronyism has become endemic. Since the 1990s, the traditional Whitehall model has been usurped as part of an 'ideologically driven reduction in the status and responsibilities of the State, a triumph of the market State, and an acceptance of businesses elites as important partners of political elites' (Wilks, 2013: 62). The civil service, once the preserve of public servants, has been opened up to business, with individuals with commercial interests in promoting privatisation acquiring both top appointments and influential consultancy role. 'In the dark undergrowth of entanglements between commercial interests and government' (Rawnsley, 2021), business interests have increasingly encroached upon the body politic: the traditional Whitehall model of administrative discretion, due process and the 'ideals of public service' has been transformed (Wilks, 2013: 104).

With new privatisation and partnerships embedded in the State apparatus, a new 'public service industry' has emerged in which no area of public service delivery is immune to corporate penetration. Thanks to an emergent ideological hegemony, large multi-national corporations have assumed the mantle of effective political actors, increasing their political power and shaping both criminal justice policy and the delivery of criminal justice services to serve their commercial interests. As successive UK governments have abrogated responsibility for the delivery of their policy agenda to a small number of large corporations to (e.g. the awarding of the contract to reduce the numbers of claimants entitled to disability benefits to Atos), the emergent symbiotic relationship between policy makers and commercial interests in the UK exhibits features that resemble the US corrections commercial complex described by Lilly and colleagues.

In common with the US, private companies in the UK form part of the elite network of interest groups, lobbyists, advocacy coalitions and neoliberal think tanks, as well as ideologically like-minded politicians, government officials and journalists who have been highly successful in promoting public policy which reflects business and free market ideology, ensuring the expansion of the role played by commercial interests in delivering the government of the day's policy priorities. Mirroring the US, as privatisation has become the mainstay of successive UK governments of different political affiliations, the public and private domains have become increasingly co-dependent and enmeshed. As Froud *et al.* (2017) remind us:

> Public sector outsourcing extends private business into the sphere of state ownership and de-commodified state production in ways that bind together

the state with private interests. In high income economies, outsourcing has . . . created huge opportunities for big business and organised finance as franchised providers of . . . services.

(2017: 78)

The emergent privatisation political consensus as expressed through the scale and growth of the outsourcing State has normalised the convergence of government and commercial interests. As traditional boundaries have become thinned and blurred, the door between Whitehall and lucrative jobs in outsourcing businesses revolves ever smoothly. In this context, it can be argued that 'public policy in the UK increasingly reflects not the democratic will of the public, but the interests of a "corporate elite"' of wealthy business interests that control large companies and increasingly have 'colonised' the government policy realm (Wilks, 2015: 4).

The revolving door

A particularly pernicious contemporary feature of the UK variant of the corrections commercial complex is the 'revolving door' through which 'people from corporate background, with sympathies towards corporate interests revolve into government (in 2013/14, 30% of senior civil servant appointments were made that way), and through which civil servants and ministers recruited for their knowledge, are led out' (Wilks, 2015: 5–6). Moving in two directions, the 'revolving door' both spins company executives into Whitehall to sit on task forces and other committees where they can promote policies and regulatory enforcement that favour business interests and spins out an increasing number of public sector managers, civil servants and other government officials, including government ministers and mandarins, into private sector posts where they can financially benefit from expertise, know-how and connections developed in the public sphere. As Brooks and Hughes (2016) argue:

> The beauty of the revolving door is that it . . . removes all tension between the state and private sector with which it should deal objectively. Both sectors end up employing the same people and they think in the same way . . . Perhaps even more than lobbying and hospitality, the revolving door creates the uniformity of thinking between gamekeeper and poacher, purchaser and provider or even regulator and the regulated, that invariably ends in disasters, up to and including the financial crisis.
>
> *(2016: 24)*

Although successive governments, in the face of embarrassing scandals (e.g. the 'cash for question' in 1994), have taken some limited measures to 'clean up' the process[5] (most recently in opposition, Cameron condemned 'crony capitalism' and 'ex-ministers, and ex-advisers for hire, helping big business to find the right way to get their own way', extending the ban on ex-ministers and ex-mandarins lobbying the government from one year to two), as successive governments have pursued policies of forging closer links between the public sector and private business (Brooks and Hughes, 2016: 22), the 'flawed regulatory process'[6] means that little has been done in recent years to stem the flow of public service personnel joining the firms that they 'were, until recently, responsible for commissioning' (White, 2016: 198).

The advantages of the 'revolving door' for the private sector are considerable: the recruitment of staff from the public sector not only opens up lobbying conduits to the 'old-boy network' of former employers affording considerable competitive advantage in commercial negotiation with ministers and officials, but also provides a much sought after veneer of legitimacy to businesses whose range of global activities is at times highly controversial and not infrequently contravenes international agreements on human rights (Wood, 2003). In recent years the 'revolving out' has acted as 'an important source of mutual understanding and cross fertilisation', and the pace at which the door spins has accelerated (White, 2016).

'Revolving out' places individuals in a position whereby they can 'exert undue influence on their old colleagues or exploit information they gained when they were on the inside, to the (commercial) benefit of their new employer' (White, 2016: 198–199), bringing the transparency and integrity of tendering processes and contract procurement into disrepute. It also poses the risk that, in an abuse of office, ministers and civil servants whilst still in office curry favour with potential employers by 'giving a company preference treatment' (Wilks, 2015: 5). Regardless of these risks, between 2000 and 2014, the ACBA, the toothless Advisory Committee on Business Appointments, approved 1,020 business appointments for ministers and top-level civil servants (Wilks, 2015: 15).

In the criminal justice field (as elsewhere), as terms and conditions of employment have deteriorated and job security has been reduced as part of the austerity agenda, enforced retirements, redundancies and the amalgamation of services and posts have made 'revolving out' increasingly attractive for public employees. Indeed, with gamekeepers happy to turn poachers, the active recruitment by private companies of staff from the public sector with privileged, insider knowledge has been accompanied by considerable financial inducements for those seeking to carve out second careers, often supplementing pensions or other payments from the public purse. In the 'revolving out' process the big four providers have been major beneficiaries, enhancing their capacity to attract new contracts.

Noteworthy case examples of 'revolving out' include John Reid, former Labour home secretary, who joined G4S in 2009; Phil Wheatley, the former head of NOMs, who joined G4S in 2010; Tom Wheatley (the son of Phil Wheatley), former prison governor at HMP Nottingham and HMP Moorland, who joined G4S in 2010 (Corporate Watch, 2012); Roger Hill, the former Director of Probation and a NOM commissioner of private service, who joined Sodexo in 2011 as they prepared their bid for probation contracts (Brown, 2011); and former police commissioner John Stevens, who from 2000–2005 served on numerous boards of companies bidding to provide traditional police services. In August 2015, it came to light that Sir Martin Narey, previously the Director General of Prisons, was receiving payments as a consultant for G4S at the time that an independent report to the Youth Justice Board exonerating the Rainsbrook Secure Training Centre in the wake of a excoriating report by Ofsted, HM Inspector of Prisons and the Care Quality Commission that condemned its failings was being compiled (White, 2016).

In November 2015 Nick Gargan, the former Chief Constable of Avon and Somerset (he resigned his post in October 2015 following a disciplinary process that found him guilty of eight counts of misconduct), signed a four month contract with G4S as programme director (Peachey, 2015). Additionally, probably the most controversial appointment was that of Malcolm Stevens to Group 4 Rebound Ltd. as operations director in the 12 months before the opening in 2008 of the Medway Special Training Centre, a young offenders' centre which has been recently returned to the public sector after staff were arrested for the mistreatment of the children and abuse of public office. As a senior civil servant, Stevens had drawn up the blueprint for the STC, and such was the sensitivity of his appointment that it had to be referred to the Cabinet Office for approval. Despite the fact that his entire job in the Home Office and Department of Health had involved decisions about who should be placed in STCs (each place cost £125,000 a year), and that real concerns were voiced that his insider knowledge of bid preparation and tendering was being exploited for 'commercial advantage' (Hattersone and Allison, 2016), the appointment was approved.

Think tanks

As well as recruiting staff from the public sector, commercial providers increasingly benefit from the expansion of the expert governance network to include right wing think tanks advocating the outsourcing of public services to private contractors, such as Reform,[7] which, despite claims of independence, counts three of the 'big four' providers (G4S, Serco and Sodexo) among its 'corporate partners', as well as Policy Exchange, Centre for Social Justice and Centre for Crime Prevention. Since the 1980s, with the decline in the influence of the traditional penal experts (senior civil servants, academics and penal reformers), a marketplace in research has emerged (Hobbs and Hamerton, 2014), in which right leaning think tanks (aided and abetted by private company sponsors [White, 2016]), under the guise of political neutrality, publishing and disseminating 'research reports', have flourished. With the 'narrowing of the range of (academic) knowledge . . . admitted as policy-relevant' (Morgan and Hough, 2008: 60) and the expansion of expert governance networks, the 'research' produced by think tanks, frequently headed up by former or serving ministers (the Centre for Social Justice was established in 2004 by Ian Duncan Smith, the former leader of the Conservative Party), has been afforded greater status (Hope, 2004; Hammersley, 2005), providing both an influential and lucrative conduit through which corporations with a vested interest in the privatisation of criminal justice can promote ideas and policy initiatives that serve their commercial interests. Indeed, such is the importance of the think task to policy makers that in 2013 Francis Maude, the then minister for the Cabinet Office, went so far as to suggest that all government policy making should be outsourced to them (White, 2013).

Insider groups

Finally, with privatisation policies mainstreamed by both of the main political parties, successive governments have become increasingly dependent on private industry, in particular the large multi-national businesses that dominate the sector. One of the consequences of their market strength and ideological proximity to government is that, despite being traditionally seen as outside the 'closed world' of penal policy making (Jones and Newburn, 2007), the oligopoly of multi-national companies that dominate the provision of previously publicly delivered services have been able to reposition themselves, moving from the outside to the inside of the policy making process. As an insider group they enjoy 'close, consultative relationships with ministers and government departments' (Savage and Charman, 2010: 446), benefit from privileged access to the executive and have a much better chance of affecting policy making than those of the 'outsider group' (Page, 1999). Between 2010 and 2013, G4S, one of the largest providers of services to the Ministry of Justice and the Home Office, despite claims by Reform that it was 'left out of the Whitehall policy discussion', held 17 meetings with ministers (White, 2013).

Recent examples of the insider status of corporate interests include both Roger Hill, Director of Community and Partnerships at Sodexo, and Peter Neden, a managing director of G4S, appearing among the group of 'experts' that included senior academics, senior police and probation staff, directors of penal reform groups and government ministers who were invited to present oral evidence to the House of Common's Justice Select Committee on Transforming Rehabilitation (HOC, 2011): a committee that was tasked to make recommendations on the privatisation of probation services. Although in the event G4S, as a consequence of the tagging scandal, had to withdraw from bidding for contracts to deliver probation services, Sodexo, with the charity Nacro playing second fiddle, was awarded 6 of the 21 community rehabilitation company contracts, making it the biggest single supplier.

Fault lines in the 'regulatory' apparatus: poor governance

As Edmiston (2014) points out, 'in a somewhat self-defeating logic', the regulation of privatised services 'can only be granted by the state', and even then the extent and mode of control is determined by what Blomqvist (2004) has identified as 'the choices of policy makers, for example with respect to the financial conditions and legal restraints under which private actors are allowed to operate' (2004: 152–153). Outsourcing is dependent on a contract between the State and private companies: a process that 'represents a complex interweaving of power with uncertain outcomes'. The process is fraught with problems and 'frequently goes wrong, with fiascos creating political embarrassment for states and financial problems' (Froud et al., 2017: 77).

Whilst it is irrefutable that privatisation spawned a plethora of different regulatory systems, as the scope, speed and scale of privatisation have ratcheted up, concessions that favour industry have proliferated, and fault lines in the governance system have been exposed. The fault lines that businesses exploit include: less than coherent configuration of divergent service-level agreements, contract targets and audits; the watering down of inspection legislation and standards; the withdrawal of funding from inspections; the pressure on inspectors not to enforce; the replacement of qualified with less qualified regulators; the increasing outsourcing of inspection and regulation to the private sector;[8] and the introduction of the controversial 'black box' procurement system, whereby the invitation to tender, devoid of 'detailed prescription of service provision by central government', affords private contractors operational freedom to design and deliver services as they deem fit, so long as the overall policy objective is met, coupled with 'light touch' scrutiny[9] of the actual service delivered (Grayling's Work Programme and the Probation Service part privatisation were both subjects of 'black box' contracts) (Finn, 2013: 4).

What is more, a lack of commercial knowledge, skills and curiosity on the part of civil servants has led to the poor procurement and oversight of contracts: a situation which has gifted business the upper hand in both negotiation and management contracts and has created an environment in which 'there is a lack of useful information in Government', effecting a 'blind reliance on what companies tell the government, instead of a genuine exchange of information and a continual appraisal of the contractor's performance over the life time of the contract' (HOC, PACAC, 2018: 4). This is compounded by big companies' capacity to hide their performance and value for money 'behind the cloak of commercial confidentiality' (Trade Union Co-Ordinating Group, 2013: 35). With the 'Chinese walls between companies and the Whitehall officials who contract them too often paper thin' (White, 2016), and a 'revolving door' that provides unfettered access to a lucrative business career, an all too cosy cronyism between the Whitehall purchaser and the private provider, exacerbated by collusive auditors,[10] has developed. As Carillion exemplifies, all too often contractors have acted in their own interests with few constraints and little/no consideration of the impact on the public to whom a service is due. Nebulous lines of responsibility, lax oversight and a lack of transparency have left government tasked with repairing and managing the political and/or financial fallout from contractual failure: failure that they were supposed to prevent.

Contract non-compliance and underperformance are to a significant extent the inevitable byproducts of the 'race to the bottom' created by a price-competitive market. With price, not value for money, the key determinant, there is an inbuilt incentive for private contractors to overstate their case to secure the contract, and, in the knowledge that the price agreed on will lead to a default on some aspect of the contract delivery, to even factor in the payment of fines or the loss of performance bonuses. As discussed in a previous chapter, gaming the procurement process is endemic to the system. As cost cutting has become the number one policy priority, private contractors, reliant on public sector contracts, and Whitehall procurers, constrained by budgetary cuts, have been caught up in a cycle of underfunding, undercutting and underpricing: a 'race to the bottom' in which providers, aware that a procurement process structured on a most economically advantageous tenders process rewards the cheapest bidder, game the procurement process to gain advantage over competitors in the expectation that when delivery costs outstrip the bid, government departments, dependent on the private sector to deliver its services, are faced with three options: to let the contractor hand the contract back, to terminate the contract early (a fiscally and politically expensive option) or to bail the contractor out by paying it enough to fulfil its contractual obligations. Options which favour business at the expense of the public, the service user and the Treasury. The price imperative means that

> [o]utsourcers have been squeezed by the need to provide services more cheaply . . . The first time a government outsources . . . it is relatively easy for someone to make savings, to do it more cheaply . . . [however] . . . when the contract comes up for retender, you have to bid cheaper than you did the first time you did it, so you get downward pressure on prices.
>
> (Davies, 2018b)

Although government contracts are a lucrative source of income, with some outsourcing companies wholly dependent on this source of income, the consequence of the downward spiral on prices is that companies can become overstretched and unable to fulfil their contracts. Despite the fact that since 2016, the government has been forced to renegotiate more than £120m of contracts to maintain public services, with contracts awarded on the basis of cost, not quality, in the 'race to the bottom', businesses, undercutting the actual cost of delivering the service, can become overwhelmed and even when bailed out by the Treasury can collapse under mounting debts (Weardon, 2018). The recent collapse of three outsourcing firms, Carillion, Interserve and Working Links, is proof of the long-term costs to staff, subcontractors and suppliers, service users and the public purse of short-term financial expediency.

Rewarding failure: the power of the 'big four'

Although the recent collapses have been a wakeup call, an oligopoly of private contractors, banking on government's growing dependence on their services, has built overclaiming what is possible (gaming the procurement process) and misrepresenting what has been achieved (gaming the delivery system) into the privatisation business model. The operational activities of private industries have been beset with corner cutting, contract non-compliance and financially risky behaviour in the expectation that not only will government seek to avoid the fiscal and political costs associated with terminating contracts early by bailing firms out (see earlier chapter), but also that, even when substantial sanctions are imposed following high-profile debacles (such as the army providing 3,500 personnel to act as security guards at the Olympics when G4S failed to fulfil their contract) or financial scandals (such as G4S and Serco overcharging for EM), the privatisation gravy train may temporarily stall[11] but will not be derailed.

Companies debarred from tendering for one contract as a consequence of misdoing have been able to take for granted that this will be only a temporary censure and that there will be every likelihood that, in the absence of alternative providers, they will be able re-enter the contractual fold at a later date. Indeed, in the case of G4S and Serco, when the companies were facing fraud charges and their contracts for delivering EM had supposedly been removed, it came to light that they were continuing to receive payments for supplying EM tags because the Ministry of Justice, despite initially offering and then quickly rescinding the contract to technology firm Buddi, had 'failed to find a suitable firm to provide the equipment'(White, 2016: 212–213).

Although ministers may take a sharp intake of breath and pronounce that they 'can't always rely on the private sector' (Wright, 2012), ideologically and politically driven privatisation carries on apace, and multi-national commercial providers with large and diverse portfolios can rest assured that another contract awaits just around the global corner. A case in point is G4S, which, after being barred for six months from bidding for government contracts following the 'tagging debacle', was (once the ban was lifted in April 2014) awarded a contract to manage work placements for long-term unemployed from the Department of Work and Pensions, and had its contract to run Rainsbrook Secure Training Centre renewed (Moulds, 2014). In the event, the contact was withdrawn in the following year as a consequence of an excoriating Ofsted report highlighting poor care, poor management and '[p]oor staff behaviour (which) has led to some young people being subject to degrading treatment, racist comments, and being cared for by staff who were under the influence of illegal drugs' (Ofsted, 2015: 8).

As recent reports by the NAO and the House of Commons Public Accounts Committee have identified, poorly drawn-up contracts, as well as lax oversight and enforcement of contract compliance, have created opportunities for private companies to avoid sanction for poor performance and to engage in fraudulent behaviour. They concluded that failure by government departments to identify and act on instances of poor performance has cost the public purse. In 2008, a value for money survey of private contractors conducted by the NAO (2008) pointed out:

> While there are examples of good practice, central government's management of service contracts is not consistently delivering value for money. Nearly all the organisations we surveyed thought that value for money could be improved through better contract management, in terms of more or better services, and/or lower costs. Based on the survey, we estimate that better contract management could potentially generate efficiency savings of between £160 million and £290 million a year across the organisations we surveyed through reduced contract expenditure, and this may well be a conservative figure as it is based on estimates the organisations themselves provided in our survey. As well as financial savings, better contract management

could bring improvements in the quantity and/or quality of services, the avoidance of service failure, and better management of risk.

(2008: 8)

Similar findings were reached by the House of Commons Committee of Public Accounts in 2014, following a series of high-profile cases in which some private companies not only failed spectacularly to meet their contractual obligations in terms of performance, but also overcharged respective Whitehall departments for their services. Examples cited in the report included the poor performance of G4S in supplying security guards for the Olympics, which resulted in a very public bailout by the army, Capita's failure to deliver court translation services, and issues with Atos's work capability assessments, as well as the submission of fraudulent claims for services that had not been delivered, including misreporting of out of hours GP services by Serco and years of overcharging by G4S and Serco on electronic tagging contracts. With concern expressed by penal reformers and trade unionists that 'accelerating privatisation' in the run up to the 2015 election meant that the conservative Minister of Justice, fearing a change of administration, was signing government contracts with undue haste in the hope of thwarting the plans of the incoming government (NAPO, 2015), a report compiled by NAPO in 2014 drew attention to fundamental weaknesses in the procurement of services, the failure of central government to 'adequately protect the taxpayer and citizens' interest in the writing of contracts', as well as a lack of vigilance in respect of 'contractors' operations and delivery of services to users'.

Citing a tendency to make managing contractors' performance overly complicated by imposing multiple targets, and a failure of contract managers to consistently apply sanctions for contract non-compliance, the report was particularly scathing regarding the 'scandalous' overcharging of the taxpayer by tens of millions of pounds for electronic tagging, which had gone undetected for eight years. Recommending investment in 'developing experience and expertise in commercial issues and contract management', as well ensuring that those 'who are responsible for day-to-day contract management have sufficient authority, commercial skills and experience', the report concluded:

> The rapid growth in public sector business by some contractors, often achieved through acquisitions, has in some cases outpaced their ability to keep tight controls over all aspects of their government funded business; and, in turn, government bodies have not done enough to gain assurance that contractors have adequate governance and internal controls.
>
> *(NAPO, 2014: 6–7)*

Carillion collapse

Although 'examples of private sector incompetence are legion' (the fitting of a 'tag' to a prisoner's false leg was one of the more amusing incidents) (The Trade

Union Co-Ordinating Group, 2013: 4), and privatisation has from its early days been bedevilled by scandals, crises and expensive failures, these have in the main been contained, confined to one sector, and have attracted little or no public attention. With the exception of the G4S Olympic debacle, where there was wide media coverage, this has been restricted to a few columns in the inside pages of redtop papers. Notwithstanding this, in January 2018, an outsourcing and PFI crisis erupted which eclipsed all others. Carillion, one of the largest PFI construction companies as well as a major outsourcing company with contracts across a wide range of government departments (e.g. defence, education and justice), despite efforts by the government to keep it afloat by awarding new outsourcing contracts after it announced a profit warning in July 2017, went into liquidation with 'liabilities of nearly £7 billion and just £29 million in cash' (HOC, 2018: 7): an example of what happens when a 'too big to fail' company fails.

Through a series of debt-fuelled mergers and acquisitions, at the point of its collapse, Carillion, whose attitude towards executive pay and shareholder dividends was as misaligned from the 'public interest as . . . could be' (Innes, 2018), was in effect one of the biggest recipients of public funding, managing a huge variety of public sector projects, from the rebuilding of Battersea Power Station to the cleaning and building maintenance of 50 prisons (HOC, 2018). With tentacles reaching into the deepest recesses of Whitehall, the sheer size and scope of its operations, and the unprecedented expense of its failure, mean that it has become the prophetic example of not only what happens when a 'too big to fail' company fails, but also what happens when underbidding becomes the business model and investor dividends and directors' bonuses are given precedence.

Although the company published 'rosy accounts' of its 2016 activities in March 2017, and in the months before its collapse paid 'a record dividend of £79 million and large bonuses to senior executives for performance in 2016' (HOC, 2018: 7)—£55 million was paid out in June 2017—the subsequent report by the Business, Energy and Industrial Strategy and Work and Pensions Committees excoriated not only the reckless business model adopted and the lamentable State of corporate governance, but also the complicity of the big four accountancy firms (HOC, 2018). The report stated:

> Its business model was a relentless dash for cash, driven by acquisitions, rising debt, expansion into new markets and exploitation of suppliers. It presented accounts that misrepresented the reality of the business, and increased its dividends every year, come what may. Long term obligations, such as adequately funding pension schemes, were treated with contempt. Even as the company very publicly began to unravel, the board was concerned with increasing and protecting generous executive bonuses.
>
> *(2018: 3)*

If this was not sufficient to condemn PFI as a costly failure, in July 2018 the HOC Public Administration and Constitutional Affairs Committee produced its own findings on the Carillion collapse, which underscored the 'folly of using contractors to drive down costs'. The report concluded that the procurement system, driven by price, was fundamentally flawed. The prioritising of cost had exposed contactors to excessive risk, jeopardising the quality of services delivered (Weardon, 2018).

Whilst other scandals have come and gone, the enormity of the collapse of a company which has become synonymous with 'recklessness, hubris and greed' (HOC, 2018: 3), and its ramifications for suppliers, service users and workers who have lost their jobs and risk losing their pensions, temporarily ignited a debate about privatisation: a debate which was further inflamed by the collapse of Working Links and Interserve (one of the big four). With the government paying out £150 million to date to keep essential services running in the face of contract default (HOC, 2018), and public sector providers clawing back control of privately provided services by bringing services back in house to mitigate the impact on service users (the MOJ created a new government owned company to take over the delivery of prison services), a debate about the provision of public services that not restricted to the usual liberal voices has exploded into the public realm.

Conclusion

Although private ownership and competitive markets are 'normally thought to go hand in hand' in the neoliberal State, with competition welcomed by neoliberal proponents as the 'critical spur' to cost effectiveness and efficiency, recent developments in the UK suggest that 'ownership and market structure are often separate' (Starr, 1989: 27). Indeed, as privatisation has increased in scope and scale, an oligopoly of private providers of public services has emerged that militates against competition. With governments held captive by a cartel of multi-national providers that are that are 'too big to fail', a 'Shadow State' (White, 2016) has emerged.

As recent scandals have demonstrated, balancing the risks/benefits in favour of the public requires robust, transparent and accountable internal and external governance. However, as the sheer volume of contracts awarded has outstripped the capacity of civil servants to enforce the necessary checks and balances, the lines between the State and business have become blurred, and a culture of complacency and cronyism has developed in which regulatory oversight has been compromised. Ideological adherence to market fundamentalist theory has left successive governments inured to the reality that outsourcing is more flawed the more complex the task and the more uncertain the contingencies. As Innes, writing in 2008, before the Carillion debacle and the Grenfell tragedy, asked:

> [N]ot only is a lot of outsourcing conducted in markets characterised by monopoly and oligopoly, the impossibility of writing 'complete' long term contracts that cover all eventualities means that both the competitive pressures on performance and buyers control are weak . . . How many failures

will it take to prove that really existing public services are a far cry from the paradigm of competitive efficiencies in performances?

Notes

1 Although deregulation is primarily associated with Thatcher, there was no *volte-face* under New Labour. In accordance with the Third Way agenda, in 2005 Gordon Brown, the chancellor, keen to prove New Labour's pro-business credentials, proposed to crack down on red tape about boring stuff like health and safety standards that got in the way of profit-making. 'No inspection without justification, no form filling without justification, and no information requirements without justification, not just a light touch but a limited touch'. He also called for 'light touch regulation', in other words less regulation on the city and finance capital.
2 Since 2010 G4S alone has been the organisation running facilities and services: associated with the death by restraint of deportee Jimmy Mubenga—staff were charged with manslaughter (2010); tagging overcharging (2013); gross misconduct at Rainsbrook, a secure training unit—s6 members of staff were dismissed (2015); suspension or sacking of 11 staff at Medway STU for inappropriate restraint of inmates and falsifying records (2016); riots at HMP Birmingham (2016); and the stepping in of public-sector managers to run HMP Birmingham after HMI evoked the urgent notification process.
3 Sodexo was launched in France in 1966 as a catering company serving hospitals, schools and staff restaurants. In 1997, the group's holding company changed its name to Sodexho. In the same year Sodexho joined forces with Universal Ogden Services, the leading remote site service provider in the United States.
4 TUPE is an acronym for the Transfer of Undertakings (Protection of Employment) Regulations 1981.
5 In 1994 in response to the cash for questions scandal, the then–prime minister, Major, set up the Commission on Public Life to tighten up the regulation of what Gordon Brown called 'jobs for the boys'. In relation to the 'revolving door', Major extended to ministers the requirement that applied to civil servants to submit their applications to join the private sector to the Advisory Committee on Business Appointments, a weak and under-resourced body with no monitoring powers that cannot check if former ministers and civil servants are abiding by its rulings (White, 2016).
6 The government regulator, which oversees the appointments to the private sector of public officials, provides a solely advisory role, has little/no power of sanctions, is biased in favour of approval of applications by ministers and senior civil servants to join the private sector and applies only to ministers and the most senior civil servants (e.g. NHS and local government officials are exempt) (Wilks, 2015: 5).
7 In 2013 Reform, established in 2001 by Nick Herbert, currently a Conservative MP, and Andrew Haldenby (former director of studies at the Centre for Policy Studies and head of the Political Section of the Conservative Research Department) produced an 'independent' report entitled *The Case for Private Prisons*, which suggested private prisons offer better value for money and lower reoffending rates, an argument which was disputed by the Prison Reform Trust and was even described as highly selective and simplistic by the then–prisons minister, Jeremy Wright. It had previously produced reports promoting the benefits of privately run custody suites and recommending the idea of G4S 'bobbies on the beat' (these reports were given favourable coverage in the *Times* and the *Telegraph* [White, 2013]).
8 The Grenfell fire investigation received evidence that while building inspections had been the responsibility of the fire service, this had been privatised and regulations relaxed to facilitate light-touch inspections.

9 In 2010 the Dept. of Work and Pensions announced that Ofsted, the independent regulator, would no longer inspect the Work to Welfare programme. Instead the remit of DWP's own provider assurance teams was extended to cover, 'in a light touch way', some of the quality issues that formed part of the external inspections
10 Early findings in relation to the Carillion collapse indicated that auditors had failed to disclose the real state of the business's perilous financial position, giving rise to concerns that they were in collusion with the firm. With KPM criticised by the parliamentary committee for signing off accounts prior to its collapse, in January 2018 the head of the Financial Reporting Council called for an investigation into whether the Big Four accounting firms should be broken up in the wake of Carillion's collapse, amid concerns that auditors failed to spot major financial malpractice at the contractor.
11 Despite some police forces revising their plans to outsource custody suite provision to G4S in 2012/13, in November 2015 Leicestershire Police announced proposals to merge the 999 control room with neighbouring forces in Nottinghamshire and Northamptonshire—and outsource it to private security firm G4S—as a way of saving money.

References

Blomqvist, P. (2004) 'The Choice Revolution: Privatization of Swedish Welfare Services in the 1990s' *Social Policy & Administration* 38 (2): 139–155

Braithwaite, J. (2000) 'The New Regulatory State and the Transformation of Criminology' *British Journal of Criminology* 40 (2): 222–238

Brooks, R., and Hughes, S. (2016, September 2) 'Public Servants and Private Paydays' *Private Eye* 1426

Brown, J. (2011) 'Roger and Out' http://probationmatters.blogspot.co.uk/2011/03/roger-and-out.html. Retrieved 6 December 2015

Chakrabortty, A. (2017, June 20) 'Over 170 Years after Engles, Britain Is Still a Country that Murders Its Poor' *The Guardian*

Christie, N. (2003) *Crime Control as Industry: Towards GULAGs, Western Style?* (3rd edition) London: Routledge

Corporate Watch (2012) *G4S: A Company Profile,* London: Corporate Watch

Crawford, A. (2006) 'Networked Governance and the Post-Regulatory State? Steering, Rowing and Anchoring the Provision of Policing and Security' *Theoretical Criminology* 10 (4): 449–479

Crawford, A., and Lewis, S. (2007) 'Global Processes: National Trends and Local Justice: The Effects of Neo-Liberalism on Youth Justice in England and Wales (translated from French)' in F. Bailleau and Y. Cartuyvels (eds) *Les Evolutions Entre Modèle Welfare et Inflexions Neo-Liberales,* Paris: L'Harmattan

Davies, R. (2017, June 16) 'Complex Chain of Companies That Worked on Grenfell Tower Raises Oversight Concerns' *The Guardian*

Davies, R. (2018, February 1) 'Prognosis for Outsourcing Sector Is Poor as Capita Joins the List of Troubled Firms' *The Guardian*

Deakin, N., and Walsh, K. (1996) 'The Enabling State: The Role of Markets and Contracts' *Public Administration* 47 (1): 33–34

Drakeford, M. (2000) *Privatisation and Social Policy,* Harlow: Longman

Edmiston, D. (2014) 'Social Security Privatisation in the UK' *People, Place and Policy* 8 (2): 113–128

Finn, D. (2013) *The Design and Delivery of 'Payment-By-Results' and 'Black Box' Contracts: The Case of the UK Work Programme,* Portsmouth: ICJS University of Portsmouth

Froud, J., Johal, S., Moran, M., and Williams, K. (2017) 'Outsourcing the State: New Source of Elite Power' *Theory Society and Culture* 34 (5–6): 77–101

Garside, R. (2014, March 17) 'This Market Isn't Working. UK Government Contractors Exploit Secrecy and Weak Competition' *Open Democracy UK* online

Goodin, R., Rein, M., and Moran, M. (2003) 'The Public and Its Policies' in M. Moran, M. Rein and R. Goodin (eds) *The Oxford Handbook of Public Policy*, Oxford: Oxford University Press

Grierson, J., and Siddique, H. (2017, June 30) 'Grenfell Tower Management Company Chief Quits to "Focus on Inquiry"' *The Guardian*

Hammersley, M. (2005) 'Is the Evidence-Based Practice Movement Doing More Good Than Harm? Reflections on Iain Chalmers' Case for Research-Based Policy Making and Practice' *Evidence & Policy* 1 (1): 85–100

Hatterstone, S., and Allison, E. (2016, February 26) 'G4S Youth Jails: A Story of Revolving Doors, Dangerous Restraints and Death' *The Guardian*

Hobbs, S., and Hamerton, C. (2014) *The Making of Criminal Justice Policy*, Oxford: Routledge

Hope, T. (2004) 'Pretend it Works: Evidence and Governance in Evaluation of the Research Burglary Initiative' *Criminology and Criminal Justice* 4 (3): 287–308

House of Commons (2014) *Contracting out Public Services to the Private Sector*, London: HMSO

House of Commons (2018) *Carillion. Second Joint Report from the Business, Energy and Industrial Strategy and Work and Pensions*, London: Parliament Publications

House of Commons Justice Committee (2011) *The Role of the Probation Service*, London: HMSO

House of Commons, Public Administration and Constitutional Affairs Committee (2018) *After Carillion: Public Sector Outsourcing and Contracts*, London: HMSO

Innes, A. (2018, February 5) 'Risks of Outsourcing Have Been Laid Bare' *The Guardian*

Jones, T., and Newburn, T. (2007) *Policy Transfer and Criminal Justice*, Maidenhead: Open University

Loughlin, M., and Scott, V.C. (1977) 'The Regulatory State' in P. Dunleavy, A. Gamble, I. Holliday and G. Peele (eds) *Developments in British Politics*, London: Palgrave Macmillan

Ludlow, A. (2017) 'Marketizing Criminal Justice' in A. Liebling, S. Maruna and L. McAra (eds) *The Oxford Handbook of Criminology* (6th edition), Oxford: Oxford University Press

Mitchell, W. (2000) *E-topia: "Urban Life, Jim—But Not as We Know It"*, Cambridge, MA: MIT Press

Moran, M., and Proser, T. (1994) *Privatisation and Regulatory Change in Europe*, Bucks: Open University Press

Morgan, R., and Hough, M. (2008) 'The Politics of Criminological Research' in R. King and E. Wincup (eds) *Doing Research in Crime and Justice* (2nd edition), Oxford: Oxford University Press

Moulds, J. (2014, August 13) 'G4S Revenues Bounce Back from Prisoner-Tagging Scandal' *The Guardian*

NAO (2008) *Central Government's Management of Service Contracts*, London: NAO

NAO (2013) *The Role of Major Contractors in the Delivery of Public Services*, London: NAO

NAPO (2014) *Probation Transforming Rehabilitation Concerns*, London: NAPO

NAPO (2015) *Probation Union Anger at Justice Secretary Signing Off Probation Outsourcing Contracts*, London: NAPO

Nellis, M. (2011) 'The Complicated Business of Electronic Monitoring' in R. Taylor, M. Hill and F. MacNeil (eds) *Early Professional Development for Social Workers*, Birmingham: Venure Press/BASW

Ofsted (2015) 'Inspection of Rainsbrook Secure Training Centre: February 2015' http://reports.ofsted.gov.uk/sites/default/files/documents/secure-training-centre-reports/rainsbrook/Rainsbrook%20STC%20Ofsted%20report%20February%202015%20%28PDF%29.pdf. Retrieved 10 March 2016

O'Neil, S., and Karim, F. (2017, June 30) 'Keep Costs of Cladding Down, Grenfell Tower Experts Told' *The Times*

Padfield, N. (2016) 'The Magnitude of the Offender Rehabilitation and "Through the Gate" Resettlement Revolution' *Criminal Law Review* 2: 98–114

Page, E. (1999) 'The Insider Outsider Distinction: An Empirical Investigation' *The British Journal of Politics and International Relations* 1 (2): 205–214.

Paterson, C. (2004) 'Technocorrections' and the Future of Crime Control' *Criminal Justice Matters* 58 (1): 8–9

Paterson, C. (2013) 'Commercial Crime Control and the Development of Electronically Monitored Punishment: A Global Perspective' in M. Nellis, K. Beyens and D. Kaminski (eds) *Electronically Monitored Punishment: International and Critical Perspectives*, London: Routledge

Peachey, P. (2015, December 1) 'Nick Gargan: Former Chief of Avon and Somerset Police Hired by G4S Weeks after Being Found Guilty of Misconduct' *The Independent*

Rawnsley (2021, April 18) 'David Cameron and the Greenshill Scandal Is Just the Tip of the Fatberg' *The Observer*

Savage, S., and Charman, S. (2010) 'Public Protectionism and "Sarah's Law": Exerting Pressure Through Single Issue Campaigns' in M. Nash and A. Williams (eds) *Handbook of Public Protection*, Cullompton: Willan

Shelden, R., and Brown, W. (2000) 'The Crime Control Industry and the Management of the Surplus Population' *Critical Criminology* 9 (1/2): 39

Starr, P. (1989) 'The Meaning of Privatisation' (reprinted) in S. Kamerman and A. Kahn (eds) *Privatization and the Welfare State*, Princeton: Princeton University Press

The Trade Union Co-Ordinating Group (2013) *The Real Cost of Privatisation*, London: Centre for Legal and Social Studies

Weardon, G. (2018, July 9) 'Carillion Collapse Shows How PFI Has Been a Costly Failure, Say MPs' *The Guardian*

West, K. (2018, January 14) 'Carillion in Crisis as Outsourcing Operation Crumbles Under Debt' *The Observer*

White, A. (2013, April 25) 'Four Reasons Why Policy-Making Shouldn't Be Outsourced to Right-Wing Think Tanks' *New Statesman*

White, A. (2016) *Shadow State: Inside the Secret Companies that Run Britain*, London: Openworld

Wilks, S. (2013) *The Political Power of the Business Corporation*, Cheltenham: Edward Elgar

Wilks, S. (2015) *The Revolving Door and Corporate Colonisation of UK Politics*, London: The High Pay Centre

Wright, O. (2012, August 14) 'Exclusive: G4S Proves We Can't Always Rely on Private Sector, Says Minister' *The Independent*

Wood, P. (2003) 'The Rise of the Private Prison Industrial Complex' in A. Coyle, A. Campbell and R. Neufeld (eds) *Capitalist Punishment: Privatization and Human Rights*, London: Zed Books

6
THE PRIVATE AND PUBLIC POLICE, OR THERE AND BACK

> My policies are based not on some economics theory, but on things I and millions like me were brought up with: an honest day's work for an honest day's pay; live within your means; put by a nest egg for a rainy day; pay your bills on time; support the police.
> (Margaret Thatcher, *The News of the World*, September 1981)

Introduction

In the opening paragraph of his seminal work, *Crime Control as Industry*, Nils Christie considers the State of the field of crime control in terms of development and scope. Writing at the turn of the millennium, his warning still rings true two decades on as he reflects and predicts:

> Societies of the Western type face two major problems: Wealth is everywhere unequally distributed. So is access to paid work. Both problems contain potentialities for unrest. The crime control industry is suited for coping with both. This industry provides profit and work while at the same time producing control of those who otherwise might have disturbed the social process.
> *(2000: 13)*

At the very tip of the criminal justice spear in terms of controlling those who might cause unrest and otherwise disturb the social process are public police officers; as a consequence the uniformed public police are perhaps the most obvious of our official crime control agencies and for the majority of the public the only agency that they regularly see, hear, and interact with in everyday life. In terms of a politicised privatisation strategy which has sought to engage all aspects of the criminal justice system, this places the police in a unique position, with operating

DOI: 10.4324/9781315709819-6

requirements to act as credible and viable keepers of the peace and upholders of the rule of law—agents of the State in plain sight.[1] However, this existence as a 'special case' has not rendered policing immune to private sector style restructuring in the quest for operational efficiency from within or economic interventions to provide cost effectiveness from without. This provides the focus for this chapter, which seeks to examine some of the central developments in public and private policing as counterpoints, primarily in the historical context of England and Wales from the early modern development of the public sphere to the neoliberalism of the 1980s. As such it is necessarily selective.

Historically, the standing of public policing is largely dependent on image ostensibly linked to notions of duty, trust and force—or at the very least recognition. If we are to view criminal justice as a process akin to a conveyor, the police are the pickers, discretionary quality control, at the head of Herbert Packer's production line—gatekeepers to further processing, classification, or rejection (1964). Over the last decade, within a prevailing setting of economic austerity, a series of widely mediated global events which have resonated glocally have brought issues of public police force to the fore and with them considerations of service, accountability and faith. In the UK, the G20 Summit protests in 2009 saw widespread condemnation of the use of 'kettling' crowd control techniques by the Metropolitan Police and the deployment of its Territorial Support Group (TSG) (the replacement for the controversial Special Control Group [SPG]) in an attempt at coercion and dispersal, leading to public injury and the unlawful killing of a bystander, Ian Tomlinson, having been pushed to the floor by a TSG officer (Walker and Lewis, 2012). Despite condemnation, similar policing techniques were used against student demonstrators in London during large-scale protests against cuts in higher education during November and December of the following year. This led to 30 protestors receiving emergency treatment for head injuries and 50 complaints being made to the Independent Police Complaints Commission (IPCC) concerning excessive police conduct. The complaints included that of Jody McIntyre, a disabled man who was dragged from his wheelchair after being struck with batons, he later reflected 'I wasn't the only one to suffer that day. The police deliberately used violence to try and provoke the protesters into fighting back and in that way losing public support' (Sawer, 2010).

In comparative context, during 2013, the acquittal of George Zimmerman in the murder trial of unarmed black teenager Trayvon Martin led to the foundation of the Black Lives Matter (BLM) activist movement in the United States. Zimmerman, a local neighbourhood watch captain in Sanford, Florida, pursued and shot Martin whilst he was visiting his relatives in their gated community but was found not guilty at trial with the case overlooked in terms of perceptible civil rights violations by the Department of Justice, leading to accusations of complicity between criminal justice agencies. This case proved the catalyst for substantial and sustained criticism of the police and the US criminal justice system more generally as institutionally racist whilst highlighting multiple deaths of African Americans following police contact or custody under the #BlackLivesMatter hashtag. The BLM campaign, which made connections to the preference for reactive zero-tolerance 'broken windows' policing strategies in US inner cities since the 1980s (Friedersdorf, 2017), became turbocharged after May 2020 following viral global media coverage of the public murder of a handcuffed black man, George Floyd, at the hands of a white police officer (Barrie, 2020).

Within the recent European sphere at the time of writing, memories of prolonged violent disturbances between police and Catalan separatist protesters in Catalonia, Spain, during the 2018 referendum are still fresh, as are the regular 'Gilets Jeunes' clashes that occurred throughout France during 2019 and 2020, a scenario only dissipated by the global emergency of the coronavirus pandemic during 2020 and 2021. In France, members of the populist grassroots political group the 'Mouvement des Gilets Jeunes' (Yellow Vests—chosen as a recognisable symbol of blue-collar solidarity) were pitched against the Police Nationale in a series of violent stand offs following mass demonstrations. Emerging in late 2018 as an anti-globalist left and right wing coalition of convenience demanding economic justice and political accountability (the very issues around wealth, work and unrest foreseen by Nils Christie), their self-styled attempt at 'popular insurrection' over a period of some 16 months saw skirmishing protesters and bystanders alike killed, injured and subjected to barricading, tear gas and water cannons amidst the most widespread episode of civil unrest in France since the Second World War (Lichfield, 2019).

Extraordinary and provocative events such as these have led to a renewed debate on public police power, its function and origins, with considerations of an often-idealised past, a transitory and 'challenging' present and an obscure future. Such idealism in terms of historical and developmental research on policing can direct towards a linear path—from informal to formal, darkness to light and moreover private to public. Here the State-agency functions of the police are often shown as intact and unencumbered by the private sector; from this it emerges as something of a sacred cow. Newburn and Reiner argue that this view has become a fixation, a *fetish*, with the concept of social control in contemporary global societies susceptible to increasingly wide social, cultural, political and technical cues. They state:

> Understanding the nature of policing requires conceptual deconstruction of this assumed idea of *the police*. Modern societies are characterized by what can be termed 'police fetishism': the ideological assumption that the police are a functional prerequisite of social order, the thin blue line defending against chaos. In fact many societies have existed without a formal police force of any kind. The limitations of thinking in terms of *the* police are increasingly apparent, as contemporary societies are experiencing a pluralization of policing.
>
> *(Newburn and Reiner, 2007: 912)*

Such pluralism includes testing the enduring allure of the *fetish* and evaluating the development and relevance of *the police* as a public service alongside policing which increasingly engages and embraces private enterprise.

Private responsibility and public sphere

As Les Johnston points out in terms of historical development in the UK, 'policing' is a concept that has endured for a lot longer than that of *the police*, with the arrival of the 'new police' via Robert Peel and the *Metropolitan Police Act* in 1829 augmenting private provision in terms of social control rather that replacing it (Johnston, 1992). This conceptual 'widening' in terms of social history is identified by Dodsworth as central to early modern European political thought and applicable to the English developmental model. He argues:

> 'Police' in this archaic sense did not mean a uniformed force employed by the State to govern law and order, it implied a much more general system of government, the task of which was to regulate broad aspects of communal existence with the aim of establishing the common good of the community and was closely associated with maintenance of the moral order, security and the maximisation of national resources.
>
> *(Dodsworth, 2008: 583)*

This is encapsulated by what Foucault referred to as 'governmentality' (Foucault, 1979: 5) and links to Habermas's concept of public sphere which emerged in the midst of the age of enlightenment, founded upon the identification and debate of social issues worthy of political attention and spanning both the private and public realms. Essentially a commercially driven democratising extension of the State—the social discovery of public opinion. Habermas, focusing on eighteenth-century London, demonstrates the proximity and importance both of public and private to burgeoning civil society, and he argues that the public sphere should be conceived as a bulwark 'against the public authorities themselves, to engage them in a debate over the general rules governing relations in the basically privatized but publicly relevant sphere of commodity exchange and social labor' (1989: 27).

Against this progressive backdrop of social change, policing in the UK for much of the long eighteenth century was administered through local delegation as a reactive amateur concern rather than a centralised proactive public service, as had been the case since the Statute of Winchester of 1285. Essentially policing had developed from custom in step with the common law rather than anything approaching intervening governmental policy. Alongside entrepreneurial thief-takers paid by the collar, the hierarchy of what might be deemed organised 'policing' in 1700 emanated from the magistracy, unpaid justices of the peace (JPs), who would often come to the role with either an active interest in law and order or merely a desire for the prestige of public office or personal gain (hence the appearance of the derogatory term 'trading justices'). Alongside their judicial office, the function of the magistrate was mainly administrative and occasionally active, in terms of raising hue and cry or forming a posse of men to restore public order, apprehend a dangerous felon or retake an escaped convict. Consequently, there was a voluntary oath attached to office to take an operational role in keeping the peace, which was only taken by around three out of four at installation. The remainder who avoided the active service commitment were accused by Lord Cowper, England's first Lord High Chancellor between 1714 and 1718, of weakness in not 'giving themselves the trouble of doing the duty' (cited in Beattie, 1986: 59).

Under the direction of the magistracy were the parish constables (derived from the Latin *comes stabuli*), an office traditionally pertaining to universal obligation which required 'buying out' to avoid, ostensibly a force appointed by the presiding magistrate from local parishioners. This rather vague ancient office, usually running for one year, conferred few powers beyond active citizenship and was well summarised by Critchley as: 'not merely as an officer appointed for the preservation of the King's peace, nor as the mere officer of the parish, but as the direct representative of the old vill or township' (1967: 17). Thus, the parish constable system that existed in the early eighteenth century was essentially to service an informative link between parishioners and their magistrate. In practice, this meant patrolling the local district ensuring that the lanterns required of dwelling houses were lit, pathways were clear, locks were secure and any strangers within the vicinity were observed or asked their intentions—an early form of preventative beat policing. As these duties were time consuming, they were often viewed as a distraction from earning, and the majority of men of means able to do so paid the fee required to avoid serving their term. This included Daniel Defoe, who described the imposition of the office of constable in 1714 as: 'an unsupportable hardship; it takes up so much of a man's time that his own affairs are frequently neglected, too often to his ruin' (cited in Webb and Webb, 1906: 62). Consequently many constables 'sub-contracted', employing low-paid deputies privately to undertake these duties on their behalf, and as this cost was self-funded, opted for the cheapest appointee within their means. This in turn brought about a geographical lottery, with significant divergence in quality between the parish watch operating in affluent parishes and those serving the poor, whose watchmen were often, according to Henry Fielding:

> Chosen out of those poor old decrepit people who are, from their want of strength, rendered incapable of getting a livelihood by work. These men, armed only with a pole, which some of them are scarcely able to lift, are to secure the persons and houses of his majesty's subjects from the attacks of gangs of young, bold, stout, desperate and well-armed villains.
>
> *(1751: 15)*

This pessimistic depiction of deputy-constables and parish watchmen as incompetent bumbles, often seen clutching lantern and pole in illustration, was an established cultural construct by the reign of Elizabeth I, with Shakespeare providing comic relief in the pompous caricatures of Dogberry, Verges and Sexton in *Much Ado about Nothing* (1599), with the unfolding farce in Sicily purposely transposable to an English town (Draper, 1961: 273). Indeed, such ingrained cultural portrayals of inadequacy were likely to have been encouraged by the early police reformers,

Fielding and Patrick Colquhoun (Tobias, 1972: 201), serving to speed calls for a public police force along the lines of the French model. However, as Emsley argues with reference to developments in London, for many the customary policing system was working well without the need for radical change and its associated financial burden: '[it is] clear that at least in some metropolitan parishes there were determined attempts to ensure that the night watch was competent and capable a hundred years before the Metropolitan Police took to the streets' (Emsley, 1996: 219). Policing coverage had improved somewhat for some of the capital's wealthier residents after the *Metropolitan Watch Act 1735*, which levied a parish tax to pay for salaried watchmen in the more affluent parts of the city (initially Piccadilly, St Georges and St James), but this levy system did not operate consistently until 1800, by which time a professional standing police force was under serious consideration.

As an awareness of crime as social problem began to percolate, particularly in terms of impediment to commerce and threat to moveable property, it was recognised that the historical reliance on parish constables and the watch, essentially a local government function, was proving wholly inadequate. Attempts were made at reform, notably via the *Westminster Watch Act 1774*, which sought to regulate watch numbers, function and pay, and the formation of an armed blue-coated 'City Patrole' in 1785, with the object of controlling anti-social behaviour. The preventative function of the Patrole augmented the detective disposition of the group of ex-constables hired by Fielding to act as a reactive force from his house in Bow Street in 1749. Fielding's house became a central hub for criminal intelligence in the capital, with stipendiary constables (runners) paid for by the reward money they acquired as private thief takers, by this juncture a practice increasingly seen by the public as archaic and discredited (Harris, 2004: 74). By 1797 there were 62 constables working from Bow Street, comprising both foot patrols and mounted units (Babington, 1969: 176).

The year after, in 1798, Colquhoun formed the London River Police, a private force, paid for and in sole service of the West India Company, whose large cargo ships were vulnerably anchored in the Pool of London for loading and unloading. This was a direct response to widespread violence, looting and petty theft on the river that was estimated to be costing traders in excess of £500,000 per year.[2] In response, Colquhoun enlisted an experienced ex-mariner soldier and justice of the peace, John Harriot, to devise an effective cost-benefit model of preventative policing for the Thames at the behest of the West India Company (Dalton, 1935). Harriot's model was formed as The West India Merchants Company Marine Police Institute, comprising three branches: a Magistracy staffed by Colquhoun and Harriot; a Lumping Department, which regulated the dockers and lightermen unloading West India Company ships; and a Police Establishment, with 50 constables warranted by Customs and Excise. Within two years this well-drilled and highly visible structured force had been extremely successful in limiting losses and fostering a brand of lawfulness, leading to its incorporation as England's first genuinely professional police force under the Marine Police Bill in July 1800 (Budworth,

1997). September of the same year saw the formation of the City of Glasgow Police, Scotland's first standing municipal force based upon preventative principles, after over a decade of Parliamentary lobbying for its establishment. The drive towards public responsibility in matters of law and order was increasing.

Enter the new public police

By the early nineteenth century support for the idea of a standing public police force had gained considerable momentum, not least due to increased fears over the apparent lack of morality amongst London's 'dangerous classes' and the insanitary nature of their living conditions (Hobbs, 1988). Colquhoun, a vocal supporter flush from his success with the River Police, had published his influential *Treatise on the Police of the Metropolis* in 1800, describing the existing amateur and private provision as 'without energy, disjointed, and governed by as many Acts of Parliament as there are Parishes' (Colquhoun, 1800: 107). With the development of the public sphere, modernising cities and eyes across the channel towards revolutionary France, crime, radical protest and its control became a subject of increased political debate, leading to a series of Royal Commissions and Acts of Parliament. The drive towards professionalisation was aided exponentially by the appointment of Robert Peel as Home Secretary in 1822, a politician who saw the value of political arithmetic (here crime statistics) in garnering both Parliamentary and public support. Aged 34 and a rising star and moderniser within the Tory party, Peel sought to centralise public control of criminal justice in terms of prisons and policing. This led to the establishment of the Metropolitan Police under the *Metropolitan Police Act 1829*, with amalgamation of the River Police (Marine Police Force) in 1839, and the establishment of a separate force to cover the City of London under the *City of London Police Act 1839*.

Professional duty was to be guided by the 'General Instructions', commonly referred to as the nine 'Peelian principles' (a designation, however, likely imposed retrospectively by Reith in the 1940s [Emsley, 2014: 12]), issued as a guide on powers and conduct to every police officer and unwritten by the concept of policing by consent (Lentz and Chaires, 2007). As a model, policing by consent was both innovative and key, allowing the previously sceptical public to (tentatively) view these new uniformed public police as 'citizens in uniform' rather than agents of surveillance and coercion—that swarm of 'blue locusts' they had feared (Storch and Engels, 1975). However, Peel's new force still attracted a good deal of criticism, particularly in terms of the increased cost to the public purse, suspicion over their potential martial ambitions to develop as a British *gendarmerie* and disagreements tantamount to class interest versus public benefit (Watts-Miller, 1987).

Despite such opposition, the Royal Commission on Constabulary (1836–39) recommended the creation of a national police force or forces, leading the *Rural Constabularies Act* of 1839 (RCA) (also known as the *County Police Act*) and the amendment of 1840 (which responded to funding concerns). This enabled the magistracy to establish forces in their areas on a non-compulsory basis, resulting in a take-up of 25 of the 55 counties. The provisions on formation under the RCA had been underwritten in terms of governance by the *Municipal Corporations Act 1835*, which as well as establishing a uniform system of municipal boroughs served by councils elected by rate-payers, compelled these boroughs to establish a Watch Committee (later police authority). The scope of each Watch Committee included the recruitment of a constabulary in order to keep the peace within jurisdiction and its regulation—thus investing a great deal of local control over local policing arrangements. Further legislation was to follow with the *County and Borough Police Act 1856*, which finally compelled the remaining 30 local authorities to modernise their policing provision to a uniformed professional force, which would be scrutinised and overseen by a national inspectorate.

The establishment of the new police, though geographically comprehensive by the mid-nineteenth century, was slow to dominate culturally, supplementing rather than displacing the longstanding traditions of private/hybrid policing and security, with the continuance in many areas of the parish constabulary and watch systems to the turn of the twentieth century.[3] Moreover, new industries such as the rail companies sought to organise their own uniformed 'private police forces' under the *Special Constables Act 1831* to guard and secure their property in coexistence with public policing provisions (a system that endured as a quasi-public entity until nationalisation into the British Transport Police in 1948). Similar private forces of special constables policed other key commercial and industrial settings, including harbours, docks, canals and mines, later being established as the specialist police agencies with constabulary powers that endure to this day (Button and Wakefield, 2018: 145).

Desired discipline and private-sector innovation

The growth of disciplinary society and the perception of a need for externalised control during the Victorian era also saw an increased availability of private security measures to order labour and leisure and safeguard property. Factories appointed charge-hands and foremen who supervised behaviour and levied fines for lack of productivity or insubordination, whilst pubs, fairs and racecourses recruited doormen to restrict and eject unruly or undesirable customers. The rich, as had been the case for some time, placed a premium on the security credentials of their senior servants, as Linebaugh argues: 'the hierarchy of servants within households corresponded to their security responsibilities' (1991: 336). Demographic change and economic growth also created a need for secure deposit, storage and the protection of valuables. This was to be met by an ever-responsive banking industry with an eye for procedural compliance and technical development in terms of locks, vaults, alarms and accompanying personnel. The Chubb ironmongery company, having received a royal license from George IV for its locks and strongboxes, patented the 'burglar proof' safe in 1835 and had set up a safe-making factory in London by 1837. These mechanical deterrents were often accompanied by human overseers, particularly in the banking industry, the Corps of Commissionaires being founded in 1859 with royal patronage (which continues to this day) and providing employment for ex-servicemen as static and active guards to meet this need.

Alongside these trends in overt private policing, the market in covert servicing was remodelling too. The lineage of what would become known as civil agents, private detectives or private investigators could be traced to longstanding concepts of paid informing and thief taking (Moore, 1997: 59). Both practices relied on surveillance, intelligence gathering, covert enquiry and the use of established official and non-official networks prior to informing or apprehension (Emsley and Shpayer-Makov, 2006). In 1833, just four years after the establishment of the Metropolitan Police in London, a former criminal with convictions for fraud, forgery and violence, Eugène François Vidocq—in true poacher turned gamekeeper style—was setting up his fledgling detective agency in Paris, Le bureau des renseignements (the office of information). Le bureau quickly became popular, offering both private 'policing' and detection services to individuals and the government and employing mainly ex-criminal associates of Vidocq. He later reflected on the necessary skillset required for private detective work in his memoirs:

> I believe I might have become a perpetual spy, so far was every one from supposing that any connivance existed between the agents of the public authority and myself. Even the porters and keepers were in ignorance of my mission with which I was entrusted. Adored by the thieves, esteemed by the most determined bandits (for even these hardened wretches have a sentiment which they call esteem), I could always rely on their devotion to me.
>
> *(Vidocq, 1834: 190)*

Vidocq's memoirs in several volumes were widely published in Europe and the Americas from around 1829, and agencies similar to his model began to appear in the following decades. Amongst the most famous of these was the Pinkerton National Detective Agency (now part of Securitas AB), which was founded in 1850 in Chicago by Allan Pinkerton—a Scottish immigrant whose former career as informer, agent provocateur, spy, bodyguard, bounty-hunter and head of intelligence was at least as colourful as that of Vidocq (Mackay, 1998). Johnston suggests that though a form of 'detective agency' had existed in eighteenth-century England (the Bow Street Runners being one such example), their popular use during Victoria's reign received a considerable fillip by the provisions under the *Matrimonial Causes Act 1857*, which moved the institution of marriage from ecclesiastical sacrament to civil contract, thus widening the availability of divorce and the pursuit of evidence to prove infidelity or desertion (Cretney, 2005).

By the beginning of the twentieth century recognisable 'parishes' between private and public police function were identifiable and somewhat established. In terms of the former, private security had expanded within industrial, commercial, governmental and domestic spheres and could by now be termed a niche 'industry' in its own right. The role of the 'new' public police forces, by now 70 years young, had been apparently enlarged via practice to include social salvation as well as control, what Storch referred to as their 'moral-reform mission'. Here the individual constable can be seen as domestic missionary, gathering intelligence via presence, an applied bobby on the beat. He reflects:

> Though the full measure of the charge to police by the Victorian municipality and the State could never be lived up to, the nineteenth century saw the forging of a modern and generally effective technique of order keeping: the installation of the eyes and ears of ruling elites at the very centres of working-class daily life.
>
> (Storch, 1976: 496)

By 1900, such embedded surveillance would appear to be seen as normalised, with the policing by consent by citizens in uniform embedded into public consciousness if not universally accepted (Brogden, 1982)—with John Burns MP the first to hail the police in London as 'the best police force in the world' (Emsley, 1993: 124). This view would gather pace and support as the century developed and ensured that police leaders were quick to champion both reputation and independence, culminating in what would retrospectively be vaunted as the 'golden era' for public policing in England and Wales half a century later.

Supplementing the best police in the world

The prelude to the First World War saw the police becoming involved in counter-espionage and would-be insurgency, external and internal threats (which included conscientious objectors and Labour members of police authorities) for the first time under the *Defence of the Realm Act*. Bringing senior officers into operational contact with the fledgling Secret Service Bureau (SSB), which had been founded in 1909 as a joint enterprise between the War Office and Admiralty. This relationship intensified during the onset of hostilities after 1914, as did the concept of centralisation, with Whitehall via the Home Office recognising the importance of post-war police strategy in terms of the stabilisation of social order and peacekeeping. This expanded role was formalised after the armistice in 1918 as the *Emergency Powers Act 1919*, setting out police response during states of emergency. The scope of the act extended to political demonstrations and industrial disputes, with likely due deference to the Bolshevik Revolution in Russia in 1917, and was subsequently put into action during the General Strike in 1926, with Sir Arthur Lewis Dixon of the Home Office enthusing that these recent developments had

> established the [Police] Service in what was virtually a new, and certainly important, role as an executive Force, efficient, trustworthy and versatile, and ready at a call to guide, assist or restrain the civil population in a wide variety of ways.
>
> (cited in Emsley, 1996: 138)

Dixon's triumphal tone, in particular the use of the term 'executive Force', might be viewed as a speculative puff towards greater jurisdictional control of police operations from Whitehall.

With the Home Office increasingly called in to referee disputes between chief constables and proprietorial Labour local authorities in the provinces, frustrations began to surface—with Sir John Anderson, permanent under-secretary of State for the Home Office, asserting the autonomy of the office of constable: 'the policeman is nobody's servant. He is not appointed merely as an agent of some higher authority' (1929: 192). The question of increased centralisation in terms of controlling interest had been on the agenda since at least the 1870s. With local police authorities attached to the county forces fiercely defensive in terms of their autonomy and ability to directly influence local affairs, they were able to resist change despite a series of corruption scandals until the creation of the *Police Act 1964*. This abolished the localised Watch Committee system and introduced 'police areas', thereafter overseen by independent police authorities.

Public experience of the police as executive force and civil restraint would increase prior to the Second World War, with officers increasingly called upon to monitor and control demonstrations. Alongside the increased politicisation of the police, the period following the First World War had also proved a watershed in the political enfranchisement of the wider public. *The Representation of the People Act 1918* and the *Representation of the People Act* (Equal Franchise) 1928 had created universal suffrage for all men and women aged 21 for the first time, swelling the male electorate by 5.2 million (Smith, 2014: 95) and creating an engaged female electorate of 8.5 million (Roberts, 2001: 1). A side effect of this was to both amplify and reconfigure the relationship between the police and working-class communities they patrolled and observed.

A minority Labour government had been elected for the first time in 1924, demonstrating capability alongside *desire* to govern, and returned for a second term in 1929, with policy commitments made during this period to improve, *inter alia*, housing, education, social insurance, tenant protection and working conditions. This political emancipation and indeed demonstrable participation resolved some of the distrust which had previously existed along class lines as the public police found their place in the burgeoning capitalist State, interacting closely with a group who were already well aware of theirs—a relational change from 'outright confrontation to an unwritten system of tacit negotiation' (Cohen, 1979, cited in Fitzgerald et al., 1981: 119). Despite this inference, public policing remained class sensitive and politically charged, with the police seen as heavy handed in their marshalling of unemployed demonstrators during the Hunger Marches that took place during 1931 and 1932 (Vernon, 2007: 56) and overtly lenient towards British Union of Fascists' activists during their charged meetings and provocative marches throughout the mid-1930s, which often descended into violence. Here, many counter-activists viewed police presence as partisan and tantamount to police approval or protection (Weinberger, 1991, 1995).

Fetishism, collectivism and the golden age of public policing

During the Second World War, with the requirement for additional duties on the home front and numbers reduced by the enlistment of younger officers into the armed forces, the police were once again drawn into closer contact with the public. This was particularly the case after September 1940, when industrial towns and cities were targeted for saturation bombing raids by the German air force. Designed to demoralise and destroy infrastructure, the strategy would ultimately result in 40,000 civilian deaths up to 1945. With the police engaged during and after air raids, often as initial information sources and official contacts for the bereaved and displaced, their esteem amongst the public who shared their challenging experiences was raised exponentially, as Godfrey and Lawrence state:

> [P]ublic opinion surveys conducted at the end of the war indicate a highly positive attitude towards the police. The wartime role and the experiences of police and public alike between 1939 and 1945 did much to shape the image of the English 'bobby' personified in the character of George Dixon in the film *The Blue Lamp* (1950) and later resurrected in the television series *Dixon of Dock Green*.
>
> *(Godfrey and Lawrence, 2005: 24)*

As the country sought to stabilise during an uncertain post-war period, the public police were embraced as a reliable constant, crossing the threshold into what has been deemed the 'Golden Age' of British policing by a series of key commentators (Emsley, 1996; Reiner, 1992, 1994, 2010; Rawlings, 2002), with the fictional hero Police Constable George Dixon leading the way into the 1950s as idealised exemplar of the chipper and stoic national character (Gorer, 1955)—Dixon was an everyman survivor who would become a *motif*. Reiner traces the symbolic emergence of the bobby as icon from the Battle of Britain to the Festival of Britain as a by-product of the relative social peace that followed extreme social conflict, citing the large scale survey conducted for the Royal Commission on the Police in 1962 which confirmed 'an overwhelming vote of confidence in the police . . . No less than 83% of those interviewed professed great respect for the police' (1992: 763).

O'Morgan suggests that the construction of a post-war 'people's peace' was built upon shared experience and responsibility, a façade of unity (1999). During wartime the existence of such a façade was crucial, with national unity described by Sir William Beveridge as 'the mutual understanding between Government and people . . . the determination of the British people to look beyond victory to the uses of victory' (1943: 109). Polar to the grim reconstructionism firmly aligned class lines that had followed the First World War when Lloyd-George's rhetorical 'fit country for heroes to live in' had patently failed to materialise (1918), post-Second World War Britain possessed ambition, momentum and crucially optimism. If the success of the Festival of Britain in 1951 had provided the cultural veneer, the social framework had been constructed by the Attlee led Labour government that had won a landslide victory in the general election of July 1945. Despite post-war austerity, the wounded country had full employment, with the government launching a program of nationalisation targeted towards vital sectors of the economy and critical infrastructure—notably the Bank of England, coal, health, utilities, railways and steel (Chick, 2002). Nationalisation was coupled with radical social policy based upon welfarism. This saw the creation of a publically funded national health service under the *National Health Service Act 1946*, providing free treatment to all at the point of use, and a new system of social security offering 'cradle to grave' support in terms of unemployment, child sickness, funeral benefits and pensions which would be founded by the *National Insurance Act 1946*. An ambitious housebuilding program was also initiated under the Town and Country Planning Act 1947, including the provision of affordable housing and the construction of a number of 'new towns' (Jefferys, 1992).

This backdrop of intense public sector activity provides the setting for consideration of public policing's 'golden age'—offering social stability as a counterpoint to political flux. Certainly by the early 1950s the police had made significant gains towards the acceptance of policing by consent, the legitimation of their office as public servants. Police constables on the whole were still recruited from working-class backgrounds, a strategy employed since the earliest days of the new police to ensure a degree of familiarity and foster acceptance and understanding in the communities that they served (Emsley and Clapson, 1994). Policing structures and methodology in terms of public perception had also changed very little over the course of a century—outside of the capital city, accountability remained local, foot patrol (the home beat method, with officers familiar and imbedded) was still standard procedure, and police powers continued to be derived from the rule of law alongside the principle of minimum force (delivering unarmed 'citizens in uniform'). By this juncture, public policing had also developed 'social service' elements of practice, offering a first response outlet to those in need (Reiner, 1992, 1994). Clearly, the presence of the police was not welcomed unanimously, but higher levels of social integration pre-war and increased affluence and social stability in its aftermath had led to greater acceptance, during an era which Fielding argues was 'marked by popular respect and obedience for authority' (1991: 36).

Commercialism, consumerism and the technological arms race

As public policing was reaching its zenith in the mid-twentieth century, the private security sector had been making steady progress in the background in terms of technology and service provision, becoming ever more commercially and technically aware in the process. This sensitivity had seen the sector concentrate on responding to three broad business streams: mechanical barriers and mechanisms, electrical security devices and systems and physical manned services. Significantly, advancement in terms of traditional hardware such as mechanical locking devices, safes and vaults had been joined by companies offering electric alarm and control systems. A rudimentary electric security alarm had been invented in America by Augustus Pope as early as 1850, with the patent registered in 1853. Pope sold the patent to Edwin Holmes, who began the manufacture of alarm systems commercially in 1860s New York off the back of his persuasive pamphlet *A Treatise Upon the Best Method of Protecting Property from Burglars, and Human Life from Midnight Assassins* (1861), which included testimonials of the efficacy of the device and a list of subscribers.

With electrical power systems becoming more widespread at the turn of the century, particularly in terms of street lighting grids, Holmes's company was bought by the American Telephone & Telegraph Company (AT&T) in 1905, who saw commercial value in linking the device to their early telephony to automatically alert public police and fire services during emergencies (Lee, 2008: 26). By the time of the First World War, the use of electric alarms was relatively widespread in safeguarding banks and high-value goods in both the United States and Europe (with the remote telephone response foreseen by AT&T becoming viable during the 1920s and 30s) and often installed as part of a lucrative bilateral protection with insurance; as South argues, '[alarms] were introduced as a result of pressure from insurers on furriers in London's East End, emphasising the deterrent value of alarms' (1988: 64). By the 1950s many insurers in the UK were requesting that commercial and industrial premises be protected by electric alarms to provide cover. This saw the long-established lock company Chubb expand into providing commercial burglar and fire alarm systems and acquiring a third share in the domestic alarm supplier Burgot (manufacturers of the 'Operation Household' model since 1948) in 1959 to ensure market dominance. The pace of demand for electric alarm systems provides an example of the role that private security technology has played in shaping modern society, with good business practice, compliance or indeed active citizenry linked to participation in technological change or the purchase of security apparatus. This circular process ultimately leads to a perpetual 'arms race' between owners and those who would threaten their ownership. This links to what McGuire terms 'technomia', with technological change often pitched or perceived as a threat that requires yet further technological solution and intervention (2012: 27).

As seen in the foregoing, the antecedents of physical presence as deterrent in terms of private security are longstanding and enduring. From the Edwardian era, many large commercial and storage premises, such as department stores, factories and warehouses, began employing 'works police' forces in the form of gatekeepers and watchmen to guard premises and stock. In wartime, with certain goods seen as essential to the war effort or susceptible to fire or theft, such forces were typically increased, and during the Second World War, works police groups often liaised or worked in tandem with civil defence units, such as Air Raid Precaution (ARP) wardens or the Home Guard. What has been termed 'the guarding industry' (Johnston, 1992: 19) also gathered significant pace during the interwar years, including the foundation of Night Watch Services in 1935, a company that specialised in bicycle patrolling guards wearing the old police uniform of the affluent (paying) areas of London. Following a name change to Night Guards in 1939 and fears over the formation of private militias, the company was accused by George Lansbury, a pacifist Labour MP, of making 'the first halting step down the road to fascism', leading the company to stand down its patrols during the war (Tooher, 1996). Post-war, Night Guards, re-established as an industrial security organisation, provided operatives for commercial and industrial premises, leading to further name change in 1951 to Security Corps. As previously, the martial nomenclature soon caused concern, and in 1953 the company became Securicor, by the late 50s specialising in radio-linked armoured car cash-in-transit services (CITS). Securicor's main competition in terms of static guarding and CITS during the 1950s was Plant Protection Limited, which had been founded in 1951, later renamed Factory Guards (and currently part of G4S). The mushrooming of private policing technologies and methodologies such as these in the two decades that followed the Second World War suggest that the private security industry was experiencing a period of enlightenment alongside public policing's Golden Age as illustrated by extraordinary sector growth. George and Button reflect:

> In 1950 it was estimated that the private security industry had sales amounting to £5 million per year; by 1967 Clayton's [1967] description of the three largest companies in one sub sector illustrates the remarkable growth of the industry. For instance, in the cash-in-transit sub-sector the largest company was Securicor, with nearly 90 branches, 600 vehicles and 6,000 uniformed employees, followed by Security Express with 250 vehicles and 1,200 employees, and by Factoryguards, also with around 1,200 employees, operating in a sector reputed at the time to be worth some £50 million. Meanwhile the safe and burglar alarm manufacturers were estimated to have a turnover of some £40 to £50 million, employing over 30,000 individuals. By the late 1960s Securicor had over 18,000 employees and 3,000 armoured vehicles and provided a plethora of services.
>
> *(2000: 26)*

By the mid 1960s public policing was also succumbing to calls for enlightenment in terms of technological and social change. Despite remaining popular with the public, the traditional home beat method of foot patrol was increasingly viewed as a time-consuming drain on resources, human and financial, and increasingly as a barrier to recruitment due to its repetitive image (Skogan, 1990). Whilst public confidence in the police as an institution remained high well into the 1960s (Banton, 1964),[4] their gilt was losing some of its previous lustre, and their methods appeared lethargic and dated, with Dixon of Dock Green 'rapidly appearing out of touch with the irreverent mood at the time' (Cockcroft, 2012: 20). If the police were seen as lacking vigour, vision and mobility, their quarry certainly was not, with a notable increase in project crimes such as armed robbery and smash and grab (Morton, 2003). Significantly, this included the Great Train Robbery in 1963, where an unprecedented £2.6 million, an enormous sum at the time, was captured from a mail train, along with the public imagination. Increasingly, links were made to a growing culture of gang-related crime, particularly in London, with members seen as 'cunning, ruthless and well-informed' (Morton, 2002: 206). With Securicor and others having protected its cash-in-transit operations by the use of radio-linked modern specialist vehicles for a number of years, the public police now received its cue to modernise from the private sector, moving from its preventive policing traditions to a more reactive model as the 1960s drew to a close (Home Office, 1967).

Closing the technology gap and distancing consensus

In practice, reactive policing during the 1970s drew heavily on technology that was already commonplace in the private security sector, including the use of radio-linked vehicles to patrol set zones—the unit beat method. This system was intended to improve operational efficiency in terms of how personnel were used and the way that arrest and response figures could be recorded (aiding the compilation of accurate official statistics), with operations linked to the Police National Computer (PNC) after 1974. However, a detrimental effect of the change from home beat to unit beat was that it was seen to insulate police officers from the communities that they served, limiting their ability to build working relationships, garner trust and gather local intelligence informally. Police officers became unfamiliar, their appearance often seen as intrusive, which hampered interpersonal communication, moving away from everyday conversation towards dialogue based upon 'conflict and crisis' (Alderson, 1979: 41). Hirst, later a chief constable, reflected on the impact:

> During the late 1960s and early 1970s the Home Office unit beat policing system, introduced as an expedient to cover the shortfall in recruitment resulting from the poor salary structure, changed the nature of policing in the UK. The mobile police officer lost contact with the community in which he worked and gradually, with the demise of his credibility, his influence over it. At the same time, his continuous radio contact with his base deprived him of his independence, and he assumed a reactive stance in the community. Social control through contact with the community was undermined at a time when crime and disorder was on the increase.
>
> *(1990: 85)*

Consequently, as the decade developed the consensual distance between the police and public was seen to increase, with the highly valued social service elements of policing practice apparently discarded in favour of enforcement priorities. With finite resources attached to the reactive model, police patrolling in cars became increasingly focused on public space and as a consequence the availability of those inhabiting public space for scrutiny, resulting in friction along class lines (Fitzgerald, 1999). This was particularly the case in terms of the policing of communities which had been habitually been stereotyped as 'difficult' or 'problem' patches, with those that inhabited them seen as being worthy of particular attention and becoming over-policed. Such attention was frequently perceived as targeted, obstructive or excessive and, in the case of the use of stop-and-search powers towards black youths, racially aggravated (Hall et al., 1978; Bowling and Phillips, 2002).

These changes in terms of police role and operational priorities during the 1970s, allied to administrative constraints in terms of finance and manpower, extended the perceived 'gap in the market' for security reassurance in terms of private policing products which the private security industry was ready, willing and able to fill (Spitzer and Scull, 1977). Since 1967 the interests of the industry in the UK had been overseen by its trade association, the British Security Industry Association (BSIA), with sector organisation and self-promotion becoming more evident. South, in reflecting on industry self-confidence and placement at this juncture, quotes from a speech made by Jorgen Philip-Sorenson, director of Group 4 Security, at the Institute of Criminology at the University of Cambridge in 1971. Here, Philip-Sorenson offered his interpretation of the importance and scope of the industry; ensuring a delineation between public and private provision, he saw private policing as being utilised:

> almost always in private industrial and commercial premises, behind the traditional and legal boundary of the factory fence, which the police cannot lawfully cross unless by invitation or in other special circumstances. Our principal task is to prevent loss and minimise risk to people and property in private places and we have no function in the preservation of law and order in the private sector.
>
> *(1972, cited in South, 1988: 5)*

Such stimulation and a promise of opportunity and expansion had already drawn the attention of both industry and academic commentators, with Kakalik and Wildhorn commissioned by the Rand Corporation to produce a series of research papers on private policing to be published by the Government Printing Office in 1971. These included an evaluation of nature, purpose, extent, regulation and legal parameters, along with positive recommendations highlighting the industry's support role to the public police as 'junior partner' (Kakalik and Wildhorn, 1971). Further US and UK studies followed which positively reinforced this partnership ethos and the socio-economic opportunities of further collaboration (Braun and Lee, 1971; Scott and MacPherson, 1971; Wiles and McClintock, 1972; Anon, 1976). A constant within this literature was an expansionist interpretation which viewed private security as an appendage of the criminal justice system, jarring critically with Foucault's then forward-looking concept of pervasive power, dispersed social control and the promise of a blurred 'carceral archipelago' to deter assaults on persons and property (1977). Becker saw such developments in terms of an impending role reversal between private and public policing operatives, with the former responsible for ever more aggressive tasks in terms of crime control and apprehension (essentially those previously undertaken by a beat officer) and the latter relegated to supplementary duties around crime prevention and community service (1974). In practice, the capability of private security firms guarding 'property' by the late 1970s was certainly being interpreted very broadly, as Garner argued in the context of immigration detention in the UK, observing that 'the guarding of illegal immigrants at airports, undertaken by Securicor, does equate people with property and treats them as commodities not persons' (1978: 72). Shearing et al., reflecting on the developments of the preceding decade in 1980, saw a distinct move towards a perceived need for greater 'protection' in terms of the preservation of both property and self, a prediction that would now be realised in an era of individualism, with greed promoted as good.

Policing is for turning

With a backdrop of industrial unrest, a weak economy and the privations of the 'Winter of Discontent' still fresh in the public memory, the Margaret Thatcher led Conservative Party opposition began their electoral pitch in the spring of 1979, promising to 'restore the balance' in British society via a firm commitment to 'the rule of law'. The events of the New Year had seen mass strikes in the public sector, leading to visible signs of disarray, particularly in towns and cities, heightening public fear of crime and disorder. Tuning to this theme, the Conservative Manifesto pledged that:

> The number of crimes in England and Wales is nearly half as much again as it was in 1973. The next Conservative government will spend more on fighting crime even while we economise elsewhere. Britain needs strong, efficient police forces with high morale. Improved pay and conditions will help Chief Constables to recruit up to necessary establishment levels. We will therefore implement in full the recommendations of the Edmund Davies Committee. The police need more time to detect crime. So we will ease the weight of traffic supervision duties and review cumbersome court procedures which waste police time.
>
> *(Conservative Party Manifesto, 1979)*

The Edmund Davies Committee mentioned had focused on the longstanding problem of police pay, which, due to extreme levels of inflation, had dominated discourse on police morale during the late 1970s (Committee of Inquiry on the Police, 1977–1979, Edmund-Davies, 1979), an issue seen as so serious that it had almost forced the resignation of Jim Callaghan, the Labour Prime Minister, with the Police Federation discussing 'right to strike' and chief constables warning Merlyn Rees, Home Secretary, of 'a breakdown in law and order' (Brain, 2010: 49). Callaghan losing a vote of no confidence on 29 March triggered an early general election on 3 May, which he would ultimately lose by 43 seats, a 5.2% swing, to the Conservatives. Amongst the first actions of the incoming government was the formation of a Home Affairs Committee to examine and report on reforming criminal justice matters.

Margaret Thatcher's commitment to the police would be tested within the year with the unforeseen outbreak of inner-city rioting at the start of April 1980, commencing in the St Pauls area of Bristol and spreading sporadically to Brixton in London, Handsworth in Birmingham, Chapeltown in Leeds, Toxteth in Liverpool and Moss Side in Manchester in the following weeks, lasting until 11 July. All of these disturbances were founded upon racial tension in disadvantaged areas with large black minority ethnic (BME) communities, the very areas that had borne the brunt of the recent reactive policing strategy with its emphasis on detachment and stop and search, with these powers reinforced further by the new government under the *Vagrancy Act 1824* to resemble draconian 'sus laws' (Brake and Hale, 1991). Whilst the riots raged, a terrorist siege at the Iranian Embassy in London commenced on 30 April prior to the building being stormed on 5 May by SAS troops, resulting in the release of hostages and the killing of all but one of the terrorists—played out to the watching public live on television. Amongst the freed hostages was the embassy's Metropolitan Police liaison officer, PC Trevor Lock, who was awarded the George medal as a 'defining example of the power of the Dixon image' (Waldren, 2007: 76). In stark contrast, Thatcher's hardnosed decision to deploy Special Air Service (SAS) troops on a shoot-to-kill mission was perceived as toughness, boosting her personal popularity as the 'Iron Lady' and that of the Conservatives as the erstwhile guardians of law and order (Fremont-Barnes, 2009: 60).

The dividend of force

This uncompromising image endured for all three consecutive Thatcher ministries between 1979 and 1990, with willingness to court controversy in foreign policy demonstrated in the Falklands war of 1982 and in her dealings with Irish Republican terrorism, including further deployment of the SAS to intercept a suspected Irish Republican Army (IRA) terrorist attack on Gibraltar in 1988 (Coogan, 2002). In terms of the domestic security sphere, a rejuvenated police force were seen as an essential tool of policy implementation when necessary. They would be used most strikingly during the UK Miners' Strike of 1984–85 in response to a government programme of nationalised colliery closures resisted by the powerful National Union of Mineworkers (NUM), led by Arthur Scargill. Here, with Thatcher sensing a chance to reduce the appeal and power of trade unions early in her second term and purge the memory of the capitulation by the Heath government to the miners in the strikes of 1972 and 1974, she tactically mobilised police forces from around the country to patrol picket lines at colliery gates and to prevent 'flying pickets' from travelling in support of striking colleagues. Famously describing the striking miners as 'the enemy within' (Thatcher, 1984), the police would make over 11,000 arrests during the duration of the strike and end the dispute demonised by some as 'Maggie's army' (Mawby, 2002: 112), with one picket interviewed by Green observing 'I think they're doing more soldiering than policing—it's more violent' (1990: 69). The strike officially ended in March 1985 as an ideological victory for Thatcherism (Leeworthy, 2012); it had been the largest industrial action since the general strike of 1926, leaving Milne to observe that 'it has no real parallel—in size, duration and impact—anywhere in the world' (2004: ix). With the previously invulnerable miners broken, focus fully turned to the implementation of economic policy. Brain reflects on the era as a fulcrum of social change:

> By 1985 . . . Old industries were dying or dead; individual and collective entrepreneurialism was valued as never before, even if some of it looked like old fashioned greed and get rich quick. The public services themselves, especially health, education, local government, and housing, bastions of a service first ethos, found themselves subject to reorganization and cultural change which either practically eliminated the government's direct provision of the service, as with housing, or subjected it to the supposed rigors of private sector techniques.
>
> *(2013: 99)*

Public policing methods had been under scrutiny since the riots of 1981, and the report into the Brixton riots by Lord Scarman that followed found greatly racially disproportionate stop-and-search figures in the areas affected and a propensity towards 'hard' policing, warning that the police were in danger of losing legitimacy (1981). Additionally, despite the early law and order promises of the Conservative government, crime had continued to rise (recorded via the British Crime Survey from 1981), as would continue to be the case in every year until 1993. These factors saw a call towards what would be termed 'proactive policing' (later referred to as 'community policing'), a community-based strategy which aimed to restore public confidence in policing practice, the proactivity emanating from individual and collective action, such as residents associations and neighbourhood watch groups (Moore and Brown, 1981). This required a multi-agency approach with the identification of 'common interests' and 'community values' towards the creation of a 'village community' (Fletcher, 2005: 63). This attempt at reintegration or reassurance in terms of policing presence, usually via a partial return to foot patrol, was not, however, welcomed universally, with some communities regarding the method as intrusive or as an attempt to shift responsibility or take control (Brogden, 1982. Short, 1982).

Policing under scrutiny and the privatisation imperative

By the start of Thatcher's third and final term in office, public confidence in the police had dropped dramatically, from 77% in 1983 (the first reporting year of the British Social Attitudes Survey) to 66% in 1987 (BSAS, 1983, 1987). Further decline was recorded during 1990 in the report of Her Majesty's Chief Inspector of Constabulary Sir John Woodcock, who noted with a degree of understatement that public esteem for the service had 'slipped' (HMCIC, 1991: 3). The decade had ended as it had started, in controversy, with the police defending their image and record following media exposure of a series of historical miscarriage of justice cases, several of which challenged police integrity and competence, providing the spur for the modernising provisions provided by the *Police and Criminal Evidence Act 1984* (PACE), which attempted to modernise and regulate procedure. The summer of 1989 had seen the Hillsborough football stadium disaster, where the conduct of senior officers had been called into question in the immediate aftermath and would eventually lead to severe condemnation in the Taylor Report (Taylor, 1990; Scraton, 1999). However, it was the IRA bombing of Deal Barracks in Kent, preceding Thatcher's resignation as Prime Minister by just nine weeks, that would prick the public's consciousness of the distance policing function had travelled during her decade in office. The attack was made on 22 September 1989 when a time-bomb exploded at the barracks which housed the Royal Marines School of Music, killing 11 and wounding 21. In the aftermath, an outraged media reported that perimeter security at the base was manned by Reliance Security, a private contractor, having been provided previously by the Ministry of Defence Police or the Marines themselves. Reliance were seen as both incompetent and blameworthy for the security lapse at Deal. Allan Rogers the Labour Party MP captured public frustration towards government policy in a speech to the House of Commons the following June:

> One issue highlighted by the Select Committee report was the employment of private security firms. The practice of using such firms has increased under this Government. The Defence Select Committee and the Ministry of Defence police in its submission said that the practice was increasing because the Government were attempting to save money. When 11 Marines were killed in Deal, the firm in charge of security at that barracks was Reliance Security Services. It employed people who had criminal records and people who were badly trained and who were paid about £2 an hour . . . The employment of private security companies is simply an extension of the Government's ideological obsession of private is good and public is bad. The desire to save money has led to bad security arrangements in many establishments and perhaps resulted in needless deaths.
>
> *(Hansard, Column 553, 5 June, 1990)*

The rise in recorded crime and reported tensions in the press (particularly around terrorism and social unrest) ensured the continued growth and diversification of the private security market in the UK throughout the 1980s, including encroachment into areas of responsibility previously delivered by the public police. This was boosted considerably by a widening resource gap in terms of public policing resource and public policing expectation during the decade despite a 50% increase in policing expenditure[5] and crucially the active commitment to strategic mass privatisation by the Thatcher governments—a trend that all successors were to follow. The main socio-political developments in the area of privatisation ideology in terms of the neoliberal turn (1979–1989) (Bloom, 2017) are covered in detail in Chapters 2 and 3 of this book, but in consideration of public policing during the Thatcher era, specific reference to what Johnston terms 'the privatization mentality' (1992: 51) can be applied, whereas with private policing developments, the application of 'social markets to public services'—essentially the alignment of free-market economics with social policy—appear key (Loveday, 1995). In terms of the UK these two underlying themes have dominated the public versus private policing debate since.

Like other public agencies, police forces during the 1980s were increasingly subject to NPM principles founded on the adoption of private-sector bureaucracy, management and administrative practices. The underpinning ethos was that public services would emerge with greater operating efficiency and a citizen client centred approach—'more business like'. According to Hood, the driving force behind NPM was adherence to 'four megatrends', which can be summarised as the reversal of public spending, the shift towards privatisation and quasi-privatisation, the impact of technology (in particular automation) and an increasingly international focus and agenda (Hood, 1991: 3). Central to this was the concept of performance management via objectives, benchmarks, evaluations and audits, which provided a new level of scrutiny on public policing, as Johnston argues: 'One consequence of NPM has, however, been that performance management' may open up an organisation to public evaluation to a degree not before experienced' (Loveday, 1999: 356). Some forces received this imposition as a shock or direct attack on existing police culture (Cockcroft and Beattie, 2009) signifying a move towards consumerism as social identity, complicating governance towards a strategic 'hollowing out' of the State (Rhodes, 1994).

Johnston links the reflective use of his term 'privatization mentality' to an influential Joint Consultative Committee Operational Policing Review undertaken by the Avon and Somerset Constabulary published in 1990. The review was critical of the excessive demands in terms of managerialism, competition and value for money placed on the police during the 1980s, highlighting five specific areas of strain: application of the financial management initiative (FMI), increased influence of the Home Office and role of the Inspectorate of Constabulary, the imposition of statistical techniques and information systems and involvement of the Public Accounts Committee and Audit Commission in formulating 'efficiency exercises'—broadly falling 'into two overlapping categories [of privatisation]: policies concerned with management, and policies relating to the employment of civilians' (Johnston, 1992: 52). The instigating template for this privatising process had been provided in 1983 by Home Office Circular 114/83, which sought *inter alia* to consolidate spending after increase in the preceding three years and emphasised the apparent need for explicit statements of objectives and plans for achieving them. This would be done by limiting the availability of additional resources under the banner of 'policing by objectives' (PBO) (Lubans and Edger, 1979), the effect being that chief constables were being forced to spread existing resources thinly to consolidate services in order to meet objectives at a time when staff workloads at all levels were increasing. This led to the need for restructuring procedures in several forces, which had the knock-on effect of cutting force strength in a quest for compliance whilst attempting to balance anomalies and inequalities between diverse policing areas in an attempt to comply with set objectives, uniform Chartered Institute of Public Finance and Accountancy (CIPFA) benchmarks and annual inspections by the HMIC. It was anticipated that the adoption of such measures would create a 'performance culture' to enable efficiency and effectiveness—performance culture itself being seen as a key objective (Loveday, 1999: 357).

Hirst reflected that such an imposition of the privatisation mentality through the use of universal standards and benchmarks would often be exacerbated by centralised auditors able to add 'their own particular form of mayhem' via their advocacy of national metrics, often irrespective of the infrastructure of the force under scrutiny (1990: 86). Moreover, such measures ensured that central government, through its inspection regime, was finally able to bring some consistent pressure to bear on local police forces in terms of broad adherence to government strategy (Home Office Statistics, national and regional comparison tables and the Audit Commission) rather than authentically improving cost-effectiveness or assuming responsibility for localised crime and social disorder problems. This rigid quest for uniformity and compliance was observed to be placing the public police at a crossroads and being pulled in several directions at once. Hirst explains the impasse:

> Forces have assumed disparate sizes which means that some communities benefit from economies of scale, whilst others have to pay for expensive duplication of services at a non-cost-effective rate. Thus we have a fragmented national resource dependent on local financing but advised by central government and accountable to both central and local government as well as the local community, and increasingly the Police Complaints Authority, which is even now advocating the involvement of a Home Affairs Committee to review force policy, following serious complaints.
>
> *(1990: 87)*

The further key effect instigated by Circular 114/83 was towards civilianisation—the employment of support staff to free up time for officers to undertake operational policing tasks. The scope of civilianisation was widened by Home Office Circular 105/88, which had provided 25 roles to be filled by non-operational staff, ranging from administrative staff to gaoling, scenes of crime work, communications roles and counter and control room operatives (Home Office, 1988). As well as civilians employed directly by the police, a further move was towards the engagement of unfunded volunteers/private contractors and the recruitment of funded private contractors/agencies to outsource specific tasks—'load shedding and contracting out', respectively (Johnston, 1992: 58).

An early example of load shedding had been the organisation of Neighbourhood Watch groups to monitor community safety during the early 80s, the first of these in the UK being formed at Mollington, Cheshire, in 1982 along the lines of similar schemes in the US. This type of community-based initiative was increasingly complemented by the hiring of public-facing security staff by private individuals or organisations on a supply and demand basis—a practice which courted controversy in terms of its potential for conflict, particularly when stewarding the public at events (McArdle, 2000). Button and Wakefield provide a lucid example of load shedding in action by reference to the security arrangements for the policing of football matches during the 1980s, when typically a large contingent of public police officers would outnumber club stewards by 2 to 1, contrasting this with post Taylor Report recommendations which during the 90s would see club stewards outnumbering a token public police presence by 10 to 1, with costs supplemented accordingly (2018: 140). Crucially, the concept of contracting out sees the police retaining the responsibility for funding, seeing the hiring of the contractor or agency as cost effective (Fixler and Poole, 1988). In line with other public sector organisations during the 80s, many police forces routinely subcontracted all manner of facilities tasks, including cleaning, maintenance and catering, to outside companies. Other more specific areas seen as suitable early targets for contracting out were information technology (IT) provision, parking enforcement (McLean, 1989), forensic services (Kirby, 1989) and more controversially the civilian guarding of police stations and military installations (Johnston, 1992: 96). The private security industry was responsive in meeting such needs, its rise by now being increasingly seen as inexorable and 'recession resistant' as a low-wage, high-turnover sector (Williams et al., 1984) and through the technological advancement of refined closed circuit television (CCTV) linked to guard coordination able to offer the imminent promise of fully controlled environments—a very modern form of hegemony existing somewhere between panopticism and Disney World (Shearing and Stenning, 1985).

Conclusion

This chapter provides a social-historical examination of the development of public and private policing in the context of England and Wales via a necessarily macro analysis. This is offered as a valuable treatment, particularly given the current globalised focus on police powers and role in an era of rapid social change characterised by austerity, recession and political disenfranchisement—a genealogical respite from the immediacy that strain tends to confer. The subject matter of policing history, theory and concomitant policy is vast, ensuring that our purpose has been to select, explore and evaluate key areas.

This exploration presents a multitude of stages and events which have led to recognisable concepts of public policing and private security as possessing social and cultural cues. As Marwick reflects, 'we live in a time of rapid and far-reaching cultural change. If we are to make a rational assessment of the extent and significance of this change we have no other recourse than to look to the past' (2001: 31). Rationality is what has been attempted here. In the UK context the police have often been depicted with a sense of pride, an avatar for a nation—in heaven the police are British, supposedly—can this still be the case? The cultural exemplar of the British bobby, publically owned, was preceded by a type of private function, a duty-based form of community policing based upon shared responsibility allied to a need for order, confirming that policing existed long before *the police*.

As the public sphere developed and a need for discipline was realised, consensus was drawn towards social control, allowing for the creation of the new police for London in 1829. Bolstered by increased bureaucratic cohesion and centralised organisation, the Metropolitan Police force was able to establish itself, moving from expensive threat to liberty and limb to 'the best police force in the world' in the space of just 70 years. As has been seen, the success of *the police* did not apparently satisfy the appetite for policing, with a multitude of developments in what can now be considered private security providing a recognisable replication of the industry today, with separate operational parishes firmly established in the nineteenth century and generally unimpeded by government regulation. Moreover, commerce, technology, and the desired policy imperatives of market steering acceptance and cost defining use were impacting policing practice by the turn of the twentieth century, in very much the same way as now.

The chapter also highlights the increased politicisation of the police during the interwar years, when they were used to monitor and control demonstrations, leading to accusations of bias and what Cohen referred to as 'tacit negotiation' in their dealings with an enlarged and increasingly engaged electorate. Community mediation in the inner cities transformed from negotiation to need during the Second World War as mechanised warfare conferred the ability to destroy homes and take lives from the air, positioning the police as first point of call for reassurance and information following displacement or bereavement, a conciliating process. The immediate post-war period saw the radical use of nationalisation for the first time by a Labour government determined to provide the infrastructure for the country to re-establish itself. It is argued, in agreement with leading scholars of the discipline Emsley, Reiner, and Rawlings, that it was during this peoples' peace that public policing reached its apogee, preserved now as its 'Golden Age'. However, whilst the police enjoyed their salad days, the private security industry had been establishing itself, responding and growing to ensure that as the gilt faded they were able to provide solutions and take up the slack if need be.

As the police attempted to modernise during the economic disorder of the 1970s, the arrival of a revitalised Conservative government led by Margaret Thatcher in 1979 with the promise of investing in law and order seemed to promise stability and offer renewed relevance for the service. Thatcher, as the Iron Lady, championed the police force and was prepared to champion their role politically as guardians of order and deploy officers as enforcers when necessary, a politically pragmatic interpretation that she would later confirm in her autobiography: 'the criminal law on picketing had to be enforced by the police and courts. Although the Government would make it clear that the police enjoyed its moral support, the constitutional limits on us in this area were real and sometimes frustrating' (Thatcher, 1995: 302).

Frustration also existed in terms of a widening gap between police resources and public expectation, leading to the inclusion of the police as suitable subjects for the mass privatisation strategies attached to the neoliberal turn during the 1980s. This would register principally as the imposition of an overriding 'privatisation mentality' allied to the social marketisation of public services, with many forces on the receiving end registering these changes as a cultural shock. The centralised drive was towards service efficiency and value for money, and in attempting compliance or the satisfaction of targets, civilianisation and engagement with the private security industry were increasingly necessary.

In this chapter we have reviewed the development of policing function during its historical ascendency from private to public. In doing so it is clear that the modern history of policing emerges as an amalgam, despite a lasting fetishism or longing in terms of *the police*. One distinct effect of the neoliberal turn was to show the police in stark relief alongside their supervising civil servants and counterparts in the private security industry, transposing policing by consensus to policing by collectivism, a strategic managerialism towards dispersed governance based upon the 'collective responsibility of networks of and non-commercial "partners"' (Johnston and Shearing, 2003: 141). In the two decades that straddled the millennium, the drive towards collectivism would permeate and propagate; there would be no place for nostalgia.

Notes

1 In the historical context of England and Wales, the office of police constable has existed upon a foundation of independence. Despite the steady creep of privatisation over the past four decades, 'difference' is still seen in the responsibility of the public police, a point reinforced by Sir Ken Jones, president of ACPO. In 2008, at a time when officers were considering strike action, he rallied: 'The office of constable is the bedrock which underpins the delivery of justice in this country. It reminds us that those charged with enforcing law and order are office holders who are ultimately accountable to the law, not to any employer, politician or anyone else with a vested interest, for their actions' (Police Federation of England and Wales, 2008: 14).
2 Though historical calculation and comparisons of monetary inflation and worth are complex, this figure of £500,000 equates to a rudimentary low-end estimate of £63,000,000 in 2019, *Bank of England, Inflation calculator*—£500,000 1798 to 2018, accessed 11 February 2019: <www.bankofengland.co.uk/monetary-policy/inflation/inflation-calculator>
3 An observable image of the Parish Constable system still exists in the Channel Islands, whereby the elected head of each parish is titled *Connétable* and serves a term of duty of between two and three years.
4 Banton, in his insightful study, refers to the police as 'peace keepers', emphasising the important social dimension of the role linked via a commonality between the police and the policed during a time of escalating social and technological change (1964).
5 The Thatcherite commitment to 'less tax and law and order' was used symbolically as a contractual link towards 'decency', with policing spending 'ring fenced' for much of the 1980s despite swinging cuts to public services elsewhere—the recruitment of Maggie's army would command appropriate resourcing. In terms of the 'criminal justice budget'

overall, by the mid-point of her second ministry in 1984/85, criminal justice expenditure was already above £3.9 billion, an incredible rise from £2 billion when she entered office in 1979/80 (Evans, 2004: 57).

References

Anderson, J. (1929) 'The Police' *Public Administration* VII: 192–202
Alderson, J. (1979) *Policing Freedom*, Plymouth: McDonald and Evans
Anon (1976) *Report of the Task Force on Private Security*, Washington, DC: National Advisory Committee on Criminal Justice Standards and Goals
Babington, A. (1969) *A House in Bow Street: Crime and the Magistracy in London, 1740–1881*, London: McDonald and Co
Banton, M. (1964) *The Policeman in the Community*, London: Tavistock
Barrie, C. (2020) 'Searching Racism after George Floyd' *Socius* 6: 1–3
Beattie, J.M. (1986) *Crime and the Courts in England, 1660–1800*, Oxford: Clarendon Press
Becker, T. (1974) 'The Place of Private Police in Society: An Area of Research for the Social Sciences' *Social Problems* 21 (3): 438–453
Beveridge, W. (1943) *The Pillars of Society*, London: HMSO
Bloom, P. (2017) *The Ethics of Neoliberalism: Making Capitalism Moral*, London: Routledge
Bowling, B., and Phillips, C. (2002) *Racism, Crime and Justice*, London: Longman
Brain, T. (2010) *A History of Policing in England and Wales from 1974: A Turbulent Journey*, Oxford: Oxford University Press
Brain, T. (2013) *A Future for Policing in England and Wales*, Oxford: Oxford University Press
Brake, M., and Hale, C. (1991) *Public Order and Private Lives: The Politics of Law and Order*, London: Routledge
Braun, M., and Lee, D. (1971) 'Private Forces: Legal Powers, and Limitations' *University of Chicago Law Review* 38: 555–582
Brogden, M. (1982) *The Police: Autonomy and Consent*, London: Academic Press
BSAS (1983) 'British Social Attitudes Survey, Social and Community Planning Research, via UK Data Service' http://doi.org/10.5255/UKDA-SN-1935-1. Retrieved 4 December 2018
BSAS (1987) 'British Social Attitudes Survey, Social and Community Planning Research, via UK Data Service' http://doi.org/10.5255/UKDA-SN-2567-1. Retrieved 5 December 2018
Budworth, G. (1997) *The River Beat: The Story of London's River Police Since 1798*, London: Historical Publications
Button, M., and Wakefield, A. (2018) '"The Real Private Police": Franchising Constables and the Emergence of Employer Supported Policing' in A. Hucklesby and S. Lister (eds) *The Private Sector and Criminal Justice*, London: Palgrave Macmillan
Chick, M. (2002) *Industrial Policy in Britain 1945–1951: Economic Planning, Nationalisation and the Labour Governments*, Cambridge: Cambridge University Press
Christie, N. (2000) *Crime Control as Industry: Towards Gulags, Western Style*, London: Routledge
Cockcroft, T. (2012) *Police Culture: Themes and Concepts*, Abingdon: Routledge
Cockcroft, T., and Beattie, I. (2009) 'Shifting Cultures: Managerialism and the Rise of "Performance"' *Policing: An International Journal of Police Strategies and Management* 32 (3)
Cohen, P. (1981) 'Capitalism and the Rule of Law' *National Deviancy Conference*, London: Hutchinson, cited in Fitzgerald, M., et al. (1981) *Crime and Society: Readings in History and Theory*, London: Routledge
Colquhoun, P. (1800) *Treatise on the Police of the Metropolis*, Cambridge: Cambridge University Press (2012 edition)

Conservative Party (1979) 'Conservative Election Manifesto, April 11 1979' www.margaretthatcher.org/document/110858. Retrieved 24 October 2019

Coogan, T. (2002) *The IRA* (5th edition), New York: Palgrave Macmillan

Cretney, S. (2005) *Family Law in the Twentieth Century: A History*, Oxford: Oxford University Press

Critchley, T.A. (1967) *A History of Police in England and Wales*, London: Constable & Company

Dalton, H. (1935) 'The River Police' *Police Review* viii: 90–103

Defoe, D. (1906) 'Parochial Tyranny' by Andrew Moreton (a pseudonym of Defoe, used for critical pamphlets), London, p. 17; cited in Webb, S., and Webb, B. (1906) *English Local Government From the Revolution to the Municipal Corporations Act, the Manor and the Borough*, Vol. I, London: Longmans, Green & Co

Dodsworth, F. (2008) 'The Idea of Police in Eighteenth-Century England: Discipline, Reformation, Superintendence, c. 1780–1800' *Journal of the History of Ideas* 69 (4): 583–604

Draper, J.W. (1961) *Stratford to Dogberry: Studies in Shakespeare's Earlier Plays*, Pittsburgh: University of Pittsburgh Press

Edmund-Davies, E. (1979) *Committee of Inquiry on the Police, 1977–1979*, Cmnd. 7633, London: HMSO

Emsley, C. (1993) ' "Mother, What Did Policemen Do When There Weren't Any Motors?" The Law, the Police and the Regulation of Motor Traffic in England 1900–1939' *Historical Journal* XXXVII: 357–381

Emsley, C. (1996) *The English Police: A Political and Social History* (2nd edition), London: Longman

Emsley, C. (2014) 'Peel's Principles, Police Principles' in J. Brown (ed) *The Future of Policing*, Abingdon: Routledge

Emsley, C., and Clapson, M. (1994) 'Recruiting the English Policeman, c. 1840–1940' *Policing and Society* 3: 269–286

Emsley, C., and Shpayer-Makov, H. (2006) *Police Detectives in History, 1750–1950*, London: Ashgate

Evans, E. (2004) *Thatcher and Thatcherism* (2nd edition), London: Routledge

Fielding, H. (1751) *Amelia*, London: Penguin (1987 edition)

Fielding, N. (1991) *The Police and Social Conflict: Rhetoric and Reality*, London: Athlone

FitzGerald, M. (1999) *Searches in London Under Section 1 of the Police and Criminal Evidence Act*, London: Metropolitan Police

Fixler, P., and Poole, R. (1988) 'Can Police Services Be Privatized?' in I. Lipman (ed.) *The Annals of the American Academy of Political Science: The Private Security Industry: Issues and Trends*, Thousand Oaks, CA: Sage, p. 428

Fletcher, R. (2005) 'The Police Service: From Enforcement to Management' in J. Winstone and F. Pakes (eds) *Community Justice: Issues for Probation and Criminal Justice*, Cullompton: Willan

Foucault, M. (1977) *Discipline and Punish: The Birth of the Prison*, Harmondsworth: Penguin

Foucault, M. (1979) 'On Governmentality' *Ideology and Consciousness* 6: 5–22

Fremont-Barnes, G. (2009) *Who Dares Wins: The SAS and the Iranian Embassy Siege*, Oxford: Osprey

Friedersdorf, C. (2017, August 31) 'How to Distinguish Between Antifa, White Supremacists, and Black Lives Matter' *The Atlantic*

Garner, A. (1978) *The Guardians: A Study of the Commercialised Police in Britain*, Thesis, Manchester: Manchester Polytechnic (cited in South, 1988)

George, B., and Button, M. (2000) *Private Security, Volume 1*, London: Palgrave Macmillan

Godfrey, B., and Lawrence, P. (2005) *Crime and Justice 1750–1950*, Cullompton: Willan

Gorer, G. (1955) *Exploring English Character*, London: Cresset Press

Green, P. (1990) *The Enemy Without: Policing and Class Consciousness in the Miner's Strike*, Milton Keynes: Open University Press

Habermas, J. (1989) *The Structural Transformation of the Public Sphere: An Inquiry into a Category of Bourgeois Society*, Cambridge, MA: MIT Press

Hall, S., et al. (1978) *Policing the Crisis: Mugging, the State, and Law and Order*, London: Palgrave Macmillan

Hansard (1990) 'The Army' Volume 173: Debated on Tuesday 5 June 1990, Column 553

Harris, A.T. (2004) *Policing the City: Crime and Legal Authority in London, 1780–1840*, Columbus: The Ohio State University Press

Hirst, M. (1990) 'The Police Service' in Association of County Councils (ed) *New Directions in Public Services: The County Council Experience*, London: Policy Studies Institute

Her Majesty's Chief Inspector of Constabulary (HMCIC) (1991) *Report of Her Majesty's Chief Inspector of Constabulary for the Year 1990*, London: HMSO

Hobbs, D. (1988) *Doing the Business: Entrepreneurship, the Working Class, and Detectives in the East End of London*, Oxford: Clarendon

Holmes, E. (1861) *A Treatise Upon the Best Method of Protecting Property from Burglars, and Human Life from Midnight Assassins*, New York City: Holmes' Advertising Pamphlet

Home Office (1967) *Police Manpower, Equipment and Efficiency*, London: Home Office

Home Office (1983) *Manpower, Effectiveness and Efficiency in the Police Service*, London: Home Office Circular 114/83

Home Office (1988) *Civilian Staff in the Police*, London: Home Office Circular 105/88

Hood, C. (1991) 'A Public Management for All Seasons' *Public Administration* 69: 3–19

Jefferys, K. (1992) *The Attlee Governments 1945–1951*, London: Routledge

Johnston, L. (1992) *The Rebirth of Private Policing*, London: Routledge

Johnston, L., and Shearing, C. (2003) *Governing Security: Explorations in Policing and Justice*, London: Routledge

Kakalik, J., and Wildhorn, S. (1971) *Private Police in the United States, Findings and Recommendations*, Vol. 1, Washington, DC: Government Printing Office

Kirby, T. (1989, February 28) 'Rock Bottom Morale amongst Forensic Scientists Highlighted' *Independent*

Lee, S. (2008) *The Impact of Home Burglar Alarm Systems on Residential Burglaries*. Unpublished Doctoral Dissertation. New Jersey-Newark: Rutgers University

Leeworthy, D. (2012) 'The Secret Life of us, the Miners' Strike and the Place of Biography in Writing History "From Below"' *European Review of History* 19 (5): 825–846

Lentz, S.A., and Chaires, R.H. (2007) 'The Invention of Peel's Principles: A Study of Policing "Textbook" History' *Journal of Criminal Justice* 35 (1): 69–79

Lichfield, J. (2019, February 9) 'Just Who Are the Gilets Jaunes?' *The Guardian*

Linebaugh, P. (1991) *The London Hanged—Crime and Civil Society in the Eighteenth Century*, London: Penguin

Loveday, B. (1995) 'Contemporary Challenges to Police Management in England and Wales: Developing Strategies for Effective Service Delivery' *Policing and Society* 5: 281–302

Loveday, B. (1999) 'The Impact of Performance Culture on Criminal Justice Agencies in England and Wales' *International Journal of the Sociology of Law* 27: 351–377

Lloyd George, D. (1918, November 23) (Earl Lloyd-George of Dwyfor) 'Speech at Wolverhampton' quoted in *The Times*, November 25, 1918

Lubans, V., and Edger, J. (1979) *Policing by Objectives*, Hartford, CT: Social Development Corporation

Mackay, J. (1998) *Allan Pinkerton: The First Private Eye*, New York: Wiley & Sons
Marwick, A. (2001) *The New Nature of History*, Basingstoke: Palgrave Macmillan
Mawby, R. (2002) *Policing Images: Policing, Communication and Legitimacy*, Cullompton: Willan
McArdle, D. (2000) *From Boot Money to Bosman, Football Society and the Law*, London: Cavendish
McGuire, M. (2012) *Technology, Crime and Justice: The Question Concerning Technomia*, Abingdon: Routledge
McLean, A. (1989, October 6) 'Private Coppers Saving Pounds' *Police Review*: 2016–2017
Milne, S. (2004) *The Enemy Within: Thatcher's Secret War against the Miners*, London: Verso
Moore, C., and Brown, J. (1981) *Community Versus Crime*, London: Bedford Square
Moore, L. (1997) *The Thieves' Opera*, London: Viking
Morton, J. (2002) *Supergrasses & Informers and Bent Coppers*, London: Time Warner
Morton, J. (2003) *Gangland Omnibus*, vols. 1 and 2, London: Time Warner
Newburn, T., and Reiner, R. (2007) 'Policing and the Police' in M. Maguire et al. (eds) *The Oxford Handbook of Criminology*, Oxford: Oxford University Press
O'Morgan, K. (1999) *Britain Since 1945: The People's Peace*, Oxford: Oxford University Press
Packer, H. (1964) 'Two Models of the Criminal Process' *University of Pennsylvania Law Review* 113 (1): 1–68
Police Federation of England and Wales (2008, May) *The Office of Constable: The Bedrock of Modern British Policing*, Leatherhead: Police Federation of England and Wales
Rawlings, P. (2002) *Policing: A Short History*, Cullompton: Willan
Reiner, R. (1992) 'Policing a Postmodern Society' *The Modern Law Review* 55 (6): 761–781
Reiner, R. (1994) 'The Dialectics of Dixon: The Changing Image of the TV Cop' in M. Stephens and S. Becker (eds) *Police Force, Police Service*, Basingstoke: Palgrave Macmillan
Reiner, R. (2010) *The Politics of the Police* (4th edition), Oxford: Oxford University Press
Rhodes, R.A.W. (1994) 'The Hollowing Out of the State: The Changing Nature of the Public Service in Britain' *The Political Quarterly* 65 (2): 138–151
Roberts, M. (2001) *Britain, 1846–1964: The Challenge of Change*, Oxford: Oxford University Press
Sawer, P. (2010, December 13) 'Police Dragged Me from Wheelchair Twice During Protests, Says Demonstrator' *Telegraph*
Scarman, L. (1981) *The Brixton Disorders 10–12 April 1981: Report of an Inquiry by the Rt. Hon. the Lord Scarman, OBE*, London: HMSO
Scott, T., and MacPherson, M. (1971) 'The Development of the Private Sector of the Criminal Justice System' *Law and Society Review* 6 (2): 267–288
Scraton, P. (1999) *Hillsborough: The Truth*, Edinburgh: Mainstream
Shearing, C., et al. (1980) *Contract Security in Ontario*, Toronto Centre of Criminology: University of Toronto
Shearing, C., and Stenning, P. (1985) 'From the Panopticon to Disney World: The development of Discipline' in A. Doob and E. Greenspan (eds) *Perspectives in Criminal Law: Essays in Honour of John Ll. J. Edwards*, Toronto: Canada Law Book, pp. 335–349
Short, C. (1982, December) 'Community Policing—Beyond Slogans' in T. Bennett (ed) *The Future of Policing: Papers Delivered to the Fifteenth Cropwood Round-Table Conference*, Cropwood Conference Series 15, Cambridge: Cambridge Institute of Criminology
Skogan, W. (1990) *The Police and the Public in England and Wales: A British Crime Survey Report*, Home Office Research Study No. 117, London: Home Office
South, N. (1988) *Policing for Profit: The Private Security Sector*, London: Sage

Smith, H. (2014) *The British Women's Suffrage Campaign 1866–1928: Revised* (2nd edition), London: Routledge
Spitzer, S., and Scull, A. (1977) 'Privatization and Capitalist Development: The Case of the Private Police' *Social Problems* 25 (1): 18–29
Storch, R. (1976) 'The Policeman as Domestic Missionary: Urban Discipline and Popular Culture in Northern England, 1850–1880' *Journal of Social History* IX: 481–511
Storch, R., and Engels, F. (1975) 'The Plague of the Blue Locusts: Police Reform and Popular Resistance in Northern England, 1840–57' *International Review of Social History* 20 (1): 61–90
Taylor, Lord Justice (1990) *The Hillsborough Stadium Disaster, 15 April 1989, Final Report*, Cm 962, London: HMSO
Thatcher, M. (1984, July 19) 'The Enemy Within' *Speech to the 1922 Committee*
Thatcher, M. (1995) *Margaret Thatcher: The Autobiography*, London: Harper Press
Tobias, J.J. (1972) 'Police and the Public in the United Kingdom' *Journal of Contemporary History* 7: 201–219
Tooher, P. (1996, March 31) 'The Changing of the Guard' *Independent*
Vernon, J. (2007) *Hunger: A Modern History*, Cambridge, MA: Harvard University Press
Vidocq, E. (1834) *Memoirs of Vidocq, Principal Agent to the French Police, until 1827*, Philadelphia: Carey and Hart
Waldren, M. (2007) *Armed Police: The Police Use of Firearms Since 1945*, Stroud: Sutton
Walker, P., and Lewis, P. (2012, July 19) 'Simon Harwood Not Guilty of Killing Ian Tomlinson' *The Guardian*
Watts-Miller, W. (1987) 'Party Politics, Class Interest and Reform of the Police, 1829–56' *Police Studies* 10: 42–60
Weinberger, B. (1991) *Keeping the Peace: Policing Strikes in Britain 1906–1926*, Oxford: Berg
Weinberger, B. (1995) *The Best Police in the World: An Oral History of British Policing*, Hampshire: Scolar
Wiles, P., and McClintock, F. (eds) (1972) *The Security Industry in the United Kingdom*, Cambridge: Institute of Criminology University of Cambridge
Williams, D., et al. (1984) *Guarding against Low Pay*, Low Pay Pamphlet 29, London: Low Pay Unit

7
THE PUBLIC AND PRIVATE POLICE, OR BACK TO THE FUTURE

> In all I had thirty five years of service, starting in 1978 and retiring in 2013. During my time I saw a sea change in the limiting of force autonomy and with it a loss of public trust. Concerns over money and manpower became the be all and end all.
>
> (A former police chief inspector[1])

Introduction

If the 1980s are to be identified as a modern crucible for the amalgamation and blurring of public and private in criminal justice practice, what has followed since must be seen as a consolidation. In terms of criminological theory this politically charged period of the late twentieth century also provided what came to be termed *right realism*, a conformist criminology with an emphasis on responsibility over rights and common sense over uncommon sensibility. Crucially, right realism fostered administrative, neo-conservative and rational choice perspectives which staged crime as an event performed by cogent actors who could therefore be patrolled and disrupted. As such it was made for the no-nonsense 'law and order' rhetoric which had underpinned Thatcherism and chimed with public mood. The discipline of criminal justice possessed clear potential as a site for political economy. Matthews evaluates its naive appeal for neoliberal polity:

> Right realists also tend to avoid explanations that include considerations of 'root causes' and 'deep structures', such as poverty and inequality, and instead focus on the more visible but arguably more superficial aspects of crime and its control. This, in part, is the basis of its widespread appeal. By avoiding challenging conceptual issues and engaging in 'straight talking', the policies

presented often resonate not only with academics but also with politicians and the general public.

(2014: 15)

Right realism was also made for adaption to models of preventative policing, with officers at the sharp end thought most able to intervene, intersect and crucially inhibit criminal events. The best-known response in terms of a practical policing model that would be realistic *enough* is the 'broken windows' theory conceived by James Q. Wilson and George Kelling, built upon the concept of 'zero tolerance' (1982). The appeal of broken windows, then as now, was in its simplicity, the notion of the selective deployment of public police officers to address 'incivilities' in partnership with responsive local communities who would check for 'signals', a way of reclaiming and cleansing the streets. Effectively this was a return of sorts to the reinforcement of respectable community norms via contact, an antidote to the fire brigade policing and de-policing strategies of the 1970s, drawing on the experiences of a post–Golden Age generation. However, practical implementation of the thesis, despite political desirability, would require partnership and plurality to be efficient and cost effective, essentially a form of responsibilisation that has dominated public-police partnerships since (Garland, 2001).

A more critically rounded theoretical view of State response to social change from the same era was provided by Clifford Shearing and Phillip Stenning, who sought to expose the changing nature of social life through the exploration of mass private property, recognising the growth of 'hybrid' spaces where ownership and jurisdiction was unclear (1981). Later, in the midst of the Thatcher-Reagan compact, their analogy for this increasingly layered post-industrial first world was revealed as Disney World, a site of pleasure and escapism underwritten by various pervasive forms of strategic social control—direction, instruction, the limitation of choice and the erection of physical, normative and financial barriers (Shearing and Stenning, 1985). Significantly, there were no broken windows at Disney World, but civility, maintenance and security were funded by admission charge; it was a superlative model of the policing *of* profit *by* profit.

The transference of such a model to the control of hybrid space in a more comprehensive social setting would clearly require collaboration, presenting increased opportunity for an alert private security industry already aware that pluralist policing initiatives could facilitate commercial viability. Although Shearing and Stenning had based their concept on structuralism, there was also lineage to Foucault's prophetic idea of dispersal of discipline, the opportunity to construct the carceral archipelago he had envisioned with power relations visibly less overt but culturally pervasive and disparate—'not a network of forces, but a multiple network of diverse elements' (1977: 307). Such multiplicity would require consent, configuration and docility, with the foundation for this having been provided by the dominating political discourse of the 1980s, which had successfully merged and normalised uncertainty with opportunity.

Against this backdrop, the current chapter builds on its predecessor to examine developments in policing and private security over the past three decades. The loss of personal popularity by Margaret Thatcher in the late 1980s did not lead to what for many seemed an inevitable move away from Thatcherism into the 1990s. In fact what had seemed a turbulent decade of political change might now be reflected upon as a dawn rather than the light of day. For public policing the twin strategic objectives of adaptation to a privatisation mentality and the application of social markets to public service that had been established during the 1980s would now proliferate rather than diminish, and through this propagation the private security industry would gain ground towards recognition as an equal rather than junior partner—in terms of political interpretation, at least.

During the last 30 years successive governments have remained wedded to a form of neoliberalism that necessitates a minimal State and grafted it to a notion of common sense, attempting to appeal to consensus and common purpose via such soundbites as 'back to basics', the 'third way' and latterly 'big society'. Throughout, the role of *the police* and the *need* for change has remained firmly on the political agenda, weathering increased centralisation, resource constraint and civilianisation against the customary expectations of a public increasingly required to assume and absorb individual responsibility and risk for collective safety and security. These are some of the central themes that will be explored by the authors here through an examination of the impetus towards pluralism and realism that has dominated the recent history of the subject.

Business as usual

Following the resignation of Margaret Thatcher after 11 years in office, John Major became Prime Minister of the UK on 28 November 1990, with the country entering recession. After leading through the first Persian Gulf War at the end of 1990 into 1991, Major fielded repeated requests to call an early general election from the Labour party leader of the opposition, Neil Kinnock, during that year. He eventually took the country to the polls in April 1992, winning decisively and providing the Conservative Party with a fourth consecutive term in office. With the country by now in deep recession, Major was perceived as a rather dour politician but seen as the safest pair of hands on offer in terms of the economy at the time, having formerly served as Chief Secretary to the Treasury and Margaret Thatcher's last Chancellor of the Exchequer. Moreover he had been well placed in government and shared his party's commitment to the mass privatisation of public services. Reinforcing these credentials between 1994 and 1997, he took the controversial decision to privatise British Rail (BR) via the *Railways Act 1993*, despite the service and network being seen by Thatcher previously as unworkable and ideologically 'a privatisation too far' (Marr, 2007: 495). Notwithstanding his composed and mannerly appearance, Major could also be stubborn when dealing with public service resistance to policy change and impatient in terms of results thereafter, political traits shared with his predecessor that the police were soon to discover.

During the 1980s recorded crime had increased by 80%, whilst the number of sworn police officers had risen by around 13,000 to 127,000; at the start of the 1990s this was viewed as a signifier that the police were not providing efficiency or good value (HMIC, 1979–90; Home Office, 1990; Scott, 2009). To tackle this issue Major would link NPM to his key concept of a Citizen's Charter, to be launched within a year of him taking office in July 1991 and used to reform and attune public services to public expectations—fundamentally the principles of public service, with 'service first' (Citizen's Charter, 1991).

With an inspectorate and auditors already in place, the impact on police would be considerable, with 17 quality standards (QSs) and 45 key performance indicators (KPIs) added and linked to national matrices providing comparative measurement of efficiency (HMIC, 1991). In addition, an inquiry led by Sir Patrick Sheehy was instigated to examine police pay and conditions and consider introducing employment practices from the private sector, such as fixed-term contracts and performance-linked incentives and dismissal (Sheehy, 1993). These radical proposals would be considered by incoming Home Secretary Michael Howard (who would ultimately reject them) as part of his programme of 'Police Reform' (Home Office, 1993).

There was some urgency behind the installation of Howard in May 1993, who was seen as a hardliner and suitable foil for a rejuvenating Labour opposition under John Smith basking in the distinctly Thatcherite law and order rhetoric of the energetic shadow Home Secretary Tony Blair. In an interview on *The World This Weekend* programme in January 1993 Blair had stated that 'I think it's important that we [Labour] are tough on crime and tough on the causes of crime too', a message that had resonated and gained ground in the public and media outcry that followed the murder of two year old James Bulger by two older children in February that year—a case that would subsequently change the face of youth justice (Scraton, 2008) and instigate a clamour for the use of CCTV.

Howard's view of reform positioned the public police as crime-fighters first and foremost, advocating yet more load shedding to the private sector in terms of secondary tasks around licensing and escorting duties. Further streamlining was also seen to be required to ensure that police management was operated along business lines to be cost effective, with force performance and budget responsibility resting with chief constables who would be answerable as 'chief executives to their respective police authorities acting as an overseeing board of directors'. To enable the police in their crime-fighting role, additional powers were provided by the controversial *Criminal Justice and Public Order Act 1994* (CJPOA) in terms of inference drawn from the right to silence, unsupervised stop and search and restrictions on 'anti-social behaviour' and 'unauthorised assembly', with increased penalties provided for such behaviour—a statute drafted in the midst of a moral panic (South, 1999). Burgeoning methodology desired that policing should be more proactive and increasingly intelligence led (Tilley, 2003: 312), and once again the public police would be reimagined as a hard blue line, with *service* relegated as secondary to *force* (Stephens and Becker, 1994).

Howard's way also saw further centralisation with the setting out of a new relationship between the Home Secretary and territorial police forces and providing powers to determine universal objectives for the police under the *Police and Magistrates' Court Act 1994* (PMCA), a key precedent observed by Loveday as providing 'a springboard for intervention by successor administrations' (2006: 284). This would be reinforced and replaced within two years by the Police Act 1996 (PA), a radical statute which, though principally focused on structural governance, considerably extended the functions of the Secretary of State to include objective setting alongside budgetary and regulatory matters. A further commercialising effect of the PA was to allow police forces to charge for special services, goods and the use of police property whilst being able to raise 1% of their budget via sponsorship.

Demonstrating a finely tuned privatisation mentality, these changes would be overseen by an augmented HMIC and Audit Commission inspectorate to report on the now-familiar duo of effectiveness and efficiency. With the Sheehy inquiry having recommended four primary objectives of public policing—which can briefly be summarised as crime prevention, pursuit and apprehension, keeping the peace and public protection and reassurance (Sheehy, 1993)—Howard now instigated a further inquiry chaired by Ingrid Posen to review and evaluate police core and ancillary duties with a brief to 'examine the services provided by the police, to make recommendations about the most cost-effective way of delivering core policing services and to assess the scope for relinquishing ancillary tasks' (Home Office, 1995: 7).

The outcome was a final report entitled the *Review of Police Core and Ancillary Tasks* (Home Office, 1995), which, whilst broadly agreeing with the core operational areas highlighted by Sheehy, declined to confirm them, suggesting instead an incremental move towards load shedding and the application of social markets to public services. This would further position the primacy of the public police as specialist crime-fighters by allowing the relinquishing of 'inessential' tasks via interagency working and civilianisation 'setting the template for the service's composition and primary purposes for the next twenty-five years and beyond' (Brain, 2013: 54). Posen had resisted calls for a two-tiered model of police patrolling and warned of potential police disengagement leading to public service disadvantage, instead specifying 26 areas suitable seen as suitable for ancillary operatives, including the policing of events, transport and escort duties, intervening in cases of noise nuisance, stray dog catching, the issuing of summonses and provision of court security (Home Office, 1995: 12).

Active citizenship and technological treatments

One key aim of the Citizen's Charter had been to promote active citizenship and participation. This was provided with a distinctly conservative designation by John Major's 'Back to Basics' initiative launched at the Conservative Party Conference in October 1993, an event which also hosted Michael Howard's 'prison works' speech as counter to Blair's earlier challenge (Howard, 1993). This campaign had been founded on traditional values of 'neighbourliness, decency, and courtesy' and underpinned by 'a new campaign to defeat the cancer that is crime' (Major, 1993). Coming directly in the wake of the Bulger case and the raised concerns over youth crime and recreational drug use which would permeate the 1990s, it was a call for individuals to assume social responsibility for antisocial behaviour which resonated at the domestic level. In terms of crime prevention, such responsibilisation often presented as possessing private means to enable a tangible end, what Shearing and Stenning had described as the 'new feudalism' (1983: 494)—as Reiner would observe, 'Public policing is in effect increasingly restricted to a core rump. Those who are unsatisfied with this, and have the financial means to obtain private substitutes (of varying value for money and quality) are doing so' (1995: 555).

In practice this often saw individuals turning to technological innovation, a move supported by a growing body of academic research that advocated the need for physical prevention over social cure (Clarke, 1980, 1995, 1997; Clarke and Felson, 1993; Ekblom, 1991, 1994; Pease, 1994; Webb, 1994; Leigh et al., 1996). Technology, in particular microchip technology, had allowed for advances in home security by way of cost-effective photo-electric cell security lighting, alarms and safes, with vehicles increasingly sold with factory-fitted immobilisers and containing stereos with removable facias. However, the most dramatic area of private security expansion to emerge from the period would be the employment of CCTV for purposes of safety and security, a recent development which impacted domestic, commercial and social control proliferation (Gaylord and Galliher, 1991; Tilley, 1993; Taylor, 1995).

Within the UK context, the evocative image utilised by the media in the Bulger case in 1993 had been that captured by shopping centre CCTV in Bootle, Merseyside—this had informed the police that their suspects were two older children. Later that same year the conviction of serial killer Colin Ireland had been enabled by evidence provided by a security camera at Charing Cross station, London. Both cases demonstrated the apparent value of the apparatus to the attention of the public, who began to view it as a potential panacea to the apparent inexorable rise in crime and antisocial behaviour, despite concerns over civil liberties and the likelihood of displacement (Short and Ditton, 1998; Bowers et al., 1998). A further driver was provided by government regulation which increasingly demanded minimum security levels to include CCTV surveillance at public transport hubs such as ports, airports and stations and an increasing preference for its deterrent use and operational efficiency in road traffic enforcement. Moreover, from the mid 1990s the UK government provided grants to local authorities to fund CCTV systems, increasingly linking central thoroughfares and side streets to the existing coverage in shopping malls and arcades, essentially what Shearing and Stenning had described as 'mass private property' (1981). This blurring of public and private was seen to delivering an ever-expanding private security network which remained unregulated despite increasingly heated debate in Parliament. Eventually consultation in the form of a green paper focusing on the contract guarding sector of the industry would appear, but a further change of government would occur before its content would be evaluated and developed.

Costing tough on crime

Following the appointment of John Smith QC as leader in July 1992, replacing Neil Kinnock after the jolt of election defeat, the Labour party had made steady ground on the Conservatives. The experienced and respected Smith, an owlish figure, was a consummate performer at the despatch box and had recognised the need for the party to both embrace modernisation and promote young talent within its shadow cabinet. By the spring of 1994 his unruffled approach was paying dividends, with Labour leading the Conservatives in the polls by 23%, representing a significant turnaround. Smith was to die unexpectedly of a heart attack on 11 May 1994, after giving a speech where he had implored the public for 'the opportunity to serve our country, that is all we ask' (Stuart, 2005: 2). With the Labour party in shock but conscious of the need to regroup and maintain momentum, the ambitious shadow Home Secretary Tony Blair was promoted to leader by July, promising to end the party's long opposition by leading a 'New' Labour party into the millennium.

Amongst his first actions as leader, having previously been involved with ending union block voting in 1993, he sought to repeal 'clause IV', ending Labour's longstanding commitment to the common ownership of industry via renationalisation, suggesting that any future administration would be both tough on crime and fully open to the free market to fight its causes (Blair, 1995: 2). Having established his centrist credentials and commitment to the social market economics of the 'third way' with the electorate (Tansey and Jackson, 2008: 87), Blair became Prime Minister with a landslide victory in May 1997, with Jack Straw succeeding Michael Howard as Home Secretary. During Howard's tenure crime had fallen by 18% (Home Office, 1998), so being seen as the party of law and order would remain a key priority for the incoming administration.

Within New Labour's first term, it had launched its flagship Crime and Disorder Act 1998 (CDA), which had clear links to the apex of pre-emptive, pro-active partnership policing—the zero-tolerance methods popularised within the 'broken windows' concept of Wilson and Kelling (1982). The CDA included a raft of measures aimed at responsibilisation, including the much-vaunted anti-social behaviour orders (ASBOs), curfew orders and the abolition of the *doli incapax* rule. This was a clear attempt to localise social problems and by doing so spread the responsibility and cost for their containment, with government grants made available via a competitive bids process to facilitate 'Crime and Disorder Reduction Partnerships' (CDRPs) (Phillips et al., 2002). Moreover, it set a recognisably third way template for much of what would follow in terms of criminal justice policy, with an emphasis on what Reiner described as the 'Janus-faced tough/smart policy combination' simultaneously garnering popular approval with middle England, tabloid editors and the Treasury (Reiner, 2007: 136). Initiative in terms of public-private partnership was identified as a necessity to avoid risk to Labour's ambitious plans for criminal justice and to protect its recently hard won reputation; this established a clear awareness of public financial constraint to balance resource demands with those in often beleaguered communities (Butler, 2000: 309).

Such community involvement was also suggestive of a move towards the problem-oriented policing (POP) approach developed in America in the 1980s (Goldstein, 1979; Ekblom, 2002). POP emphasised the need to allocate police resources effectively to address the underlying recurrent problems within a locality (Leigh et al., 1996, 1998), thus involving local authorities as stakeholders whilst addressing efficiency and value as a response to the imperatives of NPM. The CDA effectively ensured that partnership working would become a statutory requirement, offering much scope for collaboration and tandem working with the private security industry (Wakefield, 2003: 51). However, for the public police, a key by-product of the CDA would be a further increase in bureaucracy as part and parcel of the by now customary privatisation mentality. With the launch of the government's linked national Crime Reduction Strategy (CRS) in November 1999, this manifested in the need for the police to allocate time to partnership training and consultancy alongside the creation of new units with local authorities to administer the imposition of the new measures, with augmented performance targets (Solomon, 2009: 56). It was becoming readily apparent that New Labour resembled old neoliberalism (Hay, 1997).

Private-sector involvement in the third way was seen as imperative to Labour's collaborative ethos, with Straw having addressed the BSIA within two months of gaining office to revisit the idea of the formal regulation of the industry which had been raised the previous year but also emphasising the crucial role that they would play under the new administration. He enthused, 'the private sector—and the private security industry—also have a crucial role to play . . . But in reiterating my commitment to regulation, my message is not one of mistrust, but of confidence' (Straw, 1997: paras 36–37, cited in White, 2018). Straw's confidence was in the dynamism of the industry to provide security solutions at a time when integrative CCTV was seen by a majority of the public as something of a magic bullet; this would ensure the continuation of promotion and funding for extensive CCTV schemes throughout the country, often to amalgamate partnership (Armitage, 2002). 1998 had also seen the publication of large-scale systematic research into private security by Jones and Newburn, estimating *inter alia*, that employment in the sector had grown by 240% in less than half a century, calculating over 333,000 current employees and a sector turnover of around £1.5bn. The research also stated that 29% of listed companies had been established between 1985 and 1989, and 34% since 1990, suggesting remarkable expansion which amounted to a 63% market increase in just over a decade (Jones and Newburn, 1998).

The extensive nature of private security within criminal justice was by now obvious and readily accepted, leaving Ian Blair, then chief constable of Surrey, to frankly position the police as security coordinators within interagency working, observing that with patrol, 'It [the public police] is not abandoning a monopoly of patrol. It is admitting that we haven't had one for years' (1998). However, expansion still carried controversy and a desire for regulation, leading to an announcement that a private security industry authority (PSIA) was to be established (Home Office, 1999). The corresponding Home Office report stated that over 40,000 of the people applying for posts in the private security industry per annum did so with criminal records, over 24,000 of these could be listed as serious offences (Home Office, 1999: 25). Such a move would seek to legitimise as well as regulate the industry to ensure that it was fit and able to take part in hybrid community policing initiatives, which would place an emphasis on pragmatic pluralism (Loader, 2000).

Policing a new century and extending the police family

With a new Home Secretary in David Blunkett, Labour fought the 2001 general election campaign on increased police funding, with a pledge to provide 6,000 additional officers (Labour Party, 2001). Winning a second term, the party produced a white paper, *Policing a New Century* (Home Office, 2001), which introduced the key concept of the 'extended police family' and served as a prelude to the Police Reform Act 2002 (PRA 2002) the title of which echoed the earlier 'reforming' interventions of Michael Howard. The PRA 2002 would provide a far-reaching platform for 'civilianisation', introducing police community support officers (PCSOs) as non-sworn constables, alongside investigating, detention and escort officers.

Additionally the PRA allowed chief constables to confer a limited range of powers on civilians to meet local needs under community safety accreditation schemes (CSASs), covering both local authority employees and private contractors. These developments were indicative of a radical move in the provision of visible policing strategy which effectively introduced a second policing tier via a clear dispersal of State authority, delegating robust powers which included the ability to stop vehicles, control traffic, issue fixed penalty notices and confiscate alcohol. Further provisions under the act provided the Home Secretary with enhanced influence in terms of intervention to set national priorities and objectives, directly manage failing police services and remove 'underperforming' chief officers (Loveday, 2006: 84).

The provisions conferred under the CSAS were underpinned and legitimised by the long anticipated Private Security Industry Act 2001 (PSIA), which established the Security Industry Authority (SIA). The remit of the SIA would be to regulate the private security industry in England and Wales as a self-funding independent body but reporting directly to the Home Secretary. Regulation would be carried out by a licensing process including 'fit and proper' background checks and the management of an Approved Contractor Scheme (ACS) viewable as a public register against set benchmarks alongside powers to revoke and modify licenses. These developments were generally welcomed as providing a foundation for a continuing programme of improvement, with Bruce George, MP, an industry expert and long-time advocate of regulation, reflecting that previously:

> [A]n absence of training is the norm and the public's attitude to the security industry is a combination of mirth, hostility and indifference. That will

change, and not only as a result of this long overdue legislation. The market has changed, technology has moved forward and crime levels have risen. The police realise that they must work with technology produced in the private sector with an industry to which they can relate.

(2001: cols 83–84)

Technological impact and fear of crime were indeed key, with the public police role becoming ever more specialised and refined. This rise of specialists had led to the establishment of the National Hi-Tech Crime Unit in 2001 (superseded by the Serious and Organised Crime Agency [SOCA] in 2006 and latterly the National Crime Agency [NCA] in 2013), primarily in response to the perceived threat posed by cybercrime, particularly the recognition that the advent of the World Wide Web conferred an ability for crimes to be committed across global networks, the spectre of borderless crime (Thomas and Loader, 2000: 3).

The 'policing' of cybercrime as a global entity would innately require pluralisation involving a multitude of State, quasi-State and non-State actors and agencies, its complexity and fast-moving nature ensuring a ready made market for private security measures in terms of hardware and software and the invention of online responsibilisation transforming the established concept of responsible and rational citizens into 'netizens'. Similarly, both fear and consideration of security response was greatly increased in the aftermath of the al-Qaeda terrorist attacks on September 11, 2001 (and exacerbated by the those that have followed), focusing individuals on personal risk and their exposure to potential harm whilst creating a niche market in private security for force via a significant increase in the transnational market for military security services, a practice capable of diffusing both control and potential victimisation (Avant, 2005).

As it transpired, the Labour party's commitment to extending the policing family throughout its second term would be linked to the 'national reassurance policing programme' which had been introduced in 2003 and delivered by what would be termed 'neighbourhood policing' (Home Office, 2004). Neighbourhood policing strategy, firmly founded on pluralism, involved active community engagement with second-tier policing operatives in the form of PCSOs and/or private contractors, leading to a quasi or hybrid policing approach which potentially offered 'a pluralized, fragmented and differentiated framework of policing' (Crawford, 2003: 136). Contemporary research conducted by Crawford and Lister on visible patrols in residential areas reflected a growing realisation that if householders wished to have a visible patrol in their area, they would be expected to fund it privately, signifying an end to the reassurance policing monopoly of the public police. In conclusion, they anticipated a future domestic market between technology and something approaching a tradition of duty:

> as the demand for security shows little sign of waning, the increased cost of security personnel may encourage potential purchasers to look to technological solutions, such as CCTV systems, gating, alarm response systems . . . At the same time as the cost of private security is set to increase, the introduction

of CSOs has reduced the cost of a uniformed police officer (albeit one with limited powers and training). This will seemingly allow the police to compete more effectively within this growing market.

(Crawford and Lister, 2004: 63)

By 2005 there were 6,214 PCSOs operating in England and Wales (Home Office, 2005), a figure corresponding with the '6000 additional officers' pledged in Labour's 2001 Manifesto. Along with civilianisation there had been a distinct move towards centralisation in terms of managerialism under Blunkett, who had brought online the National Intelligence Model (NIM), with its emphasis on managing both risk and resource allocation, and the National Crime Recording Standard (NCRS) following concerns that individual forces had been collecting crime data inconsistently (ONS, 2016). Such developments led to a corresponding increase in central policing costs, representing 6% of the entire national budget in 2004, garnering criticism from the Conservative opposition (Brain, 2013: 16).

Into austerity

The Labour party was to win a third election victory under Blair in May 2005, albeit with a much reduced majority, with John Reid now serving as Home Secretary. Less than two months later, policing and security in London would come under intense scrutiny following a series of coordinated terrorist attacks using suicide bombers on the capital's transport system on 7 July, leaving 52 killed and over 700 injured. A further series of ultimately unsuccessful attacks, seemingly connected to those of the 7th, were mounted on 21 July, and with the police on high alert in the aftermath, armed officers shot and killed an innocent man at Stockwell station, John Charles de Menezes, after mistakenly identifying him as a suspect (Squires and Kennison, 2010).

Directly prior to the general election, the government had passed the Serious Organised Crime and Police Act 2005 (SOCPA), which, whilst aimed primarily at the creation of the SOCA and controversially extending police powers of arrest and search, had also authorised the creation of civilian custody officers, overturning key responsibility provisions of PACE 1984. This in effect placed private security officers at the very epicentre of coercive power, a situation unthinkable a decade earlier and one which Reiner reflected on as retrograde in terms of accountability but typical of a Prime Minister increasingly attempting to hold the law and order moral high ground:

> The policing changes . . . have many echoes of premodern forms, in particular the resurgence of private and citizen policing and security services. The proliferation of gated communities enclosed and privately secured shopping and leisure complexes, and other forms of 'mass private property' have been referred to as a 'new feudalism'. While Tony Blair is of course right

that 'turning the clock back' is not possible . . . Penal regression reflects the reversal of the 'solidarity project' of post-Enlightenment modernity.

(2007: 138)

By Blair's third term in office, embroiled in an unpopular war in the Middle East since 2003, his personal popularity and public confidence in his integrity and approach toward service provision were beginning to wane, specifically in terms of the effect of performance targets and quotas in key areas such as health, education and criminal justice (Hoggart, 2005; Loveday, 2005). With the police specifically, each Labour administration under Blair had supported the use of NPM and associated performance targeting as a fundamental continuation of Conservative policy. Loveday argued that the effect of this process was that reaching targets within prescribed time boundaries had become the core focus at the potential cost of service improvement and the danger of 'perverse consequences' such as the accentuation of positive figures and the non-counting of negatives (Loveday, 2005, 2006).

Explicit examples of 'sharp practice' included that of Surrey Police, where police officers had boosted response time targets by making false calls, and Greater Manchester Police, who were found to be incentivising offenders to admit to further offences to improve their clear-up rates (Loveday, 2006: 290). Similarly, since establishment in 2003, the much vaunted regulation of the private security industry via the SIA's licensing system had experienced severe difficulties in terms of scandal, delay and error. In November 2007, amidst accusations of a cover-up, a special report by the *Guardian* newspaper revealed that since 2005 the SIA had only been conducting limited pre-licensing checks on 10% of non-European nationals, leading to a backlog of 40,000 unchecked applications. Furthermore, there were an estimated 10,000 non-EU nationals licensed to work in the security industry who were believed to be illegal immigrants, including an individual who had been responsible for Tony Blair's car whilst it was being repaired at a police facility (*Guardian*, 2007).

Following his resignation, Blair had been replaced by Gordon Brown as Prime Minister prior to the SIA revelations in June 2007, with Jacqui Smith taking up the office of Home Secretary the same month. Brown had served as Blair's Chancellor of the Exchequer throughout his tenure, overseeing radical changes to the UK's fiscal architecture, including the controversial decision to confer operational independence on the Bank of England to implement monetary policy. Brown's time as Prime Minister would coincide with the 'credit crunch' and recession that followed the global financial crisis of 2007–2008. This would ultimately lead to the largest peacetime bailout in UK governmental history, placing intense pressure on the public purse and exacerbating fears over the future viability of public service provision.

The government's response in terms of policing and other key services was to address what it called the 'confidence gap', highlighting Labour's record on modernising forces whilst providing more personnel and reducing crime, publishing *From the Neighbourhood to the National: Policing Our Communities Together* in July 2008, focusing on what it called the 'professionalisation of the police' and celebrating centralisation as a 'strategic role for government' (Home Office, 2008). However, it would soon become clear that neither New Labour's past reputation nor the imposition of further managerialism on forces would likely save Brown from the financial storm closing in, which would likely necessitate extreme cuts in the public sector regardless of party affiliation. In the approach to the general election in May 2010 opinion polls were ominous, showing raised fears over the economy and the Conservative party as possessing a 31% lead on Labour as the party of law and order (IPSOS Mori, 2010). Notwithstanding this, following the election on 6 May 2010, no party had achieved an overall majority, with the Conservatives led by David Cameron and Liberal Democrats under Nick Clegg emerging on the 12th in a coalition government to be led by the former.

We are all in this together

The much anticipated offensive on reducing public spending was to come quickly. Cameron, in his address to the Conservative Party Conference in late 2009, had declared his intention to freeze public sector expenditure in order to address austerity, pronouncing that 'we're all in this together'(Cameron, 2009)—this would become a motif for what was to follow. The sound bite was underwritten by the ideological construct of 'Big Society', a paternalistic amalgam, which sought to attach the free market economy to social solidarity—a call for cost cutting by communitarianism. According to the incoming government, this would manifest in localism by devolution of power, volunteerism, power transfer from central to local governance and support for the third sector (Scott, 2011). However, it quickly became apparent that the driving force behind Big Society was an assault to cut public services and shrink public sector provision (Farragina and Arrigoni, 2016).

Though it had long been argued that making cuts to policing was to be seen as an electoral liability this is what now occurred. The service was targeted immediately with an announcement on 27 May that cuts amounting to £135 million would be made to central budgets and spread between the 43 forces and counter-terrorism operations (Home Office, 2010), with an estimated reduction in police budgets forecast at 4% per annum (HMT, 2010). The effect of this unprecedented assault was a return to a consideration of core police and ancillary functions whilst attempting to reduce bureaucracy, which led to the loss of over 10,000 sworn officers and 16,000 civilian staff within the space of two years (Home Office, 2012) and a 20% cut in overall resources by 2014. This led to a protest by over 30,000 officers in May 2012 (Manning, 2014: 23), but the cuts would prove inexorable and cumulative. During the Labour party's final year in office, 2010, the number of sworn officers stood at 143,770, with 16,918 PCSOs in support; by 2014 these numbers had reduced to 127,909 and 13,066, respectively (Home Office, 2014), with Chief Constable Mike Cunningham, the Association of Chief Police Officers' (ACPO) workforce lead, highlighting the challenge being faced: 'With reduced recruitment and the considerable cuts made to policing budgets, it is not surprising that the number of officers and staff have reduced' (Travis, 2014).

The drive to discover fiscal solutions to the public policing budget would dominate the coalition government years, the unpredictable backdrop of austerity a constant reminder that social policies necessitated checks and balances, in both economic and political terms. 2011 would witness a good deal of service acrimony between the Police Federation and government over the Winsor Review proposals on police pay and employment conditions. Tom Winsor had been appointed as Theresa May, Home Secretary, in October 2010 to carry out a comprehensive audit of police pay and conditions with the following terms of reference:

> use remuneration and conditions of service to maximise officer and staff deployment to front-line roles where their powers and skills are required; provide remuneration and conditions of service that are fair to and reasonable for both the taxpayer and police officers and staff; and enable modern management practices in line with practices elsewhere in the public sector and the wider economy.
>
> *(Home Office, 2011)*

Following release in two parts, the final version of the report published in March 2012 was met by the Police Federation with a mixture of opposition and exasperation, lobbying the Home Secretary that the process had left its members in 'utter dismay, consternation and disillusion' (Armstrong et al., 2016: 13), but despite this, the majority of the proposals were to be adopted. Further controversy was courted after Winsor was proposed as Her Majesty's chief inspector of constabulary (HMCIC) in the aftermath. Taking up office in October that year, he would be the first HMCIC appointment from outside of the service, having previously worked as a solicitor seconded to the government legal service during the controversial privatisation of British Rail in 1993 and later serving as the rail regulator between 1999 and 2004, a tenure that witnessed the rise, fall and fallout of RailTrack.

Alongside the crusade against costs, the coalition had pledged in their Programme of Government in 2010 to 'introduce measures to make the police more accountable through oversight by a directly elected individual, who will be subject to strict checks and balances by locally elected representatives' (HM Government, 2010: 13). This saw the creation of police and crime commissioners (PCCs) to oversee designated police areas under the Police Reform and Social Responsibility Act (PRSRA) 2011. Individual PCCs would effectively replace the 'corporate' former police authorities, be empowered to hold chief constables to account in terms of operational efficiency and continue the quest for value through money by acting as the budget holders in terms of central funding—a responsibility previously met by the chief constable. Additional policing funds could also be raised by a local levy process, with the PCC able to raise a precept on council tax bills.

This conferred a great deal of exclusive power in the new office, particularly in terms of local force priorities and future service development, with the new commissioners taking up office following elections in November 2012, with the popular endorsement of the role by the Prime Minister: 'People are going to vote in their own law and order champion; one person who sets the budgets, sets the priorities; hires and fires the chief constable; bangs heads together to get things done' (Cameron, 2012: 5). These 'law and order champions' would be overseeing what still amounted to neighbourhood policing, albeit a significantly stretched version due to reduced manpower, with teams increasingly focused on crime response (HMIC, 2012).

As budget holders, PCCs would also have an eye on plural policing initiatives to provide cost effectiveness and more for less, with considerations of technological deployment (ostensibly yet more CCTV) or patrolling uniformed guards funded by local people (as Crawford and Lister had predicted) able to provide surveillance and an early warning system for the police, who could then respond (Henig, 2010). With the police advised by Home Secretary Theresa May to concentrate their efforts on being 'the tough, no-nonsense crime-fighters they signed up to become' (May, 2011), HMIC sought to provide direction for areas which might involve the private sector in their report *Policing in Austerity: One Year On* (HMIC, 2012). This highlighted key areas in terms of public-private partnership and opened up further opportunities for the 'recession proof' private security industry in the provision of policing services.

Resurrection and folly

However, the security industry itself had not escaped the attention of the coalition government, which had intended to disband the seven year old Security Industry Authority under its swinging Structural Reform Planning in 2010, alongside 904 other public regulatory bodies. This led to the formation of the 'Security Alliance' to represent the anxious industry and lobby the Home Secretary, leading to an extraordinary capitulation: 'one day later the Government announced that the SIA was no longer targeted for abolition. Contrary to the Government's assumptions, private security was not just another industry' (White, 2018: 66). This 'special' status would later be reinforced in the House of Lords by Baroness Henig, the SIA chair, who highlighted the inherent risks in the government stance, anticipating an extended role to be occupied by private security in the wake of cuts to policing budgets (Henig, 2011).

What became clear in that aftermath of the government's *volte face* was that there was a desire to position the private security industry much more centrally within the concept of plural policing. To this end community Safety Projects (CSPs) would likely prove a ripe and non-controversial area for expansion, with the Minister for Policing Nick Herbert in March 2011stating that the government would continue to back such schemes under its 'Big Society' initiative (Herbert, 2011). Such load shedding initiatives were to run without central control in terms of the setting of objectives or targets taking their cues from local priorities and be overseen by the area PCC (LGA, 2012).

At the other end of the privatisation spectrum, with contracting out by now seen as normal practice, several forces began inviting bids for large-scale outsourcing, with a landmark set by Lincolnshire police in 2011 by signing a 'strategic partnership' contract for £200 million with G4S to construct and then staff a police station for a decade, including custody services and a control room (Plimmer and Worrell, 2013). On the face of it an incredible escalation in terms of delegation of control, but of a type described by Oliver Letwin, Minister for Government policy, as 'no longer a matter of political debate but straightforward and obvious as a way of conducting business' (Mason, 2012). Lincolnshire's lead was quickly followed by the West Midlands and Surrey forces, who were offering long-term contracts totalling £1.5 billion in what appeared in retrospect to be a privatisation scoping exercise on behalf of all police forces in England and Wales (Barker and Crawford, 2013), but decided against proceeding after the G4S security debacle at the London Olympic Games, which had resembled something of a pantomime before and after the Lord Mayor's Show.

The staging of the Olympics in the summer of 2012 was supported by a liberal dose of 'Big Society', with over 70,000 volunteers involved as human infrastructure, from the performers in the opening ceremony to ticket checkers and event stewards (*Independent*, 2012). It also provided a lucrative opportunity to showcase private-sector capability en masse alongside the police in what amounted to public-private partnership on an unprecedented scale. This was to be met by the giant G4S corporation, and buoyed by its recent successful pitch to Lincolnshire police, its head of UK operations, David Taylor-Smith, had predicted:

> [G4S] have been long-term optimistic about the police and short to medium term pessimistic about the police for many years. Our view was, look, we would never try to take away core policing functions from the police but for a number of years it has been absolutely clear to us—and to others—that the configuration of the police in the UK is just simply not as effective and efficient as it could be.
>
> (*Taylor and Travis, 2012*)

After being unveiled as the Games' 'official security services provider' in March 2011, G4S had contracted to train and manage the estimated 10,000 security staff required, a mix of paid security guards, volunteers and military personnel, within an overall budget of £282 million. By December 2011 the government had announced that this initial security staffing estimate had more than doubled to 23,700, with the operating budget raised accordingly to £553 million, with the public accounts committee stating governmental need to renegotiate their contract with G4S from a 'weak negotiating position' (PAC, 2012). Despite this, two weeks prior to the opening ceremony, G4S advised the government that it was unable to meet its contractual obligation for staffing, leading to the deployment of 3,500 additional troops to provide emergency cover, the instigation of penalty clauses leading to a loss of £88 million and a drop in the G4S share price amounting to £150 million (Plimmer and Moules, 2013; Taylor and Toohey, 2017).

Alongside clear failure in terms of organisational management, it was noted that there had been considerable operating friction between the police and G4S staff in terms of contested domains and concern over competence, including the stopping and searching of vehicles and caution over the dissemination of intelligence information by the police (Armstrong et al., 2016). One effect of the debacle was a distinctive cooling off towards private-sector capability, and seeing large-scale PPPs as a ready made remedy for unfettered encroachment into the public policing domain—private-sector willingness did not necessarily amount to readiness.

Despite such reticence over the competence of policing alternatives, the strategic reorganisation of the public police power base would continue throughout the coalition period under omnipresent austerity. *The Anti-Social Behaviour, Crime and Policing Act* (ASBCPA), which came into force in the spring of 2014, had been built upon on the government's white paper *Putting Victims First: More Effective Responses to Anti-Social Behaviour* (2012), a punitive boost to the Big Society armoury. The ASBCPA was primarily designed to replace anti-social behaviour orders with criminal behaviour orders, harking back to the conservative staple of 'putting victims first'. However, a further effect was to provide newly installed police and crime commissioner with additional powers to recruit local services to address anti-social behaviour. This further eroded the traditional influence of the increasingly moribund Association of Police Officers, an act of denigration by design readily championed by May in a speech to the Police Federation in May 2014 where she stated 'If we hadn't introduced Police and Crime Commissioners and established the College of Policing, we wouldn't have been able to break the unaccountable ACPO monopoly at the head of policing in this country' (2014).

This exultation in the demise of ACPO was framed by the acrimonious negotiations on police pay wrought by Winsor which had seen collective bargaining via the Police Negotiating Board (PNB), established under the Thatcher government in 1980, replaced with the Police Remuneration Review Body (PRRB) in October 2014, a move which would lead to the Police Federation issuing instructions to commence judicial review proceedings against the government in October 2018 after two consecutive PRRB remuneration reports which recommended above-inflation increases had been disregarded as overly generous—a decision described by Cressida Dick, the Metropolitan Police commissioner, as impacting morale and recruitment in what amounted to a 'punch on the nose' (Dearden, 2018).

Though the concept of 'Big Society', or at least enthusiasm for it, faded very soon after its introduction, government commitment to pluralisation in matters of policing has been maintained, albeit chiefly in the political background since the promotion of Theresa May from Home Secretary to Prime Minister following David Cameron's resignation in the immediate aftermath of the UK EU Referendum in June 2016. However, public conception of their police service amid concern over the dwindling numbers of officers suggests that the police are still trusted as senior partners in terms of crime response—a lifeline versus a lifestyle choice. Adam White (2015) has suggested five primary reasons for the continuing public reluctance to fully embrace private security in the context of England and Wales. These he summarises as *media scaremongering* in terms of likening privatisation to a hostile takeover, *public fear* in terms of anxiety towards potential malpractice, *cultural resistance* in terms of the receptiveness or not of individual forces, *inexperience* in terms of the contracting out process linked to the laborious nature of administration and *staffing* with concerns over trust and prospective personnel change (White, 2015). White's expert headings, above all else, reveal the layering of resistance and continuing suspicions of the public towards private-sector involvement in policing, despite clear familiarity with its concept, practice and implicit necessity.

However, caution does not appear universal, and in recent years substantial inroads appear to have been made in terms of a large increase in private security patrolling as a compliment to domestic security technology. One such agency scheme is 'My Local Bobby', a subscription-based service operating mainly in the affluent areas of London, its business model likened by a director to the purchase of 'private health insurance . . . the concept of people paying for something above what the State provides—this is no different' (Provost, 2017). When reflecting as to how many people might be willing to pay for above what the State is willing to provide, transference is viewable beyond lifestyle choice. Estimates bookending an age of austerity suggest that there are currently at least 232,000 private security guards operating in the UK (CoESS, 2015),[2] a similar figure to the number of school teachers and almost double that of sworn police officers, who in 2018 numbered 122,404 (Home Office, 2018).[3] At present it appears that the political will and private enterprise exist to inevitably widen this gap yet further. Conversely, in terms of the current political landscape, the continuance of hostilities between exclusively pro-public or pro-private standpoints has been rendered somewhat meaningless, with *value* increasingly measured by *utility*. White, in discussing the case of the Lincolnshire police and G4S partnership, emphasises the need for acceptance over dogma; he reflects, 'the salient question is not so much about the ratio of private security to police, but the ratio of public good to market rationalities' (2014: 1019). Debates on policing methodologies are increasingly likely to focus on the smart over the symbolic.

Quests for utility are often met, at least temporarily in terms of criminal justice, by technology, and an examination of recent developments provides a glimpse of future opportunities for substitution or collaboration. The current watchwords are *data* and *artificial intelligence* (AI), with developing policing technologies around data science, in particular data collection, offering the potential for discipline by design—an expansion of panopticism via information glut and predictive preventative intervention based on probabilities of crime and victimisation, what Wilson has termed 'algorithmic patrol' (2018: 108). Both developments, however, are reliant on exploiting (and potentially infringing upon) venerated concepts of consensus and privacy which go to the core of liberal policing models. However, the notion of data mining to unearth information troves is a familiar commercial concept despite is newness, so the idea of developing large, or indeed comprehensive, criminal troves is a genuine possibility. In terms of recent comparative developments, the US private security giant Axon offered to supply police officers with free body cameras provided the data captured could be used to develop their AI capture systems (Coldewey, 2017). The quest is to 'join up' the elements of criminal causation so that 'policing' interventions can be formulated whether cyber or human, remote or direct.

In the United States, so often the proving ground of public private security models for global consumption, the Los Angeles Police Department currently uses a predictive policing system named PredPol in steering its officers to use 'limited resources more effectively' (PredPol, 2019). PredPol offers predictive analytics software that links historical offender behaviour and incident mapping to mathematical formulae, essentially an attempt to link technology to established positivist theory—here crime patterning with rational choice and routine activities perspectives (Brantingham and Brantingham, 1981, 1984; Cornish and Clarke, 1986; Clarke and Felson, 1993). The company describes their product as 'mathematizing criminal behaviour', drawing on the combined expertise of its co-founders George Mohler, a data scientist, and Jeff Brantingham, a criminologist at UCLA. Here, science fact mimics science fiction in providing a somewhat dilute version of the dystopian technology introduced by Philip K Dick in his influential novella *The Minority Report* (1956), with its plot focus on the curtailment of 'free will' through corrective intervention.[4] Regardless of the version and variation of such controversial practices, concerns are being expressed over the speed with which such invasive systems are being embraced and adopted, with the government of the Netherlands using predictive software which links criminal records and social welfare data and a system similar to PredPol known as the National Data Analytics Solution (NDAS) currently under advanced trial with West Midlands Police in the UK set to be rolled out nationally during 2019–2020 (Baraniuk, 2018).

Thus, between comparative criminal justice practice and academic research, the pursuit of the potential and parameters for data and AI policing is enthusiastically under way and somewhat reminiscent of the clamour and politicisation which surrounded mass CCTV adoption 30 years ago. However, the current technological trend has the potential to provide a much more lasting and fertile focus for security analysts and scientists in both government departments and private companies due to its ability to draw upon the interrelated variables of surveillance (linked dataveillance), recording, calculation, predictive tools and influence—all areas previously populated in the main by human officers or operatives which can now be undertaken by thinking machines. The development of narratives around possible technological policing 'fixes' of this type are inextricably and historically linked to 'infringements' of liberty, State challenges to the meaning of privacy and the concept of the personal. This computerised assault is in turn heightened by the fragility and precarity of post-industrial global society (Standing, 2011).

In practice, the systematic implementation of this new form of sensitive and comprehensive 'policing' by State agencies and public police forces authentically extends the capacity for abuse of power quite dramatically. A recent Human Rights Watch report on China lists a myriad of networked public/private data sources being deployed and analysed to identify 'targets' for police 'checks and controls' at security checkpoints and possible selection for detention and 'correction' thereafter. These include interlinked CCTV systems on streets and in schools, supermarkets and entertainment venues (many with facial recognition and infrared capabilities) and the use of 'Wi-Fi sniffers' to trace and track smartphones and computers and network these to individual identity cards, vehicle registrations and sensitive personal data such as health, banking and legal records (Human Rights Watch, 2018). Furthermore, any threat to human rights has to be measured alongside strategic effectiveness and public value, and the predictive policing capability currently being touted for big data analytics may yet prove illusory, particularly the claim that mass surveillance technology linked to data analysis leads to better, improved or indeed effective predictability of human behaviour in the wake of a series of unpredicted but data-informed socio-political shocks over recent years, many of which have required emergency recourse to traditional policing methodologies and human actors on the ground.[5]

When considering existing overlapping information networks, personal, commercial and public, Shearing and Stenning's disciplinary Disney World looms into plain sight. Moreover, in a relatively small country like the UK, the enthusiastic host of 90s technological evangelism in the form of CCTV surveillance, there is the possibility for preventative policing alongside deterrence, as Andrejevic suggests:

> The promise is not that information will make policing more efficient, but that information might contribute to the goal of pre-emption: intervening in real time before a crime can take place. Policing, the name change suggested, is now more about information than weaponry: or, perhaps, the weaponization of data.
>
> *(Andrejevic, 2018: 93)*

A recognisable form of this adjustment is the now familiar 'policing' of social media for instances of online hate crime, with the UK government launching an awareness campaign in October 2018 with links to its wider criminal justice planning and Crown Prosecution Service guidelines (HM Government, 2018). The expansion and normalisation of such methods into wider society is dependent on supporting organisational structure allied to desirability, with the knowledge that the physical distance and consensual gap between the police and those policed will inevitably be widened still further.

Conclusion

This chapter has explored developments in public and private policing over the last four decades. The calls for criminal justice *realism* that ushered in this period have been realised to a great extent in terms of a push towards responsibilisation that has seen the police diminish in terms of number and status and the private security industry adapt and proliferate as a result, albeit with varying degrees of success. The speed of social and technological change during this period has been extraordinary, and a tearful Margaret Thatcher leaving Downing Street in November 1990 provided reinforcement rather than respite in terms the professionalisation and privatisation of public sector services. If anything, her successor's commitment was greater, and the combination of John Major as Prime Minister and Michael Howard as Home Secretary saw a still powerful public police force placed under a great deal of scrutiny. Major and Howard's propensity for managed reform linked NPM to Citizen's Charters and league tables, with Sheehy and Posen tasked to examine, inquire and pare down role and purpose—the latter's model still enduring to a large degree. The desire was for the public police to emerge streamlined and unfettered as born-again 'crime fighters', but commitment to historical duty continued the pragmatic swing between both force and service commitments.

The 1990s also witnessed further party politicisation of law and order, Parliament and media at times resembling a rhetorical arms race between the Conservatives and Labour. Consequently with guardians clearly needed to patrol the populist punitive turn being designed, policing remained firmly on the agenda to garner public support (Hobbs and Hamerton, 2014: 124). The lauded arrival of Tony Blair as Prime Minister in 1997 was partly due to his recent success as Home Secretary in waiting, and the New Labour government quickly engaged with further police reform and the courting of the private security industry as its vanguard—pragmatic responsibilisation would require a citizenry who would take increased liability for the protection of themselves and their property. Tough on crime rhetoric was found to be insufficient as a sop in office, requiring an attempt at what Robert Reiner referred to as formulation of 'tough smart' policy (Reiner, 2011: 362). Consequently the New Labour decade developed as one populated by a series of strategic shifts in terms of the privatisation of policing augmented by legislative and regulatory flux alongside further civilianisation and technological embrace. During Blair's terms of office in particular, this drive was overseen by a series of particularly faithful and dogged home secretaries,[6] but by the onset of the credit crunch, New Labour appeared tired and tactically spent and had begun to resemble old neoliberalism.

This political lacuna, coupled with apparently 'global' austerity, was received as both gift and stimulus by the Conservative Liberal-Democrat coalition that replaced the Brown led Labour government in 2010 in terms of the opportunity to further deconstruct the already hollowed-out public sector, a practice subsequently sustained by the current Conservative administration. Since 2010 the administrative assault on public policing operations can authentically be described as unprecedented, with recent official figures suggesting the loss of at least 20,000 police officers, including 16% fewer frontline officers,[7] representing the lowest number since the early 1980s (Home Office, 2018).[8] As a joinder, centralised Police funding fell by 19% between 2010/11 and 2018/19, a stark contrast to the preceding decade under the Labour administration, when it had increased by 31% (NAO, 2018). However, alongside the political arithmetic and capitulation to the Treasury in terms of policing budgets, there has also been symbolic change, particularly in terms of the police–politico relationship. The ideological effect on the 30,000 officers who marched in the Police Federation led protests in May 2012 calling for full industrial rights and appealing to the government to 'halt its cuts and "privatisation" of the service' (Laville, 2012). The fallout in force morale and the change in the very nature of the concept of a policing career post-Winsor. Then the assertion by Theresa May, Prime Minister, in February 2019 that there is 'no direct correlation between certain crimes and police numbers' (Weaver and Pidd, 2019). This remarkable turn is brought into sharp focus by Robert Reiner, arguing as recently as 2007 that 'Nobody would claim that the police have no effect on crime, that disbanding the police, or at the other extreme saturation policing would make no difference' (Reiner, 2007: 157). For a beleaguered Conservative Prime Minister to lead the charge against a union that had previously appeared symbiotic is peculiar and singular, the special relationship seemingly long gone, to be replaced with a metaphorical 'punch on the nose' felt and expressed by the commissioner of the Metropolitan Police.

However, the collaboration of convenience between the police and the private security industry flourishes as fully strategic and, if still short of the 'obvious way of conducting business' for all, certainly an option in the foreground. The PSA in the UK, having survived the clear debacle of the titanic G4S during the London Olympics, is leading the development on algorithmic policing whilst providing the manpower for the traditional watching and patrolling of paying neighbourhoods, reinforcing the contemporary *realism* of lifeline versus lifestyle choice that allows entry into the order of Disney World at cost. The market remains open, and an idea of its potential can be gleaned from a recent research study undertaken by the financial services giant Deloitte, disseminated in September 2018 at the Police Superintendents' Association via a panel which included Home Affairs Select Committee Chair and former shadow Home Secretary Yvette Cooper, MP. The study, titled *Policing 4.0: Deciding the Future of Policing in the UK*, provides an insight into the proposed points of convergence and separation between public and private policing models in the near future and the commercial opportunities presented (Gash and Hobbs, 2018).

In this study policing evolution is presented in four discrete stages: *Policing 1.0 c1829–c1900*—the Peelian civilian policing model; *Policing 2.0 c1900–c1960*—an evolution to embrace technological advances; *Policing 3.0 c1960–present*—serving diverse society, specialisation and the adoption of managerialism; and, future *Policing 4.0 c2015–?*—the harnessing of data and cyber physical systems to create seamless connectivity with the public and other agencies. The report also contextualises the current public policing model as 'stretched' in terms of manpower and resources and likely to face recurring cyclical challenges of 'Recession, "moral panics", controversy and largescale public disorder' with concomitant threats to force legitimacy (Gash and Hobbs, 2018: 9). This suggests six 'new realities', operational challenges that will need to be met by public police forces moving towards Policing 4.0, these being *Serving a fully digital world*, the harnessing of data and digital technology; *Outgunned by private sector and civil society*, further constraint to policing resources; *Responding to a much faster pace of change in every arena*, innovation and criminal opportunity, the crime arms race; *Harnessing cyber-physical systems*, the development of the 'Internet of Things' and the blurring of the virtual and physical worlds; *Using an unknowable volume of information and knowledge*, digitisation and data analytics leading to decentralised decision making and knowledge management; and *Operating with near total transparency*, omnipresent mass surveillance of both public and police. The overriding theme reinforced throughout is that public policing needs to modernise quickly and that this is best achieved through further alliance and alignment with the private sector. The treatment and pitch are functionally familiar.

However, the discovery of such 'new realities' to a still-receptive and engaged commercial/political audience suggests that the enthusiasm for the 'privatisation' of policing is likely to continue, with data technology now providing the key driver towards something resembling a sunlit cyber-carceral archipelago—a soft panopticon, perhaps? However, regardless of future projection, it is not yet possible to move fully away from the Janus-faced reality of the police, with one face sombrely looking back and the other peeking forward—currently offering public service that one police officer described to the authors as increasingly resembling a form of 'guerrilla social work'.[9] At the time of writing, the installation of Boris Johnson as Prime Minister of the UK saw him enthusiastically express the need for a public policing renaissance—using his inaugural speech on the steps of Downing Street to make a flagship pledge to mass recruit the police officers lost since the imposition of austerity cuts to public services, stating, 'if there is one point we politicians need to remember, it is that the people are our bosses. My job is to make your streets safer—and we are going to begin with another 20,000 police on the streets and we start recruiting forthwith' (Johnson, 2019).[10] In an illuminating tableau of office and duty, as he spoke, the Metropolitan Police held at bay a large crowd of vocal protesters at the top of Downing Street. In promising a bright new future in terms of police service as succour to the people of the UK, the first instinct of the new Prime Minister was to speak of law and order and look to the past.

Notes

1 Subject (former police chief inspector) in discussion with the authors, 17 November 2019.
2 The figures produced by the Confederation of European Security Services (CoESS) state that there were 232,000 private security guards working in the UK in 2015, cited

by Provost, C. (2017) 'The Industry of Inequality: Why the World Is Obsessed with Private Security', *Guardian,* 12 May 2017 (available via www.theguardian.com/inequality/2017/may/12/industry-of-inequality-why-world-is-obsessed-with-private-security), see also www.coess.org/.
3 Such developments have been interpreted by some as a move towards a two-tiered system, in the context of England and Wales, effectively a return to the geographical lottery of privately funded watch and patrol services of the type that existed prior to the formation of the new police in the nineteenth century. In this regard, Calum Macleod, chair of the Police Federation of England and Wales, in a recent call towards Peelian principle, has argued for increased funding for patrol over change to function; he stated: 'this is dangerous territory, where the amount of money you have determines the service you get. I, for one, do not want to police a world where the haves and have-nots are treated differently—and I know most of my fellow officers would agree. We cannot have a two-tier system . . . Policing is not a consumer or lifestyle issue. Nor should it be the exclusive domain of the wealthy. When Sir Robert Peel introduced the first full-time, professional and centrally organised police force in the 1820s, that was not what he had in mind' (Home Office, 2018).
4 Dick's novella provides the fictional concept of 'pre-crime' based upon analytical intervention, prediction and determination—themes expanded in the Hollywood cyberpunk interpretation, *Minority Report* (2002), which starred Tom Cruise and was directed by Steven Spielberg.
5 For example, the Arab Spring (2010), civil unrest prior to the Libyan Civil War (2011), the London Riots (2011), the Ferguson Unrest (2014–15), the Catalan Independence Protests (2017–18), the Gilets Jaunes Protests (2018–present) and the Hong Kong 'Basic Law' Protests (2019–present).
6 Jack Straw (Home Secretary, 1997–2001), David Blunkett (2001–2004), Charles Clarke (2004–2006) and John Reid (2006–2007) all carried the 'tough on crime, tough on the causes of crime' standard during Tony Blair's premiership.
7 The current official definition of frontline encompasses response teams, neighbourhood policing, and reception officers, intelligence support, training staff or 'non-coded' frontline officers such as national policing (Home Office, 2018).
8 For demographic comparison, since 1980, the population of the UK has grown by around 7.8 million souls, equating to an equivalent increase of ten cities the size of Liverpool in under 40 years in terms of public service provision, here considering policing and criminal justice (ONS website, 2019, accessed 21 February 2019 via—www.ons.gov.uk/peoplepopulationandcommunity/populationandmigration/migrationwithintheuk/articles/thechangingukpopulation/2015-01-15).
9 Subject (Metropolitan Police sergeant) in discussion with the authors, 19 January 2019.
10 Boris Johnson 'First Speech as Prime Minister in Full' *BBC News,* 24 July 2019 (BBC News website, 2019, accessed 28 July 2019 via—www.bbc.co.uk/news/uk-politics-49102495).

References

Andrejevic, A. (ed) (2018) *Big Data, Crime and Social Control,* London: Routledge
Armitage, R. (2002, May) 'To CCTV or Not to CCTV? A Review of Current Research into the Effectiveness of CCTV Systems in Reducing Crime' in *NACRO Community Safety Practice Briefing,* London: NACRO
Armstrong, G., Giulianotti, R., and Hobbs, D. (2016) *Policing the 2012 London Olympics: Legacy and Social Exclusion,* London: Routledge
Avant, D. (2005) *The Market for Force: The Consequences of Privatizing Security,* Cambridge: Cambridge University Press

Baraniuk, C. (2018, December) 'UK Police Wants AI to Stop Violent Crime Before It Happens' *New Scientist*, p. 3206

Barker, A., and Crawford, A. (2013) 'Policing Urban Insecurities through Visible Patrols: Managing Public Expectations in Times of Fiscal Restraint' in R. Lippert and K. Walby (eds) *Policing Cities: Urban Securitization and Regulation in a 21st Century World*, Abingdon: Routledge

Blair, A. (1995) 'Let Us Face the Future: The 1945 Anniversary Lecture' *Fabian Society Pamphlet*, No. 571, London: Fabian Society

Blair, I. (1998, July 17) 'The Off-Beat Solution' *Guardian*

Brantingham, P.J., and Brantingham, P.L. (1981) *Environmental Criminology*, Beverly Hills, CA: Sage Publications

Brantingham, P.J., and Brantingham, P.L. (1984) *Patterns in Crime*, New York: Palgrave Macmillan

Bowers, K., Hirschfield, A., and Johnson, S. (1998) 'Victimization Revisited: A Case Study of Non-Residential Repeat Burglary on Merseyside' *The British Journal of Criminology* 38 (3): 429–452

Brain, T. (2013) *A Future for Policing in England and Wales*, Oxford: Oxford University Press

Butler, A.J.P. (2000) 'Managing the Future: A Chief Constable's View' in F. Leishman, B. Loveday and S. Savage (eds) *Core issues in Policing* (2nd edition), London: Longman

Cameron, D. (2009, October, Thursday 8) 'Full Text of David Cameron's Speech: The Tory Leader's Conference Address in Full' *Guardian*

Cameron, D. (2012, October, Monday 22) *Speech on Crime and Justice*, London: Centre for Social Justice

Clarke, R.V.G. (1980) '"Situational" Crime Prevention: Theory and Practice' *The British Journal of Criminology* 20 (2): 136–147

Clarke, R.V.G. (1995) 'Situational Crime Prevention' *Crime and Justice* 19: 91–150

Clarke, R.V.G. (ed) (1997) *Situational Crime Prevention: Successful Case Studies* (2nd edition), New York: Criminal Justice Press

Clarke, R.V., and Felson, M. (eds) (1993) *Routine Activity and Rational Choice*, London: Transaction

Coldewey, D. (2017, April 5) 'Taser Rebrands as Axon and Offers Free Body Cameras to Any Police Department' *Tech Crunch*

Cornish, D., and Clarke, R.V. (eds) (1986) *The Reasoning Criminal: Rational Choice Perspectives in Offending*, New York: Springer

Crawford, A. (2003) 'The Pattern of Policing in the UK: Policing Beyond the Police' in T. Newburn (ed) *Handbook of Policing*, Cullompton: Willan

Crawford, A., and Lister, S. (2004) *The Extended Policing Family: Visible Patrols in Residential Areas*, New York: Joseph Rowntree Foundation

Dearden, E. (2018, October Thursday 4) 'Police Federation Threatens Government with Legal Action Over "Derisory" Pay Rise for Officers' *Independent*

Dick, P.K. (1956) 'The Minority Report' *Fantastic Universe Science Fiction* 4(6)

Ekblom, P. (1991) 'Talking to Offenders: Practical Lessons for Local Crime Prevention' in O. Nello (ed) *Urban Crime Statistical Approaches and Analysis*, Barcelona: Institut d'Estudies Metropolitans de Barcelona

Ekblom, P. (1994) 'Proximal Circumstances: A Mechanism-Based Classification of Crime Prevention' in R.V.G. Clarke (ed) *Crime Prevention Studies*, Vol. 2, New York: Willow Tree Press

Ekblom, P. (2002, October) 'Towards a European Knowledge Base' Paper presented at the EU Crime Prevention Network Conference, Aalborg

Farragina, E., and Arrigoni, A. (2016) 'The Rise and Fall of Social Capital: Requiem for a Theory?' *Political Studies Review* 15 (3): 355–367

Foucault, M. (1977) *Discipline and Punish: The Birth of the Prison*, Harmondsworth: Penguin

Garland, D. (2001) *The Culture of Control: Crime and Social Order in Contemporary Society*, Oxford: Oxford University Press

Gash, T., and Hobbs, R. (2018) *Policing 4.0 Deciding the Future of Policing in the UK*, London: Deloitte LLP

Gaylord, M., and Galliher, J.F. (1991) 'Riding the Underground Dragon: Crime Control and Public Order on Hong Kong's Mass Transit Railway' *The British Journal of Criminology* 31 (1): 15–26

George, B. (2001) *Commons Debates*, Hansard, House of Commons, 8 May 2001, Columns 83–4

Goldstein, H. (1979) 'Improving Police: A Problem-Orientated Approach' *Crime and Delinquency* 25 (2): 234–258

Hay, C. (1997) 'Blairjorism: Towards a One-Vision Polity?' *Political Quarterly* 68 (4): 372–378

Henig, R.B. (2011) *Parliamentary Debates (Hansard)*, House of Lords, Deb [2010–11], vol. 725, col. 903, London: House of Lords

Herbert, N, (2011, March) 'The Future of Community Safety Partnerships' Speech to the National Community Safety Network Conference

HM Government (2010) *The Coalition: Our Programme for Government*, London: Cabinet Office

HM Government (2018) *It's Not Just Offensive, It's an Offence* London: HM Government https://hatecrime.campaign.gov.uk/

HMIC (1979–1990) *Annual Reports, 1979–1990*, London: HMSO

HMIC (1991) *Report of Her Majesty's Chief Inspector of Constabulary for the Year 1990*, London: HMSO

HMIC (2012, July) *Policing in Austerity: One Year On*, London: HMIC

HM Government (1991) *The Citizen's Charter: Raising the Standard*, Cm 1599, London: HMSO

HM Treasury (2010, October) *Spending Review 2010*, CM7942, London: HMT

Hobbs, S., and Hamerton, C. (2014) *The Making of Criminal Justice Policy*, London: Routledge

Hoggart, S. (2005, June 15) 'Never Mind the Results' *Guardian*

Home Office (1990) *The Victims Charter*, London: HMSO

Home Office (1993) *Police Reform: A Police Service for the Twenty-First Century*, Cm 2281, London: HMSO

Home Office (1995) *Review of Police Core and Ancillary Tasks*, London: HMSO

Home Office (1998) *Criminal Statistics England and Wales 1997*, London: HMSO

Home Office (1999) *The Government's Proposals for Regulation of the Private Security Industry in England and Wales*, Cm 4254, London: TSO

Home Office (2001) *Policing a New Century: A Blueprint for Reform*, London: Home Office

Home Office (2004) *Building Communities, Beating Crime: A Better Police Service for the 21st Century*, Cm 4254, London: TSO

Home Office (2005, July 25) 'Police Service Strength in England and Wales, 31 March 2005' *Home Office Statistical Bulletin*, London: Home Office

Home Office (2008) *From the Neighbourhood to the National: Policing Our Communities Together*, Cm 7748, London: TSO

Home Office (2010, July 27) 'Proposals for Revised Funding Allocations for Police Authorities in England and Wales 2010/11' *Home Office*, London: Home Office

Home Office (2011) *Independent Review of Police Officer and Staff Remuneration and Conditions, Part 1 Report*, March 2011, Cm 8024, London: TSO

Home Office (2012, July 26) 'Police Service Strength England and Wales, 31 March 2012' in *HOSB*, London: Home Office

Home Office (2014) 'Police Workforce, England and Wales, 31 March 2014' *National Statistics*, Published 17 July 2014, London: Home Office

Home Office (2018, July 9) *Police Workforce, England and Wales, 31 March 2018*, Statistical Bulletin 11/18, London: Home Office

Howard, M. (1993, October 6) 'Home Secretary's Speech to Conference' Conservative Party Conference, Blackpool

Human Rights Watch (2018, February 26) 'China: Big Data Fuels Crackdown in Minority Region—Predictive Policing Program Flags Individuals for Investigations, Detentions' *Human Rights Watch*, via—www.hrw.org/news/2018/02/26/china-big-data-fuels-crackdown-minority-region. Retrieved 11 February 2019

Independent (2012, August 10) 'London 2012: Olympics Success Down to 70,000 Volunteers' *Independent*

IPSOS Mori (2010) 'Issues Index, March 2010' via www.ipsos.com/ipsos-mori/en-uk/march-2010-issues-index. Retrieved 22 July 2018

Jones, T., and Newburn, T. (1998) *Private Security and Public Policing*, Oxford: Clarendon Press

Labour Party (2001) *Labour Party Manifesto*, London: The Labour Party

Laville, S. (2012, May 10) 'Police Officers March in Protest against Cuts' *Guardian*

Leigh, A., Read, T., and Tilley, N. (1996) 'Problem Orientated Policing: Brit Pop 1' *Crime Detection and Prevention Paper*, No. 75, London: Home Office

Leigh, A., Read, T., and Tilley, N. (1998) 'Problem Orientated Policing: Brit Pop 2' *Crime Detection and Prevention Paper*, No. 93, London: Home Office

LGA (2012, September) *Police and Crime Panels A Guidance to Scrutiny*, London: Local Government Association

Loader, I. (2000) 'Plural Policing and Democratic Governance' *Social and Legal Studies* 9: 323–345

Loveday, B. (2005) 'Performance Management: Opportunity or Threat to Public Services' *The Police Journal* 78 (2): 97–102

Loveday, B. (2006) 'Policing Performance: The Impact of Performance Measures and Targets on Police Forces in England and Wales' *International Journal of Police Science and Management* 8 (4): 282–293

Major, J. (1993, October 8) 'Prime Minister's Speech to Conference' Conservative Party Conference, Blackpool

Manning, P.K. (2014) 'Privatizing and Changes in the Policing Web' in J.M. Brown (ed) *The Future of Policing*, London: Routledge

Marr, A. (2007) *A History of Modern Britain*, London: Pan

Mason, R. (2012, March 1) 'Private Companies in Hospitals, Police and Schools Are Here to Stay: Says Oliver Letwin' *Telegraph*

Matthews, R. (2014) *Realist Criminology*, London: Palgrave Macmillan

May, T. (2011, March 31) *Written Statement to Parliament: Remuneration and Conditions of Service for Police Officers and Staff*, London: Home Office www.gov.uk/government/speeches/remuneration-and-conditions-of-service-for-police-officers-and-staff

May, T. (2014, May 21) 'Home Secretary's Police Federation 2014 Speech' www.gov.uk/government/speeches/home-secretarys-police-federation-2014-speech

NAO (2018, September 11) *Financial Sustainability of Police Forces in England and Wales 2018*, Report by the Comptroller and Auditor General, HC 1501 Session 2017–2019, London: NAO

ONS (2016) 'Crime in England and Wales: Year Ending June 2015' in *Statistical Bulletin: Office for National Statistics*, London: ONS
PAC (2012) *Preparations for the London 2012 Olympic and Paralympic Games*, Public Accounts Committee 74th Report via—https://publications.parliament.uk/pa/cm201012/cmselect/cmpubacc/1716/171601.htm. Retrieved 22 October 2018
Pease, K. (1994) 'Crime Prevention' in M. Maguire, R. Morgan and R. Reiner (eds) *Oxford Handbook of Criminology* (2nd edition), Oxford: Oxford University Press
Phillips, C., Jacobson, J., Prime, R., Carter, M., and Considine, M. (2002) 'Crime and Disorder Reduction Partnerships: Round One Progress' *Home Office Police Research Paper*, No. 151, London: Home Office
Plimmer, G., and Moules, J. (2013, February 12) 'G4S Takes £88m Hit for Olympics Fiasco' *Financial Times*
Plimmer, G., and Worrell, H. (2013, June 24) 'Police Hail Results of G4S Outsourcing Contract' *Financial Times*
PredPol (2019) 'Company Website' via—www.predpol.com. Retrieved 22 March 2019
Provost, C. (2017, May 12) 'The Industry of Inequality: Why the World Is Obsessed with Private Security' *Guardian*
Reiner, R. (1995, June) 'Looking through the Glass (of a Crystal Ball) Darkly' *Policing Today*: 17–20
Reiner, R. (2007) *Law and Order: An Honest Citizen's Guide to Crime and Control*, London: Polity Press
Reiner, R. (2011) *Policing, Popular Culture and Political Economy: Towards a Social Democratic Criminology*, London: Routledge
Scott, M. (2011) 'Reflections on the Big Society' *Community Development Journal* 46 (1): 132–137
Scott, P. (2009) 'The Major Governments and the Limits of Neo-Liberal Reform of the Means of State Power' *Observatoire de la Société Britannique* 7: 287–307
Scraton, P. (2008) 'The Criminalisation and Punishment of Children and Young People' *Current Issues in Criminal Justice* 20 (1): 1–18
Shearing, C., and Stenning, P. (1981) 'Modern Private Security: Its Growth and Implications' in M. Tonry and N. Morris (eds) *Crime and Justice: An Annual Review of Review of Research*, Vol. 3, Chicago: University of Chicago Press, pp. 193–245
Shearing, C.D., and Stenning, P.C. (1983) 'Private Security: Implications for Social Control', *Social Problems*, 30(5): 493–506
Shearing, C.D., and Stenning, P.C. (1985) 'From the Panopticon to Disney World: The Development of Discipline' in A.N. Doob and E.L. Greenspan (eds) *Perspectives in Criminal Law: Essays in Honour of John Ll. J. Edwards*, Toronto: Law Book, pp. 335–349
Sheehy, P. (1993) *Report of the Inquiry into Police Responsibilities and Rewards*, Cm 228, I, II, London: HMSO
Short, E., and Ditton, J. (1998) 'Seen and Now Heard: Talking to the Targets of Open Street CCTV' *The British Journal of Criminology* 38 (3): 404–428
Solomon, E. (2009) 'New Labour and Crime Prevention in England and Wales: What Worked? *IPC Review* 3: 41–65
South, N. (1999) *Drugs: Cultures, Controls and Everyday Life*, London: Sage
Squires, P., and Kennison, P. (2010) *Shooting to Kill? Policing, Firearms and Armed Response*, Chichester: Wiley Blackwell
Standing, G. (2011) *The Precariat: The New Dangerous Class*, London: Bloomsbury
Stephens, M., and Becker, S. (eds) (1994) *Police Force, Police Service: Care and Control in Britain*, London: Palgrave Macmillan
Stuart, M. (2005) *John Smith—A Life*, London: Politico's Publishing

Tansey, S., and Jackson, N. (2008) *Politics: The Basics* (4th edition), Oxon: Routledge

Taylor, I. (1995) 'Private Homes and Public Others: An Analysis of Talk about Crime in Suburban South Manchester in the Mid-1990s' *The British Journal of Criminology* 35 (2): 263–285

Taylor, M., and Travis, A. (2012, June 20) 'G4S Chief Predicts Mass Police Privatisation' *Guardian*

Taylor, T., and Toohey, K. (2017) 'The Security Agencies' Perspective' in M. Parent and J. Chappelet (eds) *The Routledge Handbook of Sports Event Management*, London: Routledge

Thomas, D., and Loader, B. (eds) (2000) *Cybercrime: Law Enforcement, Security and Surveillance in the Information Age*, London: Routledge

Tilley, N. (1993) 'Understanding Car Parks and Crime' in *Police Research Group Crime Prevention Unit Series Paper*, No. 42, London: Home Office Police Department

Tilley, N. (2003) 'Community Policing, Problem-Orientated Policing and Intelligence-Led Policing' in T. Newburn (ed) *The Handbook of Policing*, Collumpton: Willan

Travis, A. (2014, January 29) 'Police Numbers Fall by Further 3,488 Officers' *Guardian*

Wakefield, A. (2003) *Selling Security: The Private Policing of Public Space*, Cullompton: Willan

Weaver, M., and Pidd, H. (2019, March 4) 'No Link Between Knife Crime and Police Cuts, Says Theresa May' *The Guardian*

Webb, B. (1994) 'Steering Column Locks and Motor Vehicle Theft: Evidence from Three Countries' in R.V.G. Clarke (ed) *Crime Prevention Studies*, Vol. 2, New York: Willow Tree Books

Wilson, D. (2018) 'Algorithmic Patrol: The Futures of Predictive Policing' in A. Andrejevic (ed) *Big Data, Crime and Social Control*, London: Routledge

Wintour, P., and Davis, W. (2007, November 14) '10000 in Security Industry Could be Illegal Says Smith' *Guardian*

White, A. (2014) 'Post-Crisis Policing and Public-Private Partnerships: The Case of Lincolnshire Police and G4S' *British Journal of Criminology* 54: 1002–1022

White, A. (2015) 'The Politics of Police Privatisation: A Multiple Streams Approach' *Criminology and Criminal Justice* 15 (3): 283–299

White, A. (2018) 'Just Another Industry? (De)Regulation, Public Expectations and Private Security' in A. Hucklesby and S. Lister (eds) *The Private Sector and Criminal Justice*, London: Palgrave Macmillan

Wilson, J.Q., and Kelling, G. (1982, March) 'Broken Windows: The Police and Neighbourhood Safety' *The Atlantic*

8
PRISON PRIVATISATION AND THE FOUNDATION OF PUBLIC PRIVILEGE

> The right to punish has often been a great privilege. It was a display of power. In addition it was profitable. Punishments were often in the form of fines or confiscation—straight to the vault of the emperor.
> [Nils Christie (1993) *Crime Control as Industry*, p. 138]

Introduction

The act of punishment is inherently social in that its use can confer symbolism, offer a rite of passage and present retribution as rationality or irrationality. Given this symbolic and often controversial character, there is no linear State history of punishment or of the use of imprisonment, rather an attempt to interpret political contexts and social settings; as Matthews states, 'The prison has a number of characteristics which make it a unique social institution . . . it has been historically shaped through the key elements of space, time and labour' (1999: 51). Here, in a historical sketch, characteristics and elements are explored to consider and illustrate precedents, patterns and influence in terms of modern historical prison development and use in England and Wales and the wider UK: the movement towards the long-term multilinear creation and construction of what might be termed a recognisable public edifice and an evaluation of its recent fragmentation at the apparent behest of neoliberalism.

In the prelude to the introduction of the Criminal Justice Act 1991—the statute that would finally break the State monopoly on prison administration in the UK after more than a century—many influential figures and groups viewed the prospect of prison privatisation as something akin to a dereliction of duty, a retreat from governance, even as an affront to sovereignty. There was a sense of abandoning a sinking ship. During the Home Affairs Committee on the State and Use of Prisons in 1987, Andrew Rutherford, as chairman of the Howard League for Penal

Reform, made the following statement in evidence opposing the involvement of the private sector in the running of public prisons. He reasoned that: 'Prisons were a public trust to be administered on behalf of the community in the name of justice. To open the way for the private sector into the administration of prisons would undermine the very essence of a liberal democratic State' (Home Affairs Committee, 1987). Moreover, the Home Secretary at the time, Douglas Hurd, a politician who might be described as a traditional conservative, appeared similarly uncomfortable with the realistic possibility of a shift in the power to punish, stating that: 'The business of keeping convicted prisoners in Her Majesty's prisons—because Her Majesty's courts have so decreed: that is the business of Government' (Ryan and Ward, 1989: 69). Such rare equilibrium between prison reformer and Conservative Home Secretary illustrates the existence of a genuine dilemma at that time, a dilemma beyond fiscal politics, a point of socio-cultural change in terms of the penal landscape.

Politically, when considering the prevailing New Right dogma of that era, the decision to marketise the prison infrastructure of the UK under the guise of modernising it might have appeared an easier proposition—particularly in light of the much-vaunted 'special relationship' that had developed between the British Prime Minister, Margaret Thatcher, and US President Ronald Reagan. Under Reagan the US had quickly developed an outwardly successful model, the creation of a rapidly expanding prison-industrial complex through the engagement of private prison companies (Lilly and Knepper, 1992a, 1992b; Shichor, 1993). This was a sector where the UK appeared unusually reticent, particularly when considering that Thatcherism had consistently outmanoeuvred Reaganomics in the race to remodel the public sector as a cash cow in most other fields. Eisen provides a helpful synopsis:

> Although Reagan tried to privatize many government services, his administration can only point to Conrail as a successful endeavour in this arena. Nevertheless, Reagan's privatization commission paved the way for subsequent administrations. His friend, British Prime Minister Margaret Thatcher, began the privatization trend in the UK that led to the British government selling more than a trillion dollars' worth of state-owned services to investors in the 1980s and 1990s.
>
> (Eisen, 2018: 40)

Some answers in terms of political reasoning, influences and indeed attempts at social engineering might be found in the exploration of an organised penal history that traces its cultural and customary antecedents back to the seventeenth century. The prison is a peak, the high point of public censure, social control and political failure—it might be that it is worthy of special scrutiny and additional consideration. Indeed, a series of central scholars within criminology and the sociology of deviance have focused on the history of punishment as key to understanding the development of contemporary penal policies and their apparent contradictions

(Rusche and Kirchheimer, 1939; Foucault, 1961, 1975; Ignatieff, 1978; Garland, 1985, 1990, 2002; Pratt, 2002). Amongst these, within the Anglo-American context, David Garland's body of work is perhaps the most complete, his treatment the most persuasive, highlighting governmental commitment and assent to penal welfarism around the middle of the twentieth century to individual responsibilisation within a fragmented and multi-agency penality at century's end—towards a *culture of control* (2002). Certainly, at various times there have been calls for rationality and revolution in terms of the penal landscape, tussles for control and the abdication of responsibility. The principal aim of this chapter is to explore such episodes within the circuitous history of the private and public stewardship of imprisonment and the privilege to punish.

The building of a public edifice

Punishment as custom

Foucault's *Discipline and Punish*, often a customary starting point for criminologists on consideration of the effect of social change on the genealogy and methodology of punishment in western Europe, endures largely because of its theoretical power in linking censure to the desired disciplinary processes required to order and serve early modern society.[1] Prior to this period symbolic censure was frequently provided by violent retribution on the human body with its antecedents in customary and religious practice, a circular form of weighted restitutive calculus of the harm of offence and the just measure of pain in reply.

In *Discipline and Punish* Foucault uses his celebrated first chapter, 'The Body of the Condemned', as a historiographic device to demonstrate that the public destruction of Robert Damiens, the regicide in the spring of 1757, was based upon careful subjective planning, calculation and specificity, with such complex pain and spectacular torture reserved as the pinnacle of State theatre—the carnival. Whereas, the list of objective rules drawn up by Leon Faucher for the House of Young Prisoners in Paris 80 years later, used so effectively as Foucauldian counterpoint, is much more recognisable to our eyes and much less offensive to our senses in terms of conceptions of penality and civility—a truly remarkable transformation from the unsettling macabre to the enduring mundane (Foucault, 1975: 7). Unusual social change in a period of intense social change. Albion was also more than capable of staging elaborate displays of public retribution beyond its well-known preference for the noose, with John Stedman witnessing the last hours of a soldier charged with murder in 1776, two decades after Damiens had been annihilated:

> Tied on the cross [hurdle], his hand was chopped off, and with a large iron crow all his bones were smashed to splinters, without he let his voice be heard. All done, and the ropes slacked, he wreathed himself off the cross, when seeing the Magistrates and others going off, he groaned three or four times, and complained in a clear voice that he was not yet dead . . .

> He then begged the hangman to finish him off in vain, and cursed him also . . . He lived from six-thirty o'clock till about eleven, when his head was chopped off.
>
> *(Thompson, 1962: 182)*

In eighteenth-century Britain customary public spectacle in terms of criminal justice founded on physical pain was under normal circumstances provided by stocks, pillory and gallows, as it had been for centuries—the former apparatus often descending to a public trial capable of delivering death and the latter guaranteeing it. A more recent statutory addition to sentencing was exile through penal transportation via a Royal Prerogative of mercy from 1670,[2] a practice considerably augmented by the country's emergence as a colonial power which would be used widely until 1868—allowing human detritus to be banished out of sight and out of mind. All of these options required the accused, in the absence of substantial surety, to be held in custody prior to trial or punishment providing an established, if fragmented, role for incarceration as a processual form of penance—albeit as a precursor to the main event. These early small gaols, often confined rudimentary holding cells, developed as 'Lock-ups' and 'Compters' (or 'Counters') which were increasingly used to detain those breaching the peace alongside civil debtors and dissenters under the jurisdiction of a Sheriff.[3] Such facilities existed provincially outside of the capital, often supplemented by rudimentary county gaols able to hold more formed within the keeps, cellars or dungeons of fortified buildings overseen by justices of the peace. The establishment of county gaols was formalised under the 1698 Gaol Act, with local justices given responsibility for their construction and repair. This act also dictated that those accused of murder and other felonies should be held in these 'public' gaols rather than in private lockups.

Discipline by design

A key turning point can be identified in the functional change from the demand for detention towards a desire for correction. 'Houses of Correction' were not a new concept, having been founded under the Act for the Relief of the Poor in 1601, a pre-industrial statute designed to combat itinerant vagrancy and idleness alongside an attempt to formalise parochial response to poor relief.[4] Under this act adult paupers were broadly graded as *impotent, able-bodied* and *idle*, with respective destinations of *almshouse, workhouse* and *house of correction*, a specific innovation. The first House of Correction to be established in London was within the former Bridewell Palace off Fleet Street, and by the mid sixteenth-century had become known as Bridewell prison, the term 'Bridewell' synonymous as shorthand for a prison establishment thereafter (Matthews, 1999: 6). No longer a mere holding place, it was envisaged that the prison could be used as corrective and remedy for minor offenders after summary conviction, a punitive site of industry over idleness which would greatly influence the penal philosophy and burgeoning public policy that followed.

The establishment of Bridewell prisons grew considerably throughout the late seventeenth and early eighteenth centuries, corresponding with reformation of manners campaigns which crystallised the top-down idea of public morality and the perceived need for the moral guardianship of a growing and unruly population (Curtis and Speck, 1976; Hunt, 1999). For hard cases, both 'reform' and punishment could be facilitated by incarceration and demeaning hard labour, a system since identified by many leading penologists as providing a precept for the modern prison (Mannheim, 1939; Rusche and Kirchheimer, 1939; McConville, 1981, 1995; Spierenberg, 1991; Matthews, 1999). The move is towards a more generalised form of punishment with incarceration as its necessary starting point; in this sense the preference for imprisonment can be identified to be pro-active rather than reactive. Instead of breaking bodies the idea was to render them docile so they might be both useful and used. As Rusche and Kirchheimer argue, 'penal systems cannot be explained only from changing needs of the war against crime. Every system of production tends to discover punishments which correspond to its productive relations' (1939: 4). As populations grew and clustered in towns and cities, the process of punishment was increasingly linked to commercial transaction, and there was clearly a potential for profit in imprisonment.

The main profit to be had in running an eighteenth-century prison was through its administration. Sheriffs and high sheriffs were appointed in an official senior capacity, but it was customary to delegate, sublet and subcontract their duties as they saw fit, often to entrepreneurial gaolers and keepers, which allowed for the exploitation of captive prisoners whilst keeping their hands and boots clean. In a Bridewell prison the incentive was to profit from the physical labour of the inmates, with sentences able to be adjusted to link longevity with productivity. Confinement in a debtors' prison often placed the prisoner in the impossible Faustian position of being both incapacitated and thus unable to work to pay back debt. This, whilst having to meet fees and sweeteners for their personal maintenance and safety inside. Such arrangements, as with the private enterprise ethos which supported thief-taking as a form of policing and the selling of transported convicts as 'indentured servants' in the colonies (Beattie, 1986: 479), ensured that control, responsibility and costs could be delegated, localised and minimised behind the veneer of officialdom, as Ryan and Ward clarify:

> The avaricious turnkey portrayed by Hogarth [in *The Rake's Progress*, 1733–4] was not a contractor selling a service to the state, but a publicly appointed official who made most of his income by extracting fees from his prisoners. The natural consequence of this system of finance was that prisoners who had money (and owing to the intricacies of the eighteenth-century debt laws such prisoners were not uncommon) could live in considerable comfort, while those who had none lived in the most dreadful squalor.
>
> *(1989: 62)*

As the use of imprisonment increased, complex systems of inducement evolved to circumvent personal danger and the worst of conditions, for those who were able to pay. Newgate prison in London, which had been destroyed during the Great Fire in 1666, was rebuilt in 1672 by Christopher Wren. Wren's design was ingenious if polar to his customary aesthetic instinct and was lauded as a form of 'architecture terrible' a model prison conceived to dismay, debase and above all else punish (Bergdoll, 2000: 91). All new prisoners, felons and debtors alike, were received in irons outside of the condemned cell beneath the entrance gate, which was bisected by the prison sewer. They would then be held there until charges were met to free them from their manacles and establish which 'side' of the prison they would reside in. As Batty Langley, a previously respectable architect imprisoned for debt, reflected: 'It is customary when any felons are brought to Newgate to put them first in this condemned hold where they remain till they have paid two shillings and sixpence, after which they are admitted to the masters' or common felons' side' (Langley, 1724). These bribes, summarised by Langley as 'rights, privileges, allowances, fees, dues and customs', were known as 'garnish', a term in common use at the time denoting a 'debt owed', and regardless of offence, garnish dictated whether you enjoyed the relative comfort and safety of the Masters' or faced the squalor and peril of the Commons', what you ate and drank or if at all and whether you might be left unmolested or summarily beaten. Despite Newgate's notoriety, then as now, its organisation, customs and conditions were not unusual, with violence, abuse, licentiousness and disease, particularly 'gaol fever' typhus, seen as common to 'prisons'. However, the most pressing collective issue was perhaps apathy, with regime, response to accusations of abuse and the existence of inspections very localised and prone to lack of coherence and accountability.

However, as Foucault argues in the context of eighteenth-century France, the reformist agenda which began to emerge across Europe would be founded upon political efficiency as well as human mercy. He states: 'The criticism of the reformers was directed not so much at the weakness or cruelty of those in authority, as at a bad economy of power' (Foucault, 1975: 79). In England utility was required, and political arithmetic would be applied.

Construction, reform and cost

The focus of reform in terms of what passed for a criminal justice system from the mid-eighteenth century was process and censure, linking sentencing and punishment. A gradual shift away from corporal punishment towards the use of imprisonment was underway, but continuing reliance on the death penalty for social control as deterrent and retribution had seen the 50 felonies punishable by death at the end of late seventeenth century increase fourfold by the end of the eighteenth. Much of this 'Bloody Code' had evolved piecemeal, leading to great deal of overlap between statutes in a legislative scrummage which attempted to protect increasing amounts of moveable and immovable property from theft, revealing the Code as oppressive and wasteful—designed as an index of terror and class coercion (Hay et al., 1975;

Linebaugh, 1991). However, as Emsley has argued, clear disagreement in terms of its effectiveness and opposition to its continued use was underway at the time, as can be deduced from contemporary Parliamentary debates (Emsley, 2005: 15). Such political opposition was allied to increased judicial and juror 'activism' in the courts in terms of creative monetary valuations allowing verdicts for lesser felonies below the capital threshold being passed and an increase in the use of pardons (Gatrell, 1994).

Through the emergence of a bourgeois public sphere in the Age of Enlightenment, growth in literacy amongst the middling sort and the development of the popular press had stimulated public consciousness and dialogue, leading to what Habermas refers to as rational-critical discussion (1989): the chattering classes had begun to chatter. Discussion on what to do about the apparent growth of crime and disorder began to increase. Indeed, public discourse on morality and punishment in England, having been stirred by the fashionable sensationalism of newspapers and compendium publication of the *Newgate Calendar*, had received a boost from the literary pleas of John and Henry Fielding and the far-reaching impact of the moralistic visual depictions of William Hogarth throughout the mid-eighteenth century.

Henry Fielding, in his popular treatise *An Inquiry into the Causes of the Late Increase in Robbers*, 1751, recognised that the societal reaction to the public implementation of the Bloody Code was often one of mockery accompanied by disorder, advocating that punishment should be swift, processual and better served aesthetically as a wholly private affair, away from plebeian eyes and excesses. But symbolic value was not lost on Fielding; there would be a need to replace public execution with a similarly punitive organisation. He mused 'It is not the essence of the thing itself, but the dress and apparatus of it, which makes an impression on the mind' (1751: 124).

These domestic concerns were amplified further by the translation and publication of a radical short treatise, *On Crimes and Punishments*, in 1764 by the Italian jurist Cesare Beccaria. Railing against the arbitrary use of the death penalty and ignorance of justice, Beccaria advocated a fully formed penology based upon principles of social contract, utility and due process—the concepts of *free will* and *rationality* being promoted as key when considering crimes and how they are punished (Beccaria, 1764). Symbolic authority could exist in form and function rather than base terror.

Beccaria's thesis quickly attracted powerful allies, proving highly influential in terms of philosophical discourse, particularly Jeremy Bentham's concept of Utilitarianism, and in advancing calls for penal reform from a prominent lobby which included William Eden, 1st Baron Auckland, the author of the pioneering *Principles of Penal Law*, 1771, and John Howard, a fellow of the Royal Society who would become high sheriff of Bedfordshire in 1773. Choosing not to profit from his office or delegate his duties as sheriff, Howard was appalled by the conditions and practices that he witnessed in initial inspection of the county prison. Alongside obvious concerns over hygiene, Howard was particularly shocked to discover that those acquitted at trial were being returned to prison to pay the fees incurred whilst incarcerated on remand and proposed that if gaolers were salaried rather than having to rely on garnish, such procedural abuse could be eliminated. Finding that the local judiciary would only consider his views if supported by precedents, he visited gaols in neighbouring counties.

As his reputation as reformer grew, Howard gave evidence to a select committee of the House of Commons on prison conditions in 1774, during which he was thanked by the speaker, who commented that the house was 'very sensible of his humanity and zeal' before passing two bills based upon his recommendations on the need for salaried gaolers and hygiene (Godber, 1977: 9). Zeal would drive him to undertake 350 inspections of 230 separate institutions between late 1775 and early 1777—encompassing comparative research missions to France, Switzerland, the Netherlands, Flanders and Germany in addition to England and Wales, Scotland and Ireland. The body of evidence and notes accumulated were written up in 1777 to be published as *The State of the Prisons*, with Howard meeting printing costs to lower purchase price to ensure that as large an audience as possible could be acquired for his seminal work.

With a government increasingly willing to engage with political arithmetic, *The State of the Prisons* provided convincing systematic evidence of the need for reform, demonstrating the widespread nature of dysfunctional management and ill treatment of prisoners across England and Wales. Thus, a buoyed Howard returned to Parliament in 1778 to give evidence to the select committee on the retention of prison hulks. Here he emphasised his belief in the pressing need for a coherent 'penitentiary' system. These opinions and those of William Eden, by now a prominent Tory member of Parliament and lord of trade, would be considered by Sir William Blackstone in his drafting of what would become the Penitentiary Act 1779. In a letter to Eden, Blackstone outlined his innovative proposals for a penal system which would include 'experimental houses of Confinement and Labour, which I would wish to be called *Penitentiary Houses*' (Prest, 2008: 299).

The Penitentiary Act that emerged, with some further encouragement from Eden despite the distractions of the American Revolutionary War,[5] was the first to sanction centrally funded and controlled State prisons with a link to reform as well as correction. It would be firmly founded in utility, with convict labour acting as corrective and funding source for the salaries of staff; uniforms were introduced, conduct would be controlled via the use of solitary confinement and remission, male and female inmates would be segregated with separate penitentiaries constructed and reform would be enabled via the redemptive qualities of religious instruction. The act also called for the appointment of three 'supervisors' to act as overseers in determining suitable sites, construction plans and estimates, with Blackstone suggesting that 'Mr Howard (The Gentleman who has taken such laudable Pains on the Subject of Prisons) could be prevailed on to be One' (Prest, 2008: 300). Howard was indeed appointed, along with his friend Dr John Fothergill and George Whately, treasurer of the Foundling Hospital, to deliver the 'Penitentiary Plan'. However, despite the engagement of architects and costing, a series of disputes over establishing the most healthy and safe location for the project stalled, and following the death of Fothergill on Boxing Day 1780, Howard resigned at the start of the new year in January 1781—the chance of a material culmination of his life's work lost.

Howard's enduring achievement can perhaps be viewed as campaigner, publicist and catalyst, possessing a remarkable capability to engage and draw influential and powerful contemporaries to his cause—those better placed to put his ideas into effect (Cooper, 1976: 73). This ability ensured that the construction of the 'model' penitentiary would commence within Howard's lifetime, albeit via a special act of Parliament in 1785 following lobbying by Sir George Onesiphorus Paul, high sheriff of Gloucestershire, to enable the demolition of the medieval Gloucester gaol and its replacement with a purpose-built penitentiary. Paul engaged the architect William Blackburn to design the new Gloucester County Prison with a penitentiary annex. Blackburn, the winner of the design competition sponsored by the Commissioners for Penitentiary Houses in 1782, was drawn to Howard's values and ideologies, ensuring that the large modern structure that emerged, covering three acres, would exhibit corrective intent whilst providing utility and public purpose.

The polymathic Jeremy Bentham, having been drawn to Beccaria's thesis as a young man, had begun to consider penal reform prior to the doomed Penitentiary Act, with his critical pamphlet on the use of hulks entitled *A View of the Hard Labour Bill* published in 1778. However, it was whilst assisting his elder brother Samuel in Krichev, White Russia, during 1786 and 1787 that the commercial and social engineering potential of the prison would be realised. Samuel Bentham, architect, engineer and inventor, was employed by the Russian royal family to cultivate the arts of civilisation and industry. His open brief extended to social control theory with both military and civil applications; he envisaged that the large factory populations required for industrialisation would require supervision and control to ensure productivity. These difficult groups might be marshalled through central inspection by the 'Panopticon' from *Panoptes*, an all-seeing eye (Pease-Watkin, 2002: 2).

Annexing the application of the idea to the current public discourse on prisons, Jeremy Bentham, on his return to London, began to develop models and construct a penal code around his brother's concept. By 1791 he had been joined by Samuel in Westminster to advance the project, and architect Willey Reveley was commissioned to produce a series of drawings of the circular Panopticon Prison based on the Benthams' ideas. Reveley's striking illustrations revealed the commercial viability of their surveillance prison design, with clear transference to the growing needs of industry, medicine and education in terms of group scrutiny and control (Gold and Gold, 2015: 2010). The Panopticon Prison would be run on the basis of contract management, with its director paid on results in terms of improvement in prisoner health and lowering mortality. Is revolutionary cellular design would require minimal staff in terms of warders, whilst day-to-day running costs could be met by prisoner labour as a 'mill for grinding rogues honest' (Semple, 1993: 134).

With growing confidence in their technological creation, Jeremy Bentham wrote to the Prime Minister, William Pitt the Younger, suggesting that it could be developed as a model prison for London, garnering key support from the newly installed Home Secretary, Henry Dundas, and the abolitionist William Wilberforce. A verbal interpretation of the plan was provided:

> The Building circular; an iron cage, glazed; a glass lantern about the size of Ranelagh; The Prisoners in their Cells, occupying the Circumference—The Officers, the Centre. By Blinds, and other contrivances, the Inspectors concealed from the observation of the Prisoners: hence the sentiment of a sort of invisible omnipresence. The whole circuit reviewable with little, or, if necessary, without any, change of place.
>
> (Bentham, 1791)[6]

Further official endorsement came via a Parliamentary debate on the increasing cost of transportation during 1793, with the Liberal MP Sir Charles Bunbury recommending to the House the adoption of the plan conceived by 'the ingenious Mr. Jeremy Bentham' as less costly alternative to the hulks and able to offer privately contracted 'well-regulated prisons calculated to reform offenders, and to convert the dissolute and idle into good and industrious subjects' (Hansard, 1793: 958).

With £2,000 provided for preliminary works provided by the government, the Penitentiary for Convicts Act 1794 allowed the Treasury to purchase a site for Bentham's National Penitentiary to be managed by himself as 'contractor general' with his brother assisting on completion (Semple, 1993: 102). Several locations in the city and adjacent to the Thames were rejected after initial survey as unsuitable or undesirable in a drawn out process, including Bentham's preferred choice of Battersea, before land at Millbank was purchased for £12,000 in November 1799. But in the aftermath of Pitt's resignation in March 1801, with eyes fixated on foreign policy, particularly developments in France and Ireland, the project was suspended by the incoming administration headed by Henry Addington.

Addington became Prime Minister of Britain at a time of fiscal crisis, and by March 1802, with the economy in near collapse, he agreed to the Treaty of Amiens with France as respite from war expenditure. However, despite some recovery by early 1803, the need for a war chest was desired over domestic policy, and an announcement was made that Bentham's National Penitentiary prison could not be funded. His response was to accuse the government of coordinated perfidy in treating him as a gull, pointing to sinister forces at work in the establishment, he lamented on the 'destruction of eight years of the most valuable part of [my] life' which had 'murdered my best days!' (Causer, 2017: 62). Following this experience Bentham positioned himself as a political outsider committed to seeking compensation for the failed endeavour whilst developing his philosophic analyses amongst *radicals* (Thomas, 1979).

Turning point: the delicacy of punishment

Prison reform reached a watershed in 1811, with the reporting of the Penitentiary Committee formed by Richard Ryder, Home Secretary, in 1810 under the Spencer

Perceval government. The committee, chaired by George Holford MP and including William Wilberforce, had been convened to consider rationale: the form and purpose of the first centrally controlled prisons. Finding a modern penal solution had become urgent, with civil unrest and a crime wave which had been carried and aggravated by the Napoleonic Wars; as a result, between 1806 and 1820, committals for trial rose by 300% (Grass, 2003: 24). Holford considered two models: a revival of Bentham's Panopticon Penitentiary or the Howardist proposals incorporated within the Penitentiary Act 1779 that had been implemented by G. O. Paul at Gloucester. Evidence was considered, and both Bentham and Paul appeared in person before the committee, attesting to the efficacy of the respective schemes. In reaching a decision, the Panopticon was rejected as a commercial enterprise likely to lead to abuse of power in terms of administration and its perceived ability to exploit and undercut the labour market during fiscal recession. The committee opted for the burgeoning State paternalism inherent in the Penitentiary Act model, which would be publicly controlled and based upon a regime of exclusion, enabling reform through toil, reflective solitude and religion. From this position a moralising nation State could emerge as the sole entity entrusted to punish and reform its offending subjects, as Ignatieff deftly summarises:

> In place of a Benthamite conception of authority regulated by market incentives, reformers like Paul succeeded in vindicating a bureaucratic formalism that looked to inspection and rules as the means to protect inmates against cruelty and to guarantee the rigour of punishment. For opponents of the contract system, punishment was too delicate a social function to be left to private entrepreneurs. For state power to preserve its legitimacy, it was essential that it remain untainted with the stain of commerce.
>
> *(1989: 113)*

This desire for bureaucratic formalism of the prison, its legitimacy as monopoly on punishment conceived and founded during the Regency, would remain *untainted by commerce* for almost two centuries. Crucially, the desired organisation would be built as a public institution rather than a private enterprise, punishment by now perceived as too important a symbol to sub-contract.

The fledgling national public system endorsed by the Holford Committee was however open to interpretation in long-term development. However, the aspiration of a national penitentiary on the Millbank site was resurrected and given statutory weight by the passing of the Penitentiary House, etc., Act 1812. A further act of Parliament, the Millbank Penitentiary Act was passed in 1816 to push the project to completion, and its management committee was appointed, with Holford as chair. The boggy marshland at Millbank, so disliked by Bentham, ensured that the project required innovative concrete foundations, pushing the final construction cost to over half a million pounds, the equivalent of £500 per cell.[7] Millbank, conceived as a Leviathan that would accommodate 1,000 souls, became operational in June 1816, admitting male and female convicts who had been selected as most receptive to reform into separate wings. Almost from the outset problems in terms of site, design and regime became apparent, and within five years the prison was seen as an expensive debacle (Griffiths, 1884: 28). The damp site contributed to frequent outbreaks of illness and disease, staff abuse and corruption was reported and the convicts resisted and rebelled. During 1823 Millbank was evacuated and closed for fumigation following a severe outbreak of dysentery, and just 20 years later the prototype penitentiary, 27 years young, had been downgraded to a convict transfer depot (Cunningham, 1850: 337).

Despite the trials at Millbank, the modernisation of the prison estate had developed apace. Many provincial projects were driven by philanthropy at a local level following the example of G. O. Paul in Gloucester, with Paul's pioneering architect William Blackburn designing 15 further prisons prior to his untimely death aged 40 in 1790 and his work influencing many others, including George Byfield (Cambridge, 1804, Canterbury, 1808), Daniel Asher Alexander (Dartmoor, 1809, Maidstone, 1819) and Alfred Waterhouse (Strangeways, 1868). Until the Prison Act 1877, local prison provision would be overseen by various local authorities and ecclesiastical councils, ensuring that no single design dominated, though rectangular blocks (including Exeter Borough, Bodmin, Dorchester, Littledean, Oxford), circular and polygonal partial panopticons (including Lancaster, Northleach, Chester) and radials were favoured.

The radial design (including Suffolk, Berkshire, Glamorgan, Liverpool, Dartmoor, Maidstone, Tothill, Coldbath Fields), with wings radiating from a central hub resembling spokes on a wheel, offering containment and clear sight lines, emerged as the high design and has since come to epitomise both the Victorian prison and the faded glory of the British prison estate more generally due to the continued use of many examples (Bennett, 2015). It was a radial prison by Joshua Jebb, a Royal Engineers officer recently appointed as surveyor-general of prisons, that was chosen to replace Millbank as the State's model modern penitentiary in 1840. It was to be named Pentonville and sited at Barnsbury, London, over two miles inland from the natural hazards attributed to the Thames. Pentonville was operational by 1842 at around a sixth of the cost of Millbank, demonstrating that lessons were being learned in terms of both construction and organisation—many from America, with the Eastern State Penitentiary, Philadelphia, designed by John Haviland in 1829, clearly the forebear. The Eastern State Penitentiary, an innovator of a working 'separate system', also provided the British government with a guide as to reformative purpose at this point.

Imprisonment and punishment as public purpose

By the 1840s the Eastern State Penitentiary had gained a reputation for its form of the separate system, which had become known as the Pennsylvania system, with reform of both male and female convicts driven by confinement and close observation to induce silence. Eastern State's neo-Gothic front façade presented the public with a foreboding presence in their midst, whilst the radiating cell blocks of the interior incorporated redemptive cues with small doors on cells requiring the prisoners to bow to enter or exit and the only light provided by a small circular skylight suggestive of the 'eye of God' (Schmid, 2003; Dolan, 2007).

This underpinning ideology of spiritual reform in Philadelphia was seen to be influenced by both enlightenment and Quaker ideals (Kahan, 2008: 19), as had been the case in Britain since Howard. The Gaols Act of 1823 introduced by Robert Peel as Home Secretary had been influenced by prominent reformers Elizabeth Fry and her brother Joseph John Gurney, both prominent Quakers and advocates of the need for 'kind superintendence'. The 1823 act was an attempt to standardise penal practice, abolishing irons and introducing categorisation and the uniform as physical control, although consistency in terms of a form of centralised inspection and annual reporting would not be achieved until the Prison Act 1835. The indication is a movement towards consideration of the capability of the prison, its overriding purpose—alongside evangelical considerations, which system was most conducive of reform through self-reflection?

The English evolutionary experience, infused with the symbolic spirit of hard labour since the Houses of Correction, having recognised a potential for solidarity in shared toil, had selectively embraced innovation through the introduction of punitive apparatus such as the treadmill (1818). Monotonous meaningless grind could transform the prison sentence into a motif of mechanisation—moralising machines able to break minds as well as bodies (Melossi and Pavarini, 1981). The was evident in the regime at Coldbath fields, which combined attempted silence with treadmill use, ten minutes on, five minutes off, for a shift of eight hours—its only purpose to 'grind the wind' (Mayhew and Binny, 1862). By the 1830s with Millbank inept and faith in the enforcement of a silent system in associative regimes such as Coldbath dwindling, the separate system was advocated by William Crawford and William Whitworth-Russell as a reformative ideal. Crawford had been sent as a prison commissioner to America in 1933. His report on American penitentiaries, which championed the Pennsylvania system, was published by Parliament the following year, convincing the Home Secretary, Lord John Russell, of its potential. Under the Prison Act 1835, which introduced a national inspectorate, Crawford and Whitworth-Russell, the former chaplain at Millbank, were appointed as inspectors for London, the home counties and midlands. This placed the two men in a uniquely strong position to frame penal policy into the early Victorian era, ensuring that the new model prison, Pentonville, would operate on the separate system.

At its inauguration in 1842, Pentonville contained individual cells for 520 prisoners, coinciding with a change in the policy on transportation requiring felons to be held in separate confinement for 18 months before transportation to Australia, ensuring a glut of subjects for processing in the new facility. Growing confidence in the separate system saw Preston Gaol, rebuilt to a radial design in 1840, and the new Reading Gaol, an homage to Pentonville by George Gilbert Scott, opened in 1844 as early adherents. By 1850 over 60 prisons had been built or adapted to the Pentonville model, revealing the most dominant design and preferred system by the mid-nineteenth century.

Ryan and Ward (1989) highlight a key difference between the American and British system at this important juncture, that of the prison industry, arguing that the system imported by Crawford from his commission to the States and report of 1834 favoured the solitary confinement of the Philadelphia model over the 'Auburn system' of silent convict labour which was employed in the majority of prisons—reinforcing the preferred paramountcy of public penance over private profit for the national penitentiary system. Though productive convict labour continued to be employed at some provincial prisons until after the Prison Act 1865, they identify the centralising Prison Act 1877 and the socio-political conditions surrounding it as a turning point which enshrined the 'State use' system into policy until the 1970s, contending:

> Under central government [following the 1877 Act] the prison rules were tightened up and the material incentives which had often been offered to both staff and prisoners to increase production were abolished. The oakum trade collapsed as wooden ships became obsolete. Centralization coincided, too, with a period of increasing agitation by organized labour, which was especially effective in destroying the prison matting industry.
> (Ryan and Ward, 1989: 63)

Though the public nature of the British model in the second half of the nineteenth century was reinforced, penal policy was to take a punitive turn. The consecutive deaths of Crawford and Whitworth Russell during 1847 saw a movement away from reform towards a paramountcy of breaking wills. With hard labour having been reintroduced at a number of institutions, a House of Lords Select Committee was convened in 1863 to examine prison discipline. This came in the midst of a perceived crime wave and resurgent moral panic over 'garrotting' the previous year (Sindall, 1987: 351). The Committee would be chaired by Henry Herbert, Lord Carnarvon. Carnarvon was 32, an active magistrate in Hampshire, and, having previously worked with the vastly experienced Joshua Jebb on prison reform, his stance appeared to harden following his collaborator's death in June 1863.

The Select Committee Reports which followed, having utilised Carnarvon's local prison, Winchester, as a site of inquiry, advocated that the cellular system designed as a site for reflection should be used to induce deterrence. This change was an expression of growing frustration with recidivism and belief of the existence of a habitual offender incapable of reflective penance. Carnarvon's aim was to deliver a shock to the seemingly incorrigible: with prison reimagined as a fearsome place encapsulated by the phrase 'hard bed, hard board or fare and hard labour', the penitentiary was to become a site of 'painful discomfort' (Carnarvon, 1864, cited in McConville, 1995: 55).

Carnarvon was able to rely on a firm ally of penal servitude in Edmund Du Cane, a captain in the Royal Engineers and expert in fortification who had been appointed director of convict prisons in 1863 as a crusader for a regime of 'general deterrence' (Du Cane, 1885: 154). The endeavour of these two men was encapsulated in the draconian Prison Act 1865, which sought to standardise regimes in both convict and local prisons and move to full separate confinement.[8] The Carnarvon Committee recommendations overseen by Du Cane became literal, with bedding replaced with wooden planks or coarse mattresses, diets restricted and sleep deprived to induce physical weakness and the monotony of demeaning work within a silent system, often carried out in the dimly lit and insanitary confines of the individual cell (Johnston, 2016: 31).

Under Du Cane's direction large-scale commercial exploitation of productive convict labour continued to be resisted, although some prisons persisted with oakum picking and mat and clog making after the 1865 Act (McConville, 1981: 351). One established practice that was, however, readily adopted from the American model was the use of free convict labour on large-scale construction projects. In 1825, the warden of Auburn Prison in New York, Captain Elam Lynds, had used prisoners in the construction of Sing Sing Prison on the east bank of the Hudson river—Sing Sing fittingly translates as 'stone upon stone' in the Mohegan Indian language. Though clearly exploitative, Lynds' congregational model was underpinned by a robust evangelism, as Pettigrove would later enthuse:

> He led them to the spot and camped on the bank of the Hudson without a place to receive or walls to secure his dangerous companions. He made every-one a mason, carpenter or other useful laborer with no other power than the firmness of his character and the energy of his will and thus for several years the convicts were engaged in building their own prison.
>
> (Pettigrove, 1910: 34)

Having previously organised convict labour for public works when stationed on the Swan River settlement in Western Australia in the 1850s, Du Cane had begun to allocate prisoners to provide forced labour on projects of national utility in the late 1860s—the *State owned* building the owned State—with prisoners involved *inter alia* in the quarrying of stone and construction of breakwaters, sea walls and coastal defences at Portland, Chatham and Portsmouth. Between 1875 and 1891 convict labour would build Wormwood Scrubs with the bricks for the project dug from the clay underfoot and manufactured on site—the Scrubs was envisaged as a replacement for Millbank, prisoners constructing their prison *stone upon stone*, with the road outside named in honour of its architect as Du Cane Road. Though arguably less monotonous than the turning of cranks and treadmills in the unchanging gloom, involvement in these work parties was exhausting, degrading and dangerous—the breaking of backs as well as wills. The novelist Thomas Hardy recalled the prisoners toiling in the Admiralty quarries in Portland, Dorset, as a tourist attraction with the convicts surveilled from established vantage points 'one nook therein is the retreat, at their country's expense, of other geniuses from a distance: but their presence is hardly discoverable'.[9]

Edmund Du Cane's influence in ensuring that the national system developed towards severe austerity for those held within it would last for three decades, serving as chairman of the Prison Commission from 1877 to 1895. A further objective realised was uniformity via centralised control, and this was made possible by the passing of the Prison Act 1877, transferring the control of local prisons to central government to form a standardised 'nationalised' prison system for the first time. The administrative effect of the act was to confer complete control to the Home Office, the Home Secretary presiding and delegating powers to a newly established Prison Commission and centralised inspectorate whose wide remit included the review, assessment and maintenance of the estate and conditions therein. A century on from the publication of John Howard's *The State of the Prisons*, a national prison system had been constructed with centralised bureaucracy and accountability—a public model, allowing Du Cane to declare:

> The creation of this prison system and the general improvement in all matters relating to the treatment of criminals or the prevention of crime have placed England in the foremost rank in this important social reformation. Our prison establishment, particularly those in which penal servitude is carried out, are visited by foreigners from all countries, studying the subject either on their own account or on behalf of their Government, with a view to improving their own practice. They are spoken of with the highest encomiums, and are the envy of most foreign prison reformers.
>
> *(1882: 656)*

The Victorian pride evident in Du Cane's rhetoric places emphasis on the envied prison system as a site of social reformation, but at least one effect of the long-desired centralisation of the estate was to stimulate debate and contemplation about its purpose (Pratt, 2002: 123). Thus conversely, having matured towards a public bureaucracy, the prison, now identified as both rational and legitimate, would be exposed to a new level of scrutiny and ownership as well as the highest encomiums—socially, economically and politically (Beetham, 1991). Such scrutiny had been augmented by a body of knowledge about what went on beyond the prison walls encompassing both fact and fiction, with public curiosity and consciousness consistently pricked by journalistic reportage, a literature based on the memoirs of prisoners and officials and a growing elite discourse on the need for reform.[10]

From public censure towards public patronage

By the final decade of the nineteenth century, the enduring national prison regime of austere penal servitude was attracting increasing criticism, particularly in terms of nationwide disparity in sentencing, overcrowding, rates of recidivism and potential role as rookeries, particularly in terms of the exposure of young offenders (Garland, 1985: 62). Throughout the 1880s and into the 1890s, in a convincing replica of modern popular outrage, a number of newspapers had campaigned against Du Cane and his system, complete with banner headlines and leader focus on the depravity and hopelessness of life behind bars. Chief amongst the assailants was the *Daily Chronicle*, a left-of-centre and socially aware daily owned by Edward Lloyd, which by 1890 was the country's best-selling newspaper and seen as politically influential (Massingham, 1902; Stanford, 2011). The *Daily Chronicle's* campaign culminated in a series of anonymous articles apparently written by an insider exposing conditions under the title of 'Our Dark Places' which ran from January 1894. Subsequently such media assaults would position Du Cane as the instigator of a 'barbaric philosophy' and his system as 'legendary even in Russia' (Harding, 1998: 591). By June that year, in official response, a departmental committee of inquiry was convened by Herbert Asquith, Home Secretary in the Liberal government. The inquiry was to be chaired by Herbert Gladstone, Asquith's under-secretary at the Home Office, and would examine and report on both the administration of prisons and the classification and treatment of prisoners.

The report that followed, *The Departmental Committee on Prisons: 'The Gladstone Report'* (1895; hereafter 'Gladstone'), recommended a categorical transformation of the national system underpinned by a philosophical return to a reformative ideal, highlighting a number of necessary changes. 'We start', said the committee, 'from the principle that prison treatment should have as its primary and concurrent objects, deterrence and reformation' (Gladstone, 1895: 1). The report was particularly scathing towards the concept of penal servitude, describing its use as degrading and responsible for 'the crushing of self-respect, the starving of all moral instinct' (Gladstone, 1895: 8). Within days of publication, Edmund Du Cane had resigned his post, the *Daily Chronicle* celebrating the news as victory, the deposition of an autocrat, reporting on 'the inevitable end of a discredited system' (Daily Chronicle, 1895: 1).

The scope of *Gladstone* was far reaching and infused with a clear message of reformatory benevolence, a reaction and polemical contrast to what had appeared to many the State-sanctioned callousness of the preceding 30 years. Amongst its many recommendations were that unproductive labour be abolished and replaced with productive labour in association and for the extension of education provision with a wider choice of literature, that first-time offenders should be classified for inclusion on special programmes with a separate specialised juvenile reformatory established and that longer sentences be reserved as a deterrent for habitual offenders.

Early criminological theory was referenced, with the committee apparently steering a middle course between the 'embryonic' science of criminal anthropology and an innovative form of environmentalism (in terms of socialisation), accepting that whilst 'some criminals are irreclaimable'—the sufferers of disease or physiological imperfections—others might be viewed as a by-product and paradigm of urban poverty. In doing so, the report sought to engage with the concept of habitual criminality, concluding that public prisons should turn inmates out as better individuals than when they went in. This premise was reinforced by Du

Cane's replacement, as Chair of the Prison Commission Sir Evelyn Ruggles-Brise would later summarise whilst still in office:

> each man convicted of a crime is to be regarded as an individual, as a separate entity of morality, who by the application of influences, of discipline, labour, education, moral and religious, backed up on discharge by a well-organised system of patronage is capable of reinstatement in civic life.
>
> *(1911: 74)*

This concept of patronage was referenced in *Gladstone* by the recognition of a crucial need for a system of after care on release.

Implementation of the proposals, however, was frustrated by the collapse of the initiating Liberal administration in August 1895, to be replaced by the Conservatives under Robert Cecil, Lord Salisbury. The Prison Act 1898 introduced by the Cecil Conservative government provided for a somewhat watered down version of the Gladstone recommendations but retained its core reformative ethos including the adoption of classification system based on a form of *triage*, with offenders classified as 'reformable' (such as first-time offenders and juveniles), 'treatable' (such as drunkards and the feeble-minded) or 'incurable' (such as habitual offenders and the mentally ill) at admission. In practice inspectors reported that some establishments within the expanded national system were slow to adopt the reforms contained within the 1898 Act, whilst others actively resisted for as long as possible (Forsythe, 1991: 240). However, the ideological purpose of the Prison Act was clearly communicated, in providing the reassertion of reformation as the worthy rationale of a publicly accountable national prison system at the turn of the twentieth century. a system that quickly distanced itself from separation, demeaning and debilitating labour and the retributive appetite of its immediate forebears, towards nascent penal welfarism.

Thoroughly modern milieu

Within a decade of the Prison Act 1898, many of the key reformative devices that would go on to underpin reflections of penal idealism in the mid-twentieth century had been established, including Probation and distinct juvenile justice. Such developments were underwritten by varying degrees of State paternalism, moral liberalism and public obligation in the need to provide firm consistent guidance. The Probation of Offenders Act 1907, which established the status of 'officer of the court' for Probation supervisors, drew on the established ranks of volunteer court missionaries in formulating their duty to 'advise, assist and befriend' offenders released on licence (Probation). This integrative formal role conferred a great deal of public trust whilst recognising expertise and allowing a high degree of independence in practice, the Home Office Departmental Committee in 1909 stating that:

> The Probation officer must be a picked man or woman, endowed not only with intelligence and zeal, but, in a high degree, with sympathy, tact and

firmness. On his or her individuality the success or failure of the system depends. Probation is what the officer makes it.

Further departmental committees followed in 1920 and 1934, with the latter, The Departmental Committee on the Social Services in Courts of Summary Jurisdiction, a catalyst for the reform and professionalisation of the service between the wars. Essentially, the Home Office took full control in 1938, by which time the Probation Order, as a non-custodial sanction founded on ideals of welfarism, had become a familiar appendage of the penal establishment. Statutory reinforcement followed via the Criminal Justice Act 1948, which provided the foundation for the service as a 'State social service' into the 1960s and also abolished corporal punishment, hard labour and penal servitude.

Juvenile justice was also seen as an area worthy of modernisation into the twentieth century, with the Prevention of Crime Act 1908 providing for the establishment of borstal facilities, separating offenders under the age of 21 from the adult prison system. These initiating borstals were founded on a robust form of moral rehabilitation, combining physical toil and exercise with educational and technical instruction with the end goal of pragmatic diversion upon release. This act also sought to target recidivism on the basis of public protection via sentencing reform, formalising the double-track system whereby certain categories of persistent offenders would receive an indeterminate sentence on top of a fixed term as a preventative measure. This approach proved influential and was adopted in a number of European jurisdictions as a protective device to distinguish between casual and habitual criminality. However, a by-product of the approach was the intrinsic evaluation of the individual's willingness to reform, resulting in the somewhat irrational infliction of augmented repression.

Regard for academic and service evaluation in terms of criminal justice policy is evident when appraising this era—a governmental willingness to consider innovation and participate as social engineers; as Garland argues, 'Criminology would replace the ineffectual niceties of legal punishment by practical technologies involving diagnostic, preventive and curative instruments and institutions' (1985: 106). Innovative embrace such as this led to the establishment of an experimental open prison, HMP New Hall, as early as 1933, with the State penal apparatus of England and Wales increasingly seen as a persuasive and exportable model of modernity. Writing in 1939, Radzinowicz describes a three-stage evolution, from the *deterrence and retribution* of the Du Cane regime, through the *reformatory influence* of Ruggles-Brise, and into the *utilitarian and reformatory ideas* of the present. For Radzinowicz, there is a clear confidence that the centralised 'English prison system' represents a radical ideal, whilst noting that the system is a work in progress. He states:

> The English prison system not only yields nothing in comparison with the most modern systems in other countries, but even in many respects surpasses them. England's penal policy in the field of penitentiary practice has, particularly during the last few years, been a very bold, consistent and experimental

one; it is being ever better understood in that country that the prison system is not only one of the divisions of the administration of the State but that it is also a kind of specific social service in combating criminality.

(Radzinowicz, 1939: 127)

The focal point of this emphatic thesis, a high point of idealism, is State centrality—centrality in terms of control, bureaucracy and benevolence—the creation of a total institution set within a wider convention of welfarism and civilisation, what Garland has termed the 'Penal Welfare complex'. A clear rationale is evident here in terms of paternalistic scrutiny and close social control, the layered politicised bureaucratic process predicted by Weber (Waters and Waters, 2015) which would become enmeshed with many of the dominant reflections on State penal modernity in the latter half of the twentieth century (Sykes, 1958; Foucault, 1975; Melossi and Pavarini, 1981; Garland, 1985; Beetham, 1991). The possibility for individual reform in this sense is based on a process of coercive captivity to allow for processing. What might 'work' in this sense at that juncture was underwritten by State legitimacy on behalf of the public, and the decline of this outwardly utilitarian project would be linked to its insatiable appetite, spiralling costs and perceived ineffectiveness.

Idealistic decay and administrative idealism

By the 1960s the English prison system was moving towards a post-rehabilitation era which placed the model in a near perpetual state of crisis (Matthews, 1999: 73). The primary causative factor in the exacerbation and maintenance of this crisis appears to be the prison population. At the time of Radzinowicz's optimistic assessment in 1939, there were 10,326 prisoners in England and Wales; by the time of the election of the Thatcher government in 1980, this had risen to 42,220 and currently stands at 79,221 (Howard League, 2021). Accordingly, the post–Second World War trend has been steadily upwards, notwithstanding rare periods of plateau or surge linked to incremental and proportionate changes in sentencing policy, such as sentence length; offender typologies; the use of immediate custody and remand; and the availability of, or preference for, non-custodial sanctions.

The dramatic increase in the prison population and associated costs post-war frequently required the adaptation of an increasingly dilapidated Victorian prison estate, leading to a deterioration in terms of security, living conditions, personal safety and staff inmate relations. Furthermore, Pratt refers to the manifestation of a 'breakdown in civilisation', with perception of the prison moving from a site of obedience and public indifference to a site of disorder and disruption from the 1960s (Pratt, 2002: 153). Prominent episodes of disorder included a number of high-profile escapes, including that of Charlie Wilson, the great train robber from HMP Winson Green in 1964, and several riots culminating in a series of violent disturbances across the prison system over the summer of 1972, with politicised violence at HMP Albany. The Albany debacle followed the formation of a UK prisoners union, which had instigated peaceful protests against conditions and culminated in a country-wide 'prison strike' on 4 August, a significant enough global development for the *New York Times* to commission a special report from Newport, Isle of Wight, on 5 September, which makes for interesting reading:

> Prisoners at Albany protesting against all day confinement to their cells after the discovery of a mass escape plot, virtually destroyed the inside of 100 cells, by burning mattresses, blankets and sheets, breaking up furniture, and throwing the debris from the windows. The modern prison, built five years ago just outside Newport had been regarded as a model for others because each prisoner had a cell to himself . . . More than a third of the 40,000 in British prisons, most of which were built over 100 years ago, are sleeping two or three in cells designed for one. The Home Office, faced with a prison population that has doubled in the last 20 years; is now trying to modernize the system
>
> *(Shuster, 1972: 2)*

Albany was viewed as a pivotal moment for many, widely reported as an episode of extreme sustained violence, apparently organised and founded on political motives in protest against conditions and for basic rights. As a new prison, decaying Victoriana could not be held to blame in isolation for descent in this instance. Throughout the 1970s and 1980s, the idea that simmering grievance and rioting could occur in new as well as old prisons, the crowded and uncrowded and across the full range of prison types appeared to come as a repeated shock to the Home Office. The official response to apparent cultural crisis was to drift towards administrative criminology and the comforting embrace of the 'Nothing Works' doctrine, the rudimentary penal populism formulated by Robert Martinson in the US (1974). The frequency of scandal, having drawn the public eye, was affecting confidence in the constructive function of a State edifice which had been in place for almost a century. As Pratt argues:

> it was as if scandal had become systemic, symptomatic of the way in which prisons were no longer performing the functions the public expected of them and by so doing, calling into question the authority and expertise of the organisations responsible for their administration.
>
> *(2002: 153)*

Support and funding for the monopoly on punishment and the endorsement of penal welfarism were no longer assured, or apparently desired.

The Conservative government led by Margaret Thatcher, elected on a 'law and order' ticket in May 1979, appeared ready made for penal pragmatism, a position confirmed by a Home Office report that appeared later that year following a committee of inquiry into the UK prison service which advocated a service move away from 'treatment and training' towards what was termed 'positive custody'

(Home Office, 1979). The focus of positive custody was on security and conditions rather than the abandonment of rehabilitation, and its apparent effect appears to have been to provide a rhetorical device whilst maintaining status quo. The real sea change was to come from academia with the development of right realism, US neo-conservative administrative criminology based on rational choice and its promise of the deterrent effect of severe and sure punishment, a move towards popular punitiveness that Garland would later reflect upon as the foundation of a 'culture of control' (2001).

Somewhat surprisingly given their proclivity towards privatisation and marketisation elsewhere, the first two Thatcher administrations did identify the prison as an appropriate site for its large-scale use, despite possessing a convenient, if limited, historical prototype in the use of the private security firm Securicor to operate secure detention centres to process immigration detainees on airport sites during the 1970s instigated by the departing Harold Wilson Labour government. However, from the mid-1980s, it became apparent that despite an ambitious building programme designed to confer 8,000 additional places in 22 new prisons, supply continued to outstrip demand, with widespread overcrowding and police cells increasingly utilised to hold remand prisoners. Prison building was recognised to be a particularly drawn out and frustrating process in terms of planning, construction, procurement and staffing. This impasse was overseen by a growing lobby advocating privatisation and a move towards neoliberalism and marketisation; significant amongst these was the influential Adam Smith Institute, which felt that the forward direction for penality in the UK should mirror that of the United States (ASI, 1984; Young, 1987).

In early 1987, following a fact-finding visit to the US by Conservative members of the Home Affairs Committee Inquiry into Contract Prisons as guests of the Corrections Corporation of America, the idea of a limited contract model for the UK began to percolate. The Committee's concise report, amounting to three pages, *Contract Provision of Prisons* (1987), provided an enthusiastic endorsement of the US private model and recommended that the Home Office experiment in allowing private-sector companies to tender for construction and service contracts. Though the idea of the fully 'private prison' was firmly resisted by the Home Secretary, Douglas Hurd, a green paper was commissioned to gauge the ancillary areas of prison operations (such as court escort duties and the administration of remand prisons) that might 'benefit' from private-sector outsourcing and expertise. Reporting in July 1988, the green paper was received with a degree of trepidation by the Home Secretary, along with a request for further evaluation prior to decisions being made (Home Office, 1988). However, a notable fracture in the edifice had already occurred earlier that year, when in May 1988 an Army barracks had been requisitioned to temporarily house prisoners. The inmates, whilst under the guard of military personnel, were catered to by a local private company, a seemingly insignificant arrangement but the change that initiated the 'first breach in the State monopoly on imprisonment since "nationalisation" of the county gaols and recidivists prisons in the late 1870s' (Shaw, 1992: 302).

With Hurd stepping down as home secretary in October 1989, after a four year tenure, remaining government opposition to the idea of the creation of contemporary private prisons (or moreover a return to the historical model) appears to have significantly diminished, despite continued apprehension from the Home Office (Pozen, 2003). Moving into her final year as Prime Minister, Margaret Thatcher appeared at pains to ensure that privatisation would remain firmly on the penal agenda. In this regard, the Criminal Justice Bill 1990 was fundamental, proposing new legislation that provided the Home Secretary with the power to allow private-sector contractors to tender to run remand prisons and thus providing clear statutory impetus for John Major, a passionate privateer, who would succeed Thatcher as premier in November of that year. Thus, the incoming Criminal Justice Act 1991 would have the effect of overturning 114 years of State ownership of the prison system in the UK.

Conclusion

As illustrated in the foregoing, like many historical examples within criminal justice policy, the route taken in attempting resolution, or even stability, in system effectiveness or coherence has often been found to be circular. In this sense rationality dressed as revolution is often a revisitation. In the context of this chapter, which considers the development of the prison from early to late modernity, we may ask: What is being revisited? Perhaps an acceptance that the institutions of penality can be administered without the need for *noblesse oblige* or State imperative, that the market might be best suited to decide on levels of duty and responsibility?

In the specific context of the adoption of the prison in the UK, around a century separates the interventions of the pragmatists, evangelists and innovators of the late eighteenth century and the builders, administrators and crusaders of the late nineteenth. A further century posited their public legacy with the architects of the Criminal Justice Act 1991, who, seemingly exasperated by the colossus created by their visionary forebears, decided that it should best be reorganised and delegated—to paraphrase Nils Christie, a decision was taken that the *great power and privilege of punishment* would be shared by its emperors.

Foucault had of course predicted the failure of the prison edifice and to an extent the preservation of its emperors, in *Discipline and Punish*—its inherent deception—arguing that penality fundamentally is a way of dealing with illegal behaviour, drawing moral lines in the sand, neutralising certain individuals (and groups) and profiting from others. He argues: 'In short, penality does not simply "check" illegalities; it "differentiates" them, it provides them with a general "economy"' (Foucault, 1975: 172). This differentiation suggests that what was being offered as the reluctant rationalisation of prison administration in the UK at the end of the 1980s into the 1990s was an offering to the general political economy, a shift from nationalisation towards privatisation facilitated by neoliberalism.

Garland's reflective *culture of control* emerges from these fragments, the principle of publicly affirmed penal welfarism relegated and replaced with a form of managerialism that could diffuse responsibility and assuage costs to enable popular punitiveness (Garland, 2002). In an earlier work of illustrative historiography, he highlights Patrick Colquhoun, who used his position as a London magistrate to formulate a series of treatises on deviance and criminality in the capital at the end of the eighteenth century. Garland, writing 200 years after Colquhoun, makes the point that the striking thing about the common-sense 'criminology' in his *Treatise on the Police of the Metropolis* (Colquhoun 1795) is its modernity and familiarity. Colquhoun's call was for the acceptance and management of risk, resources and the channelling of rational choice—a rudimentary but recognisable form of the applied administrative criminology beloved of the proponents of right realism of the 1980s and 1990s.

In *Police of the Metropolis*, a meshed network of private-sector stakeholders (presumably overseen by public sector guardians), drawn from the wealthy and influential, would combine to play a key role in the protection and securing of property. There is no regard for structural considerations here—the role of abnormality, socialisation or deprivation—rather a format for targeted crime control. Garland, in recognising the rhetoric, contended:

> The re-emergence of the Colquhounian programme, now, at the end of the twentieth century, in tandem with the reassertion of a punitive sovereignty, threatens the eclipse of that project of solidarity which formed the central thrust of twentieth century social and penal politics. In its place, we are witnessing the emergence of a more divisive, exclusionary project of punishment.
>
> *(1996: 466)*

In the 1790s, Colquhoun above all else was calling for a regression, the abandonment of central State punitive sovereignty and a return to private administration and the responsibilisation of the British public—in terms of the British prison system, his call would finally be heeded at the beginning of the 1990s.

Notes

1. An earlier Marxian form of Foucault's thesis was provided by Rusche and Kirchheimer (1939), emphasising the concept of discipline as a key building block of industrialising society.
2. Acts of the Privy Council of England (1908), Colonial Series, Vol. I, 1613–1680.
3. For an enlightening contemporary precis of the conditions and experience of being detained in a compter, see William Fennor's remarkable *The Comptor's Common-Wealth, or A Voiage Made to an Infernall Iland*, London, 1617.
4. *An Acte for the Releife of the Poore*, 1601, 43 Eliz 1 c 2.
5. Amongst the other fiscal and human pressures imposed by the American Revolutionary War (American War of Independence—April 1775 to September 1783), Britain was unable to transport convicts to its erstwhile colony, providing yet more practical impetus for a penal solution that could punish at home and produce docile bodies for State building. Parliament contended that 'the transportation of convicts to his Majesty's colonies

and plantations in America is found to be attended with various inconveniences, particularly by depriving this kingdom of many subjects whose labour might be useful to the community, and who, by proper care and correction, might be reclaimed from their evil course' (Baseler, 1998: 124).
6 Bentham's 1791 summary, which accompanied the well-known illustrations, is cited here in an interesting later collection by the Committee of the Society for the Improvement of Prison Discipline (1826), *Remarks on the Form and Construction of Prisons*, London: Printed by Richard Taylor.
7 The equivalent cost of almost £50,000 per cell in 2018, with inflationary rise estimated by the Bank of England at £47,879 via www.bankofengland.co.uk/monetary-policy/inflation/inflation-calculator (accessed 8 August 2019).
8 At this juncture, local prisons were financed by locally collected taxes, whilst convict prisons were financed centrally.
9 Thomas Hardy (1897) *The Well-Beloved: A Sketch of a Temperament*, 1912 edition, preface via www.fullbooks.com/The-Well-Beloved1.html, Retrieved 22 September 2019.
10 Influential works of this type in this period include Dickens (1836), Symonds (1849), Hepworth Dixon (1850), Kingsmill (1854), Clay (1861), Mayhew and Binny (1862), Griffiths (1875), Cox (1870) and Tallack (1889).

References

Adam Smith Institute (1984) *The Omega Justice Report*, London: ASI
Baseler, M.C. (1998) *Asylum for Mankind: America 1607–1800*, New York: Cornell University Press
Beattie, J.M. (1986) *Crime and the Courts in England 1660–1800*, Oxford: Oxford University Press
Beccaria, C. (1764) *On Crimes and Punishments*, New York: Bobbs-Merrill (1963 edition)
Beetham, D. (1991) *The Legitimation of Power*, London: Palgrave Macmillan
Bennett, O. (2015, December 7) 'How to Build Better Prisons: New Designs and a Look at Their Purpose' *The Independent*
Bentham, J. (1791) *Panopticon: Or the Inspection House*, 2009 printing, Montana: Kessinger Publishing
Bergdoll, B. (2000) *European Architecture, 1750–1890*, Oxford: Oxford University Press
Causer, T. (ed) (2017) *Memorandums by James Martin: An Astonishing Escape from Early New South Wales*, London: UCL Press
Christie, N. (1993) *Crime Control as Industry: Towards Gulags, Western Style*, London: Routledge
Clay, W. (1861) *The Prison Chaplain*, Montclair: Paterson Smith
Colquhoun, P. (1795) *Treatise on the Police of the Metropolis*, 1806 printing, London: Bye & Law
Cooper, R.A. (1976) 'Ideas and Their Execution: English Prison Reform' *Eighteenth-Century Studies* 10 (1): 73–93
Cox, E. (1870) 'Habitual Criminals' *Law Times* 49: 158–164
Cunningham, P. (1850) 'Millbank Prison' in *The Handbook of London: Past and Present* (2nd edition), London: John Murray, pp. 337–338
Curtis, T., and Speck, W. (1976) 'The Societies for the Reformation of Manners: A Case Study in the Theory and Practice of Moral Reform' *Literature and History* 3: 45–64
Daily Chronicle (1895, April 15) 'The Inevitable end of a Discredited System' (Leader) *Daily Chronicle*
Dickens, C. (1836) 'A Visit to Newgate' in *Sketches by Boz*, London: John Macrone
Dolan, F.X. (2007) *Eastern State Penitentiary*, San Francisco: Arcadia

Du Cane, E.F. (1882) *Report of a Committee Appointed to Consider Certain Questions Relating to the Employment of Convicts in the United Kingdom*, London

Du Cane, E.F. (1885) *The Punishment and Prevention of Crime*, London: Palgrave Macmillan

Eisen, L-B. (2018) *Inside Private Prisons: An American Dilemma in the Age of Mass Incarceration*, New York: Columbia University Press

Emsley, C. (2005) *Crime and Society in England, 1750–1900* (3rd edition), London: Longman

Fielding, H. (1751) *An Inquiry into the Causes of the Late Increase in Robbers, and Related Writings*, edited by Zirker, M.A. (ed) (1988), Oxford: Clarendon Press

Forsythe, W. (1991) *Penal Discipline, Reformatory Projects and the English Prison Commission 1895–1939*, Exeter: Exeter University Press

Foucault, M. (1961) *Madness and Civilization: A History of Insanity in the Age of Reason*, New York: Pantheon Books

Foucault, M. (1975) *Discipline and Punish*, Harmondsworth: Penguin

Garland, D. (1985) *Punishment and Welfare: A History of Penal Strategies*, Aldershot: Ashgate

Garland, D. (1990) *Punishment and Modern Society: A Study in Social Theory*, Oxford: Clarendon

Garland, D. (1996) 'The Limits of the Sovereign State: Strategies of Crime Control in Contemporary Society' *British Journal of Criminology* 36 (4): 445–471

Garland, D. (2001) *The Culture of Control: Crime and Order in Contemporary Society*, Oxford: Oxford University Press

Gatrell, V. (1994) *The Hanging Tree: Execution and the English People 1770–1868*, Oxford: Oxford University Press

Gladstone, H.J. (1895) *The Departmental Committee on Prisons: 'The Gladstone Report'*, C7702, London: HMSO

Grass, S. (2003) *The Self in the Cell: Narrating the Victorian Prisoner*, London: Routledge

Griffiths, A. (1875) *Memorials of Millbank, and Chapters in Prison History, Volume 1*, London: Henry S. King & Co.

Griffiths, A. (1884) *Memorials of Millbank and Chapters in Prison History*, London: Chapman & Hall

Godber, J. (1977) *John Howard the Philanthropist*, Bedford: Bedfordshire County Council

Gold, J., and Gold, I. (2015) *Suspicious Minds: How Culture Shapes Madness*, New York: Simon and Schuster

Habermas, J. (1989) *The Structural Transformation of the Public Sphere: An Inquiry into a Category of Bourgeois Society*, Cambridge, MA: The MIT Press

Hansard (1793) *The Parliamentary History of England, Vol. XXX, Comprising the Period from 13th of December 1792 to the 10th of March 1794*, London: T. C. Hansard (1814 edition)

Harding, C. (1998) 'The Inevitable End of a Discredited System? The Origins of the Gladstone Committee Report on Prisons, 1895' *The Historical Journal* 31 (3): 591–608

Hay, D., Linebaugh, P., Rule, J., Thompson, E.P., and Winslow, C. (1975) *Albion's Fatal Tree: Crime and Society in Eighteenth-Century England*, New York: Pantheon

Hepworth-Dixon, W. (1850) *John Howard and the Prison-World of Europe*, London: Jackson & Walford

Home Affairs Committee (1987, March 25) *The State and Use of Prisons, 3rd Report, Minutes of Evidence*, Session 1986–87, London: HMSO

Home Office (1979) *Committee of Inquiry into the United Kingdom Prison Service: Report*, Cm 7673, London: HMSO

Home Office (1988) *Private Sector Involvement in the Remand System*, London: HMSO

Howard League (2021) 'Prison Watch' via https://howardleague.org/prisons-information/prison-watch/. Retrieved 4 August 2021

Hunt, A. (1999) *Governing Morals: A Social History of Moral Regulation*, Cambridge: Cambridge University Press

Ignatieff, M. (1978) *A Just Measure of Pain: The Penitentiary in the Industrial Revolution 1750–1850*, London: Penguin
Johnston, H. (2016) 'Architecture and Contested Space in the Development of the Modern Prison' in J. Simon et al. (eds) *Architecture and Justice: Judicial Meanings in the Public Realm*, Abingdon: Routledge
Kahan, P. (2008) *Eastern State Penitentiary: A History*, Charleston: The History Press
Kingsmill, J. (1854) *Chapters on Prisons and Prisoners*, London: Longman
Langley, B. (1724) *An Accurate Description of Newgate: With the Rights, Privileges, Allowances, Fees, Dues and Customs Thereof*, London: Printed for T. Warner
Lilly, J.R., and Knepper, P. (1992a) 'An International Perspective on the Privatization of Corrections' *The Howard Journal* 31 (3): 174–191
Lilly, J.R., and Knepper, P. (1992b) 'The Corrections-Commercial Complex' *Prison Service Journal* 87: 43–52
Linebaugh, P. (1991) *The London Hanged: Crime and Civil Society in the Eighteenth Century*, London: Penguin
Mannheim, H. (1939) *The Dilemma of Penal Reform*, London: Allen & Unwin
Martinson, R. (1974, Spring) 'What Works?—Questions and Answers about Prison Reform' *The Public Interest*: 22–54
Massingham, H.W. (1902) *The London Daily Press*, London: Fleming H. Revell Company
Matthews, R. (1999) *Doing Time: An Introduction to the Sociology of Imprisonment*, Basingstoke: Palgrave Macmillan
Mayhew, H., and Binny, J. (1862) *The Criminal Prisons of London and Scenes of Prison Life. With Numerous Illustrations from Photographs*, London: Griffin, Bohn and Company
McConville, S. (1981) *A History of Prison Administration, Volume 1, 1750–1877*, London: Routledge
McConville, S. (1995) *English Local Prisons 1860–1900. Next Only to Death*, London: Routledge
Melossi, D., and Pavarini, M. (1981) *The Prison and the Factory: Origins of the Penitentiary System*, London: Palgrave Macmillan
Pease-Watkin, C. (2002) 'Jeremy and Samuel Bentham—The Private and the Public' *Journal of Bentham Studies* 5 (1): 1–27
Pettigrove, F.G. (1910) 'State Prisons of the United States Under Separate and Congregate Systems' in *Penal and Reformatory Institutions*, Vol. 2, Philadelphia: William F. Fell
Pozen, D. (2003) 'Managing a Correctional Marketplace: Prisons Privatisation in the United States and the United Kingdom' *Journal of Law and Politics* XIX (253): 253–282
Pratt, J. (2002) *Punishment and Civilization: Penal Tolerance and Intolerance in Modern Society*, London: Sage
Prest, W. (2008) *William Blackstone: Law and Letters in the Eighteenth Century*, Oxford: Oxford University Press
Radzinowicz, L. (1939, October) 'The Evolution of the Modern English Prison System' *The Modern Law Review*: 121–135
Ruggles-Brise, E. (1911, October) *Report to the Secretary of State for the Home Department on the Proceedings of the Eighth International Penitentiary Congress Held at Washington*, London: HMSO
Rusche, G., and Kirchheimer, O. (1939) *Punishment and Social Structure*, New York: Columbia University Press
Ryan, M., and Ward, T. (1989) *Privatization and the Penal System: The American Experience and the Debate in Britain*, Milton Keynes: Open University Press
Schmid, M. (2003) '"The Eye of God": Religious Beliefs and Punishment in Early Nineteenth-Century Prison Reform' *Theology Today* 59 (4): 546–558

Semple, J. (1993) *Bentham's Prison: A Study of the Panopticon Penitentiary*, Oxford: Clarendon Press

Shaw, S. (1992) 'The Short History of Prison Privatization' *The Prison Service Journal* 87: 302

Shichor, D. (1993) 'The Corporate Context of Private Prisons' *Crime, Law and Social Change* 20: 113–138

Shuster, A. (1972 September 5) 'British Prisons Rocked by Disturbances' Special to *The New York Times*

Sindall, R. (1987) 'The London Garrotting Panics of 1856 and 1862' *Social History* 12 (3): 351–359

Spierenberg, P. (1991) *The Prison Experience: Disciplinary Institutions and Their Inmates in Early Modern Europe*, New Brunswick: Rutgers University Press

Stanford, J. (2011) *That Irishman: The Life and Times of John O'Connor Power*, Dublin: History Press

Sykes, G. (1958) *The Society of Captives: A Study of a Maximum Security Prison*, Princeton, NJ: Princeton University Press

Symonds, J. (1849) *Tactics for the Times: As Regards the Condition and Treatment of the Dangerous Classes*, London: John Olliver

Tallack, W. (1889) *Penological and Preventive Principles*, London: Wertheimer

Thomas, W. (1979) *The Philosophic Radicals: Nine Studies in Theory and Practice, 1817–1841*, Oxford: Clarendon Press

Thompson, S. (ed) (1962) *The Journal of John Gabriel Stedman*, London: Mitre Press

Waters, T., and Waters, D. (2015) *Weber's Rationalism and Modern Society: New Translations on Politics, Bureaucracy, and Social Stratification* (original 1914–1919, translation-2015), London: Palgrave Macmillan

Young, P. (1987) *The Prison Cell*, London: ASI

9
PRISON PRIVATISATION AND NORMALISATION IN THE NEOLIBERAL STATE

Between dispersal of decency and diffusion of duty

> I believe that contracting out prisons to the private sector has been a serious mistake. It is something I refused to do as a member of Margaret Thatcher's cabinet, but not because I was hostile to privatisation generally . . . Incarceration should be administered by servants of the State and not by private companies in Britain or elsewhere.
>
> (Sir Malcolm Rifkind, *Financial Times*, 13 April 2019[1])

Introduction

When considering the rapid assimilation of the private prison into the criminal justice system of the UK over the past three decades, the apparent outward hesitancy, even reluctance, of the final Thatcher administration towards establishment belies a steady momentum throughout the 1980s. This goes well beyond admiration from afar towards the prison industrial complex model that had been created by Reagan in the US, rather an observant evaluation of what might work in a country with a population density eight times that of America and a land mass smaller than that of Oregon, a medium-sized State. In these circumstances, it might be argued that prison privatisation was a question of timing rather than aspiration—with the die likely cast with the totem of the financial management initiative adopted within months of Thatcher taking office. The FMI, with its emphasis on accountability and value for money, established as policy by 1982, had been in preparation by the Civil Service for a quarter of a century and would fuel and underwrite the neoliberal assault on the public sector towards the millennium—crucially, it provided the necessary symbolic shift towards a new methodology (Sharifi and Bovaird, 1995: 469), and symbolism is often a necessary driver during times of rapid social change.

Further 'economic' catalysts—encouragements and prompts—would follow in the coming decade. Amongst these the increasing influence of the Adam Smith Institute, the right wing fiscal think tank. This was particularly the case in the aftermath of the publication of its *Omega File: A Comprehensive Review of Government Functions*, in 1985 (Butler et al., 1985). This large-scale manifesto laid out over 600 New Right policy initiatives with privatisation and the hollowing out of State services at its core. Marketed as an almanac of the future of Britain, it augmented the growing concept of Thatcherism, though not all in cabinet were convinced of its overriding utility nor its inclination for speed. Carvel reported at the time,

> It is a brave counter blast to the advice of cabinet consolidators, such as Lord Whitelaw and Mr John Biffen, who are seeking to persuade Mrs Thatcher to tone down the ideological contents of the next Queen's Speech for fear of presenting the electorate with more radicalism than it can take.
>
> *(1985)*

Significantly, the *Omega File*, seen as far fetched in the mainstream at the time, had pitched that the private sector should be utilised in both prison construction and operation. Thereafter, seeing an opportunity and increasingly enjoying the ear of government, the ASI's radicalism in lobbying for prison privatisation would grow through direct attacks on the capability, resourcefulness and 'imagination' of the Prison Service and later in representations and overtures towards the Home Office in terms of the need for modernisation and managerialism (Young, 1987; James et al., 1997).

The committed privateers within Parliament would use the overtures of the ASI to sell the concept of penal privatisation of as part of a drive for elusive efficiency and decency in criminal justice, a tangible opportunity for wholesale reform of a problematic sector—a last throw of the dice. On taking office in 1979 the Conservatives had been quick to point to their inheritance of a prison system at a breaking point. Reflecting on the recommendations of the May Report on the administration of the Prison Service in August 1980, the Home Secretary, William Whitelaw, pointed to a crisis, with the 'dangerously high' prison population of 44,500 causing severe overcrowding. He stated,

> The problems were set out by the May committee in stark relief—a decaying prison estate, the poor working and living conditions for staff and prisoners, the decline in the belief that imprisonment can have a positive effect and the deterioration in industrial relations.
>
> *(Hansard, 1980)*

The Conservatives had attempted to address these perennial issues over three terms of office, a decade of administrative reorganisation, service restructuring and prison building, without apparent success. At the end of the 1980s it was suggested that if problematic penal ethics could be navigated, privatisation might offer a solution in terms of resource and know-how. The by now seasoned exponents of neoliberalism within government argued that the engagement of private capital could act as a stimulus to replace aging infrastructure, increase capacity and bring about competition for services that would lower operating costs and modernise management practices (under pressure), as had been demonstrated in other recently privatised sectors of the public estate. Why should the penal system be seen as different? Over the next 30 years, an ideological reformation would be attempted. This chapter aims to define and critically evaluate its course and legacy.

Justification, clamour and realisation

A notable political tipping point towards the justification of privatisation of the prison system was reached in 1987 with the publication of the influential Home Affairs Committee (HAC) report, *Contract Provision of Prisons*. This came on the back of a fact finding tour the previous year as guests of the Corrections Corporation of America by two senior Conservatives, Edward Gardner, chair of the Home Affairs Select Committee, and John Wheeler, who would succeed Gardner as chair.[2] The tour had clearly been compelling, with the members noting that there was nothing to warrant criticism in what they had been shown by CCA, stating in their report that the Home Office should experiment in enabling private-sector companies to tender for the construction and management of custodial institutions:

> Such contracts should contain standards and requirements and failure to meet them would be grounds for the Government's terminating a contract. The standards should be made legally enforceable against contractors. We also recommend that tenders should be invited in particular for the construction and management of new remand centres, because it is there that the worst overcrowding in the prison system is concentrated.
>
> *(Home Affairs Committee, 1987)*

Despite initial resistance by the incumbent Home Secretary, the long serving Douglas Hurd, and trepidation from the Home Office towards this proposed sea change in penal policy around remand custody, a green paper was published in July the following year, *Private Sector Involvement in the Remand System*, with requests for further evaluation in terms of benefit prior to decisions being made. Within the green paper, in order to aid and speed the evaluation process, the Home Office sought to engage management consultants 'to examine in detail the practical feasibility of the various options for involving the private sector', including management and outsourcing practice (Home Office, 1988: 9). Deloitte were appointed to undertake the audit, reporting with unsurprising enthusiasm the manifold opportunities for development of private-sector involvement in the prison system (Deloitte Haskins & Sells, 1989). Following the publication of the report, a contemplative Hurd addressed the House of Commons on 1 March 1989 on 'Remand System Privatisation' and, after offering reassurance on the paramountcy of prisoners' rights and public safety, proposed to move forward on the privatisation of prison escort and remand centres following further consultation. He concluded:

> The introduction of the private sector into the management of the prison system in the way I have outlined would certainly represent a bold departure from previous thinking and practice. It offers the prospect of a new kind of partnership between the public and private sectors in this important, though often sadly neglected, aspect of our national life. We should not be scornful of new ideas which, if successful, will make an important contribution to the Government's programme of providing decent conditions for all prisoners at a reasonable cost.
>
> (Hansard, 1989)

Hurd's position throughout the consultation was that private provision must not be extended to convicted prisoners as a matter of principle. Consequently, the Criminal Justice Bill 1990 was set out as an experiment, restricting the Home Secretary to allow the private sector to tender in servicing unsentenced prisoners in newly built facilities. However, by November 1990, John Major had replaced Margaret Thatcher as Prime Minister, with Kenneth Baker, party chairman and a more committed privateer than Hurd, installed as Home Secretary.[3] As the Criminal Justice Bill navigated Parliament, a crucial 'technical' amendment was added at the report stage, greatly extending the initial legislative scope to empower the Home Secretary to invite private-sector companies to tender in service and facility provision for sentenced convicted prisoners in newly built facilities as well as those unsentenced on remand. Thus, the Criminal Justice Act 1991, enacted on 25 July 1991, was *the* turning point, providing the fledgling Major government with the legislative tools to privatise the penal system—with Part IV, Provision of Services, covering Prisoner Escorts (ss 80–83), Contracted Out Prisons (ss 84–88) and Contracted Out Functions (ss 88a).[4]

However, neoliberal zeal allied to governmental appetite for privatisation was only part of the story in terms of reaching this fundamental point—the overturning of 114 years of State ownership of the prison system in the UK. The much maligned public sector would now have competition. This experimental proposition—with a quiet echo of the 'what works' debate of the 1970s—was met with a good deal of political and media interest from across a broad cross section of positions, left, right and centre, well beyond the predisposed diktat of the ASI, though Neil Kinnock's Labour Party, by now attempting distance from its traditional ties to the unions in favour of Croslandite values of 'equality' over public ownership, maintained public opposition to private-sector involvement in prisons throughout his leadership. This climate of relative media compliance acted as a boost to the conception of privatised penality, as did the timing, coming in the twilight of the Thatcher era at the end of *the* decade of mass privatisation. Ryan and Ward, in their forensic content analysis of press machinations during this period, demonstrate that whilst some elements of the British media had retained scepticism and partisanship in terms of what privatisation might deliver, the issue was seriously considered and remained relatively free from sensationalism by the majority. They contended at the time:

> Overt support came from the leader writers. While the *Guardian's* editorial after arguing that privatization should not be discussed out of hand, finally came down against it, the *Sunday Times Business News* ('Memo to Maggie' 18 August 1985), *The Economist* (13 December 1986), *The Times* (8 May 1987), the *Telegraph* (15 May 1987) and the *Independent* (15 September 1987 and 26 July 1988) all unequivocally supported privatization, interpreting the American experience as showing how, in the *Independent's* words, 'the market could . . . become the agent of reform in an area which desperately needs it.
> (Ryan and Ward, 1989: 56)

Such desperation for an agency of improvement within the public sphere was also keenly felt within consequentialist elements of academic criminology, with some suggesting that aspects of correctional privatisation might provide a 'middle way' towards reform (Fulton, 1989; Gardiner, 1989; Hutto, 1990; Logan, 1990, 1993). Foremost amongst these, Logan, in *Private Prisons: Cons and Pros*, argued for a move beyond the hypothetical, essentially that whilst private prisons face challenges, they do so primarily because they are *prisons*, not because they are *private*. Within this persuasive thesis Logan advocated that private penality should not be seen as unique or overwhelming, rather that private and State might exist as cooperative entities in attempting the efficient delivery of safety and humanity (1990). The call was for strategic social policy to improve material conditions, the identification and delegation of core and ancillary tasks (as had already been used elsewhere in the 'modernisation' of criminal justice agencies) which might then be exposed to the requirements and accountability of the competitive market. The established theoretical counter to this, in many ways then as now, was opposition to the delegation of State control in terms of coercive authority and legitimacy, appearing for many a compounding regression which weakened the concept of power to punish and opened the way to punishment for profit—a convenient processing development for the crisis of surplus populations (Box and Hale, 1985; Mathiesen, 1990; Lilly and Knepper, 1992; Shichor, 1993). Lilly and Knepper, in particular, argued forcefully that mass privatisation would likely lead to unfettered expansionism, a normalised sub-governmental complex which would blur corrections with commerciality, resulting in speculative diversification and industrial capacity growth in the prison estate, wedded to loss of political accountability. This in turn would likely provide a fertile ground for vested interest and potential misconduct (Lilly and Knepper, 1992).

Conscience and convention would not curtail progress, and increased capacity and the ability to demonstrate delegated accountability, the potential to manage at a distance, were clearly attractive elements for a Conservative government keen to move towards a hybrid public-private model. Further inherent appeal was vested in the opportunity to stymie an increasingly frustrated Prison Officers Association, weakening the ever present threat of industrial action, and modernise the image of a physical estate that had become wedded to dilapidated Victoriana. This familiar image of the British prison—a fading rhapsody of red brick and grey steel—had become ingrained in the psyche of generations of the British public via the dominating exterior carceral architecture that they passed in their towns and cities and the confirmation of its interior misery through popular television dramatisation during the 1970s and 80s.[5]

This stereotype of the disintegrating prison estate, and the campaign for its reconstruction, received a timely boost on 1 April 1990 with the commencement of a riot at Strangeways Prison in Manchester. Conditions at Strangeways, originally conceived as a local prison in 1868, were generally appalling but exacerbated by the remand crisis of the late 1980s, which had led to mass overcrowding, a situation that it shared with a majority of its institutional contemporaries. Single cells were being shared by three inmates, with convicted prisoners often locked in their cells up to 22 hours a day, having to use slop buckets, which served as communal toilets. Diet was consistently poor, and indignity, brutality and racism, affecting both prisoners and staff, were widespread and expected (Bastow, 2013). The Strangeways siege, including a widely reported rooftop protest, saw the prisoners in control of the institution for 25 days, causing damage amounting to £55 million and sparking copycat disturbances at 24 institutions across the prison estate. Over the 25 days at Strangeways, 147 members of prison staff were injured, along with 47 prisoners, one of whom, Derek White, a remand prisoner, later died of head injuries sustained during hand-to-hand fighting between inmates (Carrabine, 2004).

The public inquiry into the Strangeways riot, chaired by Lord Justice Woolf, presented its findings to Home Secretary Kenneth Baker on 31 January the following year. The subsequent *Woolf Report* (1991), running to 600 pages, made 12 major recommendations and 204 proposals as a template for the significant reform of the Prison Service, drawing praise from the Prison Reform Trust (PRT), who described the report as 'an authoritative statement on the condition of our prisons and what now must be done to civilise them' (Dell, 1991: i). Woolf had described conditions within the prison as 'intolerable' whilst placing the responsibility for the debacle on the failure of successive governments to 'provide the resources to the Prison Service which were needed to enable the Service to provide for an increased prison population in a humane manner' (Carrabine, 2004: 127).

Conveniently, a persuasive radical model for this reimagining and restructuring of the UK prison system appeared to already be in place—under the provisions of the Criminal Justice Act 1991 (and its Contracted Out Prisons Order, 1992)—with subsequent reform likely to lean heavily on the private sector. Kenneth Baker would soon oversee the first ever private prison contract to be awarded in Europe, with Group 4 (latterly G4S), in a competitive pitch open only to private companies, winning the tender to manage the new HMP Wolds remand centre in Yorkshire. However, just four days after its opening in April 1992, Baker was replaced by Kenneth Clarke as Home Secretary, a minister who saw private provision as a promising solution—a prospect which presented both ethical and fiscal attributes. Clarke set out how the government intended to respond to Woolf in an assertive press release dressed as an editorial later that year:

> The 1991 Woolf report into the riots at Strangeways and other jails set an agenda for reform. The Government accepted that agenda almost entirely and produced a timetable for its implementation, extending into the next century. It was then said that the programme of reforms was too slow . . . In order to speed things up, we decided to introduce a contracting out and market-testing programme into the prison system. The service I require on behalf of the taxpayer, the public and the prisoner, is effective custody, enlightened regimes and a genuine reformative content delivered efficiently at a reasonable cost. I have no ideological prejudice about whether those standards are delivered by public sector or private sector employees. There is no public interest or policy reason why the prison service should not have to demonstrate that it can compete with the private sector in delivering decent conditions and a quality regime, day in day out, at a price which demonstrates good value for money.
>
> *(1992)*

Within the space of four years, the cautious reticence of Douglas Hurd's green paper *Private Sector Involvement in the Remand System* (Home Office, 1988) had been replaced with an empowering Criminal Justice Act which bestowed muscular optimism of what the private sector could offer in revitalising Her Majesty's Prison Service. There would be no wait for an assessment of the 'experimental' HMP Wolds to be undertaken; speed was apparently of the essence. Under the Major premiership, the neoliberal principle of the free market would be provided with the means to expose where the Prison Service had been going wrong and demonstrate what needed to be improved.

Late to the privatisation party: manufacturing a private prison complex

As the ribbon was being cut at HMP Wolds on 6 April 1992, procurement arrangements for further privately managed institutions were already in place. The Wolds was to be followed by HMP Blakenhurst, which was being built in Worcestershire, the tender listed on 5 December 1991 being won by UK Detention Services Limited (UKDS), a joint venture between the CCA and two UK construction companies, McAlpine and Mowlem,[6] and HMP Buckley Hall in Lancashire, which would represent another tender win for Group 4. Significantly, both Blakenhurst and Buckley Hall would cater to convicted prisoners. As the key statutory instrument, the Criminal Justice Act 1991 (Contracted Out Prisons Order) 1992, passed through Parliament, it had become clear that HMP Wolds was not being seen as an experiment but rather a prototype. A number of dissenting voices appeared in the House of Lords, including Lords Longford and Richard. Longford, the prison reformer, had already visited Wolds first hand and pointed out that there had been three 'serious disturbances' there in the first three months of operation, concluding his submission by stating, 'I have said in this House more than once that to hand over prisons and to privatise them is obscene. I repeat that now with more emphasis after the visit which I suggest other noble Lords should imitate'. Lord Richard called for distinction in private prisons being used for remand rather than convicted prisoners as had originally been mooted and stated that given the proposed timescale to assess the Wolds experiment had been three years, the assignment of Blakenhurst to the private sector without consultation was extraordinary. Accusing the government of reneging on its promise to proceed with caution and employing a 'shroud of secrecy' over its operation at Wolds, Richard questioned its intention and ethics:

> privatisation will create a vested interest in high crime rates and full prisons. I am bound to say that I think the word 'obscene' is not too strong in this respect—in fact, it was used by my noble friend—if one imagines that, as the crime rates go up, the directors of Group 4 rub their hands and say, 'Jolly good, the Wolds will be fuller and Blakenhurst will have more prisoners. We shall make more money out of it'. I am bound to say that I find that unethical. In my view, it is unethical that the shareholders of private security firms should profit from punishment handed down by the State.
>
> *(Hansard, 1992)*

However, despite such protestations, the statutory instrument was approved, passing into law in February 1993, and by the following year, Wolds and Blakenhurst had been joined by two further new prisons, HMP Doncaster and HMP Buckley Hall, which would be managed by Premier Prison Services Ltd (a newly formed UK-US partnership venture between Serco and Wackenhut) and Group 4, respectively. The contracts for Doncaster and Buckley Hall had been awarded despite a critical report on the efficacy and standards of the operation at HMP Wolds by the Prison Reform Trust (1993).

With any vestige of penal privatisation as an experiment now fading, Clarke was also focused on hiring managerial leadership in preparation for the modernisation of Her Majesty's Prison Service, recruiting Derek Lewis, a former television company chief executive with no experience in criminal justice, during 1992. Lewis would take up the new role of director general in 1993 with a wide brief encompassing strategic planning to enable the transition of the private sector and the facilitation of a corporate approach to management and competition, plus a commitment to overseeing change (Lewis, 1997). Clarke's belief was that privatisation would create a two way street in terms of delivery, with improvements in the performance of the Prison Service driven by open competition with the private sector. He stated that the imposition of market testing would 'cause the Prison

Service to examine its own performance in the light of competitive pressure and encourage the spread of those reforms across public sector prisons much more quickly than would otherwise have been the case' (Pozen, 2003: 266).

The momentum in this rapid cultural shift towards private management of the public sector had received potential turbocharging by the Major government's creation of the Private Finance Initiative (PFI) in November 1992. In part, PFI was developed to meet the European Economic and Monetary Union (EMU) convergence requirements under the Maastricht Treaty 1993, which required EU member states to control public debt. PFI did so by requiring private companies to provide project finance and incur initial costs. The project or service would then be leased back to the government under a long-term contract, spreading cost but extending debt over decades, potentially generations. At this juncture, in terms of the planned manufacturing of a new prison estate, a service sector built primarily on hard infrastructure, the policy was received as a gift—a potential golden goose—and it was anticipated that PFI would draw private-sector investment towards the government's specification for its burgeoning public-private penal hybrid. The procurement of *materiel* was to be key. PFI would be utilised in construction and technology; indeed, the effect of the Criminal Justice and Public Order Act 1994 was to extend the Criminal Justice Act 1991 once more to allow private companies to build as well as manage prisons. Though takeup was initially slow, the increased need for custodial space during 1994 stimulated the market, and the first two contracts of the build it run it variety under PFI were signed in December 1995 and January 1996. These were to operate new prisons on designated sites in Liverpool and Bridgend, institutions which would be named HMP Altcourse and HMP Parc, both assigned to Group 4 (National Audit Office, 1997). Moreover, all of the prison contracts that were issued after HMP Doncaster in 1994 up until 2011 would employ PFI funding.

Having occupied the role of Home Secretary for just over a year, Kenneth Clarke was promoted to Chancellor of the Exchequer in May 1993, with Michael Howard becoming Home Secretary—the third appointment in three years of the Major government. The incoming Howard was a hard liner in terms of his conception of criminal justice who favoured the use of imprisonment as a tool of crime prevention. This philosophy is perhaps best encapsulated by his well known soundbite, 'prison works', delivered at the Conservative Party Conference in Blackpool in 1993 in response to a rising moral panic in the aftermath of the James Bulger murder and a swathe of media reporting on apparently unhindered anti-social behaviour, a crime wave. Less well known is the ringing endorsement of Howard's authoritarianism and 'prison works' mantra by his Prime Minister, John Major, at the same conference. In his keynote Leader's Speech, Major made the following statement:

> It's time for this party to return to its roots . . . our economic roots are clear. We're the party of Adam Smiths, not John Smith . . . I know criminals are a problem in a cell but they're much more of a problem on the street. And

> policy must be dictated by the needs of justice, not by the number of prison places we happen to have available on any given day. If someone belongs in prison, then that is where they should be and that's why we're building more prisons.
>
> *(Major, 1993)*

Thus, the increased use of imprisonment which would come to dominate Howard's time at the Home Office would be supported by the premier and facilitated by the PFI accelerated government building plans now in place. A strong stance on law and order was seen as increasingly politically necessary with the emergence of the 'New' Labour Party under John Smith and the media dynamism of his shadow Home Secretary, Tony Blair, who had begun to make hay with the increasing public disaffection around crime. With Blair pledging in an interview with Jonathan Dimbleby earlier in the year that his party would be 'tough on crime, tough on the causes of crime' firmly positioning the opposition as the new guardians of order (BBC, 1993). The answer to this affront from Michael Howard and his policy advisors, David Cameron and David Maclean, was that the Conservatives would be tougher, their brand of penal populism more popular as a result. During Howard's four year tenure at the Home Office, deterrence through incarceration moved to the forefront of the government's crime prevention strategy, with the prison population of England and Wales increasing by over 20,000 between 1993 and 1997 (Ministry of Justice, 2013: 7). Many of this number would be held in the 22 new prisons constructed in the UK by Conservative administrations between 1979 and 1997, a carceral possibility that latterly owed a great deal to privatisation.

However, the Labour opposition, despite their commitment to fighting crime and burgeoning ascendency as the party of law and order of choice, had retained their commitment to end penal privatisation if elected. During the debates over PFI, several members of the shadow cabinet had berated the government over their use of PFI, accusing them of subterfuge, using the initiative to effect unfettered privatisation through the back door to undermine public provision, with shadow Chief Secretary to the Treasury Harriet Harman stating, 'The truth is that the Government's private finance initiative is just an excuse for their refusal to invest in our infrastructure' (Hansard, 1993). Furthermore, Jack Straw, who had replaced Blair as shadow Home Secretary in October 1994, reiterated Labour's strong opposition to prison privatisation in an editorial in the Times, pledging to end the practice if his party was elected. He stated:

> It is not appropriate for people to profit out of incarceration. This is surely one area where a free market certainly does not exist . . . at the expiry of their contracts a Labour government will bring these prisons into proper public control and run them directly as public services.
>
> *(Straw, cited in Coyle, 2005: 52)*

Straw would reaffirm this party line in his address to the Prison Officer's Association Conference in 1996.

Reflecting on Howard's time as Home Secretary, penal expansionism emerges as absolutely necessary to the ability to wage a populist open ended war against crime. Julian Le Vay, the former finance director of HM Prison Service, provides a vivid analogy of the flux of government practice at this time, stating that, 'in the UK, it felt more like laying the track just in front of the engine' (Le Vay, 2016: 19).[7] Much of this metaphorical track laying had been engineered via political perception that had been in place since Margaret Thatcher had been elected on a law and order ticket in 1979—that the public needed regular reassurance that its government was sufficiently punitive in terms of crime and reactive in terms of security and control. However, the provision of additional capacity had not significantly arrested or reduced the number of prisoners being held on remand by 1995, despite this being seen as the main initial reason for give for privatisation at the close of the 1980s (Prison Reform Trust, 1995).

Concerns over prison security had also increased over Howard's tenure, partly due to conditions of overcrowding and use of inexperienced or disenfranchised staff. This situation had percolated throughout 1994 and 1995 with a series of serious breaches of security and disturbances across the prison estate, which included the escape of six Category A prisoners from HMP Whitemoor in September 1994 (a new maximum security prison opened in 1992) and the suicide by hanging of serial murderer Fred West whilst awaiting trial at HMP Winson Green on 1 January 1995. Matters came to a head on 3 January 1995 with the escape of three 'exceptional risk' prisoners from the maximum security HMP Parkhurst after they had fashioned tools and obtained a key. This, after HM chief inspector of prisons, Judge Stephen Tumim, had written to both Howard and Derek Lewis, director general of the Prison Service, the previous October, warning that rudimentary procedures such as searches and spot checks were not being carried out at the prison. Following a public inquiry chaired by Sir John Learmont in the aftermath of the Parkhurst debacle, Lewis was unceremoniously dismissed by Howard in October 1995, later accusing the Home Secretary of acting *ultra vires* in overruling him as director general on matters of staff conduct and prison security and 'improper interference in terms of the day-to-day running of the Prison Service' (Pilkington, 1999: 84). Lewis' dismissal and Learmont's review, did not, however, abate the disturbances, with serious rioting at HMP Everthorpe (a category C prison situated adjacent to the Group 4 showpiece HMP Wolds in Yorkshire) over December 1995 and January 1996. Lewis later reflected on the intensive culture of micro managerialism effected by Howard as going against any notion of independence in reasoning that the free market had been anticipated to deliver. He stated, 'It was a far cry from the "much greater autonomy from ministers and the rest of the Home Office" that Ken Clarke had publicly promised' (Lewis, 1997: 156).

As the new private-public prison system began to take shape under Howard, another historical ghost appeared as a by-product of the increased use of incarceration, *elimination*, the notion of social disappearance through incapacitation, which Andrew Rutherford referred to as the 'eliminative ideal'. Reflective examination of the eliminative ideal within contemporary Conservative governance by Rutherford provided a theoretical excursion into the darker regions of criminal policy during the mid-1990s. He argued that current and emerging social problems were being met with a legislative response that derived its validity from popular consensus allowing the problem individuals or groups involved to be identified, processed and eliminated (banished). Britain's use of transportation to its colonies during the eighteenth and nineteenth centuries provides an early modern example of such an eliminative penal practice (with added economic incentive, of course), as does Germany between 1933 and 1938 *in extremis*. But Rutherford's primary focus in terms of case study was to link the eliminative ideal to the expansion and establishment of industrialised penality in America during the 1980s and 1990s and, by close association, that of Conservative Britain (Rutherford, 1997). An emergent theme here is that the continual building of prisons to eliminate undesirable elements is likely to be as much about political appetite for social exclusion as it is about public appetite for punitiveness, its feasible grievous peak, once fully normalised, akin to crime control *as* industry supplying the gulags *western style*, as envisaged by Christie (1993). The 'positive' political effect of Howard's passion for the eliminative ideal had been a dropping crime rate (as might be anticipated with incapacitation), and this was still the case at the time of the general election on 1 May 1997 which would deliver a Labour government for the first time in 18 years. New Labour's promise to be tough on crime and tough on the causes of crime was still ringing in the ears of the electorate, underpinning their victory, less so the consistent pledge to reverse the new Conservative practice of penal privatisation, Anderson and Mann correctly predicted that the political momentum of popular punitiveness might prove too much to bear for incoming Home Secretary Jack Straw:

> Both parties locked themselves into an escalating bidding war of ever-tougher proposals, Straw took up the reins with gusto. With Blair's full backing, he came up with a host of policy proposals which indicated that once Labour got into office he would be, as one modernising member of the shadow cabinet predicted, 'the most illiberal Labour home secretary in history'.
> (Anderson and Mann, 1997: 255)

New Labour: things can only get better

Still in the immediate afterglow of Labour's landslide victory in May 1997, one of Jack Straw's first actions as Home Secretary was to reassure government contractors that he was prepared to sign off the existing PFI contracts put in place by the Conservatives – this to ensure the completion of new infrastructure; temporarily, at least, it appeared that the public-private hybrid would continue. He stated, 'If there are contracts in the pipeline and the only way of getting the accommodation in place very quickly is by signing those contracts, then I will sign those contracts' (Nathan, 2003: 168). However, the following month, in June 1997, he authorised two further contracts on new private prisons and renewed the private management contract on a third; in doing so Labour's pre-election promises to end prison privatisation looked to be have been built on quicksand. Effectively, on taking over, Labour had inherited the two new prisons under construction to be operated by Securicor and Group 4 in Bridgend and Liverpool. Both were nearing completion and would become HMP Parc and HMP Altcourse, Parc opening in November 1997 and Altcourse a month later in December 1997. Within its first seven months of government, Labour had two shiny working models of the Conservative PFI vision.

Straw did, however, in June 1997, instigate two reviews by the Home Affairs Committee into the feasibility of returning the prison estate, or parts of it, to public ownership. The first, *Public and Prison Management: Considerations on Returning Privately Managed Prisons to the Public Sector* (Home Office, 1998a), concerned itself mainly with performance indicators in terms of respective costings between public and private operations. The report highlighted the binding and long-term nature of the existing PFI contracts and the difficulties in attempting to unify the differences in employment terms between public and private staff—a prospect that would likely be resisted by both the POA and the contractors. The implied summary appeared to be a request to essentially allow the current arrangements to run their contractual course, with any intervention occurring when tenders were due for renewal (Home Office, 1998a). The second paper, *Review of Private Financing of New Prison Procurement* (Home Office, 1998b), concurred with the direction of the first, emphasising the risk in terms of cost of splitting the PFI process to allow for a private build public run system. As Le Vay argues, this advice suggested 'that any option involving public operation would be more costly than PFI and left Straw with no room to argue with Treasury for a different approach' (2016: 25).

Rosie Winterton, a Labour MP, submitted a written question under the title 'Private Sector Prisons' to Straw in Parliament on 25 June 1998 asking whether he intended to publish the reports of the two reviews. The Home Secretary replied somewhat succinctly, 'I am placing in the Library copies of the reports to the two reviews referred to in my answer of 19 June 1997. The Prison Service has already sent copies to unions and to the contractors' (House of Commons, 1998). The reviews would remain unpublished. However, with access to Home Affairs Committee information and a year in the Home Office, Straw had already revealed New Labour's long-term policy approach the previous month. At the POA Annual Conference on 19 May 1998, he had stated that the financial cost of returning private prisons to the public sector did not represent value for money and that competition in terms of prison management would remain in place, with the Prison Service permitted to participate in the tender round for private contracts when due for renewal. This effected a complete U-turn on the party's pledge when in opposition to renationalise private prisons, allowing a wholesale adoption of the Conservative legacy of popular punitivism built on economy, efficiency and effectiveness, which could and would be underwritten by PFI.

Like Howard before him, Straw's continuum approach on 'tough' crime policy was largely to placate the sensibilities of middle England, many of whom had voted for (New) Labour in their droves for the first time in May 1997. Thus, the use of custodial sentencing as a form of eliminative idealism would likely continue; prison would still *work* on Blair's watch. The point that prison might be *able to work* in reducing crime if prison regimes were adapted towards rehabilitation and preparation for release, rather than simply viewed as an extension of State penal architecture, had been strongly made in an academic collection edited by Roger Matthews and Peter Francis published in 1996. This had included a chapter from Stephen Tumim, HM chief inspector of prisons between 1987 and 1995, who had been appointed by Douglas Hurd and overseen the effect of recent policy. *Prisons 2000: An International Perspective on the Current State and Future of Imprisonment*, was primarily a Left Realist comparative response to recent New Right penal policy, but it also appeared as a realistic policy pitch towards the incoming Labour government, suggesting a possible route out of the penal crisis towards the millennium, a 'progressive paradigm'. In this regard Matthews and Francis made the following reflective point with regard to the need to separate privatisation from reactive calls to increase carceral headspace. They argued, 'It was evident in Britain for example, that even when the prison population decreased towards the end of the 1980s and while certain newly built prisons stood half empty there was still a call for the privatization of prisons' (Matthews and Francis, 1996: 9). For prison to have a chance of *working*, privatisation could not become both the means and the end.

Delivering the Prison Reform Trust Annual Lecture in December 1998, Straw chose the title *Making Prisons Work*, to lay out the government's long term policy plan, stating that for New Labour prison would still be seen to 'work' but within a wider strategy as 'one element in a radical and coherent strategy to protect the public by reducing crime'. Within this strategy, protection of the public by way of risk assessment emerged as the government's paramount concern. Straw also called for realism in terms of what might be achieved but emphasised the need for prison security and the prison as a site for restoration, rehabilitation and education but also the foundation of sentencing and a 'proper use of custody as punishment'. In summary, governmental focus would be extended to 'the causes of crime' in terms of the adoption of 'constructive prison regimes' based on values of institutional safety and fairness (security and rights) allied to individual responsibility (responsibilisation) (Straw, 1998). It was clear that new purpose was needed, as the prison population had continued to rise since Labour had taken office, and as Straw was delivering his *Making Prisons Work* lecture, it stood at over 66,000.

During its first term of office, in addition to topping out HMP Altcourse and HMP Parc during 1997, the Labour administration would open six further new private prisons in the UK. All of these projects would be financed, designed, built and operated via the use of PFI on a 25 year contract term. The six facilities and their original contracted operators were: HMP Lowdham Grange, Nottinghamshire, opened 1998 (Premier Prison Services Ltd) (PPS);[8] HMP Ashfield, Gloucestershire, 1999 (PPS); HMP Kilmarnock, East Ayrshire, 1999 (PPS); HMP Forest Bank, Lancashire, 2000 (UKDS); HMP Rye Hill, Northamptonshire, 2001 (Group 4); and HMP Dovegate, Staffordshire, 2001 (PPS). This flurry of construction activity had been administratively underwritten, to an extent, by a series of supportive reports in terms of their competitive and comparative utility; these included apparent gains across sector the in terms of the procurement process, value for money and service provision (Woodbridge, 1997, 1999; National Audit Office, 1997, 2003; Park, 2000).

However, the runaway expansion of the private sector would not continue unabated. In an open call by the Prison Service in 1999 at the end of the five year management contracts for HMP Buckley Hall and HMP Blakenhurst, both institutions were taken into public sector management, with HMPS being seen as the preferred option in terms of both quality and cost. Moreover, during 2000, HMPS retained its contract to run HMP Manchester against private competition following a competitive market testing process, a significant 'win' in that it included an arrangement with the POA to reduce established staffing ratios. This led to the expression of concerns around commercial integrity by private providers, resulting in a degree of market sensitivity, and the following year when management of the failing HMP Brixton was put out to tender, no bids were forthcoming from the private sector. These moves seemed rather convenient, politically, in terms of meeting the necessary competitive ideal that would justify marketisation. As Le Vay, who was involved with the Buckley Hall and Blakenhurst processes, argues, 'Everyone assumed a political objective: in fact, it was done entirely on cost, as in-house bids appeared cheaper. The private sector did not seem to anticipate a competitive public sector response, and were perhaps complacent' (2016: 25).

The problem of parity in public-private competition was considered in this first decade of privatisation, with consecutive Conservative and Labour governments attempting some standardisation in terms of the evaluation of institutional performance. This had gone beyond the general key performance indicators beloved of the financial management initiative and the NPM it engendered, requiring public and private-sector bidders to measure, demonstrate and target performance within the public sphere. However, a report commissioned by Straw in 2000 by the Targeted Performance Initiative Working Group headed up by Sir Bernard Laming suggested that there was some way to go, in part due to the multitude of stakeholders in the sector:

> Ministers, managers, trade unions, staff, HM Inspectorate apart from the wider world, all seem to have their own perception of what is acceptable or reasonable in the Prison Service. No organisation can hope to be confident about its performance when the benchmarks against it which it is measured vary so widely or change so often . . . It is of particular value to make such judgements [on equity] between establishments of the Prison Service and those which are separately managed by private agencies.
>
> *(Laming, 2000: 4)*

The Laming report recommended a need for a closer micro management, which might provide the desired service responsibilisation in attempting a level playing field delivering guaranteed behavioural outcomes, properties that Nellis referred to as 'total, finely calibrated control' (Nellis, 2001: 33)—an elusive target at the millennium, which still eludes Home Secretaries to this day. However, a signifier of the incremental development of a managerial culture of control in the sector can be seen in the work of Liebling, who pointed out that between 1993 and 2000 the number of key performance indicators in the Prison Service had risen from 8 to 18 (2004: 58). It might be argued that prison management requires a complex adaptable approach, a higher standard than other marketised sectors. Therein, calibrated fiscal performance is inextricably linked to often un-calibratable interpersonal variables of time and regime, centring on subjective human perceptions of order, legitimacy and decency: an amalgam of the interpersonal knowledge and experience of staff and prisoners within the overall environment, what Liebling refers to as the operation of 'moral performance' (2004: 473), but there has been little evidence of governmental interest in holistic values, existing as they often do beyond the balance sheet.

In a move to provide the coveted *total, finely calibrated control*, the flagging private prison industry was given critical stimulation by the Carter Review of 'correctional services' in 2003. The review titled *Managing Offenders, Reducing Crime—Changing Lives*, led by Patrick Carter, a private health care entrepreneur and school friend of Jack Straw,[9] was founded on the doctrine of 'contestability' as a device to drive up service standards and provide yet more value for money—a conclusive crossing from the customarily *sacred* to the contemporary *profane*, a Trojan Horse, keenly summarised by Nellis as representative of 'messianic managerialism' (2006: 53). Carter recommended the creation of the National Offender Management Service (NOMS) to provide end-to-end management of offenders through a merger of prison and probation services, transferring Martin Narey, director general of the Prison Service and proponent of the 'decency agenda', as its first chief executive. The focus of the Carter Report was the most effective use of resources in lowering the number of offenders in prison and under supervision in the community; it was proposed that this would be enabled by the management of each offender from initial contact to completion of sentence, with a division between service commissioners and service providers ensuring contestability between these disparate agencies. Here, contestability through direct management would act as a threat in bringing failing institutions into line by splitting the commission and provision elements within NOMS. A further hope was that a growing cadre of private and third-sector organisations would enter the fray in competing to manage prisoners, with NOMS 'offender managers' able to purchase custodial places or community interventions from a varied choice of providers. However, the introduction of a mixed economy for prisons and probation based on payment by results (PbR) also came with a degree of service risk, potentially introducing a divisive effect of deconstructed bifurcation and potential net-widening (Sim, 2009: 120).

Indeed, many of the desired reforming effects of NOMS in stimulating the market failed to materialise, including the first group of prisons earmarked for contestability in May 2005. Here, the Home Secretary, Charles Clarke, halted plans to allow private companies to tender for a cluster of three public prisons HMP

Elmley, HMP Standford Hill and HMP Swaleside on the Isle of Sheppey, Kent, after an advance agreement on a revised programme in terms of standards and performance was reached with union representatives to run for a duration of three years. Clarke's decision had wide significance for the involvement of private and voluntary organisations in terms of the expansion along the lines proposed by Carter, with much of the internal opposition from the public sector garnered in deterrence of the suspected threat of US corrections operators muscling into the UK marketplace. Overall, the element of contestability seen as instrumental to the successful operation of NOMS failed to materialise, Le Vay reflecting:

> Heroic targets were set: 10% of probation work by value to be subcontracted by 2007–08, and one quarter of all adult services operated by NOMS, to a value of £9 billion, to be completed within five years. It seemed competition policy was finally moving up several gears, from short term incrementalism to major strategic commitment. But none of this happened. The grand strategy was gradually forgotten—in fact, there was *less* competition in prisons for some years after 2006 than before, while competition for Probation was hobbled by a well organised opposition.
>
> *(2016: 31)*

In May 2007 the Prison Reform Trust's *Bromley Briefing* was able to provide a valuable penal snapshot of a decade of New Labour, just as Tony Blair was stepping down as Prime Minister. The Trust noted that the period represented frenzied activity in the sphere, with the government taking administrative pride in the delivery of over 20,000 additional prison places at enormous expense in that time. Privatisation had been key to the rescaling of the penal system of the UK, with 11 private prisons in operation at that time accounting for 8,243 prisoners, all running at a comparably higher cost in most categories than their public counterparts (Prison Reform Trust, 2007: 37). Blair's tenure had seen the creation the most privatised prison system in Europe, a multi-layered hybrid, which according to Sim had 'perfectly symbolized the nature and direction of the country and its desperate search for political and cultural modernisation' (2009: 122).

One of Gordon Brown's first actions on taking over as Prime Minister from Blair was to appoint Jack Straw to the recently created post of Justice Secretary. This brief conferred power over the correctional service elements formerly within the purview of the Home Office to the Ministry of Justice. In January 2008 Straw announced that the director general of the Prison Service would become chief executive of NOMS (latterly director general), thus assuming responsibility for both the Prison Service and the National Probation Service. On the back of these changes, NOMS emerged as an executive agency within the Ministry of Justice with oversight and control of private contracts within the sector. In the midst of deepening economic recession during 2010, Straw announced the 'social impact bond' (SIB) in a final attempt to stimulate the corrections market that Carter's vision for NOMS had promised. The SIB was set up as a financial instrument that operated as a commissioning tool, enabling organisations to bid on service contracts conditional on achieving results with the investors who funded the project at start up paid on the basis of agreed upon results. Early adoption of this model saw SIBs operating in the sphere of rehabilitation via a private and voluntary 'alliance' between Serco and two prison charities, Catch 22 and Turning Point at HMP Doncaster (Wright and Jones, 2012: 55). Although initial pilot results for the alliance were encouraging (including a successful bid to provide resettlement services for HMP Belmarsh West),[10] plans to extend the initiative would be interrupted by the incoming coalition government and its demand for austerity. As a browbeaten Labour Party left office after a term of 13 years in May 2010, the prison population stood at 85,000, a dramatic rise of around 20,000 during this period (Ministry of Justice, 2013). Under the Blair and Brown governments, prison privatisation and mass incarceration had become an augmented reality within an unceasing environment of penal populism.

The last decade: peak rationalisation or a model of denigration

As has been discussed at length elsewhere in this book, the Conservative Liberal Democrat coalition government led by David Cameron that entered office May 2011 did so in the midst of global recession, emphasising the need for a term of enforced national austerity. The coalition's first justice secretary would be Kenneth Clarke, seen as an experienced and safe pair of hands by Cameron, a figure instrumental to the establishment of prison privatisation in the UK as Home Secretary in 1992. His first action in this arena now was to attempt regeneration of the sector via an increase in competition. This was published, at pace, in July 2011 as *Competition Strategy for Offender Services*, with Clarke stating:

> This strategy sets out our principles for how we will change the way we use competition to meet these aims. My approach is based on ensuring an effective balance between making services more efficient while reforming them so that they provide better outcomes for the public. In doing so, we will draw on a wide range of expertise from the private and voluntary sector, which will work in partnership with a strong, vibrant and newly empowered public sector.
>
> (Ministry of Justice, 2011: 2)

The strategy would cover all services within the criminal justice sector, existing and planned, with an ambitious push towards increased privatisation and third-sector involvement. Specifically, the Ministry of Justice, and by association, NOMS under Michael Spurr, committed to the creation of what was described as a 'functioning market' for offender services, with the by now usual emphasis on innovation and cost effectiveness, declaring that the impact of its competition strategy would see the first round of contract awards made by 2012 (Ministry of Justice, 2011: 4).

The desired acceleration did occur, with a competition opened in July 2011 that represented the biggest penal tendering round ever seen in the context of the UK prison estate. In this phase the Ministry of Justice expressed an intention to close two prisons, Latchmere House prison and HMP Brockhill, and a desire to privatise nine: HMPs Birmingham, Acklington and Castington (which would merge to become HMP Northumberland), Coldingley, Durham, Hatfield, Lindholme, Moorland and Onley—all of which were currently within the public sector—along with a re-tendering process for HMP Wolds, which was contracted to G4S. HMP Birmingham, an early Victorian prison, would become the first publicly built, owned and operated UK prison to be fully transferred to the private sector, with G4S taking over both operations in October 2011 and full ownership by April 2012 (Liebling and Ludlow, 2017). The chaotic competitive scramble surrounding the acquisition of HMP Birmingham was later summarised by Ludlow in the following terms:

> Following a process that cost £5.84 million; the Birmingham competition produced a contract between the Government and G4S with a value of £316.5 million that is impenetrable to all but lawyers in its length and language, which is more focused upon NOMS' needs than prisoner needs, and which lacks vision and ambition for future service improvement and the important role of the workforce in delivering it.
>
> *(2015: 194)*

Another key aspect of Clarke's strategy had been to adopt the rehabilitation rhetoric of his immediate predecessor Jack Straw in an attempt at reduction in the overall prison population—a position necessitated to reduce public spending rather than a move towards penal liberalism. The device of choice considered to facilitate a reduction in numbers, via a reduction in reoffending as with Straw, would be the private third sector service collaboration with payment by results. A model anticipated along the lines of the 'Alliance' (Serco, Catch 22, Turning Point) pilot running at HMP Doncaster described in the foregoing.[11] This initiative was to be combined with increased competition for Probation and the management of low-risk offenders in the community across the public, private and third sectors, as laid out during March 2012 in a further NOMS competition initiative, *Punishment and Reform: Effective Probation Services*, with the by now familiar emphasis on volunteerism, technology and cost effectiveness:

> Extending the partnership between the Probation Service and the private, public and voluntary sectors, and giving Probation Trusts more control of local budgets of offender management services like electronic monitoring of curfews and joint commissioning for drug and mental health treatment, will help cut crime by driving down reoffending. This will better support the Government's priorities for wider reform of the justice sector, including the development of payment by measured results to cut reoffending.
>
> *(Clarke, 2012)*

However, Clarke's ambitious proposals would not be realised, with Chris Grayling's appointment as Justice Secretary in September 2015 signifying a move away from the prison market test towards an austerity led agenda in criminal justice. Indeed, by November 2012 Grayling had overseen the suspension of the extant competitive tendering processes for HMPs Coldingley, Durham and Onley and the decision to take HMP Wolds (the original private model) into the public sector, defending the decision to Parliament on the basis of an overriding need for 'further and faster' cost reductions:

> [T]he competition for these prisons [HMPs Coldingley, Durham and Onley], is not proceeding and they will remain in the public sector. For the Wolds—currently managed by G4S—the benefits of the competition when compared to the option of clustering the Wolds with the nearby prison Everthorpe, did not represent best value to the public. I have therefore decided not to progress with the competition. This means that when the current contract expires in July 2013, the prison will move to public sector management.
>
> *(Hansard, 2012)*

Grayling's apparent U-turn on competition was received as an unexpected shock by the private security industry, particularly in the light of the public humiliation of G4S in the security debacle, which had preceded the recently concluded London Olympic Games (Armstrong et al., 2016). The concern was that the Ministry of Justice would now begin to move away from competition within the prison sector, preferring to attempt close fiscal management by public control; others saw it as the prelude to a more radical approach to marketisation. In practice he would employ both approaches.

In September 2013 Grayling announced that the financing of two 2,000 place 'superjails' (formerly suggested as titan prisons) had received Treasury approval, with sites for their construction secured in London and Wrexham (Travis, 2013). At the same time, the Ministry of Justice had instigated public sector cost cutting in an attempt to meet the government target of reducing the prisons budget by an additional £500 million per annum in addition to the austerity cuts already in place, identifying that this could be accelerated by direct management of the public estate. Le Vay argues that this restructuring was approached in three ways: 1. The rationalisation of the prison estate, 2. the development and deployment of a new cost and operational model for public prisons and 3. cuts to staffing costs (pay and pensions) planned for the longer term (Le Vay, 2016: 36). Here, the prison estate would be rationalised via a programme of closures on the basis of operating and maintenance costs and strategic geography rather than performance—a factor which spared a number of poorly performing PFI prisons at this point. NOMS would oversee the new private-sector developed model for public sector operations, driving towards leaner staff prisoner ratios, a development which cut costs as desired but also disregarded previously accepted conventions on performance and safety. The governmental assault on staff pay and pensions would be more nuanced, incremental, but nevertheless the long-term strategy was made clear through the adoption of adjusted pay scales and streamlined management structures during Grayling's tenure at the Ministry of Justice.

Cost effectiveness did not exist as a given in the new private prison estate, with a National Audit Office Report in December 2013 stating that NOMS had implemented a policy of closure exemption for privatised prisons in England and Wales due to the prohibitive timescale and cost implications of withdrawing from the contracts (National Audit Office, 2013). Similarly, during the Public Accounts Committee which sat in April 2014, it was revealed that HMP Oakwood and HMP Thameside (two large contracted-out prisons) were two of only three establishments across the estate to have been awarded the lowest performance ratings for 2012–13, stating that HM chief inspector of prisons, Nick Hardwick, had said the quality and quantity of purposeful activity across the prison system had 'plummeted' over the course of a year (House of Commons, 2014)

The negative social impact of unprecedented change driven by coalition-rendered austerity on the prison system was also apparent very quickly and given further clarity by Hardwick in his next Annual Report for 2013–14, which was published in October 2014. In this report, Hardwick highlighted an existential safety crisis in the system, focusing on managing diminishing resources and central policy pressures alongside a prison population at 96% usable capacity. He stated,

> there remains a real risk that the price of restoring stability and safety to prisons will not just be the costs involved but a prolonged period in which prisoners have reduced access to the work, education and resettlement activities on which the rehabilitation of many depends.
>
> *(HMCIP, 2014: 17)*

This report was compounded by a critical House of Commons Justice Committee Report which appeared the following March. This largely supported Hardwick's view, paying particular attention to the strain being caused by overcrowding, with a number of institutions operating beyond their baseline capacity, and the resultant impact on safety, noting that levels of assaults, self harm and suicide had been steadily rising since 2011, representing a 45% increase in the space of four years and remarkably a 38% rise between 2012 and 2014 (House of Commons Justice Committee, 2015: 29–30). The committee concluded by expressing concern that *inter alia*, 'there is a real danger that savings and rehabilitation could become two contradictory policy agendas. The question of the sustainability of the system cannot continue to be ignored' (HCJC, 2015: 73). These two assessments of the penal landscape in the middle of the last decade perhaps encapsulate Grayling's relatively short, but now notorious, term as Minister of Justice between September 2012 and May 2015, with the painful cuts to the fabric of the criminal justice system dispatched at great speed with the compassion and alacrity of an enthusiastic executioner. Following the election of a Conservative government with a working majority led by Cameron in May 2015, he would be replaced at the Ministry of Justice by Michael Gove.

The Conservatives, having been re-elected with a prison population at 97% capacity, announced in their Spending Review of November 2015 another 'prison building revolution' that would deliver nine new institutions at a cost of £1.3 billion during the following decade. This was a return to the rhetorical model of 'old for new' central to previous coalition government policy, which had seen the closure and sale of ten prisons between 2010 and 2015—a public spirited form of asset stripping. These closures, which were deemed necessary to finance the building programme, would in this round include the lucrative real estate occupied by HMPs Reading and Holloway, with the land to be sold off for housing. Moreover, in terms of long-term indication regarding infrastructure planning, the new super-jail in Wales was nearing completion in Wrexham, eventually opening in February 2017 as HMP Berwyn, with its unprecedented capacity for 2,106 prisoners, the biggest in Europe.

Conservative prison policy on the front foot for the remainder of the decade would often be focussed on construction; indeed the mantra adopted, or adapted, by Boris Johnson following his successful election in December 2019 was to 'build back better' in an appeal to the public to endorse apparent activity as progress. Policy on the back foot meanwhile would increasingly resemble baton passing and reactive crisis management to tackle the errors and incivilities of previous policy decisions, with initiatives delivered towards a point on the horizon. Arguably, the most complete recent example of this concept was contained in the white paper *Prison Safety and Reform* published in November 2016 during Theresa May's term as Prime Minister following the resignation of Cameron in the aftermath of the Brexit referendum (Ministry of Justice, 2016).

Prison Safety and Reform utilised the plans previously drawn up by Cameron and Gove which attempted to arrest the deterioration in prison morale and conditions that had been created, to an extent, by the accelerated implementation of coalition austerity measures, principally during the Grayling era. Gove, as Minister of Justice, had expressed a desire to rebuild and reform the prison estate which had culminated in the commitment to build the nine new institutions outlined in the November 2015 Policy Review. This idea was harnessed by Cameron as a campaign to develop a series of 'reform prisons', setting out his vision as 'the biggest shake up in the way our prisons are run since Victorian times' and promising a Prisons Bill during the next Parliamentary session to stimulate the private and voluntary sectors. He stated:

> because we know that State monopolies are often very slow to change themselves, and because the involvement of the private and voluntary sectors in prisons has been one of the most important drivers of change in this system since the 1990s, we'll ensure there is a strong role for businesses and charities in the operation of these reform prisons and the new prisons we will build in this Parliament.

Post Cameron, May's white paper proposed to realise these ideals in building a framework setting out a clear set of purposes for the prison system, committing to raising standards in terms of staffing and governance with prison governors empowered via a degree of budget autonomy over services, all within the safe and secure environment of a modernised estate. Key to this would be the by now tried and tested method of PFI resourcing and the implementation of commercial performance agreements to benchmark prison population and performance expectations. Oversight of strategy and standards and operations would be provided by the Ministry of Justice and the Prison Service, respectively. However, the legislation required to bring the provisions in the white paper into law contained within the Prison and Courts Bill 2017 was interrupted by the general election called by May during June and was subsequently withdrawn, and with it perhaps the best hope for meaningful reform of the prison system of the UK in a generation.

By 2018, an increasingly beleaguered Conservative government with a precarious majority was preoccupied with the implications of Brexit, and considerations of the State of the prisons had been relegated to fire-fighting once more. By this point, private penality as a concept was normalised and had integrated to a large extent with the public prison estate as a persistent cause of concern. However, an explosive turning point in terms of perception would come in August 2018, with the G4S managed HMP Birmingham being taken over by the Ministry of Justice through the use of emergency powers. Ministry intervention followed a catalogue of serious failings, culminating in a unannounced inspection by Peter Clarke, HM chief inspector of prisons, which led to the invocation of the Urgent Notification (UN) Process. In a summary to his emergency report to the Justice Secretary, David Gauke, Clarke concluded:

> I was astounded that HMP Birmingham had been allowed to deteriorate so dramatically over the 18 months since the previous inspection. A factor in my decision to invoke the Urgent Notification process is that at present I can have no confidence in the ability of the prison to make improvements. There has clearly been an abject failure of contract management and delivery . . . The inertia that seems to have gripped both those monitoring the contract and delivering it on the ground has led to one of Britain's leading jails slipping into a state of crisis that is remarkable even by the low standards we have seen all too frequently in recent years . . . First, however, there is an urgent and pressing need to address the squalor, violence, prevalence of drugs and looming lack of control that currently afflict HMP Birmingham.
>
> (Clark, 2018: 6–7)

The emergency measures recommended in the report for HMP Birmingham saw its management and staffing operations immediately transferred to the Prison Service for six months. However, in April 2019 the remainder of the contract with G4S was terminated, and the prison fully returned to the public sector. Following the Birmingham debacle, a Prison Reform Trust briefing in October 2018 reported that at that juncture, 19% of prison population, 15,813 individuals, were being held in the 14 private prisons across England and Wales. Furthermore, alongside the 'serious concern' of HMP Birmingham, under the Government Prison Performance Ratings, two private prisons, HMPs Doncaster and Northumberland, had returned 'overall performance is a concern' ratings in 2016–17, and three, HMPs Lowdham Grange, Northumberland and Thameside, the following year in 2017–18. HMP Birmingham was not to be viewed as an exception or a one off (Prison Reform Trust, 2018: 18).

Alongside concerns over the regime management capabilities of private contractors, financial instruments and the structuring of commercial arrangements has also received greater scrutiny in recent years. In the aftermath of the collapse and liquidation of the multi-national infrastructure and facilities management company Carillion plc in January 2018, responsibility for the maintenance contracts of 52 prisons was predictably returned to the public sector at vast public expense (Ministry of Justice and House of Commons Justice Committee, 2018). Carillion had been a repeated recipient of PFI funding for government contracts. In the wake of the collapse, two cumulative unfavourable official reviews, questioning governmental reliance on PFI funding which straddled it, came to the fore (Office for Budget Responsibility, 2017; House of Commons Committee of Public Accounts, 2018). Subsequently, Philip Hammond, the Chancellor of the Exchequer, in his Budget Statement of October 2018, announced immediate cessation of the use of the PFI (and its planned replacement PF2) in government projects. Whilst making clear that the mechanism should be viewed as a burden on public financing and a source of serious financial risk, he stated, 'I have never signed off a PFI contract as Chancellor . . . and I can confirm today that I never will. I can announce that the Government will abolish the use of PFI and PF2 for future projects' (Hammond, 2018).

Despite the debacle at HMP Birmingham, the collapse of Carillion and the abandonment of the PFI model, UK government policy remains wedded to the mixed market competitive model in terms of prison construction and operations. Launching the Prison Operator Services Framework (POSF) in November 2018, inviting private companies to tender, the Minister for Prisons, Rory Stewart, reaffirmed commitment to the private sector, stating:

> This Government remains committed to a role for the private sector in operating custodial services. The competition launched today will seek to build on the innovation and different ways of working that the private sector has previously introduced to the system. The sector has an important role to play, and currently runs some high performing prisons, as part of a decent and secure prison estate.
>
> *(Ministry of Justice, 2018)*

The purpose of this framework, in addition to acting as policy ratification, is to provide specificity in the choice of contractor for prison operations with the government. In answering a Parliamentary question on 9 July 2019, the Minister of Justice, Robert Buckland, confirmed that six bidders had been successful in meeting the initial call and would join the POSF for a six year tenure; these were G4S Care and Custody Services UK Limited, Interserve Investments Limited, Management and Training Corporation Works Limited, Mitie Care & Custody, Serco Limited and Sodexo Limited. Thus, the continuance of private-sector operations in the sector was assured, with some familiar names recruited.

A month after Boris Johnson had become Prime Minister, during August 2019, his Justice Secretary, Robert Buckland, issued a press release with the title '10,000 Extra Prison Places to Keep the Public safe' to provide a template for likely policy direction on prisons for the Johnson administration. The content was very familiar, with the suggestion that the additional headspace of 10,000, and colossal expense, was required to prevent crime and reassure the public. He argued that the strategy would dovetail with other asserted governmental aims within criminal justice in the coming years, notably the promised recruitment of 20,000 additional police officers, and furthermore, that the replacement of the ageing prison estate was necessary to ease overcrowding and provide a suitable site for rehabilitation (Ministry of Justice, 2019). On reflection, Buckland's rallying call to popular punitiveness could have been issued at any point in the preceding 30 years, its approach by now ubiquitous in the performance of public reassurance in terms of supplying deterrent incarceration. Like the colloquial expression of painting the Forth Bridge, governmental approach to prison reform has descended to cliché, in that it is approached as an insurmountable perpetual task, with ever more paint required to be thrown at the job.

The Johnson government, like the six that immediately proceeded it, will continue to build on, over and beyond the prison estate, employing the use of private capital in harness to the commercial ethos of competition. Current major construction projects include the superjail HMP Five Wells, at Wellingborough in Northamptonshire, due to complete phased construction in November 2021, and a replacement for the former HMP Glen Parva in Leicester, due to open in spring 2023. Both prisons are being built with public money but will be privately managed—the superjail HMP Five Wells by G4S. In addition, advanced planning for four more new prisons is in progress to supplement the already vast estate over the next six years, a prison each for East Yorkshire and the North West and two for the South East (Ministry of Justice, 2020a). However, despite this further expansion of the estate, a research report by the Chartered Institute of Public Finance and Accountancy in April 2020 argued that the system will likely continue to operate in crisis mode in the coming years, particularly with regard to overcrowding and staffing matters. It concluded:

> The government has a poor record at building new prisons, but even if all the Wellingborough, Glen Parva and Full Sutton places are ready quickly, the number of prisoners will exceed the capacity of the estate in 2023/24 under the central and high demand scenarios. Existing prisons cells may also be lost

quicker than expected if HMPPS doesn't clear its backlog of major capital works, estimated at nearly £1bn.

(Pope et al., 2020: 26)

In Pope et al.'s study, three demand scenario models were developed in terms of *low*, *central* and *high* prison place demand within UK prison population and projected alongside Ministry of Justice data for the next four years. In each scenario in this study, the forecasted prison population was higher than the Ministry of Justice estimate, the central (median) and high demand scenarios remarkably so, recording a projected central figure of 90,000 places by 2023/24 and a high figure of 95,378 in comparison to the official estimate of 81,700 (Pope et al., 2020: 24). This research suggests that the UK prison population will comfortably exceed its previous record high figure of 88,167[12] by 2025. Moreover, the long-term creation of new places is not likely to assuage perennial crises of population, regime and purpose. Thus, the contemporary policy landscape suggests a commitment to build, frequently bigger, perhaps even, in the rhetoric of Boris Johnson, to 'build back better'. Consequently, whilst meaningful penal reform remains elusive for the UK, the private sector will remain central in contributing to the eliminative ideal—in its normal manner.

Conclusion

Policy analysis of the contemporary penal landscape of the UK acts as a prompt in revisiting Foucault's well used theoretical paradox: that the use of imprisonment survives despite its perpetual and obvious failure (1975). This brings one to consider the development of the private prison in the UK over the last four decades and moreover its place and purpose. When the revolutionary Criminal Justice Act 1991 appeared, the idea of private-sector involvement in the UK prison system was still seen as highly controversial, for many unethical. In 2021 it appears completely conventional, normalised—cultural change achieved in the space of three decades. Acknowledgement of this remarkable expansion in the apparatus of punishment reveals a principal contention of this chapter: that in reflective evaluation of this intense period of unusual penality, we can perceive immense symbolic growth but very little structural improvement.

Currently there are 13 private-sector operated prisons in the UK; there were 14 until 2019 with the highly public repossession of HMP Birmingham (Beard, 2021: 3). It is notable that the damning inspection of Birmingham by Her Majesty's chief inspector, Peter Clarke, in August 2018 was preceded by a similarly damning inspection of HMP Liverpool in January of that same year, two large Victorian prisons built within five years of each other in the middle of the nineteenth century to serve two large industrial cities of the fledgling empire—though during 2018, HMP Liverpool was operated by HM Prison Service (public) and HMP Birmingham by G4S (private). The striking contemporary similarity between Liverpool and Birmingham lies in the detail of Clarke's reports, with both institutions described as poorly maintained places of violence and squalor, with drugs widely available, chaotic regimes overseen by abject managerial failure. Such close symmetry suggests a high degree of equality, a fusion of public and private, two peas in a pod, perhaps. Arguably, debate around public and private penality in the UK has now shifted far beyond controversy, through normalisation, and towards mundane amalgamation.

The core difference at present appears to be in construction, where private continually leads the charge—if there is currently a secure return on private investment within the contemporary penal landscape in the UK, it is to facilitate expansionism, *building back better*. Whilst on the surface the actual act of prison building might not appear controversial, considered historically alongside public policy, a pattern emerges, as is often the case (Garland, 1990, 2001). Recent research by Jones, Gray and Farrall is both interesting and supportive in this regard. In *Coal Today, Gone Tomorrow: How Jobs Were Replaced with Prison Places*, the authors argue within the context of the UK that the deindustrialisation seen as necessary to usher in the neoliberalism of the 1980s can be linked to expansionism in the prison population and prison building, with many new prisons built, or destined for, former industrial areas over the past half century—in sum, penal expansionism supporting the eliminative ideal underwritten by privatisation (Jones et al., 2021). Former coal mining areas were highlighted in the study, which conferred remarkable results in terms of the density and spread of the prison population, suggesting that ten times as many prisoners are located in former coal mining areas as elsewhere, a stratified demographic trend likely to continue given the location of the sites chosen for the Conservative government's current programme of mass construction and their continuing preference for the 'revolving door' inherent to the eliminative model (Maguire, 2020). They conclude:

> the vestiges of neo-liberal economic policy in former coal mining areas has been a far reaching expansion of criminal justice infrastructure. While deindustrialisation in the 1980s could be described as a dramatic and hard hitting process, with time we can also recognise it as a 'slow moving' process, the consequences of which may not become fully realised for several decades (Pierson, 2004). Our analysis points towards the value of thinking geographically and theoretically about the rise of the carceral State and the context of the where exactly prisons are built.
>
> (Jones et al., 2021: 16)

Indeed, longitudinal and macro study of the constituent aspects of prison privatisation would likely reveal many more legacies of control, particularly in terms of the effectiveness and utility of free market competition as a tool of social reform. In this instance, the concept appears to be fatally flawed, principally because the marketplace that has developed as the 'corrections industry' in the UK is far from free, with less than ten private-sector corporations and their conglomerates, amalgamations and subsidiaries dominating the sector since its inception in the early 1990s.

The vast scale of operation required to compete, allied to a need for corporate assets and associated infrastructure, precluded small and medium sized enterprises (SMEs) from entering the competitive tendering process. This goes well beyond a loaded system; it is a closed system, open only to select large corporates. However, as has been seen with Carillion and GS4 in recent years, even collapse or abject failure does not lead to political sanction or censure, merely substitution or resurrection. Repetition is a distinct theme within this field, both in policy and practice. A constant is that risk and cost remain with the public throughout.

Such vestiges of neoliberal socio-economic policy can also be clearly identified in the political methodologies that have been used to drive and justify expansion of the prison system over the past 40 years and the use of private enterprise to accelerate and supplement this process in terms of both infrastructure and service provision. Again, as we continue to manufacture the prison, the suggestion by Nils Christie of the possibility of *crime control as industry towards gulags, western style* (1993) that appeared somewhat pessimistic, even dystopian, in 1993, has taken on a much clearer form 40 years on.

Notes

1 Rifkind, M. 'Why Prisons Should Never Be Privatised', *Financial Times*, 13 April 2019. Malcolm Rifkind was first elected to Parliament as an MP in 1974, serving as a cabinet minister and key strategist in the Thatcher and Major administrations and latterly as chairman of the Intelligence and Security Committee of Parliament under Cameron. Though never Home Secretary, his 40 year career in government included a number of positions informing State security, spanning the entirety of the contemporary prison privatisation era.
2 Since retiring from Parliament in 1997, Wheeler has worked in a number of senior roles in the private security industry, including a three year tenure as chairman of Reliance Custodial Services between 1997 and 2000.
3 David Waddington, a traditionalist with a reticence towards large scale penal privatisation, had been appointed by Margaret Thatcher to replace Douglas Hurd as Home Secretary on 26 October 1990, but was only in the role for a little over a month, as the incoming John Major appointed an ally, Kenneth Baker, to the key post on 28 November.
4 Criminal Justice Act 1991, UK Public General Acts 1991 c. 53, via legislation.gov.uk— www.legislation.gov.uk/ukpga/1991/53/contents (accessed 22 July 2021).
5 Key amongst these pop culture examples were *Porridge*, a critically acclaimed BBC situational comedy set at a fictional men's prison, HMP Slade (using HMP Maidstone for its exterior identity in the well known title sequence) that ran between 1974 and 1977, and *Within These Walls*, an ITV drama series that ran between 1974 and 1978 set at the fictional HMP Stone Park, which focused on the staff perspective at a women's prison.
6 UKDS as a US-UK joint venture was created in 1987 between the Corrections Corporation of America and the UK construction giants McAlpine and Mowlem. The trio formed a very powerful lobby towards the creation of a private prison estate in the UK based upon the US model, signing a memorandum in January 1988 agreeing to 'promote the design, financing, construction and management by private contractors of prisons and remand facilities in the UK' (Nathan, 2003: 164). Both McAlpine and Mowlem were corporate donors to the Conservative party during this period. CCA acquired full ownership of UKDS during 1996 and sold a 50% share to a French

provider. During 2000 Sodexho bought CCA'S 50% stake to acquire full ownership of UKDS.
7 The authors, like many academic researchers who venture into the field of private prison development within the contemporary UK context, are much indebted to Julian Le Vay for the close practitioner analysis and insider expertise expressed in his excellent *Competition for Prisons* (2016), Bristol: Policy Press, and subsequent publications.
8 Premier Prison Services (PPS) was a US-UK joint venture between the corrections division of the Wackenhut Corporation and Serco Group PLC. In 2002, Wackenhut Corporation was acquired by Group 4, with Group 4 securing a 57% share in WCC and consequently a 50% stake in PPS, PPS becoming jointly owned by the two conglomerates.
9 Carter and Straw had met as boys in the same year at Brentwood School; Straw, in his autobiography, *Last Man Standing: Memoirs of a Political Survivor*, London: Pan, describes Carter as his 'closest friend' (page 49).
10 The contract was awarded in July 2010 by the newly installed Conservative–Liberal Democrat coalition government. HMP Belmarsh West was opened in 2012 by Serco as HMP Thameside.
11 The Alliance contract at HMP Doncaster required a reduction in reconviction rates of 5% in terms of released prisoners after a one year period, with reconviction resulting in financial penalty.
12 Ministry of Justice (2011) Offender Management Statistics Quarterly, Prison Population, Table 1.1, November 2011, London: Ministry of Justice.

References

Anderson, P., and Mann, N. (1997) *Safety First: The Making of New Labour*, London: Granta
Armstrong, G., Giulianotti, R., and Hobbs, D. (2016) *Policing the 2012 London Olympics: Legacy and Social Exclusion*, London: Routledge
Bastow, S. (2013) *Governance, Performance and Capacity Stress: The Chronic Case of Prison Crowding*, London: Palgrave Macmillan
BBC (1993) 'On the Record, Tony Blair Interview' Recorded from Transmission BBC2, 4 July 1993 via www.bbc.co.uk/otr/intext92-93/Blair4.7.93.html. Retrieved 11 June 2020
Beard, J. (2021, October 8) *The Prison Estate*, London: The House of Commons Library
Box, S., and Hale, C. (1985) 'Unemployment, Imprisonment and Prison Overcrowding' *Contemporary Crises* 9: 208–229
Butler, E., Pirie, M., and Young, P. (eds) (1985) *The Omega File: A Comprehensive Review of Government Functions*, London: Adam Smith Institute
Carrabine, E. (2004) *Power, Discourse and Resistance: A Genealogy of the Strangeways Prison Riot*, London: Ashgate Publishing
Carvel, J. (1985) 'Omega File Maps the Way of the Right: Adam Smith Institute Publishes Compendium of Right Wing Policies' *Guardian*, Tuesday 11 June
Christie, N. (1993) *Crime Control as Industry: Towards Gulags, Western Style*, London: Routledge
Clarke, K. (1992) 'Prisoners with Private Means: As a TV Executive Becomes Head of Britain's Jails, Kenneth Clarke, the Home Secretary, Defends His Free Market Policy' *Independent*, Tuesday 22 December, via www.independent.co.uk/voices/prisoners-with-private-means-as-a-tv-executive-becomes-head-of-britain-s-jails-kenneth-clarke-the-home-secretary-defends-his-freemarket-policy-a3139561.html. Retrieved 17 July 2021
Clarke, K. (2012) 'Punishment and Reform' Press Release: Ministry of Justice and The Rt Hon Kenneth Clarke QC, 27 March 2012 via www.gov.uk/government/news/punishment-and-reform. Retrieved 12 August 2021

Clarke, P. (2018) 'Urgent Notification: HM Prison Birmingham' 16 August 2018, via www.justiceinspectorates.gov.uk/hmiprisons/wp-content/uploads/sites/4/2018/08/16-Aug-UN-letter-HMP-Birmingham-Final.pdf. Retrieved 22 September 2021

Coyle, A. (2005) *Understanding Prisons: Key Issues in Policy and Practice*, Maidenhead: Open University Press

Dell, E. (1991) *The Woolf Report: A Summary of the Main Findings and Recommendations of the Inquiry into Prison Disturbances*, London: Prison Reform Trust

Deloitte Haskins & Sells (1989) *Report to the Home Office on the Practicality of Private Sector Involvement in the Remand System*, London: Deloitte Haskins & Sells

Foucault, M. (1975) *Discipline and Punish: The Birth of the Prison*, London: Penguin

Fulton, R. (1989) 'Private Sector Involvement in the Remand System' in M. Farrell (ed) *Punishment for Profit*, London: ISTD

Gardiner, E. (1989) 'Prisons—An Alternative Approach' in M. Farrell (ed) *Punishment for Profit*, London: ISTD

Garland, D. (1990) *Punishment in Modern Society: A Study in Social Theory*, Oxford: Clarendon Press

Garland, D. (2001) *The Culture of Control: Crime and Social Order in Contemporary Society*, Oxford: Oxford University Press

Hammond, P. (2018) 'Budget 2018: Philip Hammond's Speech' HM Treasury and The Rt Hon Philip Hammond, 29 October 2018, via www.gov.uk/government/speeches/budget-2018-philip-hammonds-speech. Retrieved 22 July 2021

Hansard (1980) *Prison System*, HC Deb 1 August 1980, Volume 989 cc1900–28, The Secretary of State for the Home Department, Mr William Whitelaw, 9.37am

Hansard (1989) *Remand System Privatisation*, HC Deb 1 March 1988, Volume 148, The Secretary of State for the Home Department, Mr Douglas Hurd, 3.31pm

Hansard (1992) *Criminal Justice Act 1991 (Contracted Out Prisons) Order 1992*, HL Deb 7 July 1992, Volume 538, Lord Richard, 6.17pm

Hansard (1993) *Budget Resolutions and Economic Situation*, Commons Sitting, Orders of the Day, HC Deb 07 December 1993, Volume 234 cc145–277, Harriet Harman MP

Hansard (2012) *Prison Competition and Efficiency*, Volume 552: HC Deb 8 November 2012. The Lord Chancellor and Secretary of State for Justice, Chris Grayling, Column 45WS

HM Chief Inspector of Prisons (2014, October 21) *Annual Report 2013–14, Session 2014–2015 HC 680*, London: HMCIP

Home Affairs Committee (1987) *Contract Provision of Prisons*, London: Home Affairs Committee

Home Office (1988, July) *Private Sector Involvement in the Remand System*, Cmnd. 434, London: HMSO

Home Office (1998a) *Public and Prison Management: Considerations on Returning Privately Managed Prisons to the Public Sector*, London: Home Office [unpublished]

Home Office (1998b) *Review of Private Financing of New Prison Procurement*, London: Home Office [unpublished]

House of Commons (1998) *Private Sector Prisons* [25 June 1998] HC Deb 1998, col. 387W, via https://publications.parliament.uk/pa/cm199798/cmhansrd/vo980625/text/80625w09.htm#80625w09.html_sbhd0. Retrieved 24 September 2021

House of Commons (2014) 'Public Accounts Committee, Fifty Third Report' Ministry of Justice and National Offender Management Service: Managing the Prison Estate, 7 April 2014 via https://publications.parliament.uk/pa/cm201314/cmselect/cmpubacc/1001/100102.htm. Retrieved 7 July 2021

House of Commons Committee of Public Accounts (2018) *Private Finance Initiatives, Forty-Sixth Report of Session 2017–2018*, London: House of Commons
House of Commons Justice Committee (2015) *Prisons: Planning and Policies, Ninth Report of Session 2014–15 Report*, 4 March 2015, HC 309, London: The Stationery Office Limited
Hutto, T. (1990) 'The Privatization of Prisons' in J. Murphy and J. Dison (eds) *Are Prisons Any Better? Twenty Years of Correctional Reform*, Newbury Park: Sage
James, A., Bottomley, A., Liebling, A., and Clare, E. (1997) *Privatizing Prisons: Rhetoric and Reality*, London: Sage
Jones, P., Gray, E., and Farrall, S. (2021, January) *Coal Today, Gone Tomorrow: How Jobs Were Replaced with Prison Places*, Centre for Crime and Justice Studies, Briefing 24, London: CCJS
Laming, H. (2000) *Modernising the Management of the Prison Service*, London: Home Office
Le Vay, J. (2016) *Competition for Prisons: Public or Private?* Bristol: Policy Press
Lewis, D. (1997) *Hidden Agendas: Politics Law and Disorder*, London: Hamish Hamilton
Liebling, A. (2004) *Prisons and Their Moral Performance: A Study of Values. Quality, and Prison Life*, Oxford: Oxford University Press
Liebling, A., and Ludlow, A. (2017) 'Privatising Public Prisons: Penality, Law and Practice' *Australian and New Zealand Journal of Criminology* 50 (4): 473–492
Lilly, J.R., and Knepper, P. (1992) 'An International Perspective on the Privatization of Corrections' *Howard Journal* 31 (3): 174–191
Logan, C.H. (1990) *Private Prisons: Cons and Pros*, Oxford: Oxford University Press
Logan, C.H. (1993) 'Well Kept: Comparing Quality of Confinement in Private and Public Prisons' *The Journal of Criminal Law and Criminology* 83 (3): 577–613
Ludlow, A. (2015) *Privatising Public Prisons: Labour Law and the Public Procurement Process*, Oxford: Bloomsbury
Maguire, D. (2020) *Male, Failed, Jailed: Masculinities and "Revolving-Door" Imprisonment in the UK*, London: Palgrave Macmillan
Major, J. (1993) *Leader's Speech*, Conservative Party Conference, Blackpool 8 October 1993, British Political Speech via www.britishpoliticalspeech.org/speech-archive.htm?speech=139. Retrieved 12 August 2021
Mathiesen, T. (1990) *Prison on Trial*, London: Sage
Matthews, R., and Francis, P. (eds) (1996) *Prisons 2000: An International Perspective on the Current State and Future of Imprisonment*, London: Macmillan
Ministry of Justice (2011) *Competition Strategy for Offender Services*, London: Ministry of Justice
Ministry of Justice (2013) *Story of the Prison Population: 1993–2012 England and Wales*, London: Ministry of Justice
Ministry of Justice (2016, November) *Prison Safety and Reform*, London: Ministry of Justice, London: Ministry of Justice
Ministry of Justice (2018) *Press Release: Prison Operator Services Framework Competition*, 29 November 2018 via www.gov.uk/government/speeches/prison-operator-services-framework-competition. Retrieved 10 September 2021
Ministry of Justice (2019) *Press Release 10,000 Extra Prison Places to Keep the Public Safe*, 11 August 2019 via www.gov.uk/government/news/10-000-extra-prison-places-to-keep-the-public-safe. Retrieved 11 June 2021
Ministry of Justice (2020a) *Press Release Four New Prisons Boost Rehabilitation and Support Economy*, Ministry of Justice, 28 June 2020 via www.gov.uk/government/news/four-new-prisons-boost-rehabilitation-and-support-economy. Retrieved 10 September 2021

Ministry of Justice and House of Commons Justice Committee (2018, November 6) *Work of the Ministry of Justice, Oral Evidence Session*, London: HM Stationery Office

Nathan, S. (2003) 'Prison Privatization in the United Kingdom' in A. Coyle et al. (eds) *Capitalist Punishment: Prison Privatisation and Human Rights*, Neufeld: Zed Books

National Audit Office (1997, October 31) *HM Prison Service: The PFI Contracts for Bridgend and Fazakerley Prisons, Report by the Comptroller and Auditor General*, HC 253 Session 1997–98, London: NOA

National Audit Office (2003) *The Operational Performance of PFI Prisons*, HC 700 Session 2002–2003, London: NAO

National Audit Office (2013, December 12) *Managing the Prison Estate, Report by the Comptroller and Auditor General, Ministry of Justice and National Offender Management Service*, HC 735 Session 2013–14, London: NOA

Nellis, M. (2001) 'Community Penalties in Historical Perspective' in A. Bottoms, L. Gelsthorpe and S. Rex (eds) *Community Penalties: Change and Challenges*, Cullompton: Willan, pp. 16–40

Nellis, M. (2006) 'NOMS, Contestability and the Process of Technocorrectional Innovation' in M. Hough, R. Allen and U. Padel (eds) *Reshaping Probation and Prisons: The New Offender Management Framework*. Bristol: Policy Press, pp. 49–68

Office for Budget Responsibility (2017) *Fiscal Risks Report*, London: OBR

Park, I. (2000) *Review of Comparative Costs and Performance of Privately and Publicly Operated Prisons, 1998–1999, Home Office Statistical Bulletin 6/2000*, London: Home Office

Pierson, P. (2004) *Politics in Time: History, Institutions, and Social Analysis*, Princeton, NJ: Princeton University Press

Pilkington, C. (1999) *The Civil Service in Britain Today*, Manchester: Manchester University Press

Pope, T., Davies, N., and Guerin, B. (2020, April) *The Criminal Justice System: How Government Reforms and Coronavirus Will Affect Policing, Courts and Prisons*, Institute for Governments, London: Institute for Government

Pozen, D.E. (2003) 'Managing a Correctional Marketplace: Prison Privatization in the United States and the United Kingdom' *Journal of Law and Politics* 19: 253–284

Prison Reform Trust (1991) *The Woolf Report: A Summary of the Main Findings and Recommendations of the Inquiry into Prison Disturbances*, foreword by the Rt. Hon. Edmund Dell, London: PRT

Prison Reform Trust (1993) *Wolds Remand Prison, Contracting Out: A First Year Report*, London: PRT

Prison Reform Trust (1995) *The Prison Population Explosion*, London: PRT

Prison Reform Trust (2007, May) *Bromley Briefings Prison Factfile*, London: PRT

Prison Reform Trust (2018, Autumn) *Bromley Briefings Prison Factfile*, London: PRT

Rutherford, A. (1997) 'Criminal Policy and the Eliminative Ideal' *Social Policy & Administration* 31 (5): 116–135

Ryan, M., and Ward, T. (1989) *Privatization and the Penal System: The American Experience and the Debate in Britain*, Milton Keynes: Open University Press

Sharifi, S., and Bovaird, T. (1995) 'The Financial Management Initiative in the UK Public Sector: The Symbolic Role of Performance Reporting' *International Journal of Public Administration* 18 (2–3): 467–490

Shichor, D. (1993) 'The Corporate Context of Private Prisons' *Law and Social Change* 20: 113–138

Sim, J. (2009) *Punishment and Prisons: Power and the Carceral State*, London: Sage

Straw, J. (1998, December 1) *Making Prisons Work: The Prison Reform Trust Annual lecture 1998*, London: Prison Reform Trust

Travis, A. (2013, September 4) 'Dartmoor Prison Facing Closure as Ministers Announce Shakeup of Jails' *Guardian*

Woodbridge, J. (1997) *Review of Comparative Costs and Performance of Privately and Publicly Operated Prisons, 1996–1997*, Prison Service Research Report, 3, London: HMPS

Woodbridge, J. (1999) *Review of Comparative Costs and Performance of Privately and Publicly Operated Prisons, 1997–1998*, Prison Service Research Report, 4, London: HMPS

Wright, C., and Jones, P. (2012) 'Something Old, Something New: Catch22's Work in Doncaster Prison' in V. Helyar-Cardwell (ed) *Delivering Justice. The Role of the Public, Private and Voluntary Sectors in Prisons and Probation*, London: Criminal Justice Alliance, pp. 55–59

Young, P. (1987) *The Prison Cell: The Start of a Better Approach to Prison Management*, London: Adam Smith Institute

10
THE ASCENDENCY OF THE BUSINESS IDEAL AND THE MARKETISATION OF OFFENDER SERVICES

> Do you know why the Home Office has made so many changes to the Probation Service in the last thirty years? It is because it can.
> (A former Chief Probation Officer)

Introduction

The establishment of the State as the sole provider of criminal justice, one of the defining features of industrial capitalism, was heralded by Elias as indicative of the civilisation process: a process by which the power to punish is 'vested almost exclusively in the state and exercised through its bureaucratic and administrative organs of the state' (Pratt, 2005: 263). In the case of the management of offenders in the community, the administrative organ of the State was the Probation Service. Set up initially as a charitable organisation in the late nineteenth century under the auspices of the church missionary movement to assuage middle class fears of the threat to social order by dangerous classes, particularly those under the influence of demon drink, (Vanstone, 2004), the 1948 Criminal Justice Act, which abolished the remnants of the Victorian penal system (birching, penal servitude, prison with hard labour and whipping) provided the legal and administrative framework of the Probation Service. Management of the service was assumed by local committees of magistrates, with its day-to-day operations defined by Home Office policy (Nellis, 2001: 20).

Although for most of its history, the Probation Service, in common with the other 'Penal Welfare' agencies (Garland, 2003), operated semi-autonomously, as a relatively benevolent justice agency focused on changing rather than containing its clients, unfettered by the interference from political parties, the politicisation of law and order in the last quarter of the twentieth century (Downes and Morgan, 2002) and changes to the political economy in the nineties and noughties, alongside the commodification of punishment (Christie, 2003), transformed the service. The Probation Service changed from an organisation embracing social work values to a 'more punitive, target driven agency driven by the key imperative of law enforcement' (Teague, 2013: 17): a beleaguered agency, vulnerable to the changing political landscape, and the whims and vaguries of ministers.

Whilst the bigger players in the criminal justice system, particularly police, were able to rely on powerful interests to fight their corner and, in contrast, successfully positioned themselves to fend off the worst excesses of the government plans (Ashworth, 2009), the Probation Service, 'largely invisible to the public and one of the least well understood areas of the criminal justice system' (Hedderman and Murphy, 2015: 219), has been uniquely vulnerable to the political predilections of successive governments. The victim of an unparalleled level of incursion by the private sector it was denuded of all but a quarter of its services the service has been dismantled, diminished and demoralised.

The privatisation of probation has its roots in two parallel but ultimately interrelated developments, which have transformed the 'justice system into a competitive market place where the attainment of financial return rather than social justice is a primary drive' (Teague, 2013: 18). The two developments are the introduction of electronic monitoring as the first exclusively private provision of offender services in the UK, which with the benefit of hindsight signalled the demise of probation, and the series of incremental changes to the Probation Service, which constitute 'privatisation by stealth' (Burgess and MacDonald, 1999: 8). The later include: the inculcation of efficiency and management techniques from the private sector, intended to inject a greater 'commercial orientation' into its ethos and functioning; the creation of an internal market, splitting purchaser and provider functions (this was first trialled by the NHS); and the introduction of competition and contracting out of the delivery of both ancillary and direct public services to non-public service providers–providers that have been predators rather than partners, carving out the space to expand their sphere of influence in the interests of making more and more from punishment.

A brief history of the origins of the Probation Service

Although the origins of the probation officer can be traced back to the police courts in Boston in 1841 and the campaigning activities of the Howard Association, which promoted the American model in England, the orthodox history focuses on the figure of Frederic Rainer, a volunteer with the Church of England Temperance Society (an organisation which employed missionaries in general rescue work and the promotion of temperance), who in 1876 wrote to the society of his concern about the lack of hope and help for those appearing before the courts, and donated five shillings towards a fund for practical rescue work in police courts. The society responded by appointing a 'missionary' to Southwark Police Court, which became the base of the fledgling London Police Court Mission. Between 1876 and 1902 eight full time court missionaries were appointed. The mission opened homes and shelters for offenders and provided vocational training for the court missionaries.

Although there has been a tendency in historical accounts of the Probation Service to emphasise the humanitarian and philanthropic ideals of its founders, as revisionist historians are keen to point out, it is no coincidence that the probation movement emerged at 'a time of rising concern at the moral degeneration of the working class' (Whitfield, 1998: 12), a period of moral panic about demon drink and its effects (Mair, 1997), and deep-seated fears of the Victorian middle and upper classes about dangerous classes. Indeed, in common with other 'rescue' movements that characterised the 'Golden Age' of voluntary organisation (e.g. the rescue of prostitutes and abused children), the benevolence of social welfare activists was not merely altruistic but rather 'confirmed the rightness of a middle class view of society' (Vanstone, 2004: 37), promoting middle class notions of morality and respectability: 'charity was, among other things, about changing and improving people who represented a threat and a source of social infection'(Vanstone, 2004: 36). As Young argues, 'probation emerged as a policy measure generated out of a relationship between classes in the later nineteenth century'(1976: 55): a relationship that was defined by a preoccupation with the maintenance of social order and the process of controlling the lives of the working poor.

In 1879 the *Summary Jurisdiction Act* was passed, which enabled offenders to be released on their own recognisance (binding over). Following the implementation of this Act, police court missionaries began to offer informal supervision to this group of offenders. This was followed in 1907 by the *Probation of Offenders Act*. The Act allowed courts to suspend punishment and discharge offenders if they entered into a recognisance of between one and three years, one condition of which was supervision by a person named in the 'Probation Order'. The Probation Service remained within the voluntary sector until 1938, when the Home Office assumed its control (cc. Whitehead and Statham, 2006). With the post-war heyday of the Welfare State, and the rise of the autonomous welfare professional, who was entrusted to rehabilitate the deviant, the service became closely aligned with social work, sharing key elements of its training and practice. Simultaneously it assumed a greater range of roles and responsibilities. This period, which Garland (2001) refers to as one of penal welfarism, lasted until the late 1970s, when the rise of the New Right penology and neoliberalism ushered in a new era of law and order policy making: one characterised by the punitive sentencing and the management of offenders, as well as fiscal efficiency, the imposition of private market discipline on the workforce, marketisation of services, and ultimately privatisation of over three quarters of delivery of the Probation Service.

New Public Management: the first phase of privatisation

Neoliberalism and NPM

As discussed earlier, privatisation, the government policy of 'rolling back of the state' (Dorey, 2005: 215), removing an increasing number of State-owned industries and services from the public sector, was a key feature of the 1980s and 1990s. Fiscally and ideologically driven, it formed part of a wider public policy imperative to dismantle the much reviled public sector (Collett, 2013), and to reduce 'the role of the state in the disposal of the Gross National Product (GNP)' (Massey, 2001: 19). However, whilst the selling off of key assets in terms of industries and utilities and the privatisation of some aspects of local authority provision proved relatively easy, the residual problem of how to expand the market into the 'rump' of public services, thereby reducing public spending and avoiding tax increases, remained.

With organisational change 'a major part of neoliberalism' and the 'profit-seeking corporation promoted as the admired model for the public sector' (Connell et al., 2009: 334), the mode of privatisation adopted in relation to offenders services can been traced back to the imposition of a range of overlapping strategies, known collectively as NPM, intended to exert disciplinary control. Imported from the business world, NPM aimed to impart greater 'commercial orientation' into the ethos and functioning of public services (Vickers and Wright, 1989: 3). Substituting the 'passive' public service ethos of public administrators with 'active' private sector modes of management, NPM, which drew its inspiration from a privatisation approach informed by public choice theory (see Chapter 1), sought to replace social welfare professionals, who were decried as disguising or rationalising their self-interest under a public good façade, with managers who (in common with their counterparts operating in competitive markets) were accountable for their actions, and could reap both the 'rewards (e.g. performance-related pay) and the penalties' for their actions. For Drakeford (2000), paraphrasing Ranade:

> The set of techniques thus imported into social welfare systems—accountability mechanisms, performance indicators and reviews, staff appraisals, performance related pay, league tables of performance, quality standards and so on-amount to 'privatisation from within'.
>
> *(2000: 26)*

Underpinned by neoliberal principles of competition, individual and organisational accountability, the 3 Es—economy (cost), effectiveness and efficiency—NPM reforms, which shifted the emphasis from public administration to public management, became synonymous with: 'a profound scepticism about professional ideals ... the profession of practitioners' (Connell et al., 2009: 335) and self-regulation; an increasing emphasis on command and control modes of functioning, denoted by the introduction of institutional and individual objectives to clearly define and establish key performance indicators against which outputs could be measured (Massey, 2001: 19); and (in later phases) the promotion of a mixed economy of provision and the creation of an internal market with a provider/purchaser split.

NPM in the Probation Service

Although criminal justice agencies lagged behind other public services, being in effect 'the last public sector body to be subject to private sector disciplines'

(Loveday, 1999: 351), once under the political gaze, they 'did not get off lightly' (Ashworth, 2009: 63). Viewed as 'spendthrift, idiosyncratic and unaccountable', criminal justice agencies were subjected to a three-pronged approach which included: the imposition of cash limits to promote greater economic efficiency; the introduction of national standards (NS) into policies and practice to reduce professional autonomy and to iron out individualised idiosyncrasies; and structural reorganisation backed up by performance management. The new measures, which imposed centralised disciplinary control (Raine and Wilson, 1993), were intended to ensure that criminal justice implemented government's New Right penal policy and fiscal agenda, the rationale being that if services could not be sold off, they could at least be made to bend to the political will.

The Tory years: 1979–1997

In terms of probation practice, from the early 1980s, new forms of governance to 'establish new boundaries of state responsibility and new modes of regulation' emerged that had two primary objectives. These were the inculcation of the business ethos of organisational efficiency and cost effectiveness (Gelsthorpe, 2001: 107 as cited in Ashworth, 2009: 65), and the New Right penal policy programme (Nash, 2003: 96). Perceived as a 'soft touch', the Probation Service, with its outmoded principles of welfare led practice (Garland, 2001), was set on a collision course with its political masters. The treatment paradigm, with 'its soft social work values' of help and assistance, which shaped its ideology and practice (Mair, 1997: 1202), was at odds with penal policy ideals that 'erred more towards retributionist thinking' (Chui and Nellis, 2003: 6). With a showdown inevitable, the new form of bureaucratic governance offered by NPM provided the government with the means of coercing probation officers into adopting practice and policies prescribed by its new punishment oriented political agenda (Nash, 2008): policies which were anathema to practitioners.

Committed to the expansion of 'law and order services (police, courts and prisons)', expenditure reduction in other areas of public service and 'tougher sanctions for criminals' (Downes and Morgan, 2002: 289), the Conservative administration of the 1980s recognised early on that imposing a new centralised discipline over devolved local probation areas, which, in common with the police, operated as autonomous, idiosyncratic 'personal fiefdoms' (Mair, 2008: 21), was pivotal to driving through its penal policy changes. Deriving their authority and legitimacy from unelected local Probation Committees (Morgan, 2007), the chief officers, 'unfettered by government prescription', exercised considerable freedom over the practice initiatives and policy priorities implemented in their local areas (Chui and Nellis, 20003: 6). This high degree of 'operational independence' meant that there was no standardised model, and services to offenders were something of a post code lottery.

Statement of National Objectives and Priorities

The earliest introduction of NPM into the Probation Service can be identified with the Home Office's issuing of the Statement of National Objectives and

Priorities (SNOP) (Davies and Gregory, 2010: 402; Nash, 2008). Predated by the launch in 1982 of the financial management initiative, SNOP 'was associated with the language of the 3Es (economy, efficiency, effectiveness), improvements in performance and greater accountability, cash limits, but also the setting of objectives, priorities, and later targets' (Whitehead, 2007: 85). Intended to 'persuade' local probation services to adopt modes of intervention that complied with its penal policy agenda, it was underpinned by the threat of the imposition of cash-limited budgets, which directed probation funding into government priority areas rather than those of CPOs (May, 1991; Raynor, 2002).

Although, the Home Office's first attempt to achieve centralised control through the introduction of SNOP was met with resistance, and delivered little in the way of tangible results (Lloyd, 1986; Chui and Nellis, 2003), the initiative itself was highly significant. Foreshadowing things that would come to pass, it signalled a radical realignment of relationship between criminal justice and the State: the creation of new forms of governance that would prescribe 'in ever greater detail . . . what work should be resourced and how tasks should be undertaken' (Morgan, 2007: 92). As May (1991), writing when NPM was in its infancy, observed, SNOP indicated a 'hitherto unprecedented acknowledgement of Home Office involvement in local policy initiatives'. Further, with its emphasis on efficiency and effectiveness, it was an indication that financial management could be applied to agencies in the criminal justice system as a means of exerting centralised control (1991: 41–42).

National standards and KPIs

Following the government's initial failure to persuade the Probation Service to implement SNOP (Nellis, 2001: 27), measures to control the Probation Service from the centre (Nash, 2003) became progressively more 'assertive and . . . more directive' (Canton, 2011: 185). In 1991, underpinned by the then Home Secretary's belief that 'prison is an expensive place that makes bad people worse', the watershed 1991 *Criminal Justice Act* was passed, which sought to reduce the prison population by restricting prison to the most serious offenders and creating new, more punitive community sentences. Extending the pre-existing 'bifurcation' sentencing framework (Bottoms, 1977), the Act reserved the custody threshold for those offenders whose offences were deemed 'so serious'; those whose offences were deemed 'serious enough' would receive a punishment in the community. With its emphasis on punishment, the Act represented a radical departure from the service's 'Penal Welfare' (Garland, 2003) tradition, informed by welfare principles, values and ethos. It was met with opposition from probation staff, who had been trained to 'advise, assist and befriend'; The Magistrates' Association; and some of the judiciary. Long standing magistrates resigned on principle, and in the higher court, several judges flatly refused to implement key aspects of the new legislation.

Despite resistance to the new legislation, spurred on in part by the damning 1989 Audit Commission report, which concluded that the Probation Service was not good value for money, the Home Office in 1992 issued the first of a series of 'top down' NSs. With the aim of standardising practice, national standards developed in tandem with KPIs provided the practice framework against which to gauge and manage performance (Davies and Gregory, 2010: 402). Reducing the tasks and routines of probation officers to a series of transparent, standardised, formulaic activities, NSs, which stipulated the what, when and how of probation activities (Ashworth, 2009), provided a benchmark against which performance could be measured, and were a cornerstone of the development of KPIs and targets (Merrington and Stanley: 2007).

Although Her Majesty's Inspectorate of Probation (HMIP) had been conducting effectiveness and efficiency inspections since the mid-1980s, it was not until the mid-late 1990s that performance targets became embedded in the governance of the Probation Service (Whitehead, 2007: 85). In common with other public services, under New Labour, the Probation Service was subjected to 'command and control' strategies most commonly associated with the Soviet economic system: 'management through targets' (Hood, 2006: 515)

The New Labour years 1997–2010: micromanagement

In 1997, after an unprecedented four terms of Conservative administration, a Labour government was elected espousing the virtues of the Third Way: a new approach to politics which transcended the old categories of left and right. Whilst its adherents, in particular the sociologist Giddens, maintained that it represented a non-ideological, pragmatic approach, the acceptance by its proponents that 'there is no alternative to the market' (encapsulating the free market principles of labour deregulation, privatisation of public services and removing the barriers to commerce) ensured that the New Way was merely an 'ideological shell for neoliberalism' (Anderson, 2000: 9). As critics have observed, 'New Labour . . . embraced the market with a passion and enthusiasm which often leaves the Conservatives standing' (Ferguson, 2004: n.p.). Third Wayers resembled 'free marketers who [had] learnt to play the chords of Stairway to Heaven' (Elliott, 2003).

The electoral mandate of the incoming administration espoused a vision for criminal justice that would be both 'tough on crime and tough on the cause of crime'. Whilst many in the Probation Service welcomed this as signalling a return to the old values of service, reversing the punitive penal policies of the previous administration, early optimism turned to disappointment when it became apparent that 'New Labour (had) not turned back the clock to some halcyon period dominated by inclusivist welfare and anti-punishment sensibilities', but rather intended to accompany acknowledgments of differential opportunities, social deprivation and social exclusion with punitive sanctions (Whitehead, 2010): developments which led many to form the view that 'tough on the causes of crime' agenda was an early victim of the pragmatic politics of electoral success (Ashworth, 2009: 69).

Following an early dalliance with a 'weaker version' of social inclusion agenda (Young and Matthews, 2003), intended to ameliorate the worst excesses brought about by global social and economic transformation, the focus was placed on imposing measures aimed at manipulating the 'conduct' of the individual. With the emphasis on the agency of the actor rather than structurally induced inequality, causes of crime were relegated to 'simple context' (Squires, 2006). The dominant theme in policy making was a profound social authoritarianism encompassing the management and surveillance of offenders: a policy development which, when coupled with the cost efficiencies offered by new technologies and the enthusiasm of commercial interests to supply both the equipment and the managerial oversight, was to provide the impetus for the full-scale implementation of electronic monitoring on a purely commercial basis.

At an institutional level, one of the central tenets of the New Labour Third Way was the modernisation of public services. In 2001 the National Probation Service (NPS) was created (Raynor and Vanstone, 2007: 71), extending rather than reversing centralist managerialism, it was characterised by command and control governance. Very welcome increases in expenditure were performance related and became synonymous with measures to improve efficiency, heralding in 'a plethora of targets and performance indicators' (Dorey, 2005: 112). Backed up by cash-linked targets and national league tables, these measures ensured that services, in order to 'maintain the budget and staff' (McGarva, 2007: 202), complied with top-down performance criteria. Between 1997 and 2010 the performance management culture became more pervasive, intrusive and directive.

Concerned with the 'fragmentation of governance' and the perceived lack of accountability of local services to central government (Whitehead, 2010), in 2000, the *Criminal Justice and Court Services Act* (the statutory instrument that enabled the establishment of the NPS) was passed, creating a unified national service coterminous with the pre-existing 42 police areas of England and Wales. Under the new structure local Probation Boards were given devolved powers to employ all staff, with the exception of chief officers, who, centrally recruited and accountable to the Director of Probation, were civil servants. As 'accountable officers', chiefs were expected to do the government's bidding in a cost-efficient way. The achievement of Whitehall set goals, reflecting government penal policy priorities, was reinforced by the creation of a new budgetary formula, under which budgetary allocation was dependent on the meeting of targets.

Although at the outset 'national targets were agreed with ministers and divided pro rata according to resources', as the scheme developed, attention was directed towards individual services, and punitive sanctions were imposed. With the introduction of 'cash-linked' targets (subsequently rebranded as a 'performance bonus scheme'), individual services were penalised by a budgetary reduction if the previous year's targets were not met (Hill, 2007). 'Once the scheme was established, which took about three years, approximately £30 million of the national budget was distributed or withheld through this approach' (Hill, 2007: 180).

Management by targets

Traditionally viewed as professional practitioners who, free from political influence, were trusted to exercise considerable control over their day-to day practice, probation officers had been used to a 'high level of discretion and operational independence' (Loveday, 1999: 353), and had taken for granted that, by upholding the 'values and aims' of their agency, they were 'doing a good job'. However, the introduction of commercial imperatives of centralised regulation, standardisation, consistency, value for money, external auditing and scrutiny and financial accountability represented the abrupt reversal of the 'long trend towards professional autonomy and the delegation of penal powers' (Garland, 2003: 120). Sounding the death knell for probation officers as independent, reflexive and self-governing professionals with their own body of knowledge and expertise, the new measures significantly reduced the traditional high degree of autonomy and discretion (Nellis and Gelsthorpe, 2003; Loader and Sparks, 2002 Ashworth, 2009).

With 'the rise of market forces and . . . the centralisation of state power', NPM, which lay emphasis on 'competition and market testing about setting targets and performance indicators, about auditing and continuous improvement, about hierarchy and the "right to manage" rather than participatory democracy', reduced the role of the probation officer to the performance of a specific task, in a set way, by a set time (Nellis and Gelsthorpe, 2003: 238–239). Although the concepts of public accountability and effectiveness were not rejected *per se* (Gelsthorpe, 2007), the notion that practice, which depended so much on 'soft' interpersonal skills and relationship building and 'abstract concepts and processes', could be reduced to 'clearly defined performance indicators was an anathema to many probation officers' (Ashworth, 2009: 62).

The process of target setting transformed day-to-day practice: tasks became routinised, standardised and simplified to aid the auditing process. Probation staff found that a 'great deal of what they did could be discounted, ignored or invalidated' (Ashworth, 2009: 66). With NPM, auditing processes not simply measuring performance, but rather defining what activities were worth quantifying (Power, 1997), the way that tasks were undertaken and/or services were provided become distorted (Garland, 2001). The result of this was that all too often, 'audits . . . entail the tail wagging the dog' (Dorey, 2005: 260). In the alien new reality of 'target world' (Hood, 2006), practice interventions, based on experience and professional wisdom, only mattered if they could be moulded towards the meeting of centrally imposed targets. Middle managers, who had traditionally seen their role as encouraging probation officer's autonomous professional practice (Collins, 2015: 150), were transformed into auditors supplying information for increasingly demanding new data collection systems (Flynn, 1997). As practice was reduced to the performance of a set of predetermined, bureaucratised tasks, probation staff increasingly saw themselves as box tickers: 'office based computer technicians and data entry operators' (Whitehead, 2007: 92).

Effectiveness, efficiency and gaming the targets

Whilst successive governments claim that linking budgets to target attainment incentivises the public sector to improve performance, the question of how effective management by targets has been is highly contested. By definition, KPIs are selective, narrowly focused, arbitrary and at times contradictory. They are not 'some unavoidable given', but rather are an organisational and political construct

(Whitehead, 2007: 86) Their key achievement is to 'operationalise the Government's priorities' (Merrington and Stanley, 2007: 448), ensuring that the measurement of success accords with its own criteria. With policy subject to change, revision or reversal of KPIs to better ensure the delivery of ministerial priorities, or to correct anomalies in performance of their own creation, was common.

Although KPIs and targets are effective tools for the generation of statistical data (e.g. how often an offender is seen by a probation officer), they fail to capture the quality of officer/offender interaction (the empathy with and understanding of the lived lives of others) which is the bedrock of effective practice. The prescription of tasks and the preoccupation with the quantity, speed and timeliness of work were detrimental to the quality of direct work with offenders (Davies and Gregory, 2010). With political pressure on the Home Office to produce 'good news performance data' (Hood, 2006: 519), communication, engagement and reflection lost their value; outcomes and outputs became conflated; and efficiency was prioritised over effectiveness (Shapland et al., 2012). In the 'bureaucratic, mechanised (and) routinised' world of targets, 'professional creativity underpinned by social values' was narrowed and 'stifled' (Whitehead, 2007: 86).

The regime of cash-linked targets created 'a tension between doing what is appropriate for individual offenders, and a pressure to achieve centrally imposed targets' (Whitehead, 2007: 87). Targets are set in 'aspirational ways' to drive continuous improvement of performance. Consequently their achievement merely resulted in the bar being raised higher, locking practitioners into a 'narrative of perpetually increasing productivity' in which pace of work increases exponentially: a practice that eroded quality and increased the risk of errors and poor decision making (Davies and Gregory, 2010: 405). What is more, in a culture where public managers' performance-related pay and services budgets were determined by target achievement, game playing behaviours that run the gamut from outright dishonesty, where fraudulent data was submitted, to creative compliance, where targets were met but the intended outcomes were not, became normalised.

With targets the central imperative, the risk increases that service priorities become driven by financial, rather than offender, needs: doing what will generate income replaces doing what is right. In target world, playing the targets game with the treasury becomes mutually advantageous. To avoid failure and potential political embarrassment (Hood, 2006), renegotiating targets so that they can easily be met and/or lowering a target becomes commonplace. A case in point was reducing the target for accredited programmes by half when it became apparent that targets for completion of newly launched accredited programmes' initiatives set at 30,000 by April 2004 were significantly wide of the mark (Bright, 2003).

The creation of a penal market

1979–1997: partnerships and the mixed economy

The Probation Service's first foray into contracting out 'followed the paradigm of changes in delivery of health and social services' (Rumgay, 2003: 196), encapsulated in the 1990 *NHS and Community Care Act,* which established the principle of the mixed economy of provision. Although the Home Office never fully acknowledged the degree of policy transfer between the two offices of State, preferring the nomenclature of 'partnership' rather than 'contractingout', there was without doubt 'policy convergence'. Further, despite the fact that the Home Office initially stopped short of creating an internal market, it nonetheless adopted key features of the NHS delivery model, in particular the requirement for Probation Service to assume the role of 'purchasers of services' from new providers outside of the public sector (Dolowitz, 2000; Rumsgay, 2007: 544).

In 1990, the Home Office published two pivotal white papers which spelt out the government's penal policy programme. These included expanding the range of alternatives to prison through the creation of new (more punitive) community penalties—reconfiguring the service from one based on penal welfarism (Garland, 2003) to one tasked with the delivery of punishment in the community (Home Office, 1990a)—and inserting a requirement into community orders that 'elements of a supervision plan could and would be provided by organisations and individuals outside the Probation Service' (Home Office, 1990b). The intention of expanding the range of deliverers was to enhance the 'potential to solve the problem of crime by co-operating, sharing information and exploiting diverse skills and knowledge' (Minkes et al., 2005: 255). With probation officers rebranded as offender managers, the expectation was that they would be less the 'exclusive providers of services and facilities, and more . . . managers of supervision programmes', brokering services from non–public sector providers (Rumsgay, 2007: 544).

Although the Home Office initially restricted partnership working to the voluntary sector and financed it through the 'Supervision Grants' system, in 1993 the Home Office extended the definition of partnership working to include both the private or voluntary sector on the basis of direct payments or the provision of joint working services (Rumgay, 2003; 196). With some probation staff seconded to voluntary agencies (Gough, 2010), to ensure that they did not renege on their obligations local probation services were instructed to allocate 5% (rising to 7%) of their annual budget to the voluntary sector (Rumsgay, 2007: 544). In so doing, they were early adopters of the practice of outsourcing the delivery of specific services that was to prove the norm in the public sector (Crawford, 1999).

Although the provision of grants by the Probation Service to non-public sector providers was initially viewed as posing little threat to the service, representing a supplement to, rather than replacement of core probation business, it was to prove the thin end of the wedge. Further challenges to the Probation Service's monopoly position followed with the watershed roll-out of electronic monitoring, also known as 'tagging' in the late 1990s, in part a measure to circumvent probation resistance to government penal policy (Ryan and Ward, 1989) (see next section), and the publication of *Carter Review* in the noughties, which introduced the concept of contestability into the political lexicon, signalling that the Probation Service could no longer take for granted that it would be the provider of first choice.

Carter, contestability and the creation of the internal market

Whilst the outsourcing of provision developed in a limited, piecemeal manner prior to 1997, leaving the basic structure of the service intact, it was the creation of the National Offender Management Service, decried as 'simply a Trojan horse for smuggling in "contestability" to another public sector' (Stelman, 2007), which, 'copying' (Dolowitz) the restructuring that underpinned the 1990 health service reforms, formalised the creation of the internal market. The creation of an internal market in the Probation Service was the brainchild of Carter, who set out his vision for the service in his 2003 *Review of the Prison and Probation Service*. His report, which introduced 'contestability' (the opening up of the provision of offender management services to competition from the private and voluntary sector) into probation discourse (Dobson, 2004, Robinson and Burnett, 2007), was heavily influenced by neoliberal ideas of competition, effectiveness and value for money. Although Carter did not promote privatisation *per se*, under his proposals, a purchaser/provider divide was created with the establishment of regional service commissioners who would be free to purchase services from 'the public, private or voluntary sectors on an equal basis' (2003: 36).

In 2004, the Home Office, endorsing the Carter Report's key recommendations, announced the creation of the National Offender Management Service. Emboldened by inroads made into the prison system, the 2004 Home Office report, echoing Carter's views, lavished praise on the value for money and improvement in quality of service delivery that contestability would entail. It stated:

> The Government are not interested in using the private sector for its own sake, whether in prisons or in the community. We want the most cost effective custodial and community sentences no matter who delivers them. The experience with the Prison Service's use of the private sector has been extremely positive. More significantly, the threat of contestability in running prisons has led to dramatic improvements in regimes and reductions in cost at some of the most difficult public sector prisons.
>
> *(2004: 14)*

In 2006, the government, in line with its Third Way philosophy, reiterated its commitment to harnessing the 'dynamism and talents' inherent in the mixed economy approach (Home Office, 2006: 31). With the intention of further embedding this ethos into the service, in 2007 (with the passing of the *Offender Management Act*), the Home Office replaced Probation Boards (established five years previously) with Probation Trusts and authorised the Secretary of State to contract providers from charities and private providers, as well as the public sector, to deliver Probation services.

Despite the establishment of both the structural and statutory framework to create the internal market, the scope and scale of privatisation during the New Labour administration was relatively restrained. Between 2002 and 2010, the balkanisation of the Probation Service was restricted to ancillary services such as drug testing and treatment (mainly to the voluntary sector); the provision of facilities in probation hostels, including cooks, maintenance staff and cleaners by private contractors; and the management of hostel beds by a company called ClearSprings (Fletcher, 2007): 'a company with no previous experience of working with offenders, but . . . had run caravan parks in Essex', which 'quickly ran into difficulties' and had its contract cancelled after three years (NAPO, 2013).

Nonetheless, although the public Probation Service's monopoly over the provision and delivery of core offender services remained intact, with private providers predators not partners, the new arrangements established the framework for further encroachment of the private sector. As Narey (the then newly appointed chief executive of NOMS), in an interview to the *Guardian* in March 2004, predicted, contestability raised the prospect of the whole Probation services being subject to market testing (Dobson, 2004: 151).

Electronic Monitoring

Although it was to be a decade (after the Carter Report) before the true ramifications of the contestability agenda to the Probation Service manifested themselves, a parallel development, namely the introduction of electronic monitoring and the wholesale outsourcing of the management and delivery to private contractors (the realisation of the neoliberal dream) foreshadowed the way ahead. With privatisation normalised, the development of EM as a wholly commercial enterprise demonstrated that not only were ministers willing to look to the private sector to provide offender services, but also that the private sector had the capacity, know-how and infrastructure to step into the breach. With the genie out of the bottle, it was only a matter of time before privatisation moved from the periphery to the centre of the delivery of the Probation Service.

EM, a penal configuration that expands the scope of the carceral through an automation of surveillance (Garland, 1997: 192), breaking down spatial separation between the prison and the home and redefining the private space of the home as a penal space, 'an area in which movement can be monitored and contained by an *unseen* State (State mandated) personnel' (Nellis, 1991: 179), was originally promoted in the UK by the Offender's Tagging Association (OTA). The OTA, a politically non-aligned pressure group, was formed in 1982 by Stacey, an anti-custody lobbyist (Jones and Newburn, 2007: 44), who believed that other alternatives to custody were ineffective (Nellis, 2004: 228). Rejected at the outset by politicians, it developed 'slowly and experimentally' (Nellis, 2003: 247) under the Conservatives in the late 1980s before being enthusiastically adopted by New Labour, who, attracted to a strong 'techo-managerial' orientation towards offender supervision (Nellis, 2014), significantly expanded its remit (Jones and Newburn, 2007).

Novel and innovative EM, a 'product of a global industry in techno-corrections: a subdivision of the corrections commercial complex' (Paterson, 2014: 20), exemplified 'the private sector's capacity to expand the State's orbit of control by developing new forms of sanctioning' (Feeley, 2002: 322). With its origins in the US, where it was originally conceived as a 'substitute for incarceration' (Eisenberg, 2017: 129), the 'impetus for the development and marketing' of EM came primarily from the private sector and 'provides evidence of the power of the market to stimulate innovations in penal practice' (Ryan and Ward, 1989: 103), and the capacity of private entrepreneurs to expand their spheres of operations (to maximise profits), as well as the willingness of the neoliberal State to look to the private sector to provide creative, cost-effective penal solutions.

Although the Home Office initially rejected the OTA's ideas on the basis that 'house arrest' did not constitute a sufficient punitive measure (Nellis, 1991: 168), the first indication of a change of heart came in 1986 when a Home Affairs Committee (HAC) inquiry into the penal crisis (viscerally manifested in a wave of riots and rooftop protests in the 1970s and 1980s) (Cavadino and Dignan, 2007), under pressure to reduce the prison population, recommended a study of EM. To this end, a junior Home Office minister and a member of the HAC travelled to the US, the 'penal workshop of the world' (Downes and Howard, 1996), to explore the efficacy of transferring policy and practice in relation to tagging to the UK (Nellis, 2000).

EM from the outset polarised opinions of academics, reformists and practitioners. Whilst some (conservative humanitarians) cautiously welcomed the utilisation of modern technology as a pragmatic, progressive alternative to 'keep individual offenders out of the most coercive and dehumanising of penalties-prison', others opposed EM as being intrinsically wrong both 'in principle and practice' (Collett, 1998: 4). Against this backdrop, in the late 1980s, a small group of academics spearheaded a series of conferences, partly funded by American companies involved in the manufacture and delivery of EM who 'saw the UK as the next big market' (Mair, 2005: 263), at Leicester Polytechnic's School of Law. Attended by US correctional staff 'with expertise in running electronic monitoring programmes', three US private corrections businesses involved in the manufacture of electronic monitoring technology, as well as American academics who had undertaken research into EM, the events represented a hybrid of a traditional academic conference and a marketing event for private contractors, at which the American experience of EM could be disseminated, its applicability to the UK could be discussed (Nellis, 2000: 104; Jones and Newburn, 2007: 45–46), and the opinion of key stakeholders could be gauged.

In the wake of the US fact-finding visit, the green paper *Punishment, Custody and the Community* was published in 1998. The paper raised the possibility of using EM 'to enforce tracking of an order requiring the offender to stay at home for a limited period, thereby making it possible to keep out of custody offenders who might otherwise be in prison' (Home Office, 1988: 12 as cited in Mair, 2005: 263). With its over-riding objective to reduce the prison population, the green paper plans to introduce 'punishment in the community' promoted 'stand alone EM curfews [confining people to their homes for part of the day using short range radio-frequency (RF) technology] as a more viable alternative to prison than probation supervision' (Nellis, 2017a: 262). Predicated on a radical overhaul of the core ideas, beliefs and working practices of the Probation Service, plans to introduce EM, which, if implemented, would radically change the Probation Service from an agency rooted in social work to 'a more controlling agency, concerned only with surveillance and punishment' (Nellis, 1991: 169), whilst cautiously welcomed by some anti-custody liberal reformists, were met with professional resistance. The National Association of Probation Officers opposed the creeping commercialisation which EM represented, arguing that the exportation from the commercial sector of 'economies of the presence' (Mitchell, 1999), whereby technology replaces human labour and the supervision of offenders is reduced to technological surveillance, was anathema: a threat to 'incentive based, trust based and threat based means . . . which . . . traditionally comprised the social work/law enforcement repertoire' (Nellis, 2007a: 11).

The green paper proposed two models for the organisation and administration of a new community sentence of a curfew order enforced by EM (imported from the US). One included the supervision of the order by probation staff in conjunction with other agencies from the voluntary and private sector, and the other involved the establishment of a new organisation to 'contract for services from the Probation Service, the private or voluntary sector and perhaps for some purposes from the police and prison' (para. 4.4). Although the paper lay emphasis on the 'great opportunities' (para 4.2) that the new measures offered the Probation Service (creating the impression that the government was actively seeking to incorporate the service into the delivery model), it was clearly implied from the outset that the government's plans would not be thwarted, leaving most commentators in little doubt that, in the face of probation resistance, contracting-out was high on the government's agenda (Ryan and Ward, 1989).

From 1989, EM was piloted in England as a means to enforce bail curfew conditions (an option that did not require legislation [Nellis, 1991: 171]). In the planning stage of the pilot, the Home Office held a series of meetings with representatives of both the rank and file and chiefs of the Probation Service to ascertain their views. In the meetings, Probation Service representatives made it clear that EM constituted 'a controlling, oppressive infringements of civil rights' which it would not countenance (Nellis, 2001: 170). This was consistent with the position adopted by the NAPO at its AGM in 1988 where a motion of non-co-operation was passed unanimously (Ryan and Ward, 1989: 102). In the event, as the net result of intense, consistent professional opposition, the government, attracted by the novelty (Mair, 2005) and 'politically committed to the free market privatisation [and] ideologically inspired [by the] need to reduce expenditure on public services' (Nellis, 1991: 180), neatly sidestepped the Probation Service and entrusted the development of the 'new penalty to private security organisations' (Nellis, 2004: 228). In a move that led to policy and practice in relation to EM and probation developing on 'parallel tracks' (Mair and Nellis, 2013), commercial contracts were awarded to the private sector not only to provide the technological equipment, but also expanding the range of privatisation activity to provide the personnel to take on the monitoring role (Nellis, 2001: 171). With the benefit of hindsight, as Nellis recently observed, resistance was counter-productive, delivering the Probation Service little more than a pyrrhic victory:

> Probation's . . . heartfelt belief that EM surveillance was incompatible with social work unfortunately played into the government's emerging ideological interest of 'privatising' . . . public services. Over the years this policy created a pool of large commercial providers, G4S, Serco and Capita who took on work across a range of government departments.
>
> *(2017a: 262)*

The expansion of EM: research and trials

The first trials commenced 1989 in Nottingham City, North Tyneside and Tower Bridge in London. The commercial contracts were divided between private providers of equipment who had previously played 'no major role in the British criminal justice system'—Marconi Electronic Devices Ltd. in Nottingham and North Tyneside and Chubb-Racal in Tower Bridge. The contract for monitoring was awarded to Securicor Ltd. (Nellis, 1991;172), who had been running immigration detention centres since 1970 (Cavadino and Dignan, 2007). Less than enthusiastically welcomed by sentencers, the trials were marred by slow take-up, a lack of clarity about technology and the place of tagging, poor co-ordination and communication between the courts and the providers and uncertainty about who should be targeted. Despite this, those who were tagged expressed a reasonable level of satisfaction, and operational difficulties improved over time (Mair, 2005: 265).

Although the trials, described by a contemporary observer as 'disastrous and sometimes farcical' (Collett, 1998: 5), produced a set of results which were not so 'negative that further initiatives could not be justified' (Mair, 2005: 265), the prevailing political will, and the close relationship between the Conservative Party and the commercial security industry, afforded private companies involved in the trials considerable lobbying leverage. Despite the five year gap that preceded the full implementation of EM (the delay was a consequence of poorly drafted legislation in 1991, the *Criminal Justice Act)*, EM was not, as some believed at the time, dropped from the political agenda. Rather in 1994, the *Criminal Justice and Public Order Act* was passed that provided the statutory instrument for its launch (Nellis, 2001: 171). Following the passing of the legislation, a new round of trials began in July 1995. Although marred by similar problems to the first trials, poor completion rates of the first set of trials were not repeated, and the new trials produced figures of 75% successful completion of orders in the first year and 82% in the second year (Mair, 2005: 267).

EM and New Labour

Although New Labour, whilst in opposition, held out the prospect that the commercial element of EM would be reversed, this pledge was reneged upon once in office. Embracing key tenets of neoliberalism and marketisation, New Labour 'proved to be more committed to EM than the Conservatives had (ever) been' (Nellis, 2007b: 117). Indeed, following a further set of what Mair (2005) calls 'far from unequivocal' results, EM curfew orders were rolled out as a national scheme in 1998. A year later the scheme was extended to include Home Detention Curfew (HDC), which offered early from release from a prison sentence on a tag as part of the incentive for good behaviour in prison scheme. Welcomed by offenders and their families (Nellis, 2004: 233), EM positioned the private sector at the heart of penal policy delivery.

Despite the production of half a dozen major studies, carried out under close government control, which provided a wealth of useful information that could have provided a solid foundation for further development, EM evolved in a piecemeal manner with scant regard to the evidence. With the government's commitment to EM always exceeding the results warranted, it was nonetheless the case that the overwhelming findings were never so bad that they could be consigned to the penal dustbin (Mair, 2005). In common with other initiatives, legitimised by the now-debased New Labour evidence-based policy making agenda, the expansion of EM reflected the prevailing 'pick and mix' approach of ministers and Home Office officials towards officially sanctioned research (Hope, 2004 and 2005).

With findings that suited the government's political priorities 'pre-announced, post-announced and re-announced' (Dean, 2012: 7) and bad news spun as good news, EM represented one of a string of New Labour policy initiatives, contrary to claims by politicians, which, flying in the face of sound evidence or based on flimsy or limited evidence (Kendall, 2008), were moulded by the party's public relations team to fit the government's narrative. With ideological and fiscal considerations paramount, the expansion of EM was driven more by techno-economic considerations, a 'fascination' with technology, its potential to 'deliver managerialist solutions to complex social problems' more cheaply and the broader neoliberal agenda of developing 'the markets in incarceration and social control' (Paterson, 2007: 107) than evidence.

Since its inception, EM, which at the outset represented an alien American export operating at the margins of penality, has become normalised, occupying a central position in the 'reconfigured field of crime control' (Garland, 2003). Once reviled by all but a small handful of penal reformers and academics, the dramatic changes to the criminal justice system have seen the focus of attention shift, and much of the passion has been taken out of the debate. As Mair, writing in 2005, pointed out:

> Electronic monitoring, or tagging, is now firmly embedded in criminal justice as an acknowledged part of the penal landscape (indeed, a story line in Coronation Street that ran during part of 2003 showed one of the soap

opera's main characters tagged, ironically as the result of a miscarriage of justice). Within the space of 15 years, tagging has become culturally accepted and it is no longer seen as a strange, foreign import that would not suit British sensibilities.

(2005: 258–9)

To date three waves of contracts have been awarded to private providers. The first wave of contracts (1999–2004), reflecting the pivotal role played by the American corrections commercial complex in UK privatisation, were awarded to Reliance-GSSC (a partnership of UK and US security companies), Premier (a partnership between UK Serco and the US Wackenhut Corporation) and Securicor (a UK security firm). The second round of five year contracts were awarded to a 'duopoly of providers', G4S (which incorporated Securicor and Group 4) and Serco (formerly one half of Premier), trading without its former US partner. In 2009, New Labour exercised its option to extend the existing EM contract to 2012 (Nellis, 2014; Nellis, 2017a; Paterson, 2007).

EM and the coalition government

G4S and Serco: the 2013 tagging scandal

There can be little doubt that the punishment business is a highly lucrative one. Since the second set of contracts were awarded in 2005, G4S and Serco received £700 million from the treasury (NAO, 2013), and with the progressive extension of the conditions under which EM can be applied, more than 20,000 offenders were monitored on electronic tags at any one time (Travis, 2013). Despite claims that privatisation is the key to achieving cost efficiencies and raised performance, the seemingly limitless opportunities offered to business to profit from the technological development and delivery of EM have been accompanied by a series of costly fiascos and high-profile scandals: scandals that have involved failures on the part of commercial providers to fulfil contracts, leading to the public sector having to bail them out, and instances of overpayments as contractors have charged government departments for work not done.

In 2013, concerns that suppliers of EM were taking advantage of weak oversight and lax contractual management came to a head when, as part of its process of renewing the contracts to G4S and Serco, the MOJ identified anomalies in the data provided and commissioned a forensic audit of the EM contracts by PwCs. The audit focussed specifically on disputed charging processes, in particular charging on the basis of orders made rather than the number of subjects (in the case of multiple orders on one subject, only one monitoring process is necessary), charging a monitoring fee after the order has ceased and charging a monitoring fee after the first visit regardless of whether equipment was supplied (NAO, 2013: 11).

Explaining the scandal to the House, Grayling (the then Minister for Justice) told MPs that billing for non-existent services could be traced back to at least

2005, and possibly 1999. He identified that the two providers had charged for the monitoring of offenders who had been returned to prison or had left the country, as well as those who had died or had never been tagged in the first place. He concluded that, 'this is a wholly indefensible and unacceptable state of affairs. The house will share my astonishment that two of the government's biggest suppliers would seek to charge in this way' (Travis, 2013). Although the companies defended their behaviour on the grounds that contractual deficiencies obstructed the sharing of information that tagging had ceased, in 2014 G4S agreed to repay £110 million for overcharging the MOJ, followed by a similar £70.5 million settlement by Serco (Travis, 2014).

Further, in a bid to reassure Parliament and the liberal press that the failings were 'not evidence of long-suspected flaws in the entire outsourcing project', but rather the egregious behaviour of individual contractors, both companies were temporarily ejected from the 'charmed circle of favoured service providers' (Nellis, 2017a: 272) and subsequently prohibited from bidding for contracts to deliver offender management services. Despite this public shaming, in 2015 the Centre for Criminal Justice Studies disclosed that the MOJ, following a 15 month extension to contracts, was continuing to pay the 'controversial security firms G4S and Serco millions of pounds a month for electronic tagging': a development which, running counter to government claims in late 2013 that there would be 'a fresh start for' EM, called into question the ministry's openness 'about their ongoing relationship with G4S and Serco' and its 'competency to negotiate and effectively manage contracts with the private sector' (CCJS, 2015: n.p.).

In light of the findings of PwC, the matter was referred to the Serious Fraud Office (SFO), and a criminal investigation was initiated. In 2019, in addition to its initial repayment, Serco, which was accused of manipulating the costs and cross-charges incurred by a subsidiary to make its profit seem lower, by self-reporting the matter to the SFO in 2013 and co-operating with the investigation into the wrongful billing allegations, had its fine reduced by 50%. Under a Deferred Prosecution Agreement (DPA), which meant that the company avoided a criminal conviction (under a DPA a company is charged with criminal proceedings, but they are suspended if the company agrees to certain conditions, which may include a financial penalty) and would not therefore be prohibited from future government contract, Serco paid a £19.2 million fine and a further £3.7 million in costs (Vincent, 2019). Under the terms of the DPA with the SFO, Serco agreed to accept three offences of fraud and two of false accounting. Subsequent to this in April 2021, two of Serco's former senior executives, Woods and Marshall, who maintained that they were convenient 'collateral damage' for the deal between Serco and SFO, appeared at Southwark Crown Court to face charges of defrauding the MOJ by grossly inflating costs to 'artificially and dishonestly' reduce Serco's profits (Slingo, 2021). In the event, the trial, which was a culmination of eight years of evidence gathering, collapsed, as later it emerged that the SFO had failed to disclose material to the defence. An application by the SFO to adjourn for a retrial was refused by the judge (Jolly, 2021).

The following year, G4S, in a similar Deferred Prosecution Agreement, however, received a smaller discount (40%) for its plea deal. Mr Justice Davis, who approved the deal, heard that G4S 'repeatedly lied to the Ministry of Justice, profiting to the tune of millions of pounds and failing to provide the openness, transparency and overall good corporate citizenship that UK taxpayers expect and deserve from companies entering into government contracts' (Beioley and Plimmer, 2020a). Basing his refusal to apply the usual 50% guilty plea discount on the grounds that G4S's co-operation had come 'relatively late in the day', he found that, motivated by a 'desire to conceal unanticipated cost efficiencies', the company (in common with Serco) had submitted incorrect cost reports, allowing it to retain payments that should have been returned to the government. With the difference between the costs reported to the Home Office and the Ministry of Justice and the costs G4S actually incurred exceeding £70 million, G4S argued that £42 million was reported incorrectly rather than dishonestly. In spite of this, accepting responsibility for three cases of fraud, G4S agreed to pay a £38.5 million fine plus costs (Beioley and Plimmer, 2020b).

EM and the post-2015 Tory government

Grayling's over-hyped vanity project: the GPS fiasco

The third and current contract was awarded by the MOJ in 2013. Whilst some aspects of the contract remained consistent with its predecessors, it was clear that 'integral to future provision' (Nellis, 2008: 273) was the replacement of 'obsolete' RF with a 'much larger . . . "world beating" global positioning satellite (GPS)[1] technology' (Nellis, 2017b: 2): a system which since 2010 had been independently adopted by some local police services to replace costly, labour-intensive tracking of persistent and prolific offenders. Promoted by David Cameron's favourite right-wing think tank, Policy Exchange (co-founded by Francis Maude) (Geohegan, 2012; Probation Institute, 2015; Transparify, 2016), the adoption of new satellite tagging as mainstream EM was heavily influenced by the 'maverick, practical initiative by a small British GPS tracking company, Buddi': the company responsible for the setting up of a tracking system for the police which operated 'outside the framework of the existing national EM contract' (Nellis, 2014: 171). As Nellis (2008) points out, 'quintessentially neoliberal protocols helped frame the way in which the Ministry of Justice sought to implement its third EM contract' (2008: 261), with Grayling, one of the most 'doctrinaire neoliberals in the cabinet' (Nellis, 2018), its willing champion.

Seduced by the alluring utopian vision of a new world of e-governance, in which GPS surveillance would do more for less (it was argued that GPS would transform offending by expanding the numbers subject to EM curfews from 15,000 per day to 75,000) (Nellis, 2008), Grayling's vision of a bespoke system encompassed a hitherto untested delivery model. The unprecedented 'tower' model split the end-to-end electronic monitoring service, previously delivered by G4S and

Serco, into direct contracts with four different suppliers. Each would supply different elements of the service, with their work pulled together by a contracted integrator. The successful bidders were Capita (one of the 'big four' providers), who would become the single nationwide provider, with Astrium (a UK/French conglomerate specialising in military satellite communications services) supplying the software, Buddi (a UK based small to medium enterprise) the hardware (the company's involvement ended in March 2014 when it was replaced by another supplier—Steatite, the only bidder, after being unable to resolve fundamental disagreements about handling location data and protecting intellectual property), and Telefonica/O2 (a Spanish firm specialising in telecommunications) the telephone system (NAO, 2017).

Plans to create a large, advanced GPS-based EM programme were driven not by penal rationale but rather reflected ideological considerations: the government's pursuit of 'untrammelled neoliberalism . . . in respect of offender management techniques' (Nellis, 2014: 169). Due to be run out by the MOJ in late 2014, the misguided pursuit of a bespoke, rather than a tried and tested off-the-shelf system, was beset by the problems of constant changing of the technical specifications. Although it initially stalled in the face of series of costly delays (Johnstone, 2016; Nellis, 2014) and was seemingly abandoned in 2016 (Nellis, 2017b), it was, despite being condemned as a 'disgraceful waste of public money' (BBC News, 2017; House of Commons (HOC) Public Accounts Committee, 2018) by the NAO[2] in 2017, resurrected in 2019.

Indeed, on the same day as the publication of a pilot study in eight police areas testing the delivery and usage of GPS tags (Kerr et al., 2019), which

> found that tags could have a positive impact on compliance, . . . acting as a constant reminder of an offender's licence conditions, . . . and could save police investigation time by providing evidence ruling suspects in and out of crimes,

the justice secretary, in a development that would once again increase the range and scope of privatisation, announced that the costly scheme, marred by delays and false dawns, had proved 'so successful' that it would be rolled out nationally (MOJ, 2019). The costly system that never lived up to its promises remains marred in controversy.

Conclusion

Since the late 1970s the Probation Service, lacking the political influence of its larger criminal justice partners, has been in a state of almost continuous change: the soft target for successive governments of different affiliations to test out their own specific variant of neoliberal marketisation and privatisation. Buffeted by a series of measures that have incrementally opened up the service to market conditions, the service was gradually transformed from one embracing the central tenets of penal welfarism to one that functions in a marketised environment, subject to principles of performance management and accountancy imported from the business world and driven by top-down targets and KPIs, which tie it to constantly changing government law and order priorities.

In the 1990s a warning salvo was shot over the service's bows when, in the face of professional resistance, the government contracted out to private suppliers its flagship electronic monitoring initiative. In the noughties, the slippery course towards ever increasing incursion of the private sector into its sphere of operations was set with the restructuring of the service. Emulating developments in the health service, which formalised the purchaser/provider spilt, the new arrangements provided the infrastructure to implement contestability: a mechanism to increase the involvement of the private and voluntary sectors in offender management. Whilst contestability did not constitute 'out and out privatisation *per se*' (Burke and Collett, 2016: 122), it provided the mechanism by which non–public sector providers could bid to deliver probation services, enshrining the mixed economy of provision and market testing within the service's delivery model.

'With much of the ideological and practical leg work' put in place during the three terms of Labour administration (Burke and Collett, 2016: 120), by 2010, with an increasing array of its services being put out to tender, the incoming coalition government, under the auspices of austerity, was poised to embark upon the most ambitious phase of public service privatisation. The public Probation Service, a victim of neoliberal penality, faced losing all but its core responsibilities for public protection and providing information to the courts to private contractors. As the coalition government prepared to grasp the reins of power, the 'phoney war' in which the Probation Service was incrementally softened up ideologically, structurally and legislatively for privatisation was over. By the end of Labour's administration, with the service condemned as 'not fit for purpose' by John Reid during his 2006–2007 period in the Home Office:

> Probation was on the ropes just as the trumpeters of the brave new neoliberal world wanted and it facilitated the justification of significant changes to the control and structure of the Probation Service. Most importantly, under the *Offender Management Act* of 2007, the legislative provisions for dramatically differently delivery mechanisms were in place for the Coalition to carry on where New Labour had left off.
>
> *(Burke and Collett, 2016: 122)*

After more than a century of work with offenders, 'often with little encouragement or recognition for their efforts, a small island of decency and humanity in the criminal justice system (was on the brink of) . . . disappearing' (Mair and Burke, 2012: 181), to be replaced by private companies, profit-driven delivery and the commodification of offenders as financial assets. The Probation Service was effectively a dead man walking.

Notes

1 Steatite received a '£4.4 million termination fee on top of £3.3 million it was paid for its fruitless development work' when plans were seemingly abandoned in 2016 (Nellis, 2017b: 2).
2 The Public Accounts Committee stated: 'The programme so far has been a catastrophic waste of public money which has failed to deliver the intended benefits. The Ministry pressed ahead without clear evidence that it was to be operated or that it was deliverable. Its selection of a high-risk approach to procure the electronic tags, and its poor management of both the programme and potential suppliers, exacerbated these problems. The Ministry of Justice has ultimately wasted a huge amount of taxpayers' money to end up with an approach which uses the same tags and supplier it had when the programme started') (Parliament.UK, 2018: n.p.).

References

Anderson, P. (2000) 'Renewals' *New Review*, II (1)
Ashworth, P. (2009) 'What Happened to Probation? Managerialism, Performance and the Decline of Autonomy' *British Journal of Criminal Justice* 7 (3): 61–75
Audit Commission (1989) *The Probation Service; Promoting Value for Money*, London: HMSO
BBC News (2017, July 12) 'Government Criticised over Tagging Scheme' *BBC News*
Beioley, K., and Plimmer, G. (2020a, July 10) 'G4S Drafts £38.5m Deal to Settle Tagging Scandal with Fraud Office' *The Financial Times*
Beioley, K., and Plimmer, G. (2020b, July 17) 'Judge Applies Reduced Discount on Security Company's Fine over Prisoner Tagging a Seven-Year SFO Investigation Found G4S to Have Repeatedly Lied about the True Extent of Its Profits' *The Financial Times*
Bottoms, A. (1977) 'Reflections on the Renaissance of Dangerousness' *Howard Journal* 16 (2): 70–96
Bright, M., (2003, September 21) 'I'd Prefer to Do Time Than Therapy' *The Observer*
Burgess, J., and MacDonald, D. (1999) 'Outsourcing, Employment and Industrial Relations in the Public Sector' *The Economic and Labour Relations Review* 10 (1): 36–55
Burke, L., and Collett, S. (2016) 'Transforming Rehabilitation: Organizational Bifurcation and the End of Probation as We Knew It?' *Probation Journal* 63 (2): 120–135
Canton, R. (2011) *Probation: Working with Offenders*, Oxford: Routledge
Carter, P. (2003) *Managing Offenders: Reducing Crime—A New Approach*, London: Prime Minister's Strategy Unit
Cavadino, M., and Dignan, J. (2007) *The Penal System: An Introduction*, London: Sage
Centre for Crime and Justice Studies (2015) 'G4S and Serco Still Being Paid Millions for Tagging' www.crimeandjustice.org.uk/news/g4s-and-serco-still-being-paid-millions-tagging. Retrieved 10 August 2015
Christie, N. (2003) *Crime Control as Industry: Towards Gulags, Western Style* (3rd edition), London: Routledge
Chui, W.H., and Nellis, M. (2003) 'Creating the National Probation Service: New Wine, Old Bottles' in W.H. Chui and M. Nellis (eds) *Moving Probation Forward*, Harlow: Pearson Longman
Collett, S. (1998) 'Spiderman Comes to Salford Tagging Offenders: Cynical Resignation or Pragmatic Acceptance?' *Probation Journal* 45 (1): 3–9
Collett, S. (2013) 'Riots, Revolution and Rehabilitation: The Future of Probation' *The Howard Journal of Criminal Justice* 52 (2): 163–189
Collins, S. (2015) 'Then and Now: Revisiting Policy, Tasks, Theories, Skills and Experience of Probation Work in the 1970s' *Probation Journal* 62 (2): 140–155

Connell, R., Fawcett, B., and Meagher, G., (2009) 'Neoliberalism, New Public Management and the Human Service Professions: Introduction to the Special Issue' *Journal of Sociology* 45 (4): 331–338

Crawford, A. (1999) *The Local Governance of Crime: Appeals to Community and Partnership*, Oxford: Oxford University Press

Davies, K., and Gregory, M. (2010) 'The Price of Targets: Audit and Evaluation in Probation Practice' *Probation Journal* 57 (4): 400–414

Dean, M. (2012) *Democracy under Attack: How the Media Distort Policy and Politics*, Bristol: Policy Press

Dobson, G. (2004) 'Get Carter' *Probation Journal* 51 (2): 144–154

Dolowitz, D.P. (2000) 'Policy Transfer: A Framework for Analysis' in D.P. Dolowitz with R. Hume, M. Nellis and F. O'Neil (eds) *Policy Transfer and British Social Policy*, Maidenhead: Open University Press

Dorey, P. (2005) *Policy Making in Britain: An Introduction*, London: Sage

Downes, D., and Howard, M. (1996) 'Law and Order Futures' *Criminal Justice Matters* 26 (1): 3–5

Downes, D., and Morgan, R. (2002) 'No Turning Back: The Politics of Law and Order into the Millennium' in M. Maguire, R. Morgan and R. Reiner (eds) *The Oxford Handbook of Criminology* (3rd edition), Oxford: Oxford University Press

Drakeford, M. (2000) *Privatisation and Social Policy*, Harlow: Longman

Eisenberg, A. (2017) 'Mass Monitoring' *Southern California Law Review* 90: 123–180

Elliott, L. (2003, July 14) 'Third-Way Addicts Need a Fix' *The Guardian*

Feeley, M. (2002) 'Entrepreneurs of Punishment: The Legacy of Privatization' *Punishment and Society* 4 (3): 321–344

Ferguson, I. (2004) 'Neoliberalism, the Third Way and Social Work: The UK Experience' *Social Work and Society Online Journal* www.socwork.net/sws/article/view/236/411. Retrieved 18 December 2015

Fletcher, H. (2007) 'Privatization' in R. Canton and D. Hancock (eds) *Dictionary of Probation and Offender Management*, Cullompton: Willan

Flynn, N. (1997) *Public Sector Management* (3rd edition), Hemel Hempstead: Prentice Hall

Garland, D. (1997) "'Governmentality' and the Problem of Crime: Foucault, Criminology, Sociology' *Theoretical Criminology* 9 (2): 173–214

Garland, D. (2001) *The Culture of Control*, Oxford: Oxford University Press

Gelsthorpe, L. (2007) 'Probation Values and Human Rights' in L. Gelsthorpe and R. Morgan (eds) *Handbook of Probation*, Cullompton: Willan

Geohegan, R. (2012) *Future of Corrections: Exploring the Use of Electronic Monitoring*, London: Policy Exchange

Gough, D. (2010) 'Multi-Agency Working in Corrections: Cooperation and Competition' in A. Pycroft and D. Gough (eds) *Multi-Agency Working in Criminal Justice*, Bristol: Polity Press

Hedderman, C., and Murphy, A. (2015) 'Bad News for Probation? Analysing the Newspaper Coverage of Transforming Rehabilitation' *Probation Journal*, 62 (3): 217–234

Hill, R. (2007) 'National Probation Service for England and Wales' in R. Canton and D. Hancock (eds) *Dictionary of Probation and Offender Management*, Cullompton: Willan

Home Office (1990a) *Partnership in Dealing with Offenders in the Community*, London: Home Office

Home Office (1990b) *Supervision and Punishment in the Community*, London: Home Office

Home Office (2004) *Reducing Crime-Changing Lives: The Government's Plans for Transforming the Management of Offenders*, London: Home Office

Home Office (2006) *A Five Year Strategy for Protecting the Public and Reducing Reoffending,* Cm6717, London: Stationary Office
Hood, C. (2006) 'Gaming in Targetworld: The Targets Approach to Managing British Public Services' *Public Administration Review* 66 (4): 515–521
Hope, T. (2004) 'Pretend It Works: Evidence and Governance in Evaluation of the Research Burglary Initiative' *Criminology and Criminal Justice* 4 (3): 278–308
Hope, T. (2005) 'Things Can Only Get Better' *Criminal Justice Matters,* (62): 4–39
House of Commons (HOC) Public Accounts Committee (2018) *Offending—Monitoring Tags,* London: HOC
Johnstone, R. (2016, February 26) 'MoJ Scraps £23m Bespoke Electronic Tagging Contract' *Public Finance*
Jolly, J. (2021, April 26) 'Trial of Firmer Serco Executives Collapses as SFO Fails to Disclose Evidence' *The Guardian*
Jones, T., and Newburn, T. (2007) *Policy Transfer and Criminal Justice Policy,* Maidenhead: Open University Press
Kendall, K. (2008) 'Dangerous Thinking: A Critical History of Correctional Cognitive Behaviouralism' in G. Mair (ed) *What Matters in Probation,* Cullompton: Willan
Kerr, J., Roberts, E., Davies, M., and Pullerits, M. (2019) *Process Evaluation of the Global Positioning System (GPS) Electronic Monitoring Pilot.* MOJ Analytical Series 2019, London: MOJ
Lloyd, C. (1986) *'Response to SNOP': An Analysis of the Home Office Document. 'Probation Service in England and Wales' and the Subsequent Local Reponses,* Cambridge: Cambridge Institute of Criminology
Loader, I., and Sparks, R. (2002) 'Contemporary Landscapes of Crime, Order, and Control: Governance, Risk and Globalization' in M. Maguire, R. Morgan and R. Reiner (eds) *The Oxford Handbook of Criminology* (3rd edition), Oxford: Oxford University Press
Loveday, B. (1999) 'The Impact of Performance Culture on Criminal Justice Agencies in England and Wales' *International Journal of Sociology of Law* 27 (4): 351–377
Mair, G. (1997) 'Community Penalties and Probation' in M. Maguire, R. Morgan and R. Reiner (eds) *The Oxford Handbook of Criminology* (2nd edition), Oxford: Oxford University Press
Mair, G. (2005) 'Electronic Monitoring in England and Wales; Evidence-Based or Not?' *Criminology and Criminal Justice* 5 (3): 257–277
Mair, G., and Burke, L. (2012) *Redemption, Rehabilitation and Risk Management: A History of Probation,* London: Routledge
Mair, G., (2008) 'The Origins of What Works in England and Wales: A House Built on Sand' in G. Mair (ed) *What Matters in Probation,* Cullompton: Willan.
Mair, G., and Nellis, M. (2013) 'Parallel Tracks: Probation and Electronic Monitoring in England, Wales and Scotland' in M. Nellis, K. Beyens and D. Kaminski (eds) *Electronically Monitored Punishment: International and Critical Perspectives,* London: Routledge
Massey, A. (2001) 'Policy, Management and Implementation' in S. Savage and R. Atkinson (eds) *Public Policy under Blair.* Basingstoke: Palgrave
May, T. (1991) *Probation, Politics and Practice,* Buckingham: Open University Press
McGarva, R. (2007) 'Performance Management' in R. Canton and D. Hancock (eds) *Dictionary of Probation and Offender Management,* Cullompton: Willan
Merrington, S., and Stanley, S. (2007) 'Effectiveness: Who Counts What?' in L. Gelsthorpe and R. Morgan (eds) *Handbook of Probation,* Cullompton: Willan
Ministry of Justice Press Release (2019) *Justice Secretary Unveils GPS Tag Roll Out to Better Protect Victims,* London: MOJ

Minkes, J., Hammersley, R., and Raynor, P. (2005) 'Partnership in Working with Young Offenders with Substance Misuse Problems' *The Howard Journal of Criminal Justice* 44 (3): 254–268

Mitchell, W.J. (1999) *E-topia: Urban Life, Jim, but Not As We Know It*, Cambridge, MA: MIT

Morgan, R. (2007) 'Probation, Governance and Accountability' in L. Gelsthorpe and R. Morgan (eds) *Handbook of Probation*, Cullompton: Willan

NAPO (2013) *Response to Transforming Rehabilitation Consultation*, London: NAPO

Nash, M. (2003) 'Pre-trial Investigation' in W.H. Chui and M. Nellis (eds) *Moving Probation Forward*, Harlow: Pearson Longman

Nash, M. (2008) 'The Policy Context' in S. Green, E. Lancaster and S. Feasey (eds) *Addressing Offending Behaviour: Context, Practice and Values*, Cullompton: Willan

National Audit Office (2013) *Ministry of Justice's Electronic Monitoring Contracts*, London: NAO

National Audit Office (2017) *The New Generation Electronic Monitoring Programme*, London: NAO

Nellis, M. (1991) 'The Electronic Monitoring of Offenders in England and Wales; Recent Developments and Future Prospects' *British Journal of Criminology* 31 (2): 165–185

Nellis, M. (2000) 'Law and Order: The Electronic Monitoring of Offenders' in D. Dolowitz with R. Hulme, M. Nellis and F. O'Neill (eds) *Policy Transfer and British Social Policy*, Buckingham: Open University Press

Nellis, M. (2001) 'Community Penalties in Historical Perspective' in A. Bottoms, L. Gelsthorpe and S. Rex (eds) *Community Penalties: Change and Challenges*, Cullompton: Willan

Nellis, M. (2003) 'Electronic Monitoring and the Future of Probation' in W.H. Chui and M. Nellis (eds) *Moving Probation Forward*, Harlow: Pearson Longman

Nellis, M. (2004) 'Electronic Monitoring and the Community Supervision of Offenders' in A. Bottoms, S. Rex and G. Robinson (eds) *Alternative to Prison: Options for an Insecure Society*, Cullompton: Willan

Nellis, M. (2007a) 'Tracking Offenders by Satellite—Progress or Cost-Cutting?' *Criminal Justice Matters* 68: 10–11

Nellis, M. (2007b) 'Humanising Justice; the English Probation Service up to 1972' in L. Gelsthorpe and R. Morgan (eds) *Handbook of Probation*, Cullompton: Willan

Nellis, M. (2008) Mobility, Locatability and the Satellite Tracking of Offenders in K.F. Aas, H.O. Gundhus and H.M. Lomell (eds) *Technologies of Insecurity: the surveillance of everyday life*. London: Routledge

Nellis, M. (2014) 'Upgrading Electronic Monitoring and Downgrading Probation: Reconfiguring "Offender Mangement" in England and Wales' *European Journal of Probation* 6 (2): 169–191

Nellis, M. (2017a) ' "The Treasure Island of the EM Market": State Commercial Collaboration and Electronic Monitoring in England and Wales' in A. Hucklesby and S. Lister (eds) *Private Sector Involvement in Criminal Justice*, Basingstoke: Palgrave Macmillan

Nellis, M. (2017b) *Grayling's Failings on Electronic Monitoring: After the Fiasco, What Next?* Centre for Crime and Justice Studies

Nellis, M. (2018) 'Electronically Monitoring Offenders as "Coercive Connectivity": Commerce and Penality in Surveillance Capitalism' in T. Daems and B. Vander (eds) *Privatising Punishment in Europe*, London: Routledge

Nellis, M., and Gelsthorpe, L. (2003) 'Human Rights and the Probation Values Debate' in W.H. Chui and M. Nellis (eds) *Moving Probation Forward*, Harlow: Pearson Longman

Parliament.UK (2019) *Offender Monitoring Tags Summary.* Retrieved 15th June 2022 from https://publications.parliament.uk/pa/cm201719/cmselect/cmpubacc/458/45803.htm#_idTextAnchor000

Paterson, C. (2007) 'Commercial Crime Control and the Electronic Monitoring of Offenders in England and Wales', *Social Justice* 34 (3–4): 98–110

Paterson, C. (2014) 'The Global Trade in (Techno) Corrections' *Criminal Justice Matters* 95 www.crimeandjustice.org.uk/publications/cjm/edition/cjm-95-electronic-monitoring Retrieved 11 August 2015

Power, M. (1997) *The Audit Society: Rituals of Verification,* Oxford: Oxford University Press

Pratt, J. (2005) 'Elias, Punishment and Decivilization' in J. Pratt, D. Brown, S. Hallsworth and W. Morrison (eds) *The New Punitiveness: Trends, Theories, Perspectives,* Cullompton: Willan

Probation Institute (2015) *Community Rehabilitation Companies and the Future of Electronic Monitoring: Ensuring a Probation Voice.* Probation Institute Background Paper PI Electronic Monitoring Workshop, 19 November 2015. London

Raine, J., and Wilson, M. (1993) *Managing Criminal Justice,* London: Harvester Wheatsheaf

Raynor, P. (2002) 'Community Penalties. Probation, Punishment and "What Works"' in M. Maguire, R. Morgan and R. Reiner (eds) *The Oxford Handbook of Criminology* (3rd edition), Oxford: Oxford University Press

Raynor, P., and Vanstone, M. (2007) 'Towards a Corrective Service' in L. Gelsthorpe and R. Morgan (eds) *Handbook of Probation,* Cullompton: Willan

Robinson, G., and Burnett, R. (2007) 'Experiencing Modernization: Frontline Probation Perspectives on the Transition to a National Offender Management Service', *Probation Journal,* 54(4): 318–337

Rumgay, J. (2003) 'Partnerships in the Probation Service' in W.H. Chui and M. Nellis (eds) *Moving Probation Forward,* Harlow: Pearson Longman

Rumsgay, J. (2007) 'Partnerships in Probation in' in L. Gelsthorpe and R. Morgan (eds) *Handbook of Probation,* Cullompton: Willan

yan, M., and Ward, T. (1989) *Privatization and the Penal System: The American Experience and the Debate in Britain,* Buckingham: Open University Press

Shapland, J., Bottoms, A., Farrall, S., McNeill, F., Priede, C., and Robinson, G. (2012) *The Quality of Probation Supervision—A Literature Review,* Sheffield: Centre for Criminological Research, University of Sheffield Occasional Paper 3

Slingo, J. (2021, March 30) 'Ex-Directors in Dock as Serco Tagging Fraud Trial Opens' *The Law Society Gazette*

Squires, P. (2006) 'New Labour and the Politics of Anti-Social Behaviour' *Critical Social Policy* 26 (1): 144–168

Stelman, A. (2007) 'From Probation to National Offender Management Service: Issues of Contestability, Culture and Community Involvement' *Probation Journal* 54 (1): 91–92

Teague, M. (2013) 'Rehabilitation, Punishment and Profit', *British Society of Criminology Newsletter* 72: 15–18

Transparify (2016) *How Transparent Are Think Tanks about Who Funds Them?* Tbilisi, GA: Transparify Org

Travis, A. (2013, July 12) 'G4S Faces Fraud Investigation over Tagging Contracts' *The Guardian*

Travis, A. (2014, March 12) 'G4S Agrees to Pay £109m for Overpaying on Tagging Contracts' *The Guardian*

Vanstone, M. (2004) 'Mission Control: The Origins of a Humanitarian Service' *Probation Journal* 51 (1): 34–47

Vickers, J., and Wright, V. (1989) 'The Politics of Industrial Privatisation in Western Europe' in J. Vickers and V. Wright (eds) *The Politics of Privatization in Western Europe*, London: Frank Cass

Vincent, M. (2019, July 3) 'Serco's £19m Fraud Fine Leaves G4S Looking Less Sure-Footed' *The Financial Times*

Whitehead, P. (2007) 'Target Practice in Probation: Take Aim for Reappraisal' *British Journal of Criminal Justice* 5 (2): 83–95

Whitehead, P. (2010) *Exploring Modern Probation: Social Theory and Organisational Complexity*, Bristol: Policy Press

Whitehead, P., and Statham, R., (2006) *The History of Probation*, Crayford: Sweet and Maxwell

Whitfield, D. (1998) *Introduction to the Probation Service* (2nd edition), Winchester: Waterside Press

Young, J., and Matthews, R. (2003) 'New Labour Crime Control and Social Exclusion' in R. Matthews and J. Young (eds) *The New Politics of Crime and Punishment*, Cullompton: Willan

Young, P. (1976) 'A Sociological Analysis of the Early History of Probation' *British Journal of Law and Society* 3: 44–58

11
INTERROGATING THE FAILED PROBATION EXPERIMENT, OR IT WASN'T BROKEN, SO WHY DID THEY TRY TO FIX IT?

> The Probation Service was recognised as a world leader until political interference . . . undermined and ultimately dismantled it.
> (Mike Worthington, a former Chief Probation Officer of Northumbria)

Introduction

The progressive incursion of the private sector into the Probation Service (under the smokescreen of 'reform') is a central feature of the last three decades of neoliberal penal policy. As 'support for privatised interventions . . . crossed the continuum of party affiliations' (Teague, 2016: 135), the Probation Service, slipping under the public radar (Rutter, 2016), was incrementally divested of its core business: a development that epitomised 'the desire to redefine the role of the state, the desire to control and discipline unionised public sector workers, [and] the desire to shift politically sensitive services to the private sector' (Kirton and Guillaume, 2015: 5).

By the time that the Labour Party left office in 2010, about 32% of offender management services were being delivered by private firms with an oligopoly of multi-national (providers G4S, Serco, Sodexo and Geo Amney accounting) for over three quarters of the expenditure (Bastow, 2014: 10). Despite this 'privatisation by stealth' (Burgess and MacDonald, 1999: 8), the Probation Service retained its core business, namely managing court orders and providing information to the courts. However, the changed political and economic landscape that ushered in 'austerity' and 'deficit reduction', coupled with Cameron's vision of the 'Big Society', in which charities, volunteers and not-for-profit organisations would prop up the Welfare State (Dominey, 2012), was to provide a new imperative for the neoliberal agenda. With outsourcing and cost cutting synonymous in the political imagination, both the pace and scale of the transformation of the probation sector, 'either put in place or aspired to' by New Labour (Collet, 2013: 166), accelerated as the Probation Service, in undignified haste, was propelled down the road to selling off 70% of its business to the private sector.

In defiance of a series of government reports disputing the efficacy of the government's proposals, as well as intensive lobbying and industrial action, in 2015 the Probation Service was subjected to 'organisational bifurcation' (Burke and Collett, 2016) with low to medium risk cases (70% of the publicly funded business of the service), in all but one of the Probation Service areas,[1] handed over to private companies in consortium with voluntary agencies. The development not only raised moral and ethical questions about neoliberal governance (e.g. making 'profits from punishment' and delegating the State's power to punish to business interests), but also signalled the degree to which crime, traditionally understood as 'a social problem to be managed or eradicated', could be reconfigured as a business opportunity (Nellis, 2011): probation services were transformed into commodities to be divvied up by big businesses in the global corrections commercial complex. A largely invisible part of the criminal justice system that few understand and fewer care about (Hedderman and Murphy, 2015), the service paid a hefty price for a short-lived and 'irremediably flawed' experiment driven by a neoliberal ideologue that wreaked havoc, putting the public at risk and squandering an estimated £500 million of taxpayers' money.

Whilst few believed that once the privatisation genie was out of the bottle that it would be replaced, on 16 May 2019, the Ministry of Justice, faced with a costly system in tatters sustained by frequent Treasury bailouts and years of damning reports by government watchdogs and inspectorates, as well as lobbying by MPs, penal reformers and professional originations, finally accepted that the widely derided delivery model was no longer viable. Under cautiously welcomed plans signalling the end of the bifurcation of services created by Grayling's flagship policy, the government announced that offender management would be brought back under public control of the NPS, which would be partnered with private sector providers who, 'rewarded' for their failures, would be able to competitively tender for highly lucrative contracts (worth £280 million annually) to deliver key face-to-face interventions (MOJ, 2019). A year later, driven more by fiscal pressures and pragmatic considerations of the COVID-19 crisis than evidence, in what amounted to a U-turn, the MOJ announced that the tendering process had been withdrawn and that the delivery of all core aspects of offenders' services (including unpaid work and programmes) would be brought back in house. Privatisation of the Probation Service a costly, short-lived experiment, which exposed the myths and fallacies at the heart of the neoliberal project, was effectively abandoned!

The coalition years: the sell off of the Probation Service

Although few in the Probation Service genuinely believed that any government would countenance the wholesale privatisation of the service, seeing this as a step too far even for the most committed neoliberal ideologue, there were a number of notable dissenters who warned that partnership working and the encouragement of a range of new providers was a slippery slope that signalled the real prospect of 'no future for probation' (Mair, 2008: 18): a spectre that loomed large with the creation of the coalition government in 2010.

In 2010, 'against a background of the global financial crisis', the coalition government, 'dominated by a neoliberally inclined Conservative party' and 'the notionally left-of-centre Liberal Democrats' (Nellis, 2014: 170), was formed, following a general election in which no single party achieved an overall majority. On 20 May 2010, the newly formed government set out its economic policy priorities, establishing that deficit reduction, to be achieved through public service funding cuts rather than taxation, was the 'most urgent issue facing Britain. With the size and nature of the public sector [attack] . . . both justified by, and obscured under the supposed reasonableness of the need for austerity' (Collett, 2013: 166), in October 2010 the Spending Review spelt out that sharp cuts to public spending would translate to a Home Office and Ministry of Justice budgetary reduction of 16% and 29%, respectively.

Rehabilitation Revolution: the Clarke years

Against the background of departmental budgetary cuts to his department, Ken Clarke, the Secretary of State for Justice and the Lord Chancellor, who was the architect of the 1990 NHS reforms, published the green paper *Breaking the Cycle* (MOJ, 2010a). Welcomed by penal reformers as one of the old-guard Tories associated with the 80s' anti-custody paradigm, Clarke, pitching himself against the 'prison works' Home Secretary, Theresa May, and the right wing press, proposed the Rehabilitation Revolution, which, paid for by the savings generated in the short term by outsourcing and in the long term by a crime reduction, would seek 'to control the use of custody' (HOC Justice Committee, 2011: 8). Offering the prospect of 'an end to the 18 year punitive arms race that has fuelled the relentless rise in the prison population' (Travis, 2010), proposals to reduce the prison population by 3,000 within four years were, despite some reservations about the new structural and governance arrangements, optimistically welcomed as the return of proportionality in sentencing principle. With rehabilitation rather than punishment at the heart of Clarke's vision, the economic and social case for investing in rehabilitation was set out in the *Evidence Report* (2010b).

The paper, building on the legacy of the previous government's post-2008 cost-cutting 'better for less' approach, which 'meant that any innovative reconfiguration of public services that saved money would be dubbed "better", regardless of quality or virtue' (Nellis, 2014: 170), outlined the government's plans to reduce expenditure by expanding contestability (Carter, 2003) and imposing new funding arrangements, Payment by Results. Under the new arrangements, which represented more of a 'funding revolution' than a Rehabilitation Revolution (Gough, 2012: 20), 'centrally controlled services dominated by the public sector [would be replaced by] a more competitive system, drawing on the knowledge, expertise and innovation from all sectors'. Local Probation Trusts were expected to 'compete with other providers from the voluntary and the private sectors' (HOC Justice Committee, 2011: 66). With the voluntary sector promoted as the source of 'specialist knowledge and experience of service delivery in many fields of social support', the mantra of Big Society diverted attention away from ideologically driven hollowing out of the State and marketisation (Rodger, 2012: 18). In the absence of a clearly defined regulatory framework, the implication was that the new funding arrangements would impose market discipline and the State would assume the 'role of market creator rather than a deliverer or a regulator' (Gough, 2012: 20).

Payment by Results

Seeking to reverse Labour's top-down, prescriptive focus on 'processes and inputs' (Gough, 2012: 20), the 2010 *Evidence Report* (2010) set out the case for introducing PbR (a new variant of management by targets originally applied in 2000 to the NHS) into the probation system, (Burke and Collett, 2016; Gosling, 2016). Despite the fact that the scheme had a chequered track record, it remained politically attractive to a government keen 'not only to reduce public expenditures, but also . . . the scale of the public sector' (Hedderman, 2013: 44), and had rhetorical appeal to a public inured to the wasteful public sector. Under PbR, a series of financially driven checks and balances would ensure that those who met contracted outcomes would be rewarded and those who failed would be penalised (Dominey, 2012). Providers would receive a basic tariff to cover their costs, with additional payments contingent upon meeting contracted targets to reduce re-offending (Fox and Albertson, 2012). In common with other PbR schemes, the rationale was to create a cost-effective, outcome-focused delivery mechanism which would transfer the risks and associated costs of ineffective interventions from the State to the provider, opening up the market to commercial providers who, freed from government regulation of what needed to be done, would be 'incentivised' to innovate (MOJ, 2010b; NAO, 2015). Although most penal reformers and criminal justice stakeholders cautiously welcomed

> the government's aim of increasing local accountability and partnership working in the justice system, and introducing local incentives that can see savings to criminal justice services achieved through reductions in reoffending reinvested into further crime prevention activity at the local level,
>
> *(Howard League, 2011: 17)*

concerns about the viability and efficacy of the payment framework featured heavily in critical responses to the paper. With an oligopoly of multi-national businesses already dominating the outsourcing market, it was feared that the precarious funding model would deter smaller organisations from bidding.

Downgrading the Probation Service

In March 2012, partly in response to the recommendation in the Justice Committee's *The Role of the Probation Service* (2011) that the MOJ clarify its 'intentions for the future of Probation and explain which elements of probation activity we consider might be commissioned from external providers' (NAO, 2014: 6), the MOJ published *Punishment and Reform: Effective Probation Services*. The consultation paper signalled the minister's intentions to pursue a twin-track approach of expanding the role of electronic monitoring 'to create the largest and most advanced electronic monitoring (EM) scheme in the world, using combined GPS tracking and radio frequency technology', whilst simultaneously downgrading the Probation Service (Nellis, 2014: 169) by outsourcing its core business.

Reversing previous manifestations of privatisation, the audacious proposals for service delivery represented an unparalleled immersion of non–public sector providers into the punishment business (Hobbs and Hamerton, 2014). The proposed delivery framework confirmed what had been suspected, namely that the previous green paper's omission of a clearly defined role for the Probation Service was indicative of 'high price' that the service would pay for the Rehabilitation Revolution (Ledger, 2010). The paper clarified the MOJ's plans for 'organisational bifurcation' (Burke and Collett, 2016). In accordance with the government's localism agenda, Probation Trusts, retaining some key functions, would act as commissioners of day-to-day probation work at a local level, rather than the default deliverers of services (Garside and Silvestri, 2013: 12–13). The service would be separated into two distinct parts, 'deep' and 'shallow', with the public service retaining responsibility for 'deep end' offenders (the highest risk of harm), leaving non–public sector providers to cherry-pick services for 'shallow end' offenders (lowest risk of harm) (Cavadino and Dignan: 2007: 252–3). Although the proposals offered the prospect of a greater role for the voluntary and not-for-profit sector, the appeal to multinational companies to bid for 'safe' interventions on a 'bulk basis' (Ledger, 2010), leaving the public service to manage the rump of cases that posed the greatest risk to the public and, by implication, the organisation's reputation, was self-evident.

The privatisation of Community Payback

In July 2012, the MOJ announced the partial privatisation of Community Payback (formerly Community Service). A four year contract worth £37m, involving 15,000 offenders, was awarded to a partnership between the London Probation Trust and Serco—one of the government's 'big four' providers (NAO, 2013). The scheme, intended to save nearly 40%, was promoted as a 'real game changer; making the payback real, driving innovation and value through the criminal justice system' (Travis, 2012). Nonetheless, in the event, in the face of claims and counterclaims about the way that the specific contract had been delivered (*Newsnight* reported claims of insufficient projects and staff, and Munro, the London Probation Trust Chief Executive, dismissed the proposed savings as 'pure fantasy' [White,

2016: 191–192]), the MOJ, in a press release (about the awarding of TR contracts) footnote, smuggled in the announcement that the contract to Serco would be terminated by the end of the year.

Transforming Rehabilitation: the Grayling years

In September 2012, a new ministerial team was appointed. Following a debacle over comments about rape, Clarke was replaced by Grayling, a dogmatic freemarketeer on a mission, who had come hot foot from the Department of Work and Pension, where he had established his privatisation credentials by introducing black box contracts and PbR (Teague, 2013). Impervious to expertise, evidence or reasoned counterargument, Grayling, a man unsuited to a role that demanded an 'instinctive' understanding of the law (Rozenberg, 2012), a man for whom 'reshaping all aspects of the criminal justice system along market lines' was the primary driver of penal policy (Nellis, 2017: 4), outlined his plans to import key features of the highly criticised Work Programme into Probation, accelerating both the intensity and pace of reform.

On 9 January 2013, the Ministry launched another consultation, *Transforming Rehabilitation: A Revolution in the Way We Manage Offenders* (NAO, 2014: 19). Retaining key features of *Breaking the Cycle*, the paper espoused an 'ambitious programme of social change, at a time of financial constraint' (MOJ, 2013a: 5), which was more far reaching than Clarke's more cautious, incremental approach. Where Clarke's strategy was predicated on 'testing and piloting the greater involvement of both the private and voluntary sector' (Hedderman and Murphy, 2015: 218) and rolling out the new measures over several years, Grayling, fearful that piloting could delay implementation until after the general election, when an incoming administration might reverse his plans (Burke and Collett, 2016), abandoned piloting in favour of 'expanding the use of PbR . . . more widely across England and Wales' (Chambers, 2013: 10). Additionally, in a bid to create a market for the delivery of probation services, he announced his intention to press ahead with splitting the service, creating a new delivery structure in which private companies would be primary providers and the not-for-profit sector would be relegated to junior subcontracted partners (Hedderman and Murphy, 2015: 218). The radical plans would shrink the public service by three quarters, constituting 'probably the most ambitious outsourcing programme that the Government had ever embarked on' (Tom Gash, Director of Research, Institute for Government in oral evidence to HOC, Justice Committee, 2013 as reported in Parliament, UK 2014).

Focusing on reconviction rates and the resettlement needs of post-release offenders, the deeply misleading paper portrayed the Probation Service as a failing service. Despite distinguishing the higher rates of reoffending among those for whom the Probation Service had neither statutory responsibility nor funding (i.e. a 57.5% reconviction rate for those serving 12 months or less) from the lower rates of those serving a sentence of more than 12 months released on licence supervision (35.9%), in a slight of hand, the figures were conflated, holding the Probation

Service responsible for the reoffending of both groups: 'despite significant increases in spending on probation under the previous government, almost half of those released from prison still go onto reoffend within 12 months' (MOJ, 2013a: 8). To remedy the discrepancy in reconviction rates and associated post-release service provision, Grayling proposed extending 'the support that a good Probation Service offers to offenders serving short sentences' (*The Guardian*, 2016) through the introduction of post-release licence arrangements for post 21 year olds, as part of his flagship Through the Gate initiative, increasing the numbers supervised by an estimated 50,000.

In the context of the government's public finance reduction programme (the MOJ was expected 'to deliver annual savings of over £2 billion by 2014–15 and a further 10% between 2014–15 and 2015–2016) (NOA, 2014: 22), outsourcing and PbR would provide the solution of doing 'more for less'. Reversing Clarke's localism agenda, Probation Trusts with knowledge of local needs and resources would be disbanded, and the MOJ would assume the role of the centralised, national commissioner of services: a procurement arrangement deemed better suited to the creation of a market that would attract the interest of big business.

Transforming Rehabilitation: the consultation phase

In response to the consultation, there was a flurry of submissions as penal reformers and other stakeholders responded. Although some respondents (e.g. the Prison Reform Trust) supported the comprehensive plans to reform the punishment, rehabilitation and sentencing of offenders outlined in *Breaking the Cycle* (PRT, 2011), and 'welcomed with caveats' extending support to a cohort whose needs 'had been neglected for too long' (PRT, 2011: 1), there was considerable opposition to the new delivery model (MOJ, 2013b). Despite government claims to the contrary, there was considerable critical concern that a system that was working well was being dismantled for ideological and financial, rather than penal reasons.

In July 2013 the House of Commons Select Justice Committee convened to scrutinise the plans. In submissions, witness after witness expressed concerns about 'the scale, the architecture, the details and the pace at which they were seeking to implement them' (HOC, Justice Committee, 2014: 3), challenging the evidence base for outsourcing of the majority of probation work. Ian Lawrence, General Secretary of NAPO, characterised the reforms as, 'a recipe for disaster. They pose a massive risk to public safety, and are untried, untested and in our view ideologically flawed'... 'destroying what works to put in place an experiment'. Similarly, probation chief representatives argued that '[the] high performing Probation Trust structure would be replaced by a system that is untested and where there is no evidence that it will perform better or deliver efficiencies as intentioned', and the Magistrates' Association observed, 'We have no evidence that anything [that is proposed] will work'.

In May 2014, the Public Accounts' Committee, reinforcing select committee concerns, highlighted the MOJ's poor record of procuring and managing private contracts, citing the high-profile EM debacle (HOC, Public Accounts

Committee: 2014) which had resulted in G4S and Serco being barred from TR tendering. It urged the ministry to grant the NAO full access to contractual information to prevent game playing and to enforce financial efficacy.

PbR: a blueprint for big business

Lauded by populist politicians keen to display their common sense business credentials, PbR, one of the Prime Minister's flagship policies, from its outset attracted a barrage of objections. Characterised as a 'technically challenging form of contract delivery', not suitable for all public service sectors, in common with other target-driven payment mechanisms, it over-relied on optimistic assumptions about providers' willingness and capacity to absorb risk: a willingness that was neither assured nor risk free. Posing the same risks associated with other 'outsourcing models, plus new specific ones related to their particular funding payment mechanism and contract structure' (Whitefield, 2012: 22), the delivery model was particularly vulnerable to 'game playing', manipulation and distortion, and required the creation and administration of robust systems to accurately measure and attribute outputs and outcomes.

Viewed as a 'highly punitive and politicised area of social policy' (Gough, 2012: 20), TR was a contentious proposal that posed ethical dilemmas both within and outside the voluntary sector. Whilst there was wide agreement that the voluntary sector would add value to the penal system, few believed that small charities would 'be in a position to compete for the new contracts'. The ministerial view that mainstreaming the voluntary sector and subjecting it to competition was the inevitable 'evolutionary journey' (Whitten, 2010) was derided. With smaller and more specialist providers particularly vulnerable to cash flow uncertainty, there was concern that the deferment of payment that underpinned the funding arrangements would place smaller providers at considerable financial disadvantage. The model, ill suited to the creation of 'a greater diversification of providers' (Fox and Alberterson, 2012: 365), favoured bigger providers with large portfolios. With the market already dominated by an oligopoly of providers, some of whom were under investigation for fraud over their previous dealings with the Ministry of Justice (Syal, 2014), the scheme looked set to further concentrate their power (HOC, Justice Committee, 2014). In the anticipated race to the bottom, the voluntary sector, which many feared would be merely 'brought in to provide a respectable veneer by the large private companies who [would] drive down costs to provide the cheapest possible' (Calder and Goodman, 2013: 178), risked becoming 'prisoners not partners' (Silvestri, 2009): unequal, minor players, dependent on the 'crumbs from the table', who would be forced to adapt 'their organisational forms, their distinctive ethos and even their goals in response to their involvement in public service delivery' (Gough, 2012: 21).

As early as 2010, Clinks, a not-for-profit organisation supporting voluntary sector providers, in a survey of the criminal justice organisation sector, pointed out that 'small VCS organisations, operating under traditional charitable governance arrangements, have neither the capacity nor the reserves' to defer payment for services delivered and warned that the funding model was 'unworkable' for most of the sector (Hayes, 2010: 8). Similarly, NCVO found that the working capital and cash flow needed to fund payments in arrears meant that providers would have to subsidise their PbR work with income from other sources, including their reserves; limit the amount of other services they could deliver; and seek loans to cover payment delays (NCVO, 2013). With only a 'handful of organisations' possessing sufficiently large incomes to deliver a 'considerable number of interventions in the criminal justice system', and only 17% of the small and 24% of the medium-sized organisations confident that they would benefit (CSJ, 2013: 9), the voluntary sector designated PbR 'flavour of the month', rather than a viable funding mechanism.

In 2019, the NAO reported that supply chains to CRCs had not been developed as planned, primarily due to financial considerations. Although two of the larger VSOs partnered with CRCs and one formed a consortium, the promise to open up the market to a diverse range of providers has been broken. By October 2018, just 11% of VSOs were providing services directly to CRCs, and those, as predicted, were in an 'unsustainable position', reliant on their own finances to fund the provision of services. Faced with the NAO's criticisms, the MOJ has little option but to accept that the rehabilitation market remained immature, and its ambition for greater third-sector involvement had not been realised (NAO, 2019).

Gaming the system: creaming and parking

Although promoted as a means of incentivising innovation, with some offenders easier to help than others and the costs of securing the desired outcome (one that would trigger a payment) unevenly distributed across different cohorts of offenders, the application of PbR to offender services raised the real possibility of replicating 'game playing' and perverse incentives, in particular 'creaming' and 'parking': a feature of the much-derided Work Programme, overseen by Grayling. With respondents to the PbR consultation less than impressed by the minister's track record, several highlighted the risk that new providers, analysing the costs/benefits, would cherry-pick 'dead certs' (House of Lords, 2013), thereby targeting resources towards the motivated and compliant with lower social needs and fewer barriers to 'going straight'—a cohort who would to be easier and cheaper to manage and more likely to release outcome payments (a process known as creaming), at the expense of the 'dead losses', the chaotic with high social needs and more substantial barriers to desistance who would be relatively unlikely to cease offending—a cohort more difficult and expensive to manage and less likely to deliver the desired outcome payment (a process known as parking) (Carter and Whitworth, 2015). Alternatively, there was a risk that providers would largely ignore the PbR component of the payment mechanism and 'maximise their profit margin on the attachment fee[2] alone by cutting costs as far as possible' (NAO, 2015: 27): with an 'eye on the prize', the focus would be on 'quick wins' rather than sustainability.

Measuring and attributing performance

Finally, with PbR bedevilled by the complexities of measuring and attributing success to specific interventions, critics warned that PbR ran the risk of organisations making claims and receiving payments for outcomes that would have happened anyway, or were either partially or wholly attributable to outputs from other organisations. As desistance literature attests, the reasons individuals go straight are contested: establishing a precise causal link between an input and an outcome is not straightforward. There is no silver bullet solution:

> a range of factors are associated with the ending of active involvement in offending: most of these factors are related to lifecycle changes, acquiring 'something' (most commonly employment, a life partner or a family) which the desister values in some way and which initiates a re-evaluation of his or her life, and for some a sense of who they 'are'.

With growing up and growing out of crime as well as environmental factors (such as the disintegration of the peer group or moving out of the area) key motivational factors in an individual's transition, it is not always clear what role, if any, intervention strategies play in shaping an individual's pathways out of crime (Farrall, written evidence to HOC, Justice Committee, 2014).

In 2011, the Howard League highlighted the problems associated with setting appropriate performance targets, and establishing accurate measurement and evaluation tools. Further, they argued that there was a risk of overlapping and duplication, with several departments making payment for the same outcome to more than one provider (Howard League for Penal Reform, 2011: 18). With this in mind, the NAO (2015) cautioned:

> It is essential that commissioners establish performance expectations at the start of a scheme, taking into account baseline performance and non-intervention rates. Commissioners should aim to define attainable but stretching performance expectations for providers that are above the non-intervention rate [the level of performance that would occur without intervention]. This avoids payment for performance that would have occurred anyway. Commissioners need good data on baseline performance, and to carry out robust modelling of likely future performance and sensitivity testing of any assumptions underpinning estimates.
> *(2015: 4)*

The splitting of the service: taking a risk with risk

Of all the concerns raised by the reforms, 'taking a risk with risk' should have been the most compelling. Organisational bifurcation and the 'inevitable fragmentation of probation work' was identified as a source of 'public risk' (Teague, 2013: 16):

> Many of our respondents have serious misgivings about how the fundamental elements of the model—the division of the management of the cases

between those deemed to represent the highest risk of harm and the less dangerous offenders—will work without jeopardising public protection.

(HOC Justice Committee, 2014)

Risk-based delivery systems are routinely exposed to problems of the uncertainties of prediction and prevention. Failure is inevitable, as 'not all risks are predictable and not all harms are preventable'; even the most robust assessment procedures and processes are not immune to the 'occasional, spectacular failures and the political costs that this entails' (McNeill, 2011: 10). Although structured risk assessment tools partially mitigate against the false negatives and positives associated with clinical judgements, they remain notoriously open to bias (Kemshall, 2008). The proposed funding model exacerbated this: inherent biases could be amplified and risk assessments distorted by financial considerations, Additionally, with risk subject to change (up to a quarter of offenders change risk classification per period of supervision), offenders could be reduced to 'parcels' passed backwards and forwards between the two agencies: a process linked to increased levels of disengagement and risk (Holt, 2000). Recognising the fluidity of risk levels and their liability to escalation, probation representatives expressed 'grave concern' that less qualified and less experienced staff in the privatised service, lacking the skills and knowledge to recognise the risk implications signified by behavioural change, and even more worryingly given the financial incentives to retain offenders (Calder and Goodman, 2013), would be reluctant to transfer cases to the public service.

Finally, with good communication sharing and information exchange between the two agencies pivotal to the management of risk fluctuation, the Probation Chiefs Association argued:

> The changing dynamics of risk of harm and case characteristics require professional and objective assessments, and continuous case management. The Government's proposals would fragment offender management, ongoing risk assessment, delivering interventions and responsibility for breach recalls across different organisations and sectors. The complexity of information exchange between new providers and the public sector would be substantial under the Government's proposed system, and this is likely to increase the risk of public protection failures.
>
> (written evidence to HOC, Justice Committee, 2014)

Reinforcing this, the Magistrates' Association warned that any diminution in sentencers' confidence if

> offenders being managed by private contractors appear in court and there appears to be any lack of communication, any lack of information on how risk was being managed or any mistrust between the private sector offender manager and the public sector official giving advice to the court

could adversely influence sentencing decisions (NAPO written evidence to HOC, Justice Committee, 2014).

Resisting the change: Save the Probation Service

Adopting the mantra 'if it ain't broke, don't fix it', trade unions and the Probation Trusts in the wake of Grayling's announcement embarked on a campaign to 'Save the Probation Service': a campaign that was supported by penal reform groups and the Magistrates Association, and was endorsed by Lord Ramsbottom, a former Chief Inspector of Prisons. Whilst some placed their trust solely in the persuasive power of government reports and inquiries, research by penal reformers and academics and reasoned argument, others adopted more activist measures to turn the tide of reform. Nonetheless, in spite of trade union campaigns, strike action and an attempted judicial review (dropped in 2014); the lobbying of MPs by stakeholders and interest groups; the publication of a positive report on the performance by HMI Probation (highlighted in the NAO report of 2013); and the leaking to the media in June 2013 of a 'restricted' internal 'code black' risk report[3] (Travis, 2013: NAPO, nd: 1), the privatisation juggernaut was unstoppable.

Grayling's choice of the Probation Service as the 'soft' target for his most ambitious privatisation programme was no accident. A small, largely invisible agency with little public support and even less political bargaining power, 'probation [,] . . . neither well understood nor highly regarded by the general public' (Hedderman and Murphy, 2015: 217), was uniquely vulnerable. Overshadowed by police, prisons and courts, the Probation Service has historically failed to attract media attention and has suffered the distortion caused by the selective, sensational reporting of atypical 'bad news' cases. Lacking the 'media savvy' to mount a defence of its actions, the Probation Service has all too often been cast in the role of the scapegoat: the naïve, idealistic 'do-gooder' who puts the offender before the victim and, like the gullible Barraclough in the sitcom *Porridge*, is easily outsmarted by those whom he is tasked to manage.

During the TR consultation and scrutiny period, '[n]either the TR strategy nor the concerns raised by commentators seemed to generate much media interest' (Hedderman and Murphy, 2015: 219). In 2013 only 24 newspaper articles (23 were in broadsheets) explicitly mentioned TR, with some aspects of the proposals (e.g. outsourcing) given more coverage than others. Coverage centred primarily on the extension of supervision to short-term prisoners and the new funding arrangements in 'ways that supported the Government's agenda to increase the role of the private sector without a principled defence of public probation provision to counterbalance this' (Burke and Collett, 2016: 127). Whilst Harry Fletcher, the NAPO spokesperson featured on three occasions in articles defending the service's performance record, and Ian Lawrence, NAPO general secretary, was quoted once in relation to probation strike action, neither the Probation Chief Association nor the Probation Board were 'quoted any stage'. Indeed, when the issue of performance was raised, even the more liberal wings of the press uncritically parroted the government's claims that the service was failing prisoners.

The problem of presenting an alternative narrative was compounded by a staff embargo on talking to the mainstream media or social media to express their opposition. In early 2013, Grayling announced that staff social taking to social media to express opposition risked disciplinary action:

> The order included 'any comments that are made in criticism or designed to undermine the justice secretary's policy or actions', and even warned that retweeting others' comments would be taken as 'incitement or approval'.
> *(White, 2016: 191)*

With probation staff gagged, a lack of pre-existing public appetite for the subject matter and coverage of the reforms concentrated in the hands of three specialist 'crime and criminal justice matters' correspondents, reporting was partial and limited. Editors, unconvinced that the casual reader would 'be prepared to devote attention to the nitty-gritty of a set of radical reforms proposals', chose simply to ignore it (Hedderman and Murphy, 2015: 229).

Whilst blaming the lack of media coverage and a publicly mounted defence for the 'unquestioning acceptance of the dismantling of the national public service' (2015: 218) would be an exaggeration, it is self-evident that the government faced no major obstacles and, unencumbered by the public outcry and the calls for politically embarrassing U-turn, features of other reform measures, was able to act with relative impunity.

Transforming Rehabilitation: the implementation phase

Once set on its policy course, the pace of implementation was breathtaking. The scheme was 'rushed through' in a 'frantic attempt to put ideology into action before an electoral deadline, rather than any considered response to reoffending' (White, 2016: 102). In May 2013, the MOJ published its final proposals, and by September of the same year, the process of putting low–medium risk work out to 'a race to the bottom' price-competitive tender process began (Harper, 2013: 39). With privatisation attracting considerable international commercial interest, particularly from corporations with US links, in December 2013, the MOJ announced that it was in formal discussions with 30 bidders from large multinational corporations to local Probation Service Mutuals (G4S and Serco were banned from tendering following the tagging scandal). In January 2014, the MOJ made a further announcement that Probation Trusts would be disbanded at the end of May 2014, and that shadow arrangements involving the creation of 21 community rehabilitation companies would be established in preparation for complete takeover by successful bidders in 2015.

The process, marked by a risky and unseemly haste to put in place contracts which would effectively tie the hands of any incoming government by 'reducing the ability to choose an alternative route' (White, 2016: 106), tied the MOJ into tenyear funding arrangements with penalties of between £300 million and £400 million for early termination (Travis and Syal, 2014). As services rolled out the new arrangements, the 17, 000 probation staff, most of whom expressed a preference to remain in the NPS, in order to retain terms and conditions of employment as well as clearer career progression and job security, were 'forcibly' transferred to private CRCs (Napo and Unison, 2014: 2) on an arbitrary 'lottery system' of literally 'drawing names from a hat' (Dunt, 2014).

In October 2014, with many of the original expressions of interest having failed to produce substantive submissions, successful bidders were announced. Confirming fears that the funding system favoured 'big business' (Harper, 2013: 39), nearly two thirds of the contracts were awarded to three companies: Interserve, a UK-based, multi-national support service and construction industry with American subsidiaries (five contracts); MTCNovo, an America-based management training company (two contracts); and Sodexo Justice Services, a multi-national French/American conglomerate (six contracts). Despite £10 million being made available to support the establishment of staff mutuals, only one (Durham and Tees) was successful in the bidding process. With promises that the voluntary and mutual sector would head up the new arrangements exposed as a smokescreen (MOJ, 2014), Frances Crook of the Howard League observed:

> As we expected, the big winner of the probation sell off is not the voluntary sector but large private companies run for profit. The Ministry of Justice will claim it has created a diverse market, but Sodexo and Interserve are the companies running half of all the contracts. A public service is being destroyed without any evidence that the fragmented landscape created will perform any better or help make communities any safer.
>
> *(Strickland, 2016: 5)*

Although charities featured heavily in the initial bids, the financial constraints, as predicted, disadvantaged charities and not-for-profit organisations. Unless they entered into subcontracting arrangements with a private provider, 'assuming the role of '"bid candy, used as window dressing by big corporates keen to buff their bid credentials' (Butler, 2011), they were effectively excluded from the procurement process. Seeking to deflect attention from its preference for less risk-averse, large multi-national providers, the MOJ 'oversold' the prospects for them winning primary contractors. Consequently, 'the time and resources they had used to participate in the competition were not well spent' (NAO, 2016: 18). Relegated to the position of Tier 2 and Tier 3 subcontractors, charities, the poor relation in the private sector/not-for-profit marriage, were from the outset exposed to uncertainty and instability in funding (NAO, 2016), arising from the prospect of receiving either insufficient of 'hard to reach' referrals (Taylor, 2012; Williams, 2012). As many had foreseen, only the larger national charities made it through the bidding process and even when they did some partnerships were short lived. In the event, with cash flow from the lead partner to the subcontracted charity an inevitable source of conflict, Addactions withdrew from their partnership with Interserve even before the ink was dry.

Black box procurement: cheaper not better services

On 1 February, 2015 the CRCs, which had operated from June 2014 under the auspices of the public sector, were transferred to commercial providers. With the imposition of 'black box' contracts (a key feature of Grayling's DWP Work Programme), which removed the requirement to enforce national standards for delivery, the CRCs were given *carte blanche* to deliver what they wanted, when they wanted and how they wanted (HOC Justice Committee, 2018). Within weeks, the largest single provider, Sodexo, taking advantage of this operational freedom, embraced the 'economies of the presence' offered by new variants of EM. Replacing costly human labour with biometric reporting machines, they curtailed face-to-face contact in favour of fingerprint recognition: a move condemned as 'dangerous' by trade unionists (NAPO News, 2015: 2).

With contractors free to pursue profit by whatever means they chose, new providers wasted no time in squeezing out the maximum profit by reducing costs. These included: 'offering jobs at lower rates than qualified probation staff' (White, 2016: 107); creating a 'two-tier workforce which over time effectively undermines the pay and job security of those who may have devoted years, even decades, of service to the public sector' (The Trade Union Co-Ordinating Group, 2013: 5); reducing staff numbers (Sodexo announced its intentions to cut staff by 436 across the six regions, with Northumbria alone facing a loss of 106 staff—a reduction amounting to one third of the workforce); reneging on 'agreed Enhanced Voluntary Redundancy terms' set out in staff transfer agreements (NAPO and Unison, 2015: 2); and introducing 'agile working' arrangements, which diminished both service provision to offenders and work conditions of employees (local offices were closed in favour of centralised delivery hubs where offenders waited for vacant interview rooms and staff searched for desks) (McDermott, 2016).

Whilst MOJ heralded its flagship enterprise as a 'success', within months of the transfer, the widely anticipated cracks were appearing. Within months (December 2015) the CRCs were facing serious funding difficulties amid claims that the MOJ's overestimation of the volume of cases (confirmed by the NAO in 2016) amounted to a 'dodgy dossier'. Although the MOJ, in its defence, maintained that it had offered no guarantees of numbers and that the CRCs had, in any case, agreed to absorb the risks, it did accept that the scale of the reduction in the volume and rate of new cases allocated had not been foreseen. At the end of 2015, in the face of CRCs' request for additional funding, the MOJ, aware of the political implications of CRCs underperforming or defaulting, and under a 'contractual obligation to act "reasonably and proportionately" when considering representations from CRCs about factors that they could not have foreseen or mitigated', entered into commercially sensitive, negotiations to revise the funding format (2016: 43).

As doubts about financial viability gained momentum, rumours of CRCs activating the break clause to extricate themselves from or being forced to terminate contracts for failure to deliver were rife, leading to speculation that one of the larger providers was poised to mop up the vacated contracts. At the end of December 2015, the *Independent* reported that Sodexo run South Yorkshire CRC, following an MOJ audit, had been placed into 'special remedial measures'. The audit, identifying 'serious gaps in obtaining domestic abuse and safeguarding information at the start and throughout the sentence', drew attention to 'shortcomings' in recording information, incorrectly recorded appointment dates, the lack of 'proactive and systematic quality assurance', and 'an absence of regular supervision and team meetings' (*Probation Matters*, 2015a). In the same month, NAPO announced that several CRCs were underperforming and had received hefty fines for failing to meet targets (*Probation Matters*, 2015b). With the precedent of failing private enterprises being returned to the public sector set by the prisons, the possibility of returning CRCs' workloads to the public was an ever present risk: a risk compounded by the rapidly diminishing NPS infrastructure and 'the residue of the NPS [which] is 'too small and [has] . . . too few qualified staff to be able to reembrace the workloads' (Fitzgibbon, 2013: 88).

Reports, inspections and investigations

From its inception, TR was the subject of excoriating reports from NAO and HM Inspectorate, as well as the subject of investigations by the PAC and the Justice Select Committee. In the period 2014–2016, HMIP published five reports on the early implementation of TR, which highlighted significant operational problems. These included: problems with risk assessment tools, leading to inaccuracies in risk assessments and incorrect allocations, as well as 'significant operational and information sharing concerns across the boundaries of the National Probation Service and Community Rehabilitation Companies' exacerbated by cumbersome and inefficient IT systems (HMI Probation, 2015: 4). In May 2016, HMI Probation released its final progress report, which, despite acknowledging that progress had been made, identified outstanding problems in terms of high NPS caseloads, staff training and morale, and pre-release prison preparation (HMI Probation, 2016a: 4). Additionally, the report identified instances of unacceptable financially driven practices by CRC staff:

> One responsible officer told us that while they: 'believed good enforcement leads to good compliance', their organisation's approach was to discourage enforcing orders or licences. Enforcement was the interface issue we heard about that was still seen as the most problematic some eighteen months after Transforming Rehabilitation. A number of responsible officers said that they had been told not to recommend 'revoke and resentence', because it would lead to a financial penalty for the CRC.
>
> *(HMI Probation, 2016a: 20)*

Cracks in the funding model

In April 2016, the NAO published the first of a series NAO critical reports, which laid bare the anticipated problems associated with funding arrangements. Focusing on the much-trumpeted PbR element of the funding, the report revealed that the MOJ had been forced to claw back its PbR plans by limiting the weight to 10% of total income and expanding the fee for service elements. Furthermore, the payment for reducing reoffending had been rescinded, being replaced by the more easily achievable and measurable successful completion of court orders.

A further report in 2018 by the NAO revealed that the MOJ, faced with the prospect of CRCs defaulting on their contracts, had acknowledged that 'contracts were not working as intended' (Parliament UK, 2018) and had adjusted them to 'reflect more accurately the cost of providing critical frontline services' (NAO, 2018: 6). Nonetheless, despite bailing the CRCs out with an additional £42 million in 2016–2017 and £22 million in 2017–2018, at a total cost of £342 million (NAO, 2018: 4), the report identified that most CRCs were running at a loss. It anticipated that 14 out of the 21 CRCs would make losses ranging from £2.3m to £43m by 2021.

In the same year, MPs were informed by the Public Accounts Select Committee that CRCs were faced with more than £100m in total losses (Travis, 2018). With CRCs 'tottering from one financial crisis to another' (Crew, 2019), on 15 February 2019, coinciding with the HMIP's publication of a damning inspection report on one of its contract areas, Working Links, the provider of services to three of the Probation Service areas, went into administration. At the point of its collapse, the company, which in a bid to stay afloat had been bought out two years earlier by Aurelius (NAPO, 2019), recorded final year losses of £2.1m (Rees, 2019). If this was not sufficient evidence of the dire financial straits of the CRC, within weeks, Interserve, the second largest provider of private probation contracts, collapsed. In the face of the irrefutable truth, the Minister of Justice reluctantly accepted that PbR was 'flawed' (BBC News, 2019 February, 16th).

Through the Gate

On 26 September 2016 the HOC PAC scrutinising the TR programme concluded that the MOJ had failed to deliver the promised Rehabilitation Revolution. Stating that lack of data transparency hindering its ability to fully assess whether the extension of supervision to short-term prisoners was having the 'desired effect', it nonetheless highlighted concerns that extending the licence would increase the numbers recalled to prison for failing to comply: an outcome it described as 'poor for offenders, the prison service and society' (HOC Public Accounts Committee, 2016: 6). Indeed, as forewarned, with the imposition of short-term licences, the number of recalls has 'skyrocketed'. Between January 2015 and September 2018, as a percentage of overall recalled prison population, recalls of short-term prisoners increased from 3% to 36% (NAO, 2019). In the 12 months up to September 2018, the number of recalls exceeded 8,000 (MOJ, 2019). In response to these figures, the PRT reminded the government had it been warned about the risks of extending mandatory supervision and opined that it had 'set offenders up to fail' (Bulman, 2019).

In October 2016 HMI Probation published the first of two independent joint thematic reports, with HMI Prisons scrutinising the government's flagship 'Through the Gate' programme.[4] The report, which superseded a highly critical thematic inspection by HMIP on women offenders and TR (2016b), whilst recognising the challenges posed by the programme's ambitious aims to provide services to an estimated 50,000 additional service users per year, concluded that the CRCs' determination to do the 'best possible job' was 'pedestrian at best' (HMI Probation and HMI Prisons, 2016: 3). Cataloguing the CRCs' failure to meet the objectives set out in the NOMS' (2015b) vision, the report found that resettlement needs were frequently neither recognised nor met (2016b: 28). In terms of innovation (a central plank of the coalition government's privatisation rationale), the report identified that not only had many of the promising new services proposed in the bids not been implemented, but also that those services that were provided failed to take 'into account research about what might help repeat offenders stop offending' (2016b: 47).

In June 2017, a second 'damning report' (Howard League for Penal Reform, 2017) based on the inspection of nine resettlement prisons and 98 cases was published. The report found that CRCS were doing little or nothing to practically improve the lives of prisoners but rather, in order to comply with the letter rather than the spirit of contractual targets, were focusing on the production of written resettlement plans. With 'good, persistent work' neither incentivised nor rewarded sufficiently, no prisoners had been helped to get education, training or a job on release; only two were found accommodation; and only one had been linked to a mentor. Concluding that the overall picture of service deliver was so 'bleak' that if the coalition government's flagship 'Through the Gate services were removed tomorrow . . . the impact on the resettlement of prisoners would be negligible', the report stated:

> None of the early hopes for Through the Gate have been realised. The gap between aspiration and reality is so great, that we wonder whether there is any prospect that these services will deliver the desired impact on rates of reoffending.
>
> *(2017: 3)*

In September 2017, speaking at the Criminal Justice Management Conference, Stacey, the Chief Inspector of Probation, summed up:

> Probation reform has not delivered the benefits that Transforming Rehabilitation promised, so far. We rarely see the innovations expected to come with freeing up the market, and instead proposed new models, new ways of

delivering probation services on the ground and supporting them with better IT systems have largely stalled. The voluntary and charitable sectors are much less engaged than the government envisaged. Promised improvements in Through the Gate resettlement—mentors, real help with accommodation, education, training and employment for short sentence prisoners—have mostly not been delivered in any meaningful way.

(Stacey, 2017)

Underperformance

With growing evidence of a widening schism between political hyperbole, hubris and on-the-ground deliverable achievements, the HOC Justice Committee announced in October 2017 that it was launching an inquiry into the Government's Transforming Rehabilitation Programme. Its terms of reference included: contractual, financial and administrative changes to CRCs in July 2017; best practice in monitoring performance; and measures for improving service delivery to provide effective rehabilitation (HOC, Justice Committee, 2017). Pre-empting the findings of the inquiry on 14 June 2018, the Minister of Justice, failing Grayling, announced plans to terminate CRC contracts in 2020, two years early, despite the insertion of financial penalty clauses into the contracts aimed to prevent this. Under the plans, the 21 contracts would be reduced to about 14 and new tenders issued to 'run the bigger probation areas'. With returning the service to the public unlikely but not ruled out, the MOJ said, 'all options remain on the table' (Ford, 2018).

Later the same year, after 18 months of evidence gathering, the Justice Committee finally delivered its verdict. Adding its endorsement to the earlier findings of NAO, PAC and HMI Prison and Probation, the committee concluded that rather than delivering any of the hyped-up benefits (e.g. improved and innovative services, opening up the Probation market to the voluntary sector, reducing reoffending) that Grayling, in his haste to privatise, had promised, the initiative had been a failure. Impervious to those who had from the outset cautioned against the proposed structure and payment framework, Grayling's pursuit of privatisation had prioritised 'ideology rather than evidence' (*The Guardian*, 2018).

With the procurement process handing private companies the freedom to provide whatever service 'in any way that they wanted' as long as it reduced reoffending (HOC, Justice Committee, 2018: 16) and penalties for poor performance not applied as envisaged, the committee identified numerous examples of poor performance (some of which could be attributed to cost cutting). These included: signposting rather than providing services to offenders on release from custody (offenders were given a leaflet), replacing face-to-face meetings with irregular telephone or kiosk contacts (examples of creaming and parking operational systems), and failing to provide a sufficient quality or quantity of unpaid work placements (some offenders were moving dirt from one pile to another). The report also highlighted the design flaw in the system which, allocating offenders on the basis of risk, had paid little/no heed to experts who had warned that risk fluctuates and can escalate quickly.

With none of the underpinning TR aims or objectives achieved by privatisation, and all of the predicted risks fulfilled, the committee concluded:

> On the longer-term future of the TR reformed . . . we are unconvinced that the TR model can ever deliver an effective or viable Probation Service. We recommend that the Ministry of Justice initiate a review into the long-term future and sustainability of delivering the Probation Service under the models introduced by the TR reforms, including how performance under the TR system, might compare to an alternative system for delivering Probation.
> *(HOC Justice Committee, 2018: 6)*

In February 2019, following a series of negative inspection reports which led Stacey to conclude that the flawed system had produced performance under contract that was 'substandard, and much of it demonstrably poor' (HMIP, 2019a), the HMIP published its excoriating findings on the performance of Dorset, Devon and Cornwall run by Working Links. The report, which exemplified the inherent risks in Grayling's ideologically driven initiative, rated the service 'inadequate' (the lowest possible rating). With the service 'trapped in a spiral of decline' in which '(t)he imperative to meet task-related contractual performance targets' dominated 'working life' (HMIP, 2019b: 12), a series of perverse incentives had been created: targets were met but meaningful practice was compromised, often dangerously so. With avoiding financial penalties incurred by failing to meet contract compliant performance targets driving service delivery, not only did inspectors find that staff were gaming the system by writing sentence plans without meeting the offender, but even more alarmingly, in order to avoid the loss of income that offenders generated, struggling with 'unmanageable' workloads (staffing had been cut by a third since 2015) and bombarded with IT generated target reminders, staff had adopted the highly dangerous practice, associated with a 'litany of high profile serious further offences' including murder (Rees, 2019), of downgrading risk to retain offenders (HMIP, 2019b). In a press release following the company's collapse, Stacey, underlining the risks associated with providers prioritising profits over people, observed that 'the ethos of Probation has buckled under the strain of commercial interest' (HMIP, 2019b).

The following month, the NAO (2019) published its own report on value for money and performance. Criticising the additional cost incurred by ending the contracts early, a total of £467 million more (including previous bailouts) than originally stipulated in the contracts, it concluded:

> The Ministry set itself up to fail in how it approached the Transforming Rehabilitation reforms. Its rushed implementation introduced significant risks that its chosen commercial approach left it badly placed to manage. The consequences of these decisions are far reaching. CRCs have underinvested

in probation services, which have suffered as a result. There is little evidence of hoped for innovation and many of the early operational issues, such as friction between the NPS and CRCs, persist. Although the number of reoffenders has reduced, the average number of reoffences they commit has increased significantly. Transforming Rehabilitation has achieved poor value for money for the taxpayer.

(NAO, 2019: 10)

Strengthening Probation, Building Confidence: throwing good money after bad

In response to the HOC Justice Committee report, in July 2018, the MOJ published the *Strengthening Probation, Building Confidence* consultation paper (MOJ, 2018). With existing contracts due to be terminated two years early in 2020 on the basis of their poor performance, the paper set out the government's future vision for the delivery of offender management services. The paper clarified that although the MOJ proposed reforming the procurement process (abandoning black box contracts), the funding formula (with a greater emphasis on the payment for services delivered rather than PbR) and the delivery of contracts (reintroducing minimum standards) and aligning CRCs and the regional NPS, reducing the number of CRCs from 21 to 11, bringing services back in house, with the exception of Wales, was not envisaged. With 'privatisation hardwired into conservative thinking' (Allen, 2018), the paper represented a relaunch, with the government reiterating its commitment to the 'mixed market approach, with scope for a range of providers, including in the voluntary sector, to continue to bring fresh, innovative ideas to probation services' (MOJ, 2018: 3).

Although the MOJ tried to limit the scope of the consultation, contributors seized the opportunity to push against the constraints by promoting the case for returning the service to the public, arguing, amongst other things, that: '(t)he mess created by the public/private split of probation (which) was foreseeable and foreseen' would not be resolved by the proposed TR2 (Howard League, 2018); that continuing to reward underperforming private companies was 'throwing good money after bad' (Howard League, 2018); and that it was incumbent upon ministers to provide 'a probation service that prioritises keeping the public safety rather than boosting the profits of private companies' (Crew, 2019).

Although the MOJ did not consult directly on the split of functions between the NPS and CRC, in the event, on 16 May 2019, with 40% of all respondents expressing 'a preference for the integration of offender management functions under the NPS' (2019: 10), the government published its consultation response, in which, contrary to its original proposals, it outlined its plans to bring all offender management back in house. With the NPS, the provider of last resort, effectively bailing the private sector out, under the revised structural arrangements, privatisation would be partially retained through public/private partnerships. In a face-saving bid to prevent the private sector vacating the criminal justice sector, private companies, despite their appalling record of delivery of TR, would be 'rewarded' with lucrative contracts worth £280 million per year to deliver key elements of sentence plans: unpaid work, accredited programmes and rehabilitative and resettlement programmes. Underlining the government's unswerving commitment to the privatisation ideal, the paper, despite a plethora of evidence to the contrary, stated:

> We are clear that there is a continued role for the private and voluntary sector in the delivery of probation services and welcome the benefits of innovation and effective delivery that this can bring.
>
> *(MOJ, 2019: 22)*

With government plans to put contracts out to competitive tendering, the proposed revision paved the way for yet another disastrous 'race to the bottom' of underbidding and over claiming, within which a new oligopoly of 'too big to fail' providers would emerge, with smaller companies, such as the one mutual CRC, being pushed aside by the bigger providers and disgraced outsourcing giants Serco and G4S (barred from bidding for the original contracts) being allowed to return to the contracting fold. Furthermore, with the MOJ held hostage by the small range of potential bidders and the lure of economies of scale, the procurement plans left open the prospect that Sodexo, the company with the largest share of contracts, which had been repeatedly named and shamed in government reports, rather than being penalised for its failures, would be rewarded with an enlarged sphere of operations.

Boris Johnson and the renationalisation of the Probation Service

In July 2019, Boris Johnson replaced Theresa May as leader of the Conservative Party and Prime Minister. Faced with a stalled Brexit, he called a snap election in December of the same year, and, having mounted a highly successful 'Get Brexit Done' campaign, was returned with a majority exceeding 80. The following year in June 2020, with attention turned to the COVID-19 pandemic, the Lord Chancellor, in a thinly disguised face-saving gesture, sidestepped the series of excoriating reports from Parliamentary committees and watchdogs, which highlighted poor performance and poor value for money, by announcing that the changed pragmatic and financial priorities of the COVID-19 crisis (rather than evidence and lobbying) had forced the MOJ to 'reassess' its 2019 plans. Brushing aside the crushing indictment of the privatisation of probation, the minister explained that the tendering process had been halted, and all core functions of offender services (to now include unpaid work as well as offender programmes) would be returned to the public sector (MOJ, 2020). What is more, with a reduced role for the private sector, the

Minister of Justice in his address to the House of Lords in May 2019 sought to reassure its members of its renewed commitment to the voluntary sector:

> My Lords, voluntary organisations play an important role in helping offenders turn their lives around. We are determined to strengthen this role. In May, the Government set out our plans for future Probation arrangements, including that the National Probation Service will directly commission specialist and voluntary sector organisations to deliver rehabilitation services. We are engaging closely with voluntary sector providers to ensure that our arrangements maximise their potential engagement.
>
> *(Hansard, 2019: n.p.)*

Mandated to turn around a complex, understaffed, fragmented service, HM Chief Inspector of Probation cautioned that, whilst welcome, renationalisation was 'not a magic bullet' that would reverse years of failure to deliver quality services to offenders:

> The *Transforming Rehabilitation* reforms have severely tested the Probation Service over the past five years. Fundamental flaws in the original design of the contracts, particularly the payment by results mechanism, have starved Community Rehabilitation Companies (CRCs) of essential funding. This has had a significant impact on the quality of supervision many CRCs have been able to deliver . . . The Probation Service must be properly funded. The quality of probation supervision will not improve merely by lifting and shifting large volumes of cases from CRCs back into the NPS next year. Vacancies for probation officers must be filled and staff properly trained for their new responsibilities.
>
> *(HMI Probation, 2020)*

With penal reformers eager to distance themselves from the government's smoke and mirrors obfuscation, one commentator eloquently summed up the humiliating U-turn:

> So, it had nothing to do with evidence, reason or argument—it was the bloody virus that 'did' for privatisation—'too complicated' what with Covid-19.
>
> *(Webster, 2020)*

Conclusion

The Probation Service, which prior to 2010 had weathered the battering of one 'reform' after another, paid a heavy price for successive governments 'driven by the obsession with freemarket principles and the belief that every department of national life can be turned into a money-spinner' (Leftly, 2015). Whilst it is axiomatic that the Grayling 'reforms' did not constitute privatisation in its purest form, as the State retained responsibility 'for setting up the new apparatus for the operation and delivery of probation services and . . . retain(ed) a role in the governance of the CRCs' (Kirton and Guillaume, 2015: 6), the outsourcing of nearly three quarters of publicly delivered offender services to private suppliers represented the most extreme example of creeping marketisation and privatisation, in its widest sense, in any aspect of public service.

In a climate of austerity and MOJ expenditure cuts (the largest of all Whitehall departments), 'the rush to marketise public services' reduced offenders to mere commodities that could be sold to the cheapest bidders (Senior, 2013: 1). With outcome-based delivery at the heart of the funding scheme (PbR), an 'array of adverse consequences' were created in which offenders, commodified as financial assets, were 'removed from the epicentre of their programme and replaced by a series of bureaucratic processes that bear no positive effect upon their journey' to cease offending (Gosling, 2016: 149).

As public probation was residualised, the bulk of probation provision was transformed by profit-driven corporations. Staff morale fell; large-scale, damaging staff resignations depleted the service of experienced practitioners (NAPO and Unison, 2014); and services became reliant on costly agency staff. 'The rush to invest in the brave new vision . . . upset established workers in the criminal justice system' (2016: 108) and contributed 'to the deterioration of employment conditions, especially for feminised professions' (Kirton and Guillaume, 2015: 54). De-professionalised, undervalued and stressed staff experienced a decline in 'working conditions and employee experiences' (2015: 25) as private providers, seeking to make money in the 'familiar fashion' of cutting costs, increased caseloads and slashed staffing numbers with the inevitable 'overburdening of staff' (McNeil, 2013: 85). With new licence arrangements adding an estimated 50,000 additional cases each year (National Audit Office, 2014), staff were staring 'into an abyss' (Rutter, 2015).

From its inception, TR attracted considerable criticism from researchers, reformers and practitioners, as well as government scrutineers responsible for budgetary oversight and governance. Financially strapped CRCs struggling to deliver the promised rehabilitation whilst turning a profit for shareholders, CRCs were plagued by performance issues due to the 'loss of expertise, conflicts of interest, [and] inconsistent practices' (Senior, 2016: 1). With the 'bifurcation of delivery integration of services for the individual service user (was) threatened' (Senior, 2016: 68) and public safety compromised (HMI Probation, 2014). Initial appeals to penal reformers' sincerely held beliefs, values and sensibilities that private providers would improve the rehabilitation and life chances of offenders were quickly exposed to be little more than a thinly disguised, placatory veneer: rhetorical devices applied to 'doing more for less', cost-cutting economies.

An unmitigated disaster, TR was plagued by a litany of undeliverable objectives (e.g. cheaper, innovative and dynamic services) in which none of the supposed benefits but all of the predicted risks were realised. A highly efficient service delivered by committed professionals was replaced by a dysfunctional, fragmented service within which CRCs, weighed down by spiralling debt and reliant on Treasury bailouts, teetered on the brink of implosion. With the collapse of two major providers in less than a month, putting 8 of the 21 CRC contracts in jeopardy, the challenges, contradictions and cracks created by the new arrangements became increasingly difficult for ministers to ignore. Consequently, in 2019, after less than four years of full operation, faced with an unremitting series of delivery debacles and financial losses, the MOJ was forced into a partial U-turn, reuniting probation under the National Probation Service.

Whilst the development was initially heralded in the liberal press as a victory for renationalisation (Grierson, 2019), a closer reading of the details revealed that this was only partial. Rather than being returned to its pre-privatisation position, the NPS, the public sector was being handed a poisoned chalice of bailing out 'yet another public service severely damaged by Chris Grayling and the Conservative obsession's with privatisation' (Crew, 2019). Under the new delivery model, although offender management would be brought back in house, the NPS would be shackled to private sector providers working to central government contractual terms who would provide the bulk of face-to-face interventions. With the buck stopping with the NPS, devoid both of the experienced staff to ensure success and the authority to hold new contract holders to account, it would be ultimately responsible for service-wide performance.

Despite the 2019 compromise, in 2020, attributing the U-turn to COVID-19 fiscal considerations rather than evidence, in a move that attracted little press interest, the Lord Chancellor announced that the Probation Service structure would effectively revert to its pre-2015 state. With the disastrous abandonment of the privatisation of probation, an indictment of the ideologically driven project, the public sector provider of last resort was once again sent in to bail out the private.

On 26 June 2021, the Probation Service was formally reunified. Commenting on the development, the NAPO (2021) Secretary General stated:

> In the decades to come let us hope that 26th June 2021 will be writ large in the annals of the Probation Service history. It's a date that signifies the final victory over a disastrous privatisation policy perpetrated by a government whose Ministers knew the price of everything but, in reality knew the value of nothing.
>
> *(2021: 6)*

Notes

1 In June 2014, 21 community rehabilitation companies, originally owned by the Ministry of Justice, were created to handle low- to medium-risk offenders, while a National Probation Service remaining in the public sector was created to supervise high risk offenders. The CRCs were sold on seven-year contracts to private and third-sector bidders as of 1 February 2015. Durham Tees Valley was the only CRC where no major private or multinational company was involved.

2 There are three main payments under the contracts: a fee for service, for the satisfactory completion of activities with offenders; a fee for use to cover work done for other parties, particularly where the NPS commissions CRC to provide services for its own higher-risk offenders; and payment by results, triggered by reductions in reoffending after two years, based on scaled payments of up to £4,000 per offender who desists and £1,000 per offence avoided.

3 A report compiled by senior officials warned Grayling that the highest-rated concerns—code black—included a more than 80% risk that an unacceptable drop in operational performance would lead to delivery failure and reputational damage, a 51% to 80% risk that insufficient support for the proposals by probation management and staff would result in a failure and a 51% to 80% risk that projected savings would not be achieved.

4 The Through the Gate programme was intended to reduce the high recidivism rates of short-term prisoners by preparing a resettlement plan within five working days of the screening being completed by prison staff; helping prisoners to find accommodation; helping prisoners retain employment held pre-custody and gain employment or training opportunities post-release; providing help with finance, benefits and debt; providing support for victims of domestic abuse and sex workers; and undertaking pre-release coordination.

References

Allen, R. (2018) 'Unlocking Potential: Back to the Future? Where Next for Probation' Reforming Prisons.blogspot.com. Retrieved 27 July 2018

Bastow, S. (2014) 'Transforming Rehabilitation: Evolution not Revolution' *Criminal Justice Matters* 97 (1): 10–11

Bulman, M. (2019, January 17) 'Number of Offenders Recalled to Prison Surges Following "Disastrous" Probation Reforms' *Independent*

Burgess, J., and MacDonald, D. (1999). 'Outsourcing, Employment and Industrial Relations in the Public Sector' *The Economic and Labour Relations Review* 10 (1): 36–55

Burke, L., and Collett, S. (2016) 'Transforming Rehabilitation: Organizational Bifurcation and the End of Probation as We Knew It?' *Probation Journal* 63 (2): 120–135

Butler, P. (2011, June 20) 'Charities: Corporate 'Bid Candy' for the Big Society?' *The Guardian*

Calder, S., and Goodman, A. (2013) 'Transforming Rehabilitation, a Fiscal Motivated Approach to Offender Management' *British Journal of Community Justice* 11 (2–3): 175–188

Carter, E., and Whitworth, A. (2015) 'Creaming and Parking in Quasi-Marketised Welfare-to-Work Schemes: Designed out of or Designed in to the UK Work Programme?' *Journal of Social Policy* 44 (2): 277–296

Carter, P. (2003) *Managing Offenders: Reducing Crime—A New Approach*, London: Prime Minister's Strategy Unit

Cavadino, M., and Dignan, J. (2007) *The Penal System: An Introduction*, London: Sage

Centre for Social Justice (2013) *The New Probation Landscape*, London: CSJ

Chambers, M. (2013) *Expanding Payment-by-Results: Strategic Choices and Recommendations*, London: Policy Exchange

Collett, S. (2013) 'Riots, Revolution and Rehabilitation: The Future of Probation' *The Howard Journal of Criminal Justice, Howard Journal of Criminal Justice* 52 (2): 163–189

Crew, J. (2019, February 16) 'Grayling Attacked over "Disastrous" Privatisation after Probation Firms Collapse' *Independent*

Dominey, J. (2012) 'A Mixed Market of Services; Can Lessons from the Recent Past Shape the Near Future?' *Probation Journal* 59 (4): 339–354

Dunt, I. (2014, July 25) 'Privatisation Admission Shows Grayling Misled the Commons' *Politics.co.uk*. www.politics.co.uk/news/2014/07/25/privatisation-lottery-a144-152dmission-shows-grayling-misled-the-co. Retrieved 10 August 2015

Fitzgibbon, W. (2013) 'Risk and Privatisation' *British Journal of Criminal Justice* 11 (2–3): 87–90

Ford, R. (2018, June 14) 'Probation Firms' Contracts Will Be Ripped Up' *The Times*

Fox, C., and Alberterson, K. (2012) 'Is Payment by Results the Most Efficient Way to Address the Challenges Faced by the Criminal Justice Sector' *Probation Journal* 59 (40): 355–375

Garside, R., and Silvestri, A. (2013) *Justice Policy Review*, London: Centre for Criminal Justice Studies

Gosling, H. (2016) 'All This Is about the Money and Making Sure That Heads Are on Beds' *Probation Journal* 63 (2): 144–152

Gough, D. (2012) '"Revolution": Marketisation, the Penal System and the Voluntary Sector' in A. Silvestri (ed) *Social and Criminal Justice in the First Year of Coalition Government*, London: Centre for Crime and Justice Studies

Grierson, J. (2019, May 16) 'Probation Will Be Renationalised after Disastrous Grayling Reforms' *The Guardian*

Hansard (2019) *Probation: Voluntary Sector Vol 708*; Debated on Wednesday 5 June 2019 Retrieved 15th June 2022 from https://hansard.parliament.uk/lords/2019-06-05/debates/D4FB1009-0F40-4A3A-B424-D7213E9AA1C0/ProbationVoluntarySector9

Harper, C. (2013) 'Transforming Rehabilitation and Creeping Marketisation' *British Journal of Criminal Justice* 11 (2–3): 37–41

Hayes, C. (2010) *Payment by Results What Does It Mean for Voluntary Organisations Working with Offenders?* London: Clinks

Hedderman, C. (2013) 'Payment by Results: Hopes, Fears and Evidence' *British Journal of Community Justice* 11 (2/3): 43–58

Hedderman, C., and Murphy, A. (2015) 'Bad News for Probation? Analysing the Newspaper Coverage of Transforming Rehabilitation' *Probation Journal* 62 (3): 217–234

HMI Probation (2014) *Transforming Rehabilitation: Early Implementation 1*, London: HMIP

HMI Probation (2015) *Annual Report 2014–2015*, London: HMIP

HMI Probation (2016a) *Transforming Rehabilitation: Early Implementation 5*, London: HMIP

HMI Probation (2016b) *A Thematic Inspection of the Provision and Quality of Services in the Community Who Offend*, London: HMIP

HMI Probation (2019a) *Annual Report of Chief Inspector of Probation*, London: HMIP

HMI Probation (2019b) *An Inspection of Dorset, Devon and Cornwall*, London: HMIP

HMI Probation (2020) *Response to Lord Chancellor's Announcement from Chief Inspector of Probation Justin Russell*. Press release, London: HMI Prison and Probation

HMI Probation and HMI Prisons (2016) *An Inspection of Through the Gate Resettlement Services for Short-Term Prisoners*, London: HMIP

Hobbs, S., and Hamerton, C. (2014) *The Making of Criminal Justice Policy*, London: Routledge

Holt, P. (2000) *Case Management: Context for Supervision Community and Criminal Justice Monograph 2*, Leicester: De Montfort University

House of Commons (HOC) Justice Committee (2011) *The Role of the Probation Service*, London: HMSO

House of Commons (HOC) Justice Committee (2014) *Crime Reduction Policies: A Co-Ordinated Approach? Interim Report on the Government's Transforming Rehabilitation Programme*, London: HOC Justice Committee

House of Commons (HOC) Justice Committee (2017) *Transforming Rehabilitation Inquiry Launched*, London: HOC Justice Committee

House of Commons (HOC) Justice Committee (2018) *Transforming Rehabilitation*, London: HOC Justice Committee

House of Commons (HOC) Public Accounts Committee (2014) *Probation: Landscape Review*, London: HMSO

House of Commons (HOC) Public Accounts Committee (2016) *Transforming Rehabilitation 17th Report*, London: HMSO

House of Lords (2013) *Offender Rehabilitation Bill*. House of Lords Second Reading www.parliament.uk/business/news/2013/november-/commons-second-reading-offender-rehabilitation-bill/. Retrieved 11 April 2016

Howard League for Penal Reform (2011) 'Response to Breaking the Cycle: Effective Punishment, Rehabilitation and Sentencing of Offenders' www.howardleague.org/fileadmin/howard_league/user/pdf/Consultations/Response_to_Breaking_the_Cycle.pdf. Retrieved 10 August 2015

Howard League for Penal Reform (2018) *Handing More Cash to Failing Private Probation Companies Is Throwing Good Money after Bad*, London: Howard League

Howard League of Penal Reform (2017) *Howard League Responds to 'Devastating' Report on Through the Gate Support for Prisoners*, London: Howard League

Kemshall, H. (2008) *Understanding the Community Management of High Risk Offenders'* (1st edition), Maidenhead: Open University Press

Kirton, G., and Guillaume, C. (2015) *Employment Relations and Working Conditions in Probation after Transforming Rehabilitation*, London: Queen Mary's University

Ledger, J. (2010) 'Rehabilitation Revolution: Will Probation Pay *the Price?*' *Probation. Journal* 57 (4): 416–422

Leftly, M. (2015, December 21) 'Privatising Probation Services Was a Foreseeable Mistake—and Now We All Stand to Pay the Price' *The Independent*

Mair, G. (2008) 'The Origins of What Works in England and Wales: A House Built on Sand' in G. Mair (ed) *What Matters in Probation*, Cullompton: Willan

McDermott, S-A. (2016) 'Probation without Boundaries? "Agile Working" in the Community Rehabilitation Company "Transformed" Landscape' *Probation Journal* 63 (2): 144–152

McNeill, F. (2011) 'Probation, Credibility and Justice' *Probation Journal* 58 (1): 9–22

McNeil, F. (2013) 'Transforming Rehabilitation: Evidence, Values and Ideology' *British Journal of Criminal Justice*. Sheffield. Sheffield Hallam University Press 11 (2–3): 83–85

Ministry of Justice (2010a) *Breaking the Cycle Effective Punishment, Rehabilitation and Sentencing of Offenders*, London: MOJ

Ministry of Justice (2010b) *Green Paper Evidence Report: Breaking the Cycle Effective Punishment, Rehabilitation and Sentencing of Offenders*, London: MOJ

Ministry of Justice (2013a) *Transforming Rehabilitation: A Revolution in the Way We Mange Offenders*, London: MOJ

Ministry of Justice (2013b) *Summary of Responses to Transforming Rehabilitation*, London: MOJ

Ministry of Justice (2014) *Voluntary Sector at Forefront of New Fight against Reoffending*, London: MOJ

Ministry of Justice (2018) *Strengthening Probation, Building Confidence*, London: MOJ

Ministry of Justice (2019) *Strengthening Probation, Building Confidence: Response to Consultation*, London: MOJ

Ministry of Justice (2020) *Government to Take Control of Unpaid Work*. Press release. Retrieved 11th June 2020 from www.gov.uk/government/news/government-to-take-control-of-unpaid-work-to-strengthen-community-sentences

NAPO (2016) *National Audit Office—Transforming Rehabilitation*, London: NAPO

NAPO (2019) *Trade Union Dismay over Failed Government Contracts Leaving Staff and the Public at Risk*, London: NAPO

NAPO (2021) *Reunification Special*, London: NAPO

NAPO and Unison (2014) 'The Truth about Transforming Rehabilitation: Voices from the Frontline' www.napo.org.uk/sites/default/files/The%20Truth%20About%20Transforming%20Rehabilitation%202.pdf. Retrieved 1h August 2015

NAPO and Unison (2015) *Sodexo Owned CRCS: Job Cuts and Redundancy*, London: NAPO and Unison

NAPO News (2015) 'Rage against the Machine' *NAPO News 263,* London: NAPO

National Audit Office (2013) *Ministry of Justice's Electronic Monitoring Contracts*, London: NAO

National Audit Office (2014) *Probation: Landscape Review*, London: NAO

National Audit Office (2015) *Outcome-Based Payment Schemes: Government's Use of Payment by Results*, London: NAO

National Audit Office (2016) *Transforming Rehabilitation*, London: NAO

National Audit Office (2018) *Investigation into Changes to Community Rehabilitation Company Contracts (Summary Report)*, London: NAO

National Audit Office (2019) *Transforming Probation: Progress Review (Summary Report)*, London: NAO

NCVO (2013) *Payment by Results: A Legal Analysis of Terms and Process*, London: NCVO

Nellis, M. (2011) 'The "Complicated Business" of Electronic Monitoring' in R. Taylor, M. Hill and F. MacNeil (eds) *Early Professional Development for Social Workers*, Birmingham: Venure Press/BASW

Nellis, M. (2014) 'Upgrading Electronic Monitoring and Downgrading Probation: Reconfiguring "Offender Management" in England and Wales' *European Journal of Probation* 6 (2): 169–191

NOMS (2015b) *A Guide to 'Through the Gate' Resettlement Services*, London: NOMS

Parliament UK (2014) Justice Committee Minutes of Evidence HC 307. https://publications.parliament.uk/pa/cm201415/cmselect/cmjust/307/131112.htm. Retrieved 21st July 2022

Parliament UK (2018) *Government Contracts for Community Rehabilitation Companies*, London: Parliament

Prison Reform Trust (2011) *Submission to Breaking the Cycle Consultation*, London: PRT

Probation Matters Blog Spot (2015a, December 21) 'Renationalistion?' *Probation Matters Blog Spot* http://probationmatters.blogspot.co.uk/. Retrieved 21 December 2015

Probation Matters Blog Spot (2015b, December 16) 'TOM Not Delivering' *Probation Matters Blog Spot* http://probationmatters.blogspot.co.uk/. Retrieved 18 December 2015

Rees, J. (2019, February 15) 'Private Probation in Wales and South West in Administration' *BBC News*

Rodger, J. (2012) 'Rehabilitation Revolution in a Big Society?' in A. Silvestri (ed) *Social and Criminal Justice in the First Year of Coalition Government*, London: Centre for Crime and Justice Studies

Rozenberg, J. (2012, September 4) 'Chris Grayling, Justice Secretary: Non-Lawyer and "on the up" Politician' *The Guardian*

Rutter, T. (2015, April 9) 'Probation Service Split: "Staff Are Staring into the Abyss"' *The Guardian*

Rutter, T. (2016, February 23) 'Privatised Probation Staff: Stressed, Deskilled and Facing Cuts' *The Guardian*

Senior, P. (2013) 'Probation: Peering through the Uncertainty' *British Journal of Community Justice* 11 (2–3): 1–8

Senior, P. (2016) 'Tragedy and Farce in Organisational Upheavals for Probation: What Next?' *British Journal of Community Justice* 14 (1): 65–70

Silvestri, A. (2009) *Partners or Prisoners: Voluntary Sector Independence in the World of Commissioning and Contestability*, London: Centre for Crime and Justice Studies

Stacey, G. (2017) *Can Probation Services Deliver What We All Want and Expect? Criminal Justice Management Conference Keynote Speech*, London: HMI Probation

Strickland, P. (2016) *Contracting out Probation Services, 2013–2016. Briefing Paper No. 06894*, London: House of Commons Library

Syal, R. (2014, September 8) 'Hodge Accuses the Government of "Shocking Complacency over G4S and Serco"' *The Guardian*

Taylor, M. (2012, June 20) 'How G4S Is Securing the World' *The Guardian*

Teague, M. (2013) 'Rehabilitation, Punishment and Profit' *British Society of Criminology Newsletter* 72: 15–18

Teague, M. (2016). 'Probation, People and Profits: The Impact of Neoliberalism' *British Journal of Community Justice* 14 (1): 133–138

The Guardian (2016, December 15) 'The Guardian View on Probation: Another Grayling Casualty' *The Guardian*

The Guardian (2018, June 25) 'Privatising Probation Has Been a Disaster. Will the Tories Ever Learn?' *The Guardian*

The Trade Union Co-Ordinating Group (2013) *The Real Cost of Privatisation*, London: Centre for Legal and Social Studies

Travis, A. (2010, December 14) 'Will Ken Clarke's Prison Green Paper Stop "Sentence Inflation?' *The Guardian*

Travis, A. (2012, July 13) 'Serco Wins First Private Probation Contract' *The Guardian*

Travis, A. (2013, June 24) 'Privatising Probation Service Will Put Public at Risk, Officials Tell Grayling' *The Guardian*

Travis, A. (2018, January 17) 'Private Probation Firms Face Huge Losses Despite £342m "Bailout"' *The Guardian*

Travis, A., and Syal, R. (2014, September 12) '"Poison Pill" Probation Contracts Could Cost £300 Million to £400 Million to Cancel' *The Guardian*

Webster, R. (2020) 'Probation Is Renationalised' www.russellwebster.com/probation-is-renationalised/. Retrieved 11 June 2020

White, A. (2016) *Shadow State: Inside the Secret Companies That Run Britain*, London: Oneworld

Whitefield, D. (2012) 'The Payments-by-Result Road to Marketization' in A. Silvestri (ed) *Social and Criminal Justice in the First Year of Coalition Government*, London: Centre for Crime and Justice Studies

Whitten, M. (2010) *Nipping Crime in the Bud: How the Philanthropic Quest Was Put into Law*, Hampshire: Waterside Press

Williams, Z. (2012, June 20) 'Public Sector Outsourcing: Finally an Unfairness That We Can Do Something about' *The Guardian*

INDEX

Note: End note information is denoted by n and note number following the page number.

Act for the Relief of the Poor (1601) 170
active citizenship 142–143, 147, 158
Adam Smith Institute 25, 188, 196
Addactions 270
Addington, Henry and administration 176
Advisory Committee on Business Appointments 94, 103nn5–6
agency theory 22–23
Airline Group 48
Air Raid Precaution wardens 120
alarm systems 72, 114, 119–120, 143
Albion 169
Alexander, Daniel Asher 178
almshouses 170
al-Qaeda terrorist attacks 147
American Telephone & Telegraph Company 120
Amersham International 29
Anderson, John 117
anti-social behavior orders 144
Anti-Social Behaviour, Crime and Policing Act (2014) 154
Approved Contractor Scheme 146–147
artificial intelligence 155–157
Asquith, Herbert 183
asset sales: Conservative-Liberal Democrat coalition policies of 53; Conservative party policies on 28–30, 53; history of privatisation and 5; industrial *versus* Welfare State 8, 27, 28–30; New Labour party policies on 41, 44, 47–48; privatisation defined by 4, 18, 19
Associated British Ports 29
Association of Chief Police Officers 150–151, 154
Astrium 248
Atos 60n5, 89–90, 92, 100
Attlee, Clement and administration 16, 118–119
Auburn Prison 181
Aurelius 272
austerity agenda: police privatisation and 11, 148–152, 158–159; prison privatisation and 12, 214–215; privatisation, generally, and 4, 9, 40, 50–53, 54, 87, 94
Austrian school of economics 21–22
Axon 156
Ayanda 58

Back to Basics initiative 142–143
Bain and Company 52
Baker, Kenneth 198, 200–201, 222n3
Balfour Beatty 46
banking industry 114–115, 120
Bank of England 119, 149
Beccaria, Cesare 173, 175
bedroom tax 50
Bentham, Jeremy 173, 175–176, 177, 191n6
Bentham, Samuel 175, 176

Best Value programme 40, 42–43, 53
Biffen, John 196
Big Society 50, 51, 140, 150, 152–154, 256, 259
black box procurement system 97, 261, 270–271
Blackburn, William 175, 178
Black Lives Matter movement 7, 108–109
Blackstone, William 174
Blair, Ian 145
Blair, Tony and administration: Interserve and 55; law and order politics of 204; police and police privatisation under 11, 141, 144, 148–149, 158, 161n6; press director for spin by 60n1; prisons and prison privatisation under 12, 208, 211, 212; privatisation, generally, under 39, 41–42, 44, 48–49
Bloody Code 172–173
Blue Lamp, The 118
Blunkett, David 146, 148, 161n6
Boots 57
Bow Street Runners 112, 115
Brantingham, Jeff 156
Breaking the Cycle (Clarke) 258, 261, 262
Brexit 9, 40–41, 53–54, 58–59, 154
bribery, in prisons 172, 173–174
Bridewell prisons 170–171
British Aerospace 29
British Aerospace Act (1980) 29
British Airports Authority 30
British Airways 29
British Army 56, 98, 100
British Coal 30
British Gas 30, 31
British Petroleum 29
British Rail 140, 151
British Security Industry Association 123, 145
British Steel 30
British Sugar 29
British Telecom 30
British Transport Police 114
British Union of Fascists 117
Britoil 29
Brittany Ferries 56
'broken windows' policing strategy 109, 139, 144
Bromley Briefing (Prison Reform Trust) 211
Brown, Gordon and administration 43, 47, 103nn1,5, 149–150, 211, 212
Buckland, Robert 219
Buddi 99, 247, 248
budget deficit reduction 40, 50, 258

Bulger, James 141, 143, 203
Bunbury, Charles 176
Burgot 120
Burns, John 116
Byfield, George 178

Cable and Wireless 29
Callaghan, Jim and administration 26, 27, 124
Cameron, David and administration: law and order politics of 204; police and police privatisation under 150, 152; prisons and prison privatisation under 212, 216; privatisation, generally, under 40; Probation Service privatisation under 256; resignation due to Brexit referendum by 53, 154; on revolving door 93
Campbell, Alastair 60n1
Capita: electronic monitoring and 243, 248; health services provision 52, 57; misconduct and malpractice of 40, 52, 54, 55–56, 100; size of 43, 55, 60n5, 89–90
capitalism: nationalism rise in response to failed 16, 20; popular 21, 30–31
Care Quality Commission 95
Carillion: collapse of 46, 54–55, 98, 100–102, 104n10, 218, 222; PFIs with 46; regulatory oversight lack for 97; size of 89
Carnarvon, Lord Henry Herbert 180–181
Carter, Patrick 210, 223n9, 239
Carter Review 210, 238, 239
Case for Private Prisons, The (Reform) 103n7
cash-in-transit services 121, 122
cash-linked key performance indicators 48–49, 235, 237
Catch 22 212, 213
CCA (Corrections Corporation of America) 74, 78, 80, 188, 197, 201, 222–223n6
CCTV (closed circuit television) 130, 141, 143, 145, 156–157
Cecil, Robert 184
Centre for Crime Prevention 95
Centre for Criminal Justice Studies 246
Centre for Policy Studies 25
Centre for Social Justice 95
China, technology and abuse of power in 157
Christie, Nils 7, 107, 109, 189, 206, 222
Chubb company 114, 120
Chubb-Racal 243

Churchill, Winston 27
Church of England Temperance Society 229
Citizen's Charter 141, 142, 158
City of London Police Act (1839) 113
Civil Aviation Act (1980) 29
civilianisation of police 129, 142, 146, 148
Clarke, Charles 161n6, 210–211
Clarke, Kenneth 34, 201–203, 205, 212–214, 258–259, 261
Clarke, Peter 217, 220–221
ClearSprings 240
Clegg, Nick 150
Clinks 263
Clinton, Bill and administration 41, 77
closed circuit television (CCTV) 130, 141, 143, 145, 156–157
Coal Today, Gone Tomorrow: How Jobs Were Replaced with Prison Places (Jones, Gray, and Farrall) 221
Coldbath fields 179
College of Policing 154
Colquhoun, Patrick 112, 113, 190
Committee on the State and Use of Prisons 167
commodification: of crime 6–7, 78; of incarceration 171–172, 181; of police services 142; of probation services 257, 279; of public services 39
Community Payback (formerly Community Service) 260–261
community policing 126, 139, 141
community rehabilitation companies 264, 268–280
community safety accreditation schemes 146
community safety projects 152
competition: Austrian school of economics on 21–22; from emerging nations 26; neoliberal goals of 102, 198; offender management services 212–213; oligopoly of privatisation reducing 89–90; prison privatisation and 198, 203, 209, 212–214, 223n7; privatisation and 27 (*see also* privatisation); Probation Service privatisation and 213, 229, 259, 263; regulation theory on 23–24
Competition for Prisons (Le Vay) 223n7
Competition Strategy for Offender Services 212
compulsory competitive tendering 32–33, 40, 42, 52
Conservative-Liberal Democrat coalition: 2010–2015 privatisation policies 49–53; electronic monitoring policies 245–247; Probation Service privatisation under 257–258

Conservative party: 1979–1997 privatisation policies 27–32; 1979–1997 Probation Service policies 232–234; 2015-current privatisation policies 53–58; electronic monitoring policies of 247–248; neoliberalism of (*see* neoliberalism)
constables 111–112, 119, 132nn1,3
contestability: prison privatisation and 210–211; Probation Service privatisation and 238, 239, 240, 249, 258
Contracted Out Prisons Order (1992) 200, 201
Contract Provision of Prisons 188, 197
contractual arrangements: black box 97, 261, 270–271; electronic monitoring 245; misconduct and malpractice with 98–100, 102–103; PFI buy-outs of 46–47; police 141, 153; prison 188, 197 (*see also under* Private Finance Initiatives); Probation Service 261, 268–269, 270–271, 274, 280–281nn1–2; regulatory system and 52, 91, 96–97, 99–100, 102–103
Cooper, Yvette 159
Corbyn, Jeremy 47
corporate service providers *see* providers of private services
Corps of Commissionaires 114–115
corrections commercial complex 65, 79–80, 92–93
Corrections Corporation of America (CCA) 74, 78, 80, 188, 197, 201, 222–223n6
costs: of COVID-19 response 57–58; of criminal justice system 75; of PFIs 45–47, 60nn3–4; of policing 121, 144–146, 148–152, 153–154, 159; of prisons 3, 73, 176–178, 186, 191nn7–8, 207, 214–215; of private provider collapse 55; of privatisation 31; privatisation to reduce 40, 87–88, 104n11, 203; of Probation Service 235; of public-sector expenditures 17; race to the bottom for 39–40, 54–56, 86, 88, 97–98, 263, 268
County and Borough Police Act (1856) 114
courts, sale of 4
COVID-19 pandemic 9, 41, 57–58, 277–278, 280
Cowper, Lord 111
Crawford, William 179, 180
creaming 264

Crime and Disorder Act (1998) 144–145
Crime and Disorder Reduction Partnerships 144–145
Crime Control as Industry (Christie) 107
Crime Control Commission (US) 87–88
Crime Reduction Strategy 145
Criminal Justice Act (1948) 185, 228
Criminal Justice Act (1991) 167, 189, 198, 200–201, 203, 220, 233, 243
Criminal Justice and Court Services Act (2000) 235
Criminal Justice and Public Order Act (1994) 141, 203, 243
Criminal Justice Bill (1990) 189, 198
criminal justice system: electronic monitoring in (*see* electronic monitoring privatisation); immigration and detention services in 1, 103n2, 124; juvenile justice system in 1–2, 95, 99, 141, 143, 183–185; offender services in (*see* offender management services); police in (*see* police); political influences on (*see* neoliberalism; politics); prisons in (*see* prisons); privatisation of (*see* privatisation of criminal justice system); Probation Service in (*see* Probation Service); providers of private services in (*see* providers of private services); risk management and 68–71
cronyism 53, 57–58, 92, 93, 97, 102
Crook, Frances 269
cultural influences: on electronic monitoring acceptance 244–245; on globalisation effects 66; on police portrayals 111–112, 118, 121, 131; on police privatisation reluctance 155; on prison portrayals 222n5; on punishment as custom 169–170; on total *versus* partial privatisation 20
culture of control 169, 188, 189–190, 210
Cunningham, Mike 150–151
curfew orders 144, 213, 241–242, 244, 247
cybercrime 147

Daily Chronicle 183
Damiens, Robert 169
data, police use of 155–157
death penalty 172–173
debtors' prisons 171
defence industry 74, 88
Defence of the Realm Act 116
Deferred Prosecution Agreements 246–247
Defoe, Daniel 111
Deloitte 57, 159, 197

demand-driven privatisation 69–70, 72
denationalisation 15, 17, 27, 28–30; *see also* privatisation
Departmental Committee on Prisons: 'The Gladstone Report', The 183, 184
Departmental Committee on the Social Services in Courts of Summary Jurisdiction 185
deregulation 27, 76, 90, 103n1
DFDS Seaways 56
Dick, Cressida 154
Dick, Philip K. 156, 161n4
Dimbleday, Jonathan 204
discipline 114, 138, 139, 170–172, 180, 190n1
Discipline and Punish (Foucault) 169, 189
Disney World 130, 139, 157, 159
Dixon, Arthur Lewis 116–117
Dixon, George (fictional character) 118, 121
Dixon of Dock Green 118, 121
Doing Time (Matthews) 7, 167
doli incapax rule, abolition of 144
Du Cane, Edmund 180–182, 183–184, 185
Dundas, Henry 176
Durham and Tees 269, 280n1

East Coast Mainline 54
Eastern State Penitentiary 178–179
economics: 1970s instability of 26; Austrian school of 21–22; Great Depression and 16; neoliberal (*see* neoliberalism); ownership theories and 21–24; recessions and 26, 149, 212; of regulation 23–24; *see also* finances
Economist, The 199
Eden, William 173, 174
Edmund Davies Committee 124
electronic monitoring privatisation: Conservative-Liberal Democrat coalition policies on 245–247; Conservative party policies on 247–248; contractual arrangements for 245; GPS technology and 247–248; industry growth 12, 229, 238; Matthews on 1; misconduct and malpractice with 99–100, 103n2, 243, 245–248, 250nn1–2, 262–263, 268; New Labour party policies on 244–245; politics and 243–248; Probation Service and 229, 238, 240–248, 249, 260, 270; regulatory oversight of 91; research and trials on 243, 244; think tank influence on 247; transatlantic transfer of 241, 242, 244–245

eliminative penal practices 205–206, 208, 219, 221
Emergency Powers Act (1919) 116
Emsley, C. 112, 116, 131, 172
Enterprise Oil 29
Ernst and Young 57
ethical and moral issues: juvenile moral rehabilitation as 185; prison privatisation and 196, 202, 220; privatisation of criminal justice as 6–7; Probation Service and 230, 257, 263; public morality as 171, 173, 177; *see also* misconduct and malpractice
European Services Strategy Unit 58–59
Eurotunnel 56
Evans, Paul 53
Evidence Report (Clarke) 258, 259
exile, as punishment 170, 171, 190–191n5, 206

Factory Guards 121
failure of private providers *see* misconduct and malpractice
Falklands war 125
Faucher, Leon 169
fetishism, police 109, 132
Fielding, Henry 111–112, 119, 173
Fielding, John 173
finances: asset sales and (*see* asset sales); budget deficit reduction and 40, 50, 258; commodification and (*see* commodification); compulsory competitive tendering and 32–33, 52; health services funding and 33–34; Private Finance Initiatives for (*see* Private Finance Initiatives); race to the bottom and 39–40, 54–56, 86, 88, 97–98, 263, 268; social impact bonds for 211–212; *see also* costs; economics
financial management initiative 128, 195, 233
Financial Times, The 18
Fletcher, Harry 267
Floyd, George 109
Fothergill, John 174–175
Foucault, M. 110, 123, 139, 169, 172, 189, 220
fragmentation, policy of 17, 23
France: police in 109, 112, 115; prisons in 169, 172, 174; Treaty of Amiens with 176
Francis, Peter 208
Friedman, Milton 24

From the Neighbourhood to the National: Policing Our Communities Together (Home Office) 149–150
Fry, Elizabeth 179

G4S (formerly Group 4): electronic monitoring and 243, 245–247, 263, 268; health care services 57; as insider group 96; misconduct and malpractice of 87, 98–99, 100, 101, 103n2, 153–154, 159, 217, 222, 245–247, 263, 268, 277; offender management services 256; police privatisation and 104n11, 121, 123, 153–154, 159; prison privatisation and 54, 79, 103n7, 200–203, 207, 208, 213, 214, 217, 219, 220, 222, 223n8; Probation Service privatisation and 243, 245–247, 263, 268, 277; revolving door with 94–95; size of 60n5, 89–90; think tanks and 95, 103n7
gaming the process: Probation Service privatisation and 236–237, 264; regulatory system and 91, 97, 98
Gaol Act (1698) 170
Gaols Act (1823) 179
Gardner, Edward 197
Gargan, Nick 95
Garland, David 7, 169, 185, 186, 188, 189–190, 230
Gauke, David 217, 274
Geo Amney 256
GEO Group 74
George, Bruce 146–147
Germany, criminal justice in 174, 206
Gladstone, Herbert 183
Gladstone Report, The 183, 184
Glasgow Police 113
Glaxo 57
globalisation: defining 66; key themes and trends with 66–72; local contexts for 66–67; neoliberalism rise with 64–65, 67; privatisation and 9, 42; risk and 67–68; transfer of penal ideas and 76–77
glocalisation 66
Gloucester County Prison 175, 177, 178
Good Law Project, The 57, 58
Gove, Michael 216
GPS (global positioning satellite) technology 247–248
Grayling, Chris: on electronic monitoring 245–246, 247–248; ferry contract fiasco of 40, 41, 56; offender management services privatisation role of 12, 97; prisons and prison privatisation under

214–215; on Probation Service privatisation 257, 261–262, 264, 267–268, 274–275, 279–280, 281n3
Great Depression 16
great leap backwards 73
Great Train Robbery (1963) 121–122
Green, Penny 7
Grenfell Tower tragedy 86–87, 103n8
Group 4 *see* G4S (formerly Group 4)
Group 4 Falck 79
Group 4 Rebound Ltd. 95
Group 4 Security 123
Guardian, The 57, 149, 199, 240
Gurney, Joseph John 179

Habermas, J. 110, 173
Haldenby, Andrew 103n7
Hammond, Philip 47, 218
Hardwick, Nick 215
Hardy, Thomas 181
Harman, Harriet 204
Harriot, John 112
Haviland, John 178
Hayek, Friedrich A. von 21, 25, 36n1
Health and Social Care Act (2012) 41, 51–52
Healthcare Environment Services 52–53
health services: compulsory competitive tendering in 40, 52; COVID-19 pandemic and 9, 41, 57–58, 277–278, 280; denationalisation of 17; funding of 33–34; internal market and 33–34; misconduct and malpractice in 40–41, 52–53; nationalisation of 16, 20, 119; *Open Public Services* on 51–53; *see also* National Health Service
Heath, Edward and administration 23, 26
Henig, Baroness 152
Herbert, Nick 103n7, 152
Hill, Roger 94, 96
Hillier, Meg 47, 56
HM Inspectorate of Constabulary 128, 129, 142, 151, 152
HM Inspectorate of Probation 234, 267, 271, 272, 273, 275
HM Inspector of Prisons 95, 103n2, 273
HMP Acklington 213
HMP Albany 186–187
HMP Altcourse 203, 207, 208
HMP Ashfield 208
HMP Belmarsh West 212, 223n10
HMP Berwyn 216
HMP Birmingham 54, 103n2, 213, 217–218, 220–221

HMP Blakenhurst 201, 202, 209
HMP Brixton 209
HMP Brockhill 213
HMP Buckley Hall 201, 202, 209
HMP Castington 213
HMP Coldingley 213, 214
HMP Doncaster 202, 212, 213, 218, 223n11
HMP Dovegate 208
HMP Durham 213, 214
HMP Elmley 210–211
HMP Everthorpe 205, 214
HMP Five Wells 219
HMP Forest Bank 208
HMP Glen Parva 219
HMP Hatfield 213
HMP Holloway 216
HMP Kilmarnock 208
HMP Lindholme 213
HMP Liverpool 220–221
HMP Lowdham Grange 208, 218
HMP Manchester 209
HMP Moorland 54, 213
HMP New Hall 185
HMP Northumberland 213, 218
HMP Nottingham 54
HMP Oakwood 215
HMP Onley 213, 214
HMP Parc 203, 207, 208
HMP Parkhurst 205
HMP Reading 216
HMP Rye Hill 208
HMP Standford Hill 211
HMP Swaleside 211
HMP Thameside 215, 218, 223n10
HMP Whitmoor 205
HMP Winsome Green 186, 205
HMP Wolds 3, 200–202, 213, 214
Hodge, Margaret 46, 90
Hogarth, William 173
Holford, George 177
Holmes, Edwin 120
Home Guard 120
house arrest 241; *see also* electronic monitoring privatisation
House of Young Prisoners 169
Houses of Correction 170, 179; *see also* prisons
housing: bedroom tax for 50; nationalisation and provision of affordable 119; privatisation of 29, 30, 86–87, 103n8
Housing Act (1980) 29
Howard, John 173–175, 177, 179

Howard, Michael 75, 141–142, 144, 146, 158, 203–206
Howard Association 229
Howard League for Penal Reform 7, 167–168, 265, 269
Human Rights Watch 157
Hunger Marches 117
Hurd, Douglas 168, 188–189, 197–198, 201, 208

immigration and detention services 1, 103n2, 124
Independent 199, 271
Independent Police Complaints Commission 108
individual utility maximization 22
industrial privatisation 20, 28–30
Industry Act (1980) 29
inflation 24, 26
infrastructure, privately financed 40, 45
Inquest 7
Inquiry into the Causes of the Late Increase in Robbers (Fielding) 173
Insider groups 96
Institute of Economic Affairs 25
International Monetary Fund 64
Interserve: collapse and malpractice of 52, 54, 55, 98, 102, 272; PFIs with 46; prison privatisation and 219; Probation Service privatisation and 269–270, 272; size of 43
Iranian Embassy terrorist siege 125
Ireland, Colin 143
Irish Republic Army (IRA) terrorism 125, 127

Jebb, Joshua 178, 180
Johnson, Boris and administration: police and police privatisation under 160; prisons and prison privatisation under 216, 219–220; privatisation, generally, under 9, 41, 56–58; Probation Service renationalisation under 56, 277–278
Joint Consultative Committee Operational Policing Review 128
July 7 and 21 terrorist attacks 148
justices of the peace 110
juvenile justice system 1–2, 95, 99, 141, 143, 183–185

Kelling, George 139, 144
Keynesianism 24
key performance indicators: cash-linked 48–49, 235, 237; new public management requirements for 48–49, 231; police review 141; Prison Service 210; Probation Service 233–234, 235–237, 249, 265
Kier-Balfour Beatty 46
Kinnock, Neil 140, 144, 198
KPMG 57

labour unions *see* unions
Laming, Bernard 209
Langley, Batty 172
Lansbury, George 121
Latchmere House prison 213
law and order politics: police policies and 125, 138, 144, 148, 152, 158; prison policies and 187, 203–205; Probation Service policies and 232; transatlantic transfer of policies and 73, 77
Lawrence, Ian 262, 267
Lawson, Nigel 18
Learmont, John 205
Le bureau des renseignements 115
Letwin, Oliver 153
Le Vay, Julian 205, 209, 211, 214, 223n7
Lewis, Derek 202, 205
Liberal Democrat coalition *see* Conservative-Liberal Democrat coalition
Liebling, Alison 7, 210
light-touch regulation 10, 86, 97, 103–104nn1, 8–9
Lilley, Bob 7
Lloyd, Edward 183
load shedding 129–130, 141, 142, 152–153
Local Government Act (1988) 32
Local Government Act (1999) 42
Local Government Planning and Land Act (1980) 29, 32
Lock, Trevor 125
Logan, C. H. 199
London Police Court Mission 229–230
London Probation Trust 260
London River Police 112, 113
Longford, Lord 202
Lynds, Elam 181

Maastricht Treaty 203
MacAlpine, Robert 78
Maclean, David 204
Macleod, Calum 161n3
Macmillan, Harold 30
magistrates 110–111
Magistrates' Association 262, 266, 267
Major, John and administration: PFIs under 44, 47; police and police privatisation

under 11, 140–141, 158; prison privatisation under 12, 189, 198, 201, 203–204; privatisation, generally, under 9, 30, 40; revolving door response by 103n5
Making Prisons Work (Straw) 208
Management and Training Corporation Works Limited 219
Managing Government Suppliers 60n5, 89
Managing Offenders, Reducing Crime—Changing Lives 210
Marconi Electronic Devices Ltd. 243
Marine Police Bill (1800) 112
Martin, Trayvon 108
Martinson, Robert 187
Matrimonial Causes Act (1857) 115
Matthews, Roger: *Doing Time* 7, 167; *Prisons 2000: An International Perspective on the Current State and Future of Imprisonment* 208; *Privatizing Criminal Justice* 1–2, 3, 7–8
Maude, Francis 95, 247
May, Theresa and administration: Brexit dominating policy under 9, 40, 53–54; police and police privatisation under 151, 152, 154, 159; prisons and prison privatisation under 216–217; Probation Service privatisation under 258
McAlpine 201, 222n6
McIntyre, Jody 108
Medway Special Training Centre 95, 103n2
Meller, David 58
Meller Designs 58
Menezes, John Charles de 148
Metropolitan Police Act (1829) 110, 113
Metropolitan Police Scotland Yard 4, 108, 115, 131
Metropolitan Watch Act (1735) 112
Millbank Penitentiary Act (1816) 177
Millbank Prison 177–178, 179, 181
Mills, Andrew 58
Minority Report, The (Dick) 156, 161n4
misconduct and malpractice: collapse of providers and 46, 54–56, 98, 100–102, 104n10, 218, 222, 272; electronic monitoring privatisation and 99–100, 103n2, 243, 245–248, 250nn1–2, 262–263, 268; health services 40–41, 52–53; police 108–109, 117, 127, 149, 153–154, 159; prison 101, 103n2, 172, 173–174, 178, 186–187, 199–200, 202, 205, 215, 217–222; Private Finance Initiatives and 46, 101, 218; Probation Service privatisation and 257, 270–277, 279–280, 281n3; race to the bottom and 40, 54–56, 86, 88, 98; regulatory system lacks and 10, 86–87, 88, 92, 96–98, 99–100, 102–103; revolving door leading to 93–95; rewarding failure and 90, 98–100, 222, 257, 277; watchdog reports on 40–41, 88, 157
Mitie 57, 219
mixed economy of provision 238, 239
modernisation 9, 39, 42, 44, 199
Modernising Government 44, 48
Mohler, George 156
monetarism 24, 25–26
Mouvement des Gilets Jeunes (Yellow Vests) 109
Mowlem 201, 222n6
Mowlem, John 78
MTCNovo 269
Mubenga, Jimmy 103n2
Much Ado about Nothing (Shakespeare) 111
Municipal Corporations Act (1835) 114
My Local Bobby 155

Nacro 96
Narey, Martin 94–95, 210, 240
National Air Traffic Service 41, 47–48
National Association of Probation Officers (NAPO) 242, 262, 267, 271, 280
National Association of Voluntary Organisations 264
National Audit Office (NAO): on Carillion collapse 55; on contract management 99–100, 263; on councils' financial risk 50; on electronic monitoring 248; on PFIs 45–46; on post office sell-off 53; on prison privatisation 215; on Probation Service privatisation 263, 264, 265, 271, 272, 275–276; on providers of private services 57, 89
National Crime Agency 147
National Crime Recording Standard 148
National Data Analytics Solution 156
National Enterprise Board 28, 29
National Freight Company 28, 29–30
National Health Service (NHS): Best Value programme by 53; compulsory competitive tendering by 40; COVID-19 pandemic and 57–58; internal market and 33–34; nationalisation of 20; *Open Public Services* on 51–53; outsourcing opposition by 40–41; Probation Service adopting delivery model of 238; *see also* health services
National Health Service Act (1946) 119

National Health Service and Community Care Act (1990) 34, 238
National Hi-Tech Crime Unit 147
National Insurance Act (1946) 119
National Intelligence Model 148
nationalisation: cultural influences on acceptability of 21; denationalisation versus 15, 17, 27, 28–30 (see also privatisation); history of 16, 21; police and 119, 131; renationalisation policies 41, 54, 56, 277–278, 280
National Offender Management Service (NOMS) 210–215, 239–240; see also offender management services
National Probation Service (NPS) 12, 235, 269, 271, 276, 278, 280; see also Probation Service
National Union of Miners/Mineworkers 26, 30, 125
Neden, Peter 96
neighbourhood policing 147, 152
Neighbourhood Watch groups 129–130
neoliberalism: competition goals of 102, 198; defining 67; globalisation and rise of 64–65, 67; neoliberal penality 6, 72–75, 76, 249; new public management and 230–231 (see also new public management); police privatisation and 11, 128, 132, 140; policy translation of 25–26, 64–65; prison privatisation and 12, 188, 189, 195, 197, 198, 201, 221–222; privatisation, generally and 2, 5–6, 51; privatisation of criminal justice system and 71, 72–75; Probation Service privatisation and 230–231, 239, 249, 256–257; right realism and 138–139; risk management and 68–71; security provision and 70–72; State reliance avoidance in 70
Netherlands, criminal justice in 156, 174
new feudalism 143, 148
Newgate Calendar 173
Newgate prison 172
New Labour party: 1997–2010 privatisation policies 41–49; 1997–2010 Probation Service policies 234–237; deregulation under 103n1; electronic monitoring policies of 244–245; prison privatisation under 206–212; US New Democrats and 41, 77
new public management (NPM): health services and 33; neoliberalism and 230–231; New Labour privatisation policies and 42, 48–49; police

privatisation and 128, 141, 145, 149–150, 158; prison privatisation and 209; Probation Service and 231–232, 236
new punitiveness 72–73, 75
New York Times 187
NHS *see* National Health Service
NHS Support Federation 53
night watch 111–112
Night Watch Services/Night Guards 120–121
NOMS *see* National Offender Management Service
Northern Rail 56
NPM *see* new public management
NPS *see* National Probation Service

Offender Management Act (2007) 239, 249
offender management services: competition for 212–213; electronic monitoring and (*see* electronic monitoring); establishment of 210–211, 239; evolution of privatisation in 3, 12–13; outsourcing of, generally 4, 12 (*see also* outsourcing); prison privatisation and 210–215 (*see also* prison privatisation); Probation Service privatisation and 239–240 (*see also* Probation Service privatisation)
Offender's Tagging Association 240–241
Official History of Privatisation (Parker) 21
Ofsted 95, 99, 104n9
oil embargo (1973) 26
Olympics (2012) 98–99, 100, 101, 153–154, 159
Omega File: A Comprehensive Review of Government Functions (ASI) 196
On Crimes and Punishments (Beccaria) 173
Open Public Services 40, 50–53
Osborne, George 47
outsourcing: cartel and oligopoly dominating 3, 5, 10, 45–46, 51–52, 57, 60n5, 89–90, 96, 98–100, 102, 222, 256, 259; Conservative-Liberal Democrat coalition policies of 50–53; contractual arrangements for (*see* contractual arrangements); misconduct and malpractice with (*see* misconduct and malpractice); New Labour policies of 9, 44; offender management services, generally 4, 12; *Open Public Services* on 40, 50–53; partial privatisation and 20; as partnerships (*see* partnerships); police roles 104n11, 129–130, 141, 142, 144–145, 152–153 (*see also*

Index

police privatisation); politics, generally, on 39–41; prison industry 74 (*see also* prison privatisation); Probation Service 4, 237–238, 260, 261–262 (*see also* Probation Service privatisation); regulatory oversight with (*see* regulatory system); revolving door in 93–95, 103nn5–6

ownership, theories of: agency theory as 22–23; Austrian school of economics as 21–22; monetarism as 24; privatisation and 21–24; public choice theory as 22; regulation theory as 23–24

PAC *see* Public Accounts Committee
Panopticon Prison 175–176, 177
Parker, D. 15, 21
parking 264
partnerships 43–44, 144–145, 153, 237–238
patronage 184
Paul, George Onesiphorus 175, 177, 178
payment by results programme (PbR): prison privatisation and 210, 213; privatisation, generally, and 40, 51; Probation Service privatisation and 259, 261, 263–265, 272, 281n2
PCSOs (police community support officers) 146, 147, 148, 150
Peel, Robert 110, 113, 161n3, 179
penal imperialism 78
Penal State 73
penal turn 72–73, 75
Penitentiary Act (1779) 174, 175, 177
Penitentiary for Convicts Act (1794) 176
Penitentiary House, etc. Act (1812) 177
Penitentiary Plan 174–175
penology paradigm 68–69
Pentonville Prison 178, 179
Perceval, Spencer and administration 176–177
performance failures *see* misconduct and malpractice
performance review: Best Value programme requirements for 43; new public management requirements for 49, 231; payment by results and (*see* payment by results programme); police scrutiny and 128–129, 141; prisons scrutiny and 182–184, 210, 217–218; Probation Service 233–234, 235–237, 249, 265, 271–276; *see also* key performance indicators
Pestfix 58

PFIs *see* Private Finance Initiatives
Philip-Sorenson, Jorgen 123
Pinkerton, Allan 115
Pinkerton National Detective Agency 115
Pitt, William (the Younger) 175–176
Plant Protection Limited 121
Plasma Resources UK 52
police: overview 107–109, 130–132, 138–140, 158–160; austerity agenda and 11, 148–152, 158–159; centralisation of public 116–117, 142, 148; civilianisation of 129, 142, 146, 148; commodification of services by 142; community policing 126, 139, 141; concept and meaning of 110; consensual distance between public and 122–124; costs of 121, 144–146, 148–152, 153–154, 159; cultural influences on portrayals of 111–112, 118, 121, 131; discipline and 114, 138, 139; fetishism toward 109, 132; golden age for public 116, 118–119, 131; history of 110–133, 138–161; load shedding by 129–130, 141, 142, 152–153; mobilisation against union strike 125–126; nationalisation and 119, 131; neighbourhood policing 147, 152; new public police force 113–114, 115–116, 131; objectives of 142; operational challenges for 160; pay for 124, 141, 151, 154; policing by collectivism 132; policing by consent 113–114, 116, 119; policing by objectives 128–129; policing of profit by profit 139; politics and 10–11, 117, 124–128, 131–132, 138–142, 144–160; private and local responsibility for 110–113, 119, 155; privatisation of (*see* police privatisation); proactive policing by 126, 139, 141; problem-oriented policing 145; professionalisation of 113, 150; protests against and criticisms of 108–109, 113, 117, 126–127, 128; role and attributes of 108; scrutiny and performance review of 128–129, 141; specialisation of 147; supplementing 123–124, 129–130; technology and 11, 114, 119–124, 130, 143–144, 145, 147, 155–157, 159–160; wartime influences on 116, 118, 120
Police Act (1964) 117
Police Act (1996) 142
police and crime commissioners 151–152, 153, 154

Police and Criminal Evidence Act (1984) 127, 148
Police and Magistrates' Court Act (1994) 142
police community support officers (PCSOs) 146, 147, 148, 150
Police Federation 124, 151, 154, 159, 161n3
Police National Computer 122
Police Negotiating Board 154
police privatisation: overview 138–140, 158–160; active citizenship and 142–143, 147, 158; ancillary operations and 142; asset sales and 4; austerity agenda and 11, 148–152, 158–159; civilianisation and 129, 142, 146, 148; commercial and industrial implementation of 114, 120–121, 123, 130; discipline and innovation for 114–116, 138, 139; evolution of 10–11, 159–160; extending police family via 146–148; future of 159–160; history of 110–113, 114, 119–124, 126–132, 138–161; hybrid space and 139, 147; licensing system for 149; Matthews on 1; misconduct and malpractice with 127, 149, 153–154, 159; neoliberalism and 11, 128, 132, 140; new public management and 128, 141, 145, 149–150, 158; outsourcing and 104n11, 129–130, 141, 142, 144–145, 152–153; partnerships for 144–145, 153; politics and 10–11, 126–128, 131–132, 139–142, 144–160; private investigators and 115; private sector innovation for 114–116; proactive policing and 126, 139, 141; reasons for reluctance toward 155; regulatory system and 146, 151–152; supplementing public police via 123–124, 129–130; technology and 119–124, 130, 143–144, 145, 147, 155–157, 159–160; two-tiered system of 161n3
Police Reform Act (2002) 146
Police Reform and Social Responsibility Act (2011) 151
Police Reform programme 141, 146
Police Renumeration Review Body 154
Police Superintendents' Association 159
Policing 4.0: Deciding the Future of Policing in the UK 159–160
Policing in a New Century (Home Office) 146

Policing in Austerity: One Year On (HMIC) 152
Policy Exchange 95, 247
politics: agency theory on 22–23; corrections commercial complex and 65, 79–80, 92–93; electronic monitoring privatisation and 243–248; Insider groups and 96; law and order (*see* law and order politics); police and 10–11, 117, 124–128, 131–132, 138–142, 144–160; policy translation of 25–26, 64–65; prison privatisation and 12, 168–169, 188–189, 195–222; privatisation, generally, and 2, 5, 8–9, 16–17, 27–32, 35–36, 39–60; Probation Service and 228–229, 230–237, 248–249, 256–281; public choice theory on 22, 231; regulatory system and 91 (*see also* regulatory system); revolving door of business and 93–95, 103nn5–6; think tanks influencing 24–25, 95–96, 103n7, 196, 247; *see also* neoliberalism; *specific administrations and parties*
Pope, Augustus 120
popular capitalism 21, 30–31
Porridge 222n5, 267
Posen, Ingrid 142, 158
positive custody 187–188
postal services 28, 53
Pratt, John 7
predictive analytics 156
PredPol 156
Premier Prison Services 79, 202, 208, 223n8, 245
Preston Gaol 179
Prevention of Crime Act (1908) 185
PricewaterhouseCoopers 57, 245–246
Principles of Penal Law (Eden) 173
Prison Act (1865) 180, 181
Prison Act (1877) 178, 180
Prison Act (1898) 184
Prison Commission 182
Prison Officers Association 200, 204, 207
Prison Operator Services Framework 218–219
prison privatisation: overview of 168–169, 195–197, 220–222; austerity agenda effects on 12, 214–215; competition and 198, 203, 209, 212–214, 223n7; construction of prisons and 200, 203–205, 207, 208–209, 214, 216, 219, 221; contractual arrangements for 188, 197 (*see also* PFIs *subentry*); eliminative penal practices and 205–206, 208, 219,

221; evolution of 11–12; initiation of 3, 188–189, 200–201; justification for 197–201; Matthews on 1, 167, 208; media on 198–199; misconduct and malpractice with 101, 103n2, 199–200, 202, 205, 215, 217–222; neoliberalism and 12, 188, 189, 195, 197, 198, 201, 221–222; New Labour party stance on 206–212; new public management and 209; offender management services and 210–215; PFIs for 3, 4, 203–204, 206–207, 208, 214, 217; politics and 12, 168–169, 188–189, 195–222; rehabilitation goals and 208, 212, 213, 215, 219; statistics on 3, 220; think tanks influencing 103n7, 196; US 74, 168, 195, 197

Prison Reform Trust, The 7, 103n7, 200, 202, 208, 211, 217–218

prisons: overview of 167–169, 189–190; centralisation of penal system and 177, 179, 180, 182, 186; commodification of incarceration and 171–172, 181; contractual arrangements for 188, 197; convict labour and 171, 174–175, 177, 179–181, 183; costs of 3, 73, 176–178, 186, 191nn7–8, 207, 214–215; culture of control and 169, 188, 189–190, 210; debtors' 171; design and construction of 172–181, 188, 200, 203–205, 207, 208–209, 214, 216, 219, 221; discipline by design in 170–172, 180; education in 183–184, 185; escapes from 186, 205; history of 167–191; misconduct and malpractice in 101, 103n2, 172, 173–174, 178, 186–187, 199–200, 202, 205, 215, 217–222; neoliberal penality and incarceration in 73–75; patronage in 184; penal idealism and 184, 186; penal idealism decay with 186–189; population statistics for 73, 75, 186, 196, 204, 208, 220; positive custody in 187–188; prisoner rioting and protest in 186–187, 200, 205; privatisation of (*see* prison privatisation); public opinion on 182–184; public purpose of imprisonment and punishment in 178–182; punishment as custom and 169–170; reform of 172–178, 182–186, 200–201, 216–217; regulatory system and 167, 174; right realism and 188, 190; salaries of staff in 174; scrutiny and performance review of 182–184, 210, 217–218; US 73–74, 168, 178–180, 181, 187–188, 195, 197

Prisons 2000: An International Perspective on the Current State and Future of Imprisonment (Matthews and Francis) 208

Prisons Act (1835) 179

Prison Safety and Reform 216

Private Finance Initiatives (PFIs): contract buy-outs of 46–47; debt and dangers of 45–47, 60nn3–4; misconduct and malpractice with 46, 101, 218; New Labour policy of 44–47; prison privatisation under 3, 4, 203–204, 206–207, 208, 214, 217

private investigators/detectives 115

Private Prisons: Cons and Pros (Logan) 199

Private Sector Involvement in the Penal State (Home Affairs Committee) 3

Private Sector Involvement in the Remand System (Home Affairs Committee) 197, 201

Private Security Industry Act (2001) 146

private security industry authority 146

privatisation: overview of 15–17, 35–36, 39–41, 59–60; 1979–1997 Tory years of 27–32; 1997–2010 New Labour years of 41–49; 2010–2015 Conservative-Liberal Democrat coalition years of 49–53; 2015-current Conservative years of 53–58; asset sales and (*see* asset sales); context for 8–9, 15–17, 25–26; of criminal justice (*see* privatisation of criminal justice system); defining 3–4, 18–19; demand-driven 69–70, 72; denationalisation leading to 15, 17, 27, 28–30; enabling environment for 25–26, 41; forms of 19; future of 58–59; history of 5, 15–36, 39–60; ideological roots of 21–24; motives and objectives for rise of 20–21, 27; outsourcing and (*see* outsourcing); ownership theories and 21–24; partial 19–20, 32–35; partial rollback of 41 (*see also* renationalisation policies); politics and (*see* politics); think tanks influencing 24–25, 95–96, 103n7, 196, 247; total 19–20, 27

privatisation of criminal justice system: appeal of 87–88; commodification and (*see* commodification); corrections commercial complex and 65, 79–80, 92–93; of electronic monitoring (*see* electronic monitoring privatisation); of immigration and detention services 1, 103n2, 124; Insider groups influencing 96; Matthews on 1–2, 3, 7–8; misconduct and malpractice with (see misconduct and malpractice); of police (see police privatisation); politics and (see neoliberalism; politics); of prisons (see prison privatisation); of Probation Services (see Probation Service privatisation); providers of (see providers of private services); regulatory oversight of (see regulatory system); revolving door with 94–95; risk management and 71; technological innovation with 87–88 (see also technology); think tanks influencing 95–96, 103n7, 196, 247; transatlantic transfer of 9–10, 65, 76–80

Privatizing Criminal Justice (Matthews) 1–2, 3, 7–8

proactive policing 126, 139, 141

Probation Boards 239, 267

Probation Chiefs Association 266, 267

Probation Committees 232

Probation of Offenders Act (1907) 184, 230

Probation Service: overview of 228–229; 1979–1997 Tory years of 232–234; 1997–2010 New Labour policies on 234–237; centralisation of 235–236, 262; costs of 235; demise of 12, 229, 249, 279; downgrading of 260; establishment of 184; history of 228–230; key performance indicators and targets for 233–234, 235–237, 249, 265; national standards for 233–234; new public management and 231–232, 236; officers of the court in 184–185; organisational bifurcation of 4, 233, 257, 260, 261, 265–267, 276, 279, 280n1; politics and 228–229, 230–237, 248–249, 256–281; privatisation of (see Probation Service privatisation); renationalisation of 56, 277–278, 280; Statement of National Objectives and Priorities for 232–233

Probation Service Mutuals 268

Probation Service privatisation: overview of 229, 248–249, 278–280; ancillary services and 240; black box procurement in 261, 270–271; budget deficit reduction and 258; Community Payback privatisation and 260–261; competition and 213, 229, 259, 263; Conservative-Liberal Democrat coalition policies on 257–258; consultation on 262–263; contractual arrangements for 261, 268–269, 270–271, 274, 280–281nn1–2; creaming and 264; electronic monitoring and 229, 238, 240–248, 249, 260, 270 (see also electronic monitoring privatisation); evolution of 12–13, 229; gaming the process and 236–237, 264; implementation of 268–270; initiation of 3, 237–238; insider groups in 96; internal market and 239; media coverage of 267–268; misconduct and malpractice with 257, 270–277, 279–280, 281n3; neoliberalism and 230–231, 239, 249, 256–257; new public management and 231–232, 236; organisational bifurcation and 4, 233, 257, 260, 261, 265–267, 276, 279, 280n1; parking and 264; partnerships for 237–238; payment by results programme and 259, 261, 263–265, 272, 281n2; penal market creation and 237–238; performance measurement and attribution with 265; politics and 229, 248–249, 256–281; privatisation by stealth 229, 256; recidivism and 266, 272–273, 281n4; reform of 276–277; regulatory flaws with 97; Rehabilitation Revolution and 4, 258–259, 260; rehabilitation transformation and 261–263, 267–276, 278, 279–280; reports, inspections and investigations on 271–276, 281n3; reversion of 56, 257, 276, 277–278, 280; risk assessments and 265–267; 'save the Probation Service' campaign against 267–268; strengthening services 276–277; underperformance with 274–276

Probation Trusts 239, 259, 260, 262, 268

problem-oriented policing 145

profits: commodification for (see commodification); ownership theories on 21–24; PFIs and excessive 46; policing of profit by profit 139; prisons as source of 171, 199, 202, 204; Probation Service as source of 229, 270

providers of private services: Best Value programme for 40, 42–43, 53; cartel of 3; compulsory competitive tendering by 32–33, 40, 42, 52; consolidation of 89–90; contractual arrangements with (see contractual arrangements); in corrections commercial complex 65, 79–80, 92–93; for COVID-19 pandemic response 9, 41, 57–58; for criminal justice (see privatisation of criminal justice system); financial collapse of 46, 54–56, 98, 100–102, 104n10, 218,

222, 272; insider groups of 96; internal market and 33–34, 239; misconduct and malpractice by (*see* misconduct and malpractice); multinational 78–79, 89, 92, 96, 102, 256, 259; oligopoly of 5, 10, 45–46, 51–52, 57, 60n5, 89–90, 96, 98–100, 102, 222, 256, 259; outsourcing to (*see* outsourcing); partnerships with (*see* partnerships); performance review of (*see* performance review); race to the bottom by 39–40, 54–56, 86, 88, 97–98, 263, 268; revolving door with 93–95, 103nn5–6; rewarding failure of 90, 98–100, 222, 257, 277; 'too big to fail' 3, 5, 10, 54, 60n5, 90, 101, 102

Public Accounts Committee (PAC): on ferry debacle 56; on PFIs 45–47; on police policies 128; on prison policies 215; on Probation Service policies 262–263, 271, 272; on providers of private services 90, 99–100

Public and Prison Management: Considerations on Returning Privately Managed Prisons to the Public Sector (Home Office) 207

public choice theory 22, 231

Public Contracts Regulations (2015) 52

public-sector outsourcing *see* outsourcing

public service industry 92

punishment: as custom 169–170; for profit 199, 202; public prison system monopoly on 177; as public purpose 178–182

Punishment, Custody and the Community 241–242

Punishment and Reform: Effective Probation Services 213, 260

Putting Victims First: More Effective Responses to Anti-Social Behaviour 154

race: police methods and 108–109, 123, 125, 126; prison incarceration statistics by 73

race to the bottom 39–40, 54–56, 86, 88, 97–98, 263, 268

Radzinowicz, L. 185–186

RailTrack 151

railways: Great Train Robbery (1963) 121–122; partial renationalisation of 41, 56; police forces of 114; privatisation of 140, 151

Railways Act (1993) 140

Rainer, Frederic 229

Rainsbrook Secure Training Centre 95, 99, 103n2

Ramsbottom, Lord 267

Rand Corporation 123

Rawlings, P. 131

Reading Gaol 179

Reagan, Ronald and administration 9, 65, 74, 77, 168, 195

recessions 26, 149, 212

recidivism 180, 182, 185, 188, 266, 272–273, 281n4

Rees, Merlyn 124

Reform 95, 96, 103n7

regulation theory 21

regulatory system: contractual arrangements and 52, 91, 96–97, 99–100, 102–103; deregulation reducing 27, 76, 90, 103n1; economics of regulation and 23–24; erosion of 91–92; fault lines and flaws in 96–98; light-touch 10, 86, 97, 103–104nn1,8–9; misconduct and malpractice under 10, 86–87, 88, 92, 96–98, 99–100, 102–103; oligopoly under 10, 89–90; police privatisation and 146, 151–152; politics and 91; prisons and 167, 174; revolving door allowances in 93–95, 103nn5–6; rise of new with privatisation 90–91; *see also specific Acts and regulations*

rehabilitation: community rehabilitation companies 264, 268–280; juvenile moral rehabilitation 185; prison privatisation and goals of 208, 212, 213, 215, 219; Rehabilitation Revolution and Probation Service privatisation 4, 258–259, 260, 272; transforming 261–263, 267–276, 278, 279–280

Reid, John 94, 148, 161n6, 249

Reiman, Jeffrey 7

Reiner, Robert 109, 118–119, 131, 143, 144, 149–150, 158–159

Reliance-GSSC 245

Reliance Security 127

renationalisation policies 41, 54, 56, 277–278, 280

Representation of the People Act (1918) 117

Representation of the People Act (Equal Franchise) (1928) 117

Reveley, Willey 175

Review of Police Core and Ancillary Tasks (Home Office) 142

Review of Private Financing of New Prison Procurement (Home Office) 207

Review of the Prison and Probation Service (Carter) 239

Index

revolving door 93–95, 103nn5–6
Richard, Lord 202
Ridley, Nicholas 23, 28
Rifkind, Malcolm 195, 222n1
right realism 138–139, 188, 190
risk: criminal justice system and management of 68–71; globalisation and 67–68; of misconduct or malpractice (*see* misconduct and malpractice); neoliberalism and responsibility for managing 68–71; of Probation Service bifurcation 265–267
Rogers, Allan 127
Role of the Probation Service, The 260
Rolls Royce 30
Royal Commission on Constabulary 113
Royal Commission on the Police 118
Royal Mail 31
Ruggles-Brise, Evelyn 184, 185
Rural Constabularies Act (1839/1840) 113–114
Russell, John 179
Rutherford, Andrew 167–168, 205–206
Ryder, Richard 176–177
Rydon 87

sales of public assets *see* asset sales
SAS (Special Air Service) 125
Scargill, Arthur 125
Scott, George Gilbert 179
Seaborne Freight 56
Secret Service Bureau 116
Securicor 121, 122, 124, 188, 207, 243, 245
Securitas AB 115
security: inequality in provision of 71–72; police as source of (*see* police); responsibility for 70–71; *see also* criminal justice system
Security Alliance 152
Security Corps 121
Security Express 121
Security Industry Authority 146, 149, 152
Serco: electronic monitoring and 243, 245–247, 263, 268; health care services 57; misconduct and malpractice of 99, 245–247, 263, 268, 277; offender management services 256; prison privatisation and 78–79, 202, 212, 213, 219, 223nn8,10; Probation Service privatisation and 243, 245–247, 260–261, 263, 268, 277; size of 43, 51, 60n5, 89–90; think tanks and 95

Serious and Organised Crime Agency 147, 148
Serious Fraud Office 246
Serious Organised Crime and Police Act (2005) 148
Shadow State 5, 32, 46
Shakespeare, William 111
Shearing, Clifford 139, 143, 157
Sheehy, Patrick 141, 142, 158
Sim, Joe 7
Sing Sing Prison 181
Smith, Ian Duncan 95
Smith, Jacqui 149
Smith, John 141, 144, 203–204
Smith and Klein 57
social impact bonds 211–212
social media 157, 268
Sodexo/Sodexho: background of 103n3; electronic monitoring and 270; health care services 57; as insider group 96; misconduct and malpractice of 88, 271, 277; offender management services 256; prison privatisation and 78, 219, 223n6; Probation Service privatisation and 88, 269, 270, 271, 277; revolving door with 94; think tanks and 95
Spain, police in 109
Special Air Service (SAS) 125
Special Constables Act (1831) 114
Spurr, Michael 212
Stacey, G. 240, 273–274, 275
stagflation 26
State: nationalisation by (*see* nationalisation); neoliberalism avoiding reliance on 70 (*see also* neoliberalism); Penal 73; private outsourcing of criminal justice by (*see* privatisation of criminal justice system); regulatory system of (*see* regulatory system); Shadow 5, 32, 46
State of the Prisons, The (Howard) 174
Statute of Winchester (1285) 110
Steatite 248, 250n1
Stedman, John 169
Stenning, Phillip 139, 143, 157
Stevens, John 94
Stevens, Malcolm 95
Stewart, Rory 218
Strangeways Prison 200
Straw, Jack 144, 146, 161n6, 204, 206–211, 213, 223n9
Strengthening Probation, Building Confidence 276–277
Summary Jurisdiction Act (1879) 230
Sunday Times Business 199

superjails 214, 219
Supervision Grants system 238
Switzerland, prisons in 174

tagging *see* electronic monitoring
taxation 50, 74, 151
Taylor-Smith, David 153
technology: electronic monitoring with (*see* electronic monitoring); globalisation and 76; policing and 11, 114, 119–124, 130, 143–144, 145, 147, 155–157, 159–160; privatisation of criminal justice system and innovation with 87–88; risk management, security, and 68–69, 71, 72
Telefonica/O2 248
Telegraph 199
Territorial Support Group 108
Thatcher, Margaret and administration: asset sales under 28–30; cronyism by 53; deregulation under 27, 103n1; as Iron Lady 125; monetarism of 24; nationalisation and denationalisation under 16–17; police and police privatisation under 10–11, 124–128, 131–132, 132–133n5, 138–142, 154, 158; popular capitalism under 30–31; prisons and prison privatisation under 187–189, 195, 196, 205; privatisation, generally, under 2, 17, 27–32, 35, 72; Reagan and 9, 65, 77, 168; think tanks influencing 24–25; union power reduction under 17
think tanks 24–25, 95–96, 103n7, 196, 247
Third Way 9, 39, 42, 144, 146, 234–235, 239
three-day week (1974) 26
Through the Gate programme 272–274, 281n4
Times, The 199, 204
Tombs, Steve 7
Tomlinson, Ian 108
'too big to fail' providers 3, 5, 10, 54, 60n5, 90, 101, 102
Tory party *see* Conservative party
Town and Country Planning Act (1947) 119
trade unions *see* unions
Transforming Rehabilitation: A Revolution in the Way We Manage Offenders (TR) 261–263, 267–276, 278, 279–280
Transparency International UK 57, 58
Transport Act (1980) 29
treadmills, in prisons 179
Treasury Committee 45
Treatise on the Police of the Metropolis (Colquhoun) 113, 190

Treatise Upon the Best Method of Protecting Property from Burglars, and Human Life from Midnight Assassins (Holmes) 120
Treaty of Amiens 176
Tumin, Stephen 205, 208
Turning Point 212, 213

UK Detention Services (UKDS) 78, 201, 208, 222–223n6
unemployment 24, 26
unions: 1970s clashes with 26; PFI opposition by 47; police (*see* Police Federation); police mobilised against 125–126; policies to reduce power of 17, 23; popular capitalism campaign against 31; prison (*see* Prison Officers Association); prisoner 187; privatisation opposition by 30; Probation Service 267; *see also specific organisations*
United Kingdom (UK): Brexit 9, 40–41, 53–54, 58–59, 154; COVID-19 pandemic in 9, 41, 57–58, 277–278, 280; privatisation in (*see* privatisation); *see also* State; *specific administrations*
United States (US): appeal of privatisation in 87–88; corrections commercial complex in 65, 79–80, 92; crime control industry and penal imperialism emergence in 77–79; electronic monitoring in 241, 242, 244–245; neoliberal penality in 72–74, 76; police and security in 108–109, 115, 120, 145, 156; prisons and prison privatisation in 73–74, 168, 178–180, 181, 187–188, 195, 197; privatisation of criminal justice transferred from 9–10, 65, 76–80; Probation Service in 229, 269 (*see also* electronic monitoring *subentry*)
Uniting Care 52
Universal Ogden Services 103n3
Utilitarianism 173, 185–186
utility: individual utility maximization 22; in policing 155; of prisons 172, 173, 174, 181, 185–186

Vagrancy Act (1824) 125
Vidocq, Eugène François 115
View of the Hard Labour Bill, A (Bentham) 175
Virgin Care 52

Wackenhut Corrections Corporation (WCC) 78–79, 202, 223n8, 245
Waddington, David 222n3

Ward, Tony 7
Watch Committees 114, 117; *see also* Neighbourhood Watch groups; night watch
Waterhouse, Alfred 178
Welfare state and public services 19–20, 32–35
West, Fred 205
West India Company 112
West India Merchants Company Marine Police Institute 112
West London Mental Health NHS Trust 52
Westminster Watch Act (1774) 112
Whately, George 174
Wheatley, Phil 94
Wheatley, Tom 94
Wheeler, John 197, 222n2
White, Derek 200
Whitelaw, William 196
Whitworth-Russell, William 179, 180
Wilberforce, William 176, 177
Wilson, Charlie 186
Wilson, Harold and administration 188
Wilson, James Q. 139, 144
Winchester Prison 180
Winsor, Tom 151, 154
winter of discontent (1978) 26, 33
Winterton, Rosie 207
Within These Walls 222n5
Woodcock, John 126–127
Woolf Report 200–201
workhouses 170
Working for Patients (Clarke) 34
Working Links 54, 55, 98, 102, 272, 275
Work Programme 261, 264, 270
World War I 116
World War II 16, 118, 120
Wormwood Scrubs 181
Wren, Christopher 172
Wright, Jeremy 103n7

zero-tolerance 'broken windows' policing strategy 109, 139, 144
Zimmerman, George 108